To Rachael,

1-21-0?

ROCKY MOUNTAIN CHIROPRACTIC
RADIOLOGICAL CENTER

TERRY R. YOCHUM D.C., D.A.C.B.R.
Fellow, A.C.C.R.

Phone (303) 940-9400 • FAX (303) 940-9600
7500 Wadsworth Blvd. • Arvada, Colorado, 80003
E-Mail: dcrad099@aol.com

JOSEPH JANSE

Dr. Janse was my "Hero" in
chiropractic. He was the most
"Unforgettable" person I ever
met. Enjoy this gift.

With Respect,

Terry R. Yochum
NCC-72

JOSEPH JANSE: THE APOSTLE OF CHIROPRACTIC EDUCATION

By Reed B. Phillips, DC, PhD

ISBN: 1-880759-77-2 (softcover and CD-ROM)
ISBN: 1-880759-78-0 (hardcover and CD-ROM)

Library of Congress Cataloging-in-Publication Data

Joseph Janse: The Apostle of Chiropractic Education
Includes endnotes, pedigree, appendix and index

1. Janse, Joseph   2. Chiropractic history

reedphillips@scuhs.edu

This work of love is dedicated to the immediate family
of Dr. Joseph Janse.
In partial recompense for the sacrifice
all of you had to make
as you shared your brother, father, and husband with
those needy and grateful souls in the
Chiropractic Profession, we thank you.

A man filled with the love of God
Is not content with blessing his
Family alone, but ranges through
The whole world, anxious to bless
The whole human race.
(Teachings of the Prophet Joseph Smith, p. 174)

CONTENTS

FOREWORD

Dr. Joseph Janse: The Apostle of Chiropractic Education

Who is this man, Dr. Joseph Janse, revered by so many people within the profession of chiropractic? It is the question I asked myself one Saturday morning in August of 1966 as I traveled with my father, Kenneth E. Yochum, D.C., to Chicago to "meet with him and experience his passion for chiropractic," my father said. By land rights, being a native of St. Louis, I wanted to stay home to attend the Logan College of Chiropractic. With reluctance, I granted my father's wish and that meeting with Dr. Janse changed my entire professional life. As he spoke to me in his office adorned with awards and presents from all over the world about the National College of Chiropractic and the profession of chiropractic, his sincerity and character shined like a burning star. In just twenty short minutes, my mind was changed and I knew where I was going to chiropractic school, a decision that even surprised myself.

Dr. Joseph Janse was the modern-day father of chiropractic. He almost single-handedly moved the profession from the dark ages to accredited chiropractic educational institutions, his National College of Chiropractic leading the way. Joseph Janse, or J.J. as he was affectionately called by so many who loved him, had a captivating nature about his speech and demeanor. His incredible vocabulary allowed him to become one of the most sought after lecturers and motivational speakers this profession has ever seen. He used words that I never believed existed; I looked them up and they all did! Some of his most famous quotations are exemplified in his favorite poems:

Oh for the silent doer of the deed!
One that is happy in his height;
And one that, in a nation's night
Has solitary certitude of light!

So often I heard the quote when I was a student at National College from Dr. Janse when he was asked, "What is it that you do?" He would respond, "I am a chiropractor, nothing more, but incidentally, my friend, nothing less you see!"

As a great philosopher of chiropractic, a prolific authoritative author, an extraordinary anatomist, a board-certified chiropractic radiologist (one of the first three ever to write and pass the DACBR examination with Earl Rich, D.C. and Lester Rehberger, D.C.), and a superb technician of chiropractic technique, he took a position of great respect and admiration within the profession of chiropractic.

This text so appropriately establishes J.J. as one of the great humanitarians within his profession. Thank God he chose chiropractic, because he would have been successful at the highest level in anything he would have chosen. Joseph Janse was a true "legend" within the profession of chiropractic and his contributions to this chosen profession are immeasurable. I feel honored to have been a student of the great Joseph Janse and to have been invited to write a foreword in this text, which so beautifully describes his life and childhood up through his early years in Utah, as well as the memorable years as President of the National College of Chiropractic (a position he held for 38 years).

On numerous occasions I heard Dr. Janse close his inspirational lectures with one of his most memorable quotes, taken from Rudyard Kipling. It speaks of the great spirit of understanding and fellowship that Dr. Joseph Janse held for his chiropractic colleagues:

Here's to the men [and women] of my own breed,
Good or bitter bad, as they may be,
At least they hear the things I hear,
And see the things I see.

The accolades could continue, but the legacy is clear. His inspiring example allowed no room for mediocrity or compromise. Joseph Janses' commitment to excellence remains unparalleled. He was truly the "Apostle" of chiropractic education.

Terry R. Yochum, D.C., D.A.C.B.R., Fellow, A.C.C.R.
Rocky Mountain Radiological Consultants
Denver, Colorado

FOREWORD

I first met Dr. Joseph Janse in 1963 when I was on leave from the military. I was considering a career in chiropractic medicine at the time and was encouraged by an alumnus to visit National at its new campus in Lombard, Illinois. I went to the campus and almost immediately I met Dr. Joseph Janse. There was something special about this man—charisma, one would call it and perhaps something more. He often used the word "certitude," and I believe that was part of what I sensed those few minutes during which he altered my life completely.

Following my talk with him, I knew I would become a chiropractic physician and while I had known since I was four years old that I wanted to be a doctor, I had, until that moment no idea it would be as a doctor who, as Dr. Janse would say, chose to practice chiropractic.

Doubtless, the experiences of our author, Dr. Reed Phillips are quite similar—I have heard his story too, and it is clear to many of us that the same story could well be repeated countless times—such was the strength of attraction of this man Joseph Janse about whom Dr. Phillips has chosen to write.

This biography will bring to life the person most of us came to know as an adult, though it will trace his roots from his parents to his last years on this earth. It is completely appropriate that such a book should be written, for it is not often that one person can affect the lives of so many with such significance as this man did.

Dr. Janse was unique in his appearance, his demeanor, his command of the language, his oratorical and writing skills and in his knowledge of human anatomy, but most of all in his devotion to a profession and, in particular, to an institution, the National College of Chiropractic. This devotion came at some expense however, for he had such a commanding commitment to his duties at National that his family missed him and he, them.

This book serves as a window into the life of a man who was loved and admired by most. A man who stood up with unflinching conviction for the chiropractic profession which he loved so much and who never faltered in his effort to promote increased quality in chiropractic education and practice. He often quoted the words of poet Stephen Phillips; words I now use in his memory.

O for living man to lead!
That will not babble when we bleed;
O for the silent doer of the deed!

My thanks and admiration go to Dr. Reed Phillips, my contemporary, who has taken the time and dedicated his efforts to chronicling the history of a truly great man—Dr. Joseph Janse.

James F. Winterstein, D.C., D.A.C.B.R.
President National University of Health Sciences
Lombard, Illinois

ACKNOWLEDGEMENT

To accurately portray the life of an individual, after the fact, is no simple task. Had this task been undertaken while direct comment and review was available, the outcome may have differed. The reliance upon others to piece together the story of a person's life opens the doorway to multiple perspectives based upon memory. This information gathering effort extends from 1976 when the idea to write a biography was first conceived to the conclusion of a task that turned into a labor of love, and has extended to 2006.

Adriana Janse Aldous, Joseph's older sister, was especially helpful in sharing many cherished early family memories. She had gathered family stories over the years and had taken upon herself to write many of her memories of life in Holland and Huntsville. She willingly shared family photos and personal stories that only could be shared by someone who had experienced them first hand.

Many colleagues, close associates and life-long friends have contributed to this publication by sharing stories, photos and personal experiences of how their lives were moved towards greatness by the touch of Dr. Janse's hand. Lifted from despair, filled with hope, he gave them cause to aspire and achieve. It is utterly impossible to identify everyone who has been encouraged to "press on" by the gentle reminders of his own humble beginnings.

In the final crunch of time Joel Campbell, the fine tuning editor and Bryan Crockett of Book Printers of Utah have supported this work with patience and perseverance.

The Southern California University of Health Sciences (SCU/ LACC) should be recognized for their support. Many details related to gathering materials, phone calls, mailings and safekeeping of funds, lifted the burden from my desk as President allowing me to concentrate on the literary aspects of this book.

There are three associates from the National College years that have been especially helpful in providing materials, reviewing manuscripts and sharing personal experiences that should be recognized. Drs. Leonard Fay and Ronald Beideman and Ms. Marge Neely have provided insights that only they could have gained by their long years of service at National in support of Dr. Janse's leadership.

A biography could not be complete without knowing the inner workings of the family. Dr. Janse's youngest daughter, Dr. Joey Janse, and his wife Gloria, have been willing to share insights and personal possessions that have enhanced understanding few have ever been exposed to. His greatest love and his greatest challenges were often right at his own hearth. We learn from them the sacrifices made to allow Dr. Janse to help his beloved profession.

I am also appreciative of the support and cooperation granted to me by Dr. James Winterstein, President of the National College of Chiropractic (now National University of Health Sciences) by granting access to archival information, providing use of their facilities and supporting efforts to publish and distribute this book. He was also closely associated with Dr. Janse and has shared several personal experiences.

I am in debt to all who have contributed financially to this cause (see contributor list). While every dollar of support was vital to the success of this effort, special recognition is given to Dr. Terry Yochum. It was his untiring efforts that resulted in the acquisition of the necessary funds to complete the production of this book. It was also his idea and perseverance that resulted in the preservation of Dr. Janse's memory on the accompanying DVD. As he traveled about giving lectures in radiology, he always managed to create an opportunity to speak of and give special recognition to Dr. Janse and how he had changed his life. I must admit that I am also grateful that Terry has prodded my efforts by his encouragement and interest in this project. One cannot recognize Dr. Yochum without also giving due credit to his wife Inge, who also helped in gathering, sorting, and interpreting materials for this book.

Finally, this project has been a reminder of how dependent I am upon my wife's ability in the English language, starting when we were students, many years ago. Without her review of my papers for class I probably would never have graduated. Throughout my professional career she has been the most insightful critic of my letters, papers and other writings. She has burned the candle on both ends in the final weeks of production, making my book-writing dream become a reality. When Dr. Janse touched my life he also touched hers. She has also shown her gratitude for what he meant to her.

The story that follows is the story of Joseph Janse, shared by those who knew him, loved him, admired him and now miss him. We begin where he began, in his humble Holland and we end where he now rests, in Huntsville, Utah.

PREFACE

In each of our lives, there are a few individuals who have the power and influence to change our direction. Dr. Joseph Janse was one such person for me. As an impressionable nineteen-year-old in the big city of Chicago, I first encountered Dr. Janse. I was in the beginnings of my two years of missionary service for the Mormon Church that included the opportunity to be taught and encouraged by local Church leaders. Dr. Janse was frequently invited to speak to the missionaries because of his insight and inspiring style of delivery.

As I approached the end of my mission endeavors, I was charged with training new missionaries. Our living quarters were near Lincolnwood, Illinois, home of Dr. Janse. Whenever a companion missionary took ill, off to Dr. Janse's home we would go for some good chiropractic care. This was my first introduction to chiropractic.

My two-year mission in Chicago ended, followed by four years at the University of Utah. It was at this point that I needed to make a career decision. High on the list of future options was dental school at Northwestern University, back in the old mission field of Chicago. After a promising interview with the admissions department, my wife and I met with current dental students and learned about the high-rise living conditions and the struggle of living in the city. With one son already underfoot, we were not encouraged.

At the conclusion of the interview we had some time on our hands. I told my wife of Dr. Janse and thought she might enjoy meeting him. A hurried phone call and a welcomed response resulted in an immediate invitation to National College for a tour and lunch. So off to Lombard we did go, not knowing how our life was going to change.

The year was 1969 and so the campus in Lombard was new and spacious with few confining businesses nearby. The physical layout was impressive. We were met at the front door by Stephen Kesler, Student Body President and resident of our hometown, Salt Lake City. We not only received an excellent tour of this new and brightly beaming facility (in contrast to the darkened halls of Northwestern) but we received a positive introduction to chiropractic. (In the next decade, this same Dr. Kesler would become my associate, colleague and co-pilot until his untimely death in a plane crash.)

At the end of the tour we ended up in Dr. Janse's office. He seemed exuberant at our visit and took us to lunch at the Yorktown mall. We had little appreciation for the burden of responsibilities he carried yet he made us feel like we were the most important people in his life at that moment. His personal concern, his persuasive demeanor and his compassion for the challenges we then faced about our professional futures made deep and lasting impressions. He was moved to promise student housing on campus should we decide to enroll. He knew how to reach our familial concern! Janse also promised a small scholarship on entrance as an additional enticement knowing we had no prior experience with chiropractic or chiropractors, and that I would be coming with a completed four-year pre-med bachelor's degree from a major university—an achievement not common for entering chiropractic students at that time.

From this small beginning Janse made a positive difference in my life as he had done in the lives of so many others. He made a difference in the growth of National College. He affected the acceptance and expansion of the chiropractic profession.

I am acquainted with the brightest, the most famous, and the most eloquent, yet no other person has had an impact for the ultimate good of the chiropractic profession and its educational development like Dr. Joseph Janse. Thus, the appropriate title of this book, *Joseph Janse: The Apostle of Chiropractic Education*.

He changed my life. This biography is my way of saying, "Thank you, Joe, for all that you were to me personally, and for your genius in laying the incredible groundwork which has legitimized our profession."

Reed B. Phillips, D.C., Ph.D.
President
Southern California University of Health Sciences

INTRODUCTION

The painful process of writing a book is often motivated by the hope of financial gain, notoriety and prestige or for the purpose of supporting a cause, defining a purpose or paying tribute to greatness. The latter has been the source of my motivation to undertake this multi-decade effort.

Joseph Janse changed lives, and in so doing he changed his profession in all its aspects, most notably its educational process. There is no other way to tell his story than to walk with him from his humble beginnings in his native Holland to his later years in Chicago. Thus, the first Chapter focuses upon his heritage, his birth and early childhood in the land behind the dikes.

Chapter Two is pivotal, for it helps us understand how his life was changed in a most dramatic fashion. It describes how his newly acquired Mormon religion was closely entwined with family values to the extent that it caused them to pull up the roots of seven generations of progenitors in Holland and travel half way around the world to live in America.

Life for a young Dutch-speaking boy in an English-speaking farming community was a challenging cultural transition that contributed to his character development. Hard work, religious devotion and love of freedom built family traditions that carried him through years of physical hardship and meager means. Chapter Three shares insights regarding these early experiences that helped shape the man, Janse.

Many young men in the Mormon church leave home at the naïve age of nineteen or twenty to carry the gospel message of their religion to the world. Joseph Janse was called to serve a mission in the regions of Switzerland and Germany. Chapter Four recounts some of his harrowing experiences as he encountered the influence of the rising Third Reich.

A tender spot in the life of Joseph Janse was his love for his wife, Gloria, and their three children. Chapter Five opens a view through a window seldom experienced except by those who were closest to the family. A relationship of love, struggle, sacrifice and challenge welded a union that bonded for eternity.

Chapter Six puts special emphasis on how the budding and brilliant young man from Huntsville, Utah, one with the promise of a bright future doing anything he could want, decided to become a chiropractor. Community opinion and church leaders advised to the contrary but destiny prevailed in spite of a disappointing encounter with B.J. Palmer.

Chapter Seven is focused on some of the more notable achievements in the life of Dr. Janse, achievements that laid the stepping stones of his life. To include all of his accomplishments would evolve into a tome on its own. Though he enjoyed the exhilaration of "being on stage" he never sought honor or award for their own sake.

With his keen mind and driving passion for knowledge and understanding, research was a core fiber of his cloth. It was the team of Illi and Janse that set the foundation for future research and clinical investigation. Formulated in the 1940s, their concepts are as applicable to the practice and principles of chiropractic today. Chapter Eight captures the essence of their time together.

From college student to college president, we follow the academic parade of Dr. Janse's pursuit of not only his own educational excellence but that of a profession's as well. While bearing the burden of the college presidency, he was teaching in the classroom during the week and teaching in seminars on the weekends. Somehow he managed to squeeze in a decade of leadership in the National Chiropractic Association's Council on Education. It was this presence that earned him the title, "The Apostle of Chiropractic Education."

Chiropractic was a marginal profession throughout Dr. Janse's life. He was thereby forced to be on the defensive at all times. Nothing focused his defenses and brought a sharp awareness to the weaknesses of the profession more than the legal battle over the right to practice chiropractic in Louisiana. Chapter Ten sheds light on how the England Trial impacted Dr. Janse and thereby the profession.

One cannot grow within a solid shell. The old building that housed National College on North Ashland would not do and so Dr. Janse set out on the biggest and most expensive capital campaign drive in the history of the profession at that time. The end result was one of the most elite schools in the entire profession. Chapter Eleven invites one into the near daily dialogue between Dr. Janse and his Board Chair, Dr. Earl Liss, and how they directed the building of the National edifice.

Because of his influence internationally and his extensive travels, Chapter Twelve draws attention to his specific efforts on the continents or countries of Europe, Australia, Japan and South Africa. He changed lives as well as set the course for the future development of the profession in each of these places.

The final days of Janse's presidential life are fraught with heartache and misunderstandings. His transition to President Emeritus and the transition of power at the National College is a most intriguing and somewhat difficult episode to decipher as explored in Chapter Thirteen. As is often the case with great men in their era of influence, the closing years of life are more like a falling tree than a triumphant redwood.

Chapter Fourteen is an attempt to garner the gist of his writings, the philosophical interwoven with the anatomical and neurological. His was the core of what chiropractic is and should strive to be. One who was never ashamed but never one, "...to hog it all."

Chapter Fifteen is a summation of the legacy of Dr. Joseph Janse. If all who have been influenced by this man could share their stories on these pages, this chapter would extend for volumes. This chapter grants liberty to link author with subject for many common threads interweave between them.

The Appendices are an accumulation of information that does not fit well into the context of a chapter. The pedigree charts list his progenitors for five generations. The appendix, "Oft Remembered Sayings" is an accumulation of those many things we heard him repeat so many times yet they always stirred the same strong feelings.

The last two Appendices are his selected writings, both professional and personal. Key letters, speeches and articles outline his religious and philosophical foundations which shaped the spiritual and intellectual development of "The Apostle of Chiropractic Education," National College of Chiropractic and in many cases, the Chiropractic profession.

There is much more that could be said of this person whose influence remains immeasurable. I hope this humble effort to amass the highlights of his heritage and legacy will be a catalyst to ignite personal remembrances of the inspiration and motivation he instilled in each one of us who knew him. And for those who never met the man, I hope you enjoy becoming newly acquainted with an apostle of the highest order.

CHAPTER ONE

HUMBLE BEGINNINGS

Holland and the Province of Zeeland

The "Kingdom of the Netherlands" also known as Holland, is situated between Belgium and Germany, facing the harsh North Sea. The people call themselves "Nederlanders," but English-speakers often refer to them as the "Dutch."

Netherlands is interpreted to mean "low countries" and indeed one-third of the land is 20-50 feet below sea level, being protected by dikes. Two main geographic areas are 1) the coast, a low, narrow area with sand dunes helping to keep out the North Sea and 2) the Polders, lands reclaimed from lakes, sea or swamps and protected by the dikes. Polders cover most of the Netherlands in the west and they contain the country's richest soil.

Eight islands comprise the Zeeland province. The Roosevelt (Rooseveld) family of presidential fame hailed from the Island of Tholen— one of these eight. The people of the province of Zeeland live in the Polders and are referred to as the "low Dutch," not to imply any lower social status. Canals (about 4,000 miles) and train tracks crisscross the tiny, but densely populated country. Climate in the Netherlands is moderate with temperatures ranging from 80 degrees F. in the summer to 35 degrees F. in the winter. Rainfall is frequent but storms last only a short while.

During Spain's rule of the Netherlands (1500's), Catholicism was the only religion allowed. In the early twentieth century when the Janses lived in the Netherlands, Catholics represented 35% of the population, Protestants (mostly Dutch Reformed) 30%, other religions 10% and no religion 25%.

Family life was strict and children quickly learned to listen to and respect adults. Birthdays were sacred and all family members gathered to exchange gifts and celebrate. Persons having birthdays gave gifts to family members as well as received gifts.

Children were schooled in English, German and French, as well as their native Dutch. School was mandatory from ages 6 to 14 and the school year extended from August 15 to July 1. Almost everyone in the Netherlands could read and write.

On the coast of Holland is the Island of Walcheren (one of eight in the aforementioned province of Zeeland), a land literally "seized" from the sea by dikes. An oft-quoted statement is, "God created the Earth but the Dutch created the Netherlands."

During the 9th century, the Norsemen built a castle in the center of the island. As far back as the year 1103, the settlement was known as "Mitthelburgensis portus,"(harbor of Middelburg), since it was situated by the river De Arme. It was the center for trade and merchants. Two other cities on the Island were Vlissingen in the south at the mouth of the Wester Schelde River and Veere to the north, established in the 1600's. After their marriage, Pieter and Geertje Janse, Joe's parents, made their first home in Veere. Here Geertje gave birth to their first child, Debora (Joe's oldest sister).

Middelburg

During the 12th century (circa 1123), townspeople built an abbey and in time, Middelburg (Mittelburcht) became the center of the province of Zeeland, with the abbey serving as the government center. Because of its strategic location, Middelburg enjoyed a measure of prosperity during the 17th and 18th centuries as a trade center. A large warehouse called Oost-Indische Huis (East India House) and headquarters for the Oost-West Indische Compagniem (East-West India Company) were built during this period. The company traded in spices from the East Indies and sugar, tobacco and chocolate from the West Indies. They also traded with Africa in the slave market. In 1975, 1,100 homes of these wealthy merchants were restored.

The naval battles lost to England and battles lost in the Napoleonic wars (1795-1814) eventually brought a demise to the prosperous Dutch seaborne trade industry. The city of Middelburg emerged as the quiet capital of Zeeland province. The canal built through the Island of Walcheren in 1873 and the railroad in 1872, however, did not bring hoped-for prosperity back to Middelburg.

Although the Janse family roots were anchored deep in these islands reclaimed from the North Sea, the family left their homeland during the Great War (WWI) that engulfed Europe in the early twentieth century. Many in the Janse line have written that living in such a harsh environment promoted strong character among family members.

Later, during World War II, the Germans needlessly bombed the city of Middelburg (17 May 1940). In response to the German

3

invasion, the Dutch purposely opened up the dikes and inundated the entire Island of Walcheren to prevent the Germans from using their lands to wage war.

Joseph Janse's Maternal Great-Grandfather—Memories of Oud Obaatje—Old Grandfather

Oud Obaatje, as the older Janse children called him, was Geertje's grandfather. His name was **Cornelis de Voogd**, born 5 November 1819 in Oostkapelle, Zeeland, Netherlands. He was the son of Joost de Voogd and his wife was Cornelia Meijers. He died in 1905 in Vrouwenpolder, Zeeland, Netherlands.

He stayed at the Janse house in de Karelsgang, in Middelburg most of the summer of 1904. A small man, he dressed in Zeeuwse Kleederdracht (traditional dress of Walcheren Island residents). It is recorded he wore a tall beaver hat, a black coat and knee pants, gray home-knitted woolen stockings, and silver buckles on his shoes. His shirt had a long row of silver buttons down the front and five large flat silver round circles called "broekstukken" on the waist part of the pants.

As only a few of the elderly persisted in the native dress, he was chosen to open the Historical Fair in Middelburg each day of every summer. His duties were to mingle with the crowd. Dressed as he was, he attracted a lot of attention. One day Geertje took the girls to the fair to see their Oud Obaatje. They loved to sit on his lap while he told them stories and fed them licorice drops and peppermints.

Cornelis de Voogd, born 5 Nov. 1819, Joe's Maternal Great Grandfather.

He died in the winter of 1905. The grandchildren gratefully remembered their kind Oud Obaatje who lived with them his last summer.

Joseph Janse's Maternal Grandparents—Jozias de Voogd and his wife Adriana Jobse

Geertje (Mother of Joseph Janse) was the second of fifteen children (two dying in infancy) of Jozias and Adriana de Voogd. (See Pedigree Chart: Appendix A) Their grandchildren lovingly referred to Jozias and Adriana as "Oba" and "Opoe".

In an historical recollection by Adriana Janse Aldous (Joseph Janse's older sister), memories of Opoe and Oba date back to childhood experiences around the city of Middelburg. Grandchildren fondly remember Oba preventing them from touching his prized eggshell collection obtained from various birds. They soon learned that when he wrinkled his nose at them it meant, "Do Not Touch."

After Geertje was married, she and her own children would often walk from Middelburg to Vrouwenpolder (2.5 hours) and spend the night at Oba's. As time passed, two moves brought Oba and Opoe closer to Geertje, who then lived on the outskirts of Middelburg.

Father Jozias de Voogd (Oba) was unsuccessful at farming in his early married life, primarily because of drought problems. He turned his interests to raising horses and hired out as "Paardenknecht"—the best paid hired hand on a farm.

Opoe would come to the town center once a week dressed in her best clothes and white wooden shoes to do her shopping. She suffered poor health; she often complained of pains in her legs. Her trips to town were difficult. She also would work in the fields one day a week. She baked bread, buns and cookies in an outdoor brick oven for the laborers on the farm where her husband worked. She treated the grandchildren to fresh baked apples for helping around the farm.

A traditional annual event for all the grandchildren and their parents was to gather at the Opoe and Oba de Voogd home for games, good food and socializing. After eating a special stew cooked in a huge kettle, the grandchildren would gather around Oba while he would read to them from the Bible. After the reading, A prayer of thanksgiving was offered, followed by more games and a lot of singing.

Once a year, Oba would rent a large open carriage (Jan Plezier) and take his twenty-five grandchildren to the beach. They would buy candy treats (snoepjes) to eat along the way. Before returning home, all were treated to buns with cheese and ham, lemonade, and ice cream sandwiches (roomijswfaeltjes).

Opoe died in 1915 at the age of sixty-six, after suffering a severe stroke which left her unable to speak—until the night of her passing two weeks later. Before she died, she miraculously sat up in bed and scolded her son Jacob, for ridiculing his sister Geertje for joining the Mormon church. Oba then laid back down and immediately passed away. The year was 1921. Geertje and her family had already departed for America seeking a new life.

Paternal Grandparents of Joseph Janse—Adrian Janse and Debora (pronounced Day-bra) Matthysse

Pieter Janse (Joe Janse's father) was the last of six children (one died in infancy) born to Adrian and Debora Matthysse Janse. (See Pedigree Chart: Appendix A) Adrian Janse passed away in February 1874, just four years after Pieter was born. The responsibility of raising five children was left to Debora.

Debora because of improperly set fractures suffered in both legs, was unable to bend her knees. Her restricted mobility impacted the family's welfare. Being raised in poverty, the children often retired for the evening with nothing more to chew on than a piece of "zout hout" (sweet wood). In the fall, Hendrick, Jan and Pieter would go to adjacent

Debora Matthysse, born 29 Sept 1833, Joe's Paternal Grandmother

6

farms to pick up very small potatoes left over after harvesting—and often intended for the pigs—for the family.

Debora received a meager assistance from her church on occasion in the amount of fifty cents a week. One Roman Catholic priest learned of her plight when her boys went begging at his door and sent food and coal for comfort. Later, the priest promised Debora that if she and her children would join the Catholic Church they should never go without again. However, he requested that she burn her family Bible (a gift from her parents at the time of her marriage). She, with the support of her children, decided not to forsake their heritage for food and coal. Her son Hendrick spoke up and told his mother not to give up her Bible. The priest scolded the boy and told him he would burn in purgatory forever. Hendrick asked how hot that would be and the Priest lifted the lid to their stove and told the boy to put his hand inside to see how hot it would be. The boy told the priest to put his own hand in the stove. The priest left and no more food or coal came to the house. In spite of the sad incident, the family survived and the children matured to adulthood.

In her later years, Debora lived in a large room with her sister-in-law. Debora showed partiality to the grandchildren named Debora and Adrian by giving them each two cookies and two 1/2-cent-pieces, while the others (to include Joseph Janse) received only one cookie and a half-penny when they visited her.

Each of the children took their turn boarding Debora as she aged, but this proved to be difficult. She complained that Geertje (Joe Janse's mother) was too modern in how she kept her house and raised her children. Eventually, Debora was placed in "God's House," a rest home for the elderly, with several of her friends.

Father of Joseph Janse—Pieter Janse

Pieter Janse was born on 28 November 1870 in the town of Veere located on the Island of Walcheren. (See Pedigree Chart: Appendix A) The passing of Adriaan Janse on 17 February 1874, only added to the difficulties of the family's life. Pieter, his youngest child, was only four at the time. During his two years of formal schooling, Pieter became quite proficient in penmanship and mathematics.

Typically, most education came by experience and hard work. At the age of eight, Pieter was employed as a cowherder (koewatcher) and watched over stock as herds grazed upon the dikes. He continued in this work for more than a year.

Then, seeking to improve his lot in life, Pieter desired to become a baker. Considering such a momentous change prompted him to ask for approval from his mother. She wisely taught young Pieter the importance of self-reliance by telling him he was old enough to make such a decision on his own. He would have been about nine years old.

Pieter quickly learned that as a baker, freely sampling the products of his labor could be unhealthy. He spent his first night after work in bed with "an illness associated with excessive sampling of cookie dough." Mr. Giffard, the journeyman baker, was also responsible for teaching the young apprentice the skill of smoking; this was a required part of his employment. Not having the means necessary to support such an expensive habit, Mr. Giffard gave Pieter a pipe and supplemented his weekly salary with a sack of tobacco.

After working a number of years with Mr. Giffard, Pieter decided to become a fisherman and took employment on a shrimp boat (Garmalen Sloop). Fishermen used these small wooden boats on the North Sea. Pieter's fishing career abruptly stopped after a shipmate was lost at sea during a storm. His brother, Hendrik, prevented Pieter from returning to sea.

With this unexpected change, Pieter next took employment with Bude Caljouw as a freight hauler (rrachryder) between the towns of Veere and Middelburg. Pieter was treated well and continued in this job for the first 1-1/2 years of his married life.

Pieter Janse, Joe's Father, circa 1900

Pieter Janse hewing green wood, circa 1900

On 21 January 1897 Pieter, age 26, married Geertje de Voogd in Vrouwenpolder. They began married life in Veere where their first child, Debora, was born. After two years they relocated to Middelburg. Here Pieter worked for seventeen years at a lumberyard. One of his duties was hewing (by hand) large green timbers imported from South America. Workers used green timber because it could be set in water to support bridges without rotting. The green wood, however, was difficult to cut and shape.

In summer, Pieter would contract to cut grass on the dikes. Farmers used the grass to feed livestock. Since the dikes were sloped, the grass had to be cut by hand with a scythe. During World War I, because of manpower shortages, Pieter would be drafted into his grass cutting duties for several weeks at a time. He could be heard sharpening his scythe early in the morning so he could be on the dikes by dawn. Travel to and from the dikes was always on a bicycle.

In the later part of 1911, the missionaries from The Church of Jesus Christ of Latter-day Saints (Mormons) opened up their work

9

in Middelburg. The Janse family became investigators. On 9 September 1912, Pieter Janse joined the church. He was the last of the family to join; mother Geertje and the children became members a few months earlier.

He and his wife supported the foreign missionaries by having cottage meetings with investigators at their home and preparing many a meal for the hungry lads. Geertje Janse did their washing and mending each week. After the war broke out and church leaders called all missionaries home, the church meetings and special gatherings continued at the Janse home.

At the turn of the century, the Mormon church started the Perpetual Emigration Fund. The program allowed Utah church members to sponsor the immigration of foreign church members to its new state. These immigrants would pay back the debt by working for the families who sponsored their travel. The William H. Burrows family sponsored Pieter to come to Utah in 23 June 1916.[1] He worked on their farm for a year to pay his debt. On 15 December 1916[2] the rest of the Janse family was sponsored by the Burrows to come to Utah, where upon Pieter worked several more years on their farm in Huntsville, Utah to pay the debt of his family's passage.

Mother of Joseph Janse—Geertje de Voogd

Geertje was born on 3 March 1876, second child of Jozias and Adriana de Voogd, in Vrouwenpolder, Zeeland. (See Pedigree Chart: Appendix A) This was a very short distance to the north and east of Veere, where her husband-to-be, Pieter Janse, was born. Her childhood years were spent on her father's small country farm located at the base of the sea dike. Memories of those years included hearing sounds of the North Sea waves breaking on the shore, gathering flowers from the dikes, collecting sea shells from the beach, and playing with a homemade boat in the cove.

Responsibility also came to the young Geertje; she would have the duty of scrubbing wooden shoes with lime on Saturday afternoon so the whitened shoes could be worn to church on Sunday. Another unique chore, since matches were non-existent, was to carry hot coals 3/4 mile from a neighbor's home to help build a fire in her home. Geertje transported the coals covered with ashes in an earthenware pot. The children would alternate blowing through a long pipe to set the embers ablaze.

Being the second of fifteen children, Geertje worked with her father in the fields while her older sister, Cornelia, helped her mother in the house. By the age of five she was an expert at placing seeds in the rich soil prepared by her father. In the fall she would be with him again, as they threshed the grain and carried it to the windmill to be ground into flour.

Schooling began for Geertje at the age of six in the city of Veere. For three winters she trudged along the sea dikes to school, facing the cold wind from the North Sea. In the fall of 1884 hard times befell the de Voogd family. Geertje (being only eight years old) was hired out to a well-to-do-farmer. This was very hard work and she was only allowed to return home one day a month. Geertje was not treated well and her hands suffered frostbite with severe bleeding cracks. Food was scarce and one day, while the farmer and his wife were away, the hired help treated themselves to a full meal. Retribution was severe and Geertje's father finally retrieved her from her awful plight. Upon returning home, Geertje recalls being treated to large bowl of buttermilk oatmeal porridge (botermelkpap).

Geertje de Voogd Janse, Joe's Mother, circa 1900

Soon Geertje was hired out again, this time to a more considerate farmer, who fed her well and whose wife trained her extensively in domestic duties. She also undertook employment with a butcher for a short while.

After her marriage to Pieter Janse in 1897, Geertje would go two days a week to do washing for people she had worked with before her marriage. She was a familiar sight to

11

those who knew and loved her as she walked down the street with her "washboard under one arm and her new baby girl, Debora, tucked neatly under the other arm."

In Middleburg, Geertje failed in the business enterprise of operating a little neighborhood store. Failure was blamed on her kindness and her inability to deny credit.

Although deeply religious, a characteristic passed on by her parents, Geertje was unable to find complete contentment in the Dutch Reformed Church to which she and Pieter belonged in their early married years. Her religious instruction and daily family prayer formed fond memories in the hearts of her own living children today. Sundays were a day of rest since everything was made ready on Saturday, and Bible reading was the custom after each meal. This always represented a few moments of peace and tranquility no matter how hectic and worrisome the day was. After becoming a Mormon, the Book of Mormon was read. In addition to a solid religious background, Geertje learned much from her parents about the importance of honesty and making the right choices in life.

There is a family story told by their daughter about Geertje that occurred soon after the family joined the Mormon church.

> Geertje had the misfortune of falling down a very high stairway and landing with her face on a marble floor at the home of the rich people where my sister Dora (Debora) worked. She was injured very bad on her face. This was on a Thursday evening. Friday morning her face was unrecognizable and she was in much pain. The next door neighbor, Dina Geldof came over and suggested the doctor be called. Geertje desired to be administered to by the Mormon Elders. They came along with a few of the members. Prayers were offered and the sacred administration took place. On Sunday, her face was entirely healed. The power of the Priesthood and her great faith had restored her.

The next day when the neighbor Dina come again, she said, "If I had not seen you Friday, how bad you were hurt and you were to tell me how bad it was, I would call you a liar, but I have to believe what I have seen. A miracle has happened to you."

Geertje loved family gatherings. Birthdays, Thanksgiving, and the precious inspiring days of Christmas were all happy times for her. Her heart thrilled in all things of beauty, her soul sang with joy when goodness, love and affection abounded. Her spirit soared when prompted by the awareness that things were well with her children and grandchildren. She gloried in her membership in the Mormon church and lived the Gospel's commandments to the best of her abilities to the end. Her children report that a mother like her was more than a memory, she was a living presence.

In her later years, Geertje's health became poor and she was unable to take care of her household. Several winters she and Pieter lived with their second daughter Adriana. It was difficult for Adriana's husband Horace to adjust to the reserve of the Dutch manner of living. Yet, he exhibited loving patience with Adriana's parents. They were taking care of her parents when Geertje died 20 August 1937.

Just before Geertje died, Adriana could see she was failing fast. In July, she wrote both her sister Debora who lived in California and her brother Joseph who lived in Chicago. They both returned home to Huntsville, Utah to be with their mother. Joe stayed for eight days. How happy Geertje was to have her four children home with her. She perked up with remarkable response. However, a few days after Joseph and Debora had returned to their work and home, on the evening of 20 August 1937, just as the sun's last rays dropped behind the mountains she had loved, Geertje came to the end of her journey. Joseph was unable to return to Utah for the funeral.

Long before David O. McKay was called to be the ninth President of the Mormon church in 1951, he was a friend of the Janse family. He often stopped a few moments when passing the Janse home for a chat with Geertje. He had given her a blessing before Joseph left for a proselyting mission to Germany. Later, he spoke at her funeral. He said speaking of Geertje, "When I speak of her, it's from my observations. You could not be in her presence two minutes without discerning her nobleness as a wife and as a mother. I have not seen this woman more radiant and perfect than when her son was called on a mission."[3]

Early Janse Family Life as told by Adriana Janse Aldous, (sister to Joseph Janse)

"The place where I was born is called 'Een Hofje,' the house which had a straw roof. It stood at the back of a plot of ground where all kinds of vegetables, some fruit and flowers were raised, and it stood on the outskirts of the city of Middelburg.

"Father and mother made a happy home for their children. We had a dog named Bruno, several cats and a magpie who was the smartest bird. Father had slit his tongue and we (my sister and I) tried to teach him to talk without much success. But to our delight, when our kitchen door was open, he would fly in and pick up a piece of meat and fly out again.

"Our parents made a lot of lasting friends. Among these neighbors, we children enjoyed our large yard to play in. In 1905 we moved to a home in the little waterfront, 'Kleine Werfstraat.' It was a little bigger house but no front yard and a very little back yard. Father rented a small plot in back of our house which we called 'de grootetuin', the big garden, where mother, who did washings for rich people, had her clothes lines and a lawn to bleach the white clothes. Some vegetables and my father's dahlias and chrysanthemums were also raised along with mothers pink forget-me-nots. We had a small shed we called our barn for our goats and rabbits, with a small coop for a few chickens. It was painted green, trimmed with white. Father also rented a large piece of ground outside the city where he raised vegetables of all kinds, including potatoes and beans which were dried. Most of these things were sold for money. We also made large barrels of sauerkraut which was a family affair. Many evenings were spent shredding the cabbage by us children, mother putting it in the barrels and father pushing it down with a wooden thing we called a 'stamper' (pounder). Mother always had a treat for us after work.

"Our parents both had known poverty as children, and were determined their children would have a better youth than they. But they taught us that we all had to work together to accomplish this. They both had the ability to make work fun for their children.

"In this little happy home on 1 July 1907, a baby boy was born. We girls [Debora and Adrianna] were so happy to have baby Adriaan.

14

He was a pretty baby with lots of long dark hair. It turned up in the back so we told everybody he had curly hair. One of our neighbors seeing him for the first time said you girls told me he has curly hair. My sister Debora turned the baby and showed her the way it turned up in the back. The neighbor laughed and called it a duck's tail.

"He was such a good baby and we often were allowed to take him for a stroll in the baby buggy called a kinderwagen—Debora pushing it and I walking sedately by the side holding on to it (how I wished that they would let me push it too.)

"Adriaan was baptized when he was about three months in the 'Oostkerk' of the Dutch Reformed Church of which our parents were members [at that time]. Father and mother and several other parents sat in a special place close to the pulpit. The 'domince' (minister) gave a talk to the parents about their duties towards raising their children, teaching them to pray and love God, to study the Bible, to take them to church, to be honest, to obey the laws of God and the land and to be kind and loving to everyone.

"Debora and I sitting in the very back of the church (the seats you didn't have to pay for) worried that our little brother would cry when the domince would sprinkle the water on his forehead. To our relief, he didn't. After the sermon, the babies were brought in, as was the custom, the mother's presenting the baby for baptism and the father standing by the side of the mother. The baby was then taken by the one who had brought it in and taken home again, the parents remaining for the rest of the service.

"Soon after his baptism, Adriaan took very ill. The doctor came three times a day. It was a sad time in our home and many prayers were offered by us all. After many weeks, he got better. Dr. Kinderman, who had become a dear friend often came just to check on my little brother. He noticed when Adriaan was about seven months old, that he sat in his high chair in an odd way. The doctor asked my mother to undress him. After looking him over, he ordered mother to take him to the hospital. Staying there a week, our parents were told their little boy had a spine problem and would have to lay strapped on a board for 24 hours a day to straighten him out. Father made one that was covered with a soft material and had leather straps to hold

15

his little body in place. We called it 'Adriaan's plankje' (Adriaan's board). The only time he was taken off it was for his bath twice a day. It was so sad seeing our little brother suffering like that.

"Dr. Kinderman suggested he be taken off the board when he was 14 months old so he could learn to walk. It was a difficult time for all of us. He had to learn the use of his legs. Dr. Kinderman advised us what to do. After school we played with him and helped with the exercises. How happy we all were when about 16 months of age, he managed a few wobbly steps. Our kind doctors constant interest in Adriaan was so appreciated by our parents. After that he was in the hospital many times. He slept in special plaster casts until he was four and half years. He had braces of all kinds. Adriaan learned what pain meant early in his life, to be patient, to accept the difficulties. Often he would stand against the wall of our house and watch the other children play. Most of the children were kind to him.

"He had two special friends, Pieter de Ryeke, a fat rosy cheeked boy who lived on the dike close by and Corry Akkenaar, who lived across the street. They all three loved to play in the canal which had a stone walkway covered with some water. A very enjoyable place to sail little homemade sail boats, search for small crabs and of all the pleasures, three little boys could most enjoy wading in 'Voetjesbaden' often forgetting to take off their stockings and wooden shoes. We all wore wooden shoes during the week. One rule in our home was that we were to leave them in the evening by the back door turning them up side down in case it should rain during the night, the inside would stay dry. Adriaan often forgot to invert his shoes except the times he had waded or fell in the canal with his Klompen on. Years later after we came to Utah, Adriaan asked me how mother always knew when he had gone wading. Laughingly, I told him because that was the only time he would remember to turn his klompen up side down!

"One incident which gave all of us a chuckle is about a few chickens we had and a Banta rooster. Each time a chicken laid an egg, the rooster would go and sit on it and crow and crow. Adriaan would rush in the house and proclaim the fact that the rooster had laid another egg. It was a long time before we could convince him that roosters didn't lay eggs. Adriaan as a little boy was small and thin and usually had a sad look on his face. He was a good boy and didn't have a temper like the rest of us. All of us loved him and tried to protect him from unkind sayings and harm. Our brother Joe fought many boys who tried to pick on Adriaan.

"Our brother Jozias [Joseph Janse] was born early on the morning of 19 August 1909 in de Kleine Werfstraat in Middelburg. Mother had been sick in bed for about four months, my sister Debora being only thirteen years old at that time took care of the household and Adriaan. I lived with my grandparents de Voogd in the country but came each day to the school close by our home. I would stop each morning to see how our mother was. This particular morning a strange bicycle stood in the hall. Upon asking my sister to whom it belonged, she acted very upset and cross and said, 'to that midwife, we are going to have a new baby.' I being only eight and rather unconcerned about it said, 'that's fine.' She became very angry but offered a two and one half cent piece if I didn't go see the new baby. Apparently she did not want another baby to look after. In fact, she said that she would drown the baby in the rain cistern. Father told us we had a baby brother and to come in the room to see him. We refused and he called us naughty girls then offered me a dime to do with as I pleased. I went in and saw the baby, kissed my mother and asked father what his name was to be. 'Jozias after grandfather de Voogd,' he said. My sister demanded the two and half cent piece back and I happily went on my way to school with my dime clutched in my hand. When school was out for the day, I went home before going to my grandparents. Debora had forgotten about drowning the baby and we had an argument over who should hold him first. She being the oldest or I because I had gone to see him first, she won. Mother was in bed for three months longer due to ill health. Debora cared for baby Jozias. Later, she taught him to walk, to talk and he would rather go to her than anyone else.

"Jozias or Joostje as we called him, was a fat healthy but cross baby. Every time he cried, which was often, Debora would feed him as Mother still was not strong enough to care for him. Years later we decided the reason he was so cross was because he was over fed. He

17

needed a drink of water maybe more than all that food we crowded in him, giving him something to eat every time he cried.

"Adriaan and Joe, being only two years apart, were very close, always doing things together. Joe fighting Adriaan's as well as his own battles. They went to 'Kleuter School' (kindergarten) together, played on the dike and canal, came home wet, Joe often pulling Adriaan out after he fell off the little bridge that extended a few feet from the walkway and doing their chores together. Adriaan started in grade school in August, 1913. Due to his health, being absent so much, he didn't pass and spent two years in the first grade. He was in the third grade when we left for America to join our Father.

"Joe was in the second grade and they attended the same school. Adriaan was slower in his learning than Joe who was quick to grasp things. When we were ready to leave for America, his teacher gave an excellent report on Joe, stating he always wanted to do things 105%.

"While the family was yet in Holland I still have more memories. Father, who always was trying to earn a little extra money, rented

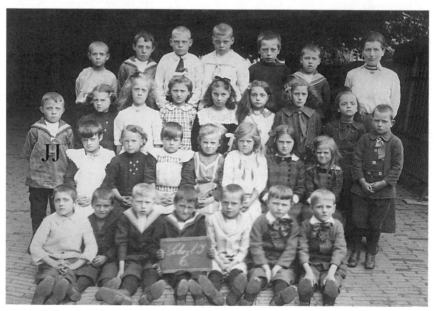

School Picture in Holland, Joe, 2nd row, left end; Adriaan, top row second from the left.

18

pieces of grass along the roads, cutting the grass for hay to feed his goats and many rabbits. What a happy evening when we all went along to bring home the hay in fathers push cart. Adriaan was the one who could sit on top of the load, while the rest of us helped pull the load or walked. Mother would have a basket of lunch and Father gave us treats when we got home. On delivering our kindling wood on Wednesday afternoon, we had fun. Father had made a beautiful wagon for his boys, a replica of the wagons the farmers use. The boys were always so proud to use it, as many people would ask, 'which wagon maker has made that?' and they would proudly say, our father did, but he is not a wagon maker by trade.

"Father bought scrap wood where he worked and sawed it in length of the same size. Adriana chopped it, Joe and Adriaan put it in gunny sacks and the three delivered each week to regular customers. The wagon was loaded and Joe would act as horse even with a bit in his mouth. Adriaan sitting on top of the load would hold the lines, Adriana walking by the side, taking care of deliveries and collecting of the money—a bushel basket of kindling for 10 cents. Half the money was for father and we received the other half of the money—to be spent for candy or toys? Oh no! Money put in our 'Spaarpot' (piggy bank) is to be used for new clothing or shoes later on. We didn't feel bad that we had to save it. Adriaan and Joe were so proud when they bought a new pair of shoes they had earned themselves and it taught us the value of money.

"In Holland, New Year's day was a happy day for the children. Everywhere you went you could see them ringing doorbells, and wishing the people in the home a very happy New Year. A cookie, piece of candy or a few pennies was given and the children went happily to the next place.

"Easter day we had eggs for breakfast. We didn't often get an egg. One year I had my heart set on a goose egg for my Easter breakfast, that was much bigger than a chicken egg. Mother tried to tell me that I wouldn't like it but I wouldn't believe her and was determined to have one. I was told by my mother that I was to earn the money to buy one, (12-1/2 cents). How I worked and saved my half

19

pennies for it! Mother cooked it for me on Easter morning. Did I like it? No! Only took one bite. 'Don't you like it father asked?' I shook my head. 'Just give it to me, I'll eat it,' and he did. No other egg was forthcoming to me that day (a lesson well learned).

"Birthdays are sacred days in Holland. The birthdays of the Royal Family are celebrated by everyone. Relatives come to visit on birthdays. They bring small gifts and also receive some.

"In the spring there was a special day to go to church and pray for the growth of the crops. In November there was a day called 'Dankdag.' This was a day to go to church to thank God for the blessing of a bountiful crop.

"What a happy time when St. Nicolaas or Sinter Klaas comes to the Dutch children on the evening of December 5th, bringing gifts to all who are good. He arrives by boat from Spain, along with his white horse and black servant called Peter. As he rides down the gangplank on his horse he is greeted by the Queen and officially welcomed to the country.

"Sinter Klaas always came in person to our house with his servant Peter, carrying a bag of presents for the good children and a bundle of twigs to use on naughty ones. Of course we told Sinter Klaas we had been good. We sang a few songs for him and candy and presents were given to us. Before going to bed we would put some hay and carrots in our wooden shoes by our front door step for Sinter Klaas's horse when he rode through the streets after midnight. We always found the hay and carrots gone but more goodies in our shoes. The thing that always bothered us was that mother always sent father after milk to our milkman and he didn't return until after Sinter Klaas had come. One year about a week before this special day, my sister who was four years older, shattered my life by saying (and looking like the cat that licked all the cream of the milk), 'Who do you think Sinter Klaas is?' 'Why Sinter Klaas of course.' She laughed, 'You dummy, its our father and black Peter is our neighbor.' I just wouldn't believe her until she took me upstairs, opened a cupboard and brought out the Sinter Klaas suit. I believed her then. She said, 'Didn't you ever wonder why father was sent after milk when he never went any other time?' Mother, when she saw how upset I was, scolded my sister and made me promise that I would not do the same to my little brothers.

"Christmas in Holland is so different from Christmas in America. Santa Claus has no place in Dutch Christmas. St. Nicolaas and gift giving is all over by December 25th and Christmas is celebrated as the birth of the babe in the manger. They have two days of 'Kerstdag' (Christmas), the 25th and 26th of December. The first day we went to church for the beautiful program of songs and talks. The last song by the audience accompanied by the organ was 'The Angel's Song,' Glory to God in the highest, peace on earth good will towards men. After the Amen, people would reverently and quietly leave the church. Outside, the music of the Carillon bell tower playing Christmas music could be heard all over, far and wide, giving every one that wonderful feeling of peace and contentment.

"'Tweede Kerstdag', the second day of Christmas, was spent visiting grandparents and other relatives and friends. Hardly anyone had a Christmas tree, only the rich. My mother wanted a tree for her children. They couldn't afford to buy one so father fashioned one out of some pine bows some one had given him. Oh it was such a little tree in a flower pot but to us children it was beautiful. It only had about ten small candles on it and homemade ornaments but mother had bought a little glass angel to put on the top. We were the only ones in the street who had a tree so we shared it with our neighbors and their children by inviting them to our house the evening of the second day of Christmas, each family bringing something for the tree. We played games, sang songs, parents told stories. After we became members of the Mormon Church, all Christmas get-togethers of the area members were held at our home.

"Some reports say that Joe came here [to the U.S.] wearing wooden shoes, that is not so. As far as I can remember, we all wore wooden shoes during the week but had regular leather shoes for Sunday and special occasions.

"The wooden shoes were warm and dry to wear when the weather was cold and wet, and easy to take off and on again. In Holland, most children wore them to school with home knitted wool stockings. Upon entering the school door, we would take off our Klompen, carry them in our hands, walking along the hall in our stocking feet, hanging our hats and coats on our assigned hook, placing our Klompen underneath on the floor. We used homemade slippers (Slofjes) that we kept in our desks to wear in the classroom. There was no noise in the school made by the children's Klompen, but on the play ground, running, jumping ropes or walking along the cobble stone streets they made quite a lot of clatter. But when there was some snow or ice, sliding on your klompen was a very enjoyable sport for all. Sometimes we got scolded a bit for having worn the bottoms off too fast.

"We always looked forward to go and pick blackberries with our father. On our island the choicest berries grew in the dunes but you needed a permit to pick there. Instead of fences to separate the different pieces of land, rows of large and high growing bushes of 'Bramen' (blackberries) were used, making very thick barriers or hedge rows. In the fall they were covered with fruit which people were allowed to come and pick. Father always made arrangements with the same farmer to come and pick in his pasture. Father's employers gave them time off on Saturday afternoons and we went to school half days on Saturdays so we were free to pick. Father outfitted us with a gallon bucket and a large stick with a hook on the end to pull down the highest branches, for that's where the choicest fruit was. Mother put long sleeved shirts on us as the branches have sharp thorns. We happily walked the hour it took us to get there. Father, who was a good singer of the old folk songs or a sprightly funny one, had us join with him. Coming home at dusk with our buckets full of fruit we saw mothers delight for now she could make jam to store for the winter use. How good those big dishes of bramen and fresh bread and butter tasted for our supper that evening.

"My Saturday afternoon job was to scrub all our klompen clean with lime so they would be nice and white for next weeks wearing. I also had to polish all our Sunday shoes as nobody, and I mean nobody, went to church or anywhere else on Sunday with unpolished shoes.

"In the fall of 1916, one Sunday, the three of us, Adriaan, Jozias and myself, decided to spend the day with our relatives in Veere. We were hoping that we would be able to follow our father to America soon and we wanted to go with our Uncle Jan and cousins to see all the places which always were of interest to us when we went there. It was a 1 1/2 hour walk. When we got to the outskirts of the city an automobile came along, stopped and asked where we were going. 'To Veere,' we said. 'Would you like a ride?' the smiling man asked. 'Climb into the back seat,' we were told. We were so excited we couldn't open the door. The young man opened it for us and helped us in. We sat on the edge of the seat but we were told to relax and sit back. We looked at each other and couldn't believe we were actually riding in a car with a rich gentleman and his son. They were so nice and talked so pleasant to us, and we were in Veere before we knew it. We thanked them and told them how much we had enjoyed the ride and their kindness. Telling our relatives about it and our mother when we got home was a happy event in our lives that day. We also wrote our father about our first ride in an automobile."

1   Immigration papers for Pieter Janse. Janse Collection. NUHS Archives.
2   Immigration papers for Janse Family. Janse Collection. NUHS Archives.
3   Personal Letter to the Janse Family. Janse Collection. NUHS Archives.

CHAPTER TWO

IMMIGRATION TO AMERICA

Conversion to Mormonism as shared by Adriana (Janse) Aldous, Older Sister of Joseph Janse

"On the 23rd of December 1911, when I was coming home from school, I was jumping over the klein straatjes (little paths) and I bumped into a tall, good looking gentleman. He said, 'Heb ik u zeer gedaan klein meisje?' (Did I hurt you little girl?) I answered, 'Nein, Mijnheer.' (No, sir.) Then he smiled at me and all I could see was that he had a lot of gold teeth…besides he was chewing gum. (Oh, an American, I thought, for only Americans had gold teeth and chewed gum.) He seemed to be selling something as he was ringing doorbells. I told my mother about it. 'Are you sure he is an American?' she asked, for the only Americans we had seen were rich and came in yachts.

"That he was selling something was hard to believe. My mother was polishing the kitchen stove and as she went back to it she shook her head, not believing me. About fifteen minutes later our door bell rang. Mother told me to answer it and if they wanted to sell something to tell them that she didn't want it. It was the American gentleman. I told him my mother didn't want what he had to sell. He then asked me to ask my mother to come to the door. 'I want to give her something.'

"Mother's hands were black from polishing the stove so she put them behind her and came to the door. This kindly American explained that he was a *'zondelingen van de De Kerk van Jezus Christus van de Heiligen der Laatste Dagen'* (a missionary of The Church of Jesus Christ of Latter-day Saints). Mother shook her head and said she never heard of that church. He then said they were more commonly known as Mormons.

"Mother explained that she and never heard of them either. He talked to her awhile and explained that they believed in baptism by immersion. Mother explained that she and been baptized and carried the sign on her forehead. He smiled and asked her to show it to him. I remember how Mother put her blackened hand to her forehead and then remembering that it was dirty quickly put it behind her again.

"He gave her a tract called *The Rays of Living Light* and asked her if she would read and study it and he would be back the next week. She did read it and it was of great interest to her. (The missionaries) came back time and time again. Mother became more interested each time. One day he asked if he could bring his senior companion in the evening when Father would be home. Mother answered that she would ask her husband and let them know. Father said that would be fine with him and they could come the following Thursday evening, so he could ask them all about the wonderful land of America, but their religion was of no interest to him.

"On Thursday, Father gave me ten cents to go to the tobacco store and get four cigars. Mother bought cookies. Even we, as children, were looking forward to the visit of these Mormons. They arrived about 7:30 PM. Father had not yet gotten home from work, so Mother very reluctantly had them come in for by this time, the ministers of the different churches were starting a vigorous campaign against those Mormons who were invading the city.

"Mother told them that she had fasted and prayed that if they were evil and from the devil, to let something happen so they couldn't come. 'But now I know what you have said is true.'

"When Mother made tea, as was the custom, and presented the (missionary) with a cup, they explained that they didn't drink tea. She then offered to make coffee. 'No thank you. we don't drink that either.' She then offered them chocolate milk which they accepted.

After the chocolate milk and cookies, Father offered them his cigars. Again they said, 'No thank you, we don't smoke.' After they had gone, Father said, 'Those Mormons are a queer lot.'

"After prayerful and thorough investigation my mother was ready to be baptized. (The missionaries) explained that she would have to have her husband's consent. At first he refused but then said, 'When somebody else wants to join that church you may be baptized, too, but I won't have my wife the only Mormon in Middelburg.' He hoped that no one would be as foolish as his wife.

"A few weeks later two other people asked to be baptized and a date was made for the following evening, 6 May 1912 at 8:00 PM in the canal which runs through the island of Walcheren on which we lived. When she told Father about it, he became very angry and refused to let her go. She reminded him of his promise. He then said, 'Go ahead, but I won't be here when you get back. You can find my body floating in the canal.'

"To us children it seemed like the devil had taken possession of our kind father. Mother was horribly upset the afternoon of May 5th. I was sent with a note to (the missionaries) to ask them to please come. They did. Mother told them about how terribly angry Father was and how he was threatening to do away with himself. Brother White, who was the senior elder, asked Mother if she really had a testimony of the gospel and did she believe that Joseph Smith was a prophet of God. He asked her more questions pertaining to the gospel and the commandments. When she answered that it was something she had been seeking for a long time and knew it was true he promised her that nothing would happen to her husband.

"So, she went alone, leaving me and my two little brothers at home. When our father came home from work he was so angry. He beat us and sent us to bed. We cried ourselves to sleep. I understood why my father was so angry but my little brothers could not understand why this terrible feeling had come into our happy home.

"Father tried to drown himself three times that evening. Twice he came back to the house and looked at us. The third time he thought he heard someone scream and thought it was us children. He told us afterwards how he came back to look at us again and then he could not go through with drowning himself.

"My mother was the first one to be baptized. As the Elder led her into the water she screamed. We often thought about that and we feel that somehow our father heard that scream when he stood by the side of the canal on the other side of the city.

"Father was ugly and angry for several days saying that he would throw the Elders out of the house. They came, as usual, on Thursday evening. Father had to work late and as we heard him come on his wooden shoes on the cobblestone streets, Elder Taylor suggested we sing. We did. As Father came into the house he put some packages of vegetable seeds on the table and began talking about what kind of things grew in America. Before the (missionaries) left that evening, he asked them to forgive him. And he asked Mother to forgive him for having been so angry. He promised that he would try to study the gospel. 'I have not been a religious man, but I will make an honest effort so my wife and I can be happy again.'

"I was baptized on 25 May 1912. My father gave his consent but said, 'Remember, as soon as your friends find out that you are a Mormon they will have nothing to do with you. They will call you names. Just look at your mother, all her friends turn away from her now, even some of her brothers and sisters.' I knew father was right so I decided not to tell anyone at school that I was a Mormon.

"The very next Monday, when we had our Bible study hour, the minister talked about baptism. He said that the Mormons were paying people 25 guilders to be baptized by immersion. Having a true Dutch temper, I put my hand up and said that was a big lie, '...they didn't pay me last Saturday evening when I was baptized.' My older sister, Debora or Dora, was baptized 19 June 1912."

End of Adriana's account

On 9 September 1912, Pieter Janse became a member of the Church of Jesus Christ of Latter-day Saints. He was the last of the family group to be baptized, Geertje and the children having become members of the church just a few months before. Adriaan and Jozias being below the age of eight required for baptism were simply blessed in the church on the 16 June 1912, by Elder Winslow R.

Adriana Janse Aldous

Elder Winslow R. Taylor, circa 1912

Taylor of Elba, Idaho, U.S.A. The family attended Sunday School and Sacrament meetings in the Middelburg Branch of the Antwerpen District of the L.D.S. Church in the Netherland Mission.

Pieter and Geertje made a home for the missionaries. They had cottage meetings with investigators at their home and many a meal was prepared for the missionaries. Sister Janse (Geertje) did their washing and mending each week. After the war broke out and all missionaries were called home, the branch meetings and special gatherings continued to be held at the Janse Home.

Pieter left on 23 June 1916 to emigrate to the United States, arriving in Huntsville in August 1916, where he made his home with the William H. Burrows family. After Pieter left for America, he was unable to send any money back to the family in Holland because the Burrows family didn't pay him for working on their farm. Brother Burrows considered Pieter's labor as payment for Pieter's passage to America.

Janse Family Oct. 1913; *(l to r)* Joe, Pieter, Debora, Adriana, Geertje and Adriaan

Brother and Sister Daniel Boone, were well-to-do members of the Middelburg Branch of the LDS Church. They often brought things the remaining Janse family needed or they invited them to their home for a delicious meal and an evening of games, songs and organ music. They went with Geertje and the kids to Rotterdam to see them off to America when the time arrived. Brother Boone was worried that their tickets on the train in America were for the immigrant train, which had a bad name in the Netherlands. He didn't think a woman alone with four children should have to be on that train for several days. Upon reaching Rotterdam he arranged with the Holland-Amerika line to have their tickets changed to the regular train, paying the extra money himself.

Brother Boone served with the Germans during the time of the occupation. His home and business was taken away from him after the war ended. The Janse family relatives and friends in Holland never approved of the Boones because of their support of the Germans during World War II. However, when Adriana visited in 1954 and

Daniel J. Boone and his wife Connie

explained how the Boones had been so helpful relatives softened their hearts. Adriana learned that Geertje had never told anyone about how the Boones had helped because the relatives were unhappy about them joining the Mormon church in the first place.

Upon visiting the Boones, Adriana found two very lonely people. She let them know how much they still were loved and had a wonderful time remembering many good things. Joe visited these kind friends several times and Adriana took her husband, daughter and her daughter's family to see them in 1963. Adriana maintained correspondence with the Boone's until they died. She is noted to say, "The Boones were dear people to all of us Janses."

Passport Photo for *(l to r)* Adriaan, Jozias and Geertje Janse, December 1916

CHAPTER THREE

LIFE IN AMERICA—HUNTSVILLE, UTAH

The Burrows' Farm

Geertje and the children left for America 15 December 1916 and arrived 3 February 1917, at William Burrows' farm in Huntsville, Utah. Pieter and Geertje wanted the boys to start school at once. Brother Burrows objected on the basis that his own son, who was Joe's age, did not go to school, so why should these peasant children go to school. "There was plenty of time for education," he would say. Pieter and Geertje were very unhappy for they had come to America not only for the Mormon church but also to better the family in other ways. So the boys helped on the farm, feeding calves, milking cows, and bringing in the wood and coal while Willis, the Burrows' son, sat by the warm stove all day. Life at the Burrows farm wasn't easy for the family but they did love the beauty of that first winter in Ogden Valley. Snow above the fence posts and the cold crisp days were so different from the weather of their homeland. Twice a week Pieter would take Geertje and the boys to feed the young stock on the Burrows' second farm, close to where the monastery in Huntsville exists. Coming from a country where all animals are stabled, the Janses all thought it odd and cruel to leave the poor farm animals out in often thirty degrees below zero weather.

About the middle of April, Pieter had made arrangements with George Burrows, a neighbor who lived about a mile farther down the road and had numerous children going to school in their own small covered wagon (called a dummy), for Joe and Adriaan to ride with them. On the first morning of school, Geertje had Adriaan and Joe dress in their Sunday best Dutch clothes and she put their lunch in a percale bag called a "boterhamzakje" she had brought from Holland. Both boys were assigned to the first grade much to their disgust. Adriaan should have been in the 3rd grade and Joe in the 2nd, but now they were in the lowly 1st grade again. They had already learned enough English so the language factor wasn't too much of a barrier for them.

The first day of school was an unhappy day for the boys. Joe sustained a black eye, scratched face and cut knuckles and his best Sunday suit was dirty and torn. When he arrived home his first words were, "We are not going to wear those old Dutch clothes to school any more. The kids made fun of us and called us names so I got in a fight and beat them all up. Tomorrow we are going to wear those overalls Bishop Petersen gave us and we don't want our lunch in that old Dutch "boterhamzakje" either. We want it in a lard bucket like the other kids." Joe had done the fighting for his brother Adriaan also because of his weakened con-

Adriaan *(left)* and Joseph, 1916

dition due to his scoliosis. They quickly learned the American way of doing things and soon had many friends at school. Their teacher was Miss Ora Engstrom, very capable and well liked by her students. She took special interest in these two Dutch boys and promoted them to the second grade after only about five weeks of schooling.

After living on the Burrows farm almost two years the family moved into Huntsville and became acquainted with the townspeople. Brother Ernest R. McKay was their ward teacher

34

Janse Family on the front porch of their Huntsville home, circa 1918

while they lived at the Burrows. He was a pleasant young man and seemed to care for the Janses. He understood how unhappy Pieter and Geertje were at the Burrows and suggested the family move away. Pieter and Geertje explained that they had promised Brother Burrows they would stay until their debt at the Pingree Bank was paid as Burrows had borrowed the money for their emigration to Utah. As soon as the debt was paid, the family moved to Huntsville and bought a house. Pieter worked for the McKay Brothers for two years and as custodian of the church house. Later he share-cropped the farm of Bishop Petersen, raising sugar beets, peas, hay and grain.

Adriaan and Joe helped with the farm work. One year the snow came early and Pieter had raised a lot of sugar beets which had to be harvested. Geertje and the boys helped to harvest those beets almost freezing their hands and feet. Adriana came home from her job in Ogden to provide good warm meals and to keep the house warm for when they came home so tired and cold. Pieter Janse, with the help of his family, was the only one in the whole valley who delivered his entire crop of beets to the sugar factory that year.

David O. Mckay

David O. Mckay was known to his brothers and sisters as "Dade," but to the townspeople of Huntsville he was David O. He had been called at a young age to become a member of the Quorum of Twelve Apostles, the governing body of the Mormon church—quite an honor to be bestowed upon a young man from a small town like Huntsville. Later he became the president of the church. He was beloved by all, young and old. For years he led the children's parade on the Fourth of July, riding his horse. In later years he and his wife, Emma Rae, would lead the parade in an open car, waving at the crowd, much to the delight of everyone (Huntsville's Royalty).

Many an ailing person was made happy by an unexpected visit from David O. He would greet Geertje in the store by saying, "Well hello Josie, haven't seen you for a long time. You sure look fine." Then he would give her a hug and kissed her on both cheeks. "You don't look so bad yourself David O.," she said back to him. Always when he and sister Mckay attended church in the Huntsville ward they sat very inconspicuously with the rest of the people. He wanted no fanfare, just to be one of them.

Pieter loved old-fashioned peppermint lozenges which he called his tobacco. (Tobacco usage was and remains a taboo in the tenets of the Mormon church.) One time he was in the store and asked for ten cents of tobacco. The storekeeper, knowing Pieter, weighed out the

David O. McKay with Joseph Felt (back turned) and Peter Johansen on right

36

peppermints saying, "Here is your tobacco Brother Janse." Father turned around and discovered Brother David O. standing behind him. Father, though surprised, opened the little sack and said, "You like my tobacco too." Brother McKay smiled and said, "You know I wondered, does Brother Janse use tobacco? But if this is the kind you use, I will take some." There is a second family story of an encounter between then President McKay and Peiter Janse. Pieter was out plowing his field when President McKay came riding by on his horse. He stopped and chatted for a while giving Pieter a much needed rest. During the conversation, President McKay asked, "Pieter, if you knew the world was coming to an end tomorrow, would you do anything different in your life?" Pieter thought for a moment and then replied, "No, I think I would go right on plowing my field." This response was always considered by the family, an example of a man who had his life in order.

Bishop Joseph L. Petersen

Through all the years of their lives in Huntsville, the Janse family's closest and most sustaining friend and counselor was Bishop Joseph L. Petersen. "From the evening we arrived he helped and sustained us on all occasions." He offered them support when needed and he never permitted them to go without. His kindness and thoughtfulness evidenced itself in many ways. Adriana stated, "Thinking about Bishop Petersen brings back so many heart warming times and wonderful memories of the kind things he did for a poor, lonely and homesick emigrant family."

Bishop Petersen and his brother Alma L. Petersen, owned and operated the Petersen Bros. Mercantile store in the center of Huntsville. The first American overalls Adriaan and

Bishop Joseph L. Petersen and his wife Ida, circa 1926

37

Joe had were given to them by Bishop Petersen. The Janse family lived in little rooms upstairs in the W.H. Burrows home when Bishop Petersen found out that after living there for about three months, they were still without furniture. Only a small stove, a bed for the parents and an old mattress for the boys on the floor to sleep on. It was a very cold winter and Joe and Adriaan often went to bed with their clothes on. Adriana and her sister Debora had jobs doing house work in Ogden at that time. Bishop Peterson told my father to come to his home the next day with a large wagon. He gave the Janse's good used furniture, a nice bed for the boys, dishes, pots and pans and a nice rug to put on the floor. Pieter asked how much he owed and offered to pay $5.00 with the promise to pay that same amount each month until the debt was all paid. Bishop Petersen said, "Brother Janse, you don't owe me anything." This furniture and things all belonged to an uncle and aunt of my brother and I know they would be so happy to know some nice people like you folks are made happy with it. How truly grateful Pieter and Geertje were for this wonderful kindness. Geertje cleaned, painted, waxed and polished until every thing shined and made her home a place where her family enjoyed coming home to, after a long days work.

During Joe's mission Bishop Petersen often provided financial aid and a needed "something" for the family, but for which there was no money.

Another time Bishop Petersen took Adriaan and Joe to Salt Lake City to the fair. First he took them to the ZCMI wholesale place and bought each boy a complete new

(l to r) Joe, Adriana and Adrian in the Great Salt Lake, circa 1919

Sunday outfit. Then he took them to the Hotel Utah for dinner and after that to the fair. Such wonderful happy boys returned home that evening with some tears shed by their parents for this kindness and love shone to their children by the bishop and his wife. They had no children of their own, but were kind to many children in the ward.

Joe was active in the Mormon church youth organization called the Mutual Improvement Association (MIA) and liked to participate in drama. He was a good dancer, and belonged to the group that competed locally, as well as at the all-church convention in June in Salt Lake City.

Basketball and baseball games were sports loved by the Janses. For several summers a roller skating rink was operated twice a week, with much success and enjoyment for all the young people. This activity was held in the old rock school house, Bishop Petersen having financed the buying of the skates for Joe and others.

The boys would often go over to Bishop Petersen's house and do some chore for him, like currying "Old King," Bishop Petersen's favorite horse, or running errands for him. One day, while there, Joe said, Brother Petersen, "Have you ever eaten great big slices of watermelon, like the black people do in the South?" "Yes Joe, he said, haven't you?" Peterson asked. " No, our mother gives us such thin slices."

In a few days, Bishop Petersen invited both boys to go with him to the lower valley to load his wagon with watermelons and cantaloupes for the store. They were delighted. Early the next morning they got the wagon out, hitched up the horses and were ready to go when Bishop Petersen came out of the house. They had a wonderful happy day—loading his wagon while eating watermelon to their heart's content. On the way home they stopped at Bishop Petersen's sister's for supper. He said, "If those boys can eat one more bite, I would like to see it. I never knew boys could east so much watermelon." Bishop Petersen invited the boys over the next day, to help unload the melons into the store. After about a dozen were taken in, Bishop Petersen told the boys to go peddle them around the valley, telling them how much to charge. They were gone all day. Mother was worried but at last she heard them coming, singing at the top of their lungs. How come you were so long? "Oh, we had to sell them all," they answered. After putting the wagon away and taking care of the horses, they were invited in the house by Bishop Petersen and explained where they had sold melons and for how much. After counting the money and finding as it should be, they handed the money to Bishop Petersen and he handed it back, saying, "you can keep the money for you are good boys." They didn't forget to thank this kind man and went home two happy boys.

Nearly every Saturday, Bishop Petersen directed groups of young men, among them Joe and Adriaan, to go and shovel snow, chop wood, and many other tasks around the homes of the widows and the aged. In the summertime it was mowing lawns, cleaning ditches and irrigating. He always gave the boys a treat afterward if they had done a good job.

One big job, which lasted several years, was the planting of hundreds of small pine trees in the park in the center of the town. It is reported that Bishop Petersen took Joe and Adriaan in his car to Logan and brought back hundreds of very small pine trees from the Agricultural College [Utah State University] as it was then called. The trees were planted in the four corners of the park by the same young men under the supervision of older ones.

The boys took turns watering them by hand every summer evening for two years, dipping the water in buckets from the town ditch, which ran along two sides of the square park. Later, irrigation ditches were plowed along the not-so-small-trees and the task became easier. The trees did well and those that died were replaced. Today, Huntsville is the proud owner of a unique, tree-lined park. One can often hear someone say, "I helped plant and water these beautiful trees, when they were only pint size, while I was a young man." Adriaan and Joe did their share of that work.

Life in a Small Utah Farming Community

Pieter Janse, Adriaan and Jozias became American citizens in 1922. At the time Pieter Janse took out his first papers to become a citizen the law allowed every one in the family to become a citizen. There was a five-year waiting period before he could actually file but during that time the law was changed. Only the head of the family and those not of age could be made citizens under the new law. Geertje, Debora and Adriana had to take out their own citizenship papers.

Jozias or "Joe" as he came to be known in America was baptized into the Mormon church Sunday, 19 August 1917 by Joseph Arnold Burrows in Spring Creek, in Huntsville. He was confirmed with a blessing and pronouncement of the Gift of the Holy Ghost on 2 September 1917, by William H. Burrows. He faithfully attended Primary, Religion class, Sunday School and Sacrament meetings. He was made a Deacon in the church on 11 September 1921 by Walter B. Scoville. He was ordained to the office of a Teacher 3 May 1924 by David I. Tracy and became a Priest 27 December 1925, ordained by Alma L. Petersen.

Joe continued to work for many people as a young boy in Huntsville, thinning beets, hauling hay and later working on a threshing machine. He was ambitious and tried to do his work to the best of his ability as taught by his parents. Joe loved working for George Aldous (who later became his sister, Adriana's father-in-law). He was paid well and had dinner at their home. Joe came home and talked about those good dinners, kind of chiding his mother about her frugality. "Mrs. Aldous always has three desserts and she serves the home made ice cream in soup bowels instead of those small ones you give us." Many years later, father Aldous would tell how much he had appreciated Joe, "He was always on time, did his work well and was always so pleased with what I paid him."

During a rest period while thinning beets, Joe climbed in a tree. He fell out landing on the hoe which his father had just sharpened. He cut his hand and forefinger badly and he was taken to Dr. Shields' office where his finger was sewed. It left him with a stiff index finger on his right hand for the rest of his life.

Like all other boys, a little bit of mischief seems to be a necessity. Halloween was a special time not just for door bell ringing, but Joe was credited for putting tick-tac-toe marks on windows and a buggy on the school roof.

The Fourth of July was always celebrated in Huntsville in grand patriotic style, starting with a salute at daybreak and the raising of

Adriaan holding the horses, Joe astride the one on the left, circa 1920

the flag in the park. The Boy Scouts and their leader were to set off the salute. The bucket containing the dynamite was to be buried in the middle of the park and than set off. This year, 1924, the scout leader, being just a young returned missionary, didn't pay too much attention to the preparation. The loaded bucket was hanging in a tree for safety until the hole to place it in was dug. One mischievous boy went over and set it off and a terrible explosion followed. Branches of the tree flew everywhere. Many windows of homes close by were broken. Arnold Renstrom, considered the most patriotic person in the community, and assigned with taking care of the flag raising, came rushing out of his home to see what happened. He was very angry and gave a lecture right there to a group of very subdued Boy Scouts and their leader, Joe and Adriaan being among them. The whole group helped pay for the damages. For many years after that, they talked about the time they tried to blow up the town on the Fourth of July, 1924.

Joe took organ lessons from Mrs. Maggie Felt and was the organist for men's Priesthood meetings at church for several years. Charles Shupe and Joseph Janse went ward teaching together. Ward teaching consisted of a monthly visit to several families to assure the

42

bishop that the families in his congregation had their spiritual and temporal needs met. Charles was a Priest and Joe a teacher in what is known as the Aaronic Priesthood. Geertje encouraged the boys to be faithful about doing their ward teaching on time each month. They met at the Janse house, Geertje discussed the message they were to present and then they would kneel in prayer, before leaving to check on their assigned families. Many years later, Charles remarked how much he had enjoyed going ward teaching with Joe and the interest Geertje had taken in their efforts.

Joe Janse as Uncle Sam and Gay Wangsgard as Miss Liberty, 4 July 1920

A young girl, Mildred Jensen, daughter of Hyrum and Ann Jensen, was very ill at the hospital in Ogden. A call for volunteers to donate needed blood was announced. Joe, along with many others, accepted the call. As blood had to be cross-typed with that of the patient, Joe was the only one of all the volunteers whose blood could be used. Many times in the next week, his blood was taken, until the doctors said no more when he almost fainted. In spite of all the efforts and his freely donated blood, the girl ultimately passed away.

Joe saved his money and paid for his schooling both in high school and Weber College. He bought his own clothes for he loved good clothes and was considered the best-dressed eligible young man in Huntsville by the girls. His very best friends were Carlyle Doman, Don Engstrom and Dilworth Jensen. They were called the four horsemen of the valley. While attending Weber College, these four young men along with Howard Stallings, a resident from the nearby town of Eden, batched it together. With some help from their families, providing food of all kinds, and their mothers or sisters cleaning the

43

few rooms they rented, they did fine and reportedly enjoyed living together.

Graduating from Weber College in the Spring of 1930, a Miss Abbot and Joe tied for first academic honors. A drawing from the hat allowed Miss Abbott first place making Joe second place. After graduation Joe rented a small farm and planted a large part of it in peas. He had a contract with a canning company in Ogden for delivery of his peas in good condition. It was hard work harvesting this crop, cutting the peas late in the evening, loading them on the hayracks and being ready to take the load as early as 2:30 A.M. to the vinery. The peas had to be threshed and quickly sent to the canning factory where they were graded. At that time, peas raised in Ogden Valley were considered the choicest and best tasting in Utah. Cans were labeled, "grown in Ogden Valley" and sold at a higher price than peas raised elsewhere.

Pea harvesting time only lasted a few weeks, but during those weeks, there were long, hard working days for all. Joe had the help of his father and his team and wagon. Also, Joseph L. Petersen allowed Joe the use of his horses and wagon. How happy both Joe and his father were when most of the crop was in the first grade. Joe also raised some hay. He also worked with Floyd Jensen on a traveling threshing crew—first in the farm communities in the lower valley, then in Ogden Valley, as the grain was slower to ripen there.

The money he earned that summer he spent outfitting himself for his church mission. Joe continued to be a very stylish dresser, so the clothes he bought were extra good quality. In October 1930, Joe and his roommate Dilworth Jensen left for the Swiss-German Mission. A farewell party (program and dance) was given for Joe and Dilworth. Members of his congregation donated enough money to nearly pay for the young men's passage to their field of labor.

Joe was ordained to the office of Elder in his church, 7 January 1930 by Elder William R. McEntire and to the office of Seventy on 1 October 1930 by Elder Charles H. Hart in the Salt Lake Temple before leaving for his mission, one week later. He served in the Swiss-German Mission with headquarters in Basel, Switzerland. While on his mission he labored in Wuppertall-Elberfeld, Kiel on the Baltic Sea and Flensborg and Zurich, Switzerland. Pieter was rather disappointed that Joe wasn't called to the Netherland Mission. Adriana happened to mention to Thomas E. McKay, brother of Mormon church Apostle David O. McKay, how their father felt. Just a few days later a letter from church headquarters came stating Joe could change to the Netherland Mission if he so desired. A family council was held and his mother's desire was that he should go where he was originally called. Joe decided he should go where his mother wanted him to labor.

His mother's health was very poor at the time of Joe's mission and the family all worried that she would not live to see the return of her son. She counseled with Apostle David O. McKay who in a formal blessing promised her that during Joe's mission she would enjoy comparative good health and that she would indeed live to see his fulfillment of an honorable mission and his return. McKay's promise was fulfilled as Joe completed an honorable mission and returned home 5 July 1933.

But during his missionary years, all family looked forward to Joe's letters. They were read over and over. When they were happy ones, the family was happy but when there were problems and worries for him, the family also worried and "many prayers were offered to a kind Father in Heaven in his behalf."

Geertje wrote him more than the rest of the family. All her spare moments were spent in writing in her own language. She had no more finished one letter then she started another. During Joe's mission it became Adriana's duty to translate her parent's letters to him. She would sometimes suggest that her mother not write so often or else compose shorter letters. Geertje would smile and say "please don't take that pleasure away from me."

Joe had almost completely forgotten his Dutch, and his parents could not write English. This translating chore helped Adriana realize what volumes of wisdom and spiritual promptings her parent's letters contained. Out of these letters she extracted a deeper understanding of her parents' spiritual integrity and propriety. Joe also expressed that each one of their letters to him was full of wisdom, inspiration and encouragement.

As the family was experiencing the sharp intrusions of the Depression, it became difficult to get the necessary money together to send to Joe to sustain him on his mission. Keeping Joe on a mission became a family project. Adriaan helped with income from his chickens. Adriana and her husband Horace made contributions, as did Debora and her family. Pieter did extra chores and work for people of the town, working almost day and night in order to make an extra dollar. But not withstanding the hard work, and sacrifices, the whole effort is remembered as "a joy and blessing to all."

One time Joe asked for an extra $50.00 to by some needed things, but his parents did not know how to get that extra money. They already owed to Joseph L. Petersen $40.00 having promised to pay it back in a certain time. They had the money but the question was weather to send it to Joe or to pay Brother Petersen as promised. The decision was made to pay the debt, having faith that some way the money for Joe would be there. Pieter and Geertje went together and paid the money. After visiting awhile they left for home but had only come to the gate when Petersen's wife called them back saying "Joseph wants to see you a minute." Joseph Petersen then came to the door, handed them back the money and said, please send this to your boy, Joseph. Pieter and Geertje cried. Brother Petersen was a person who, when you had promised a thing, he expected you to fulfill that promise, but in return could be very generous. Adriana gave Joe's parents $10.00 the next day, and the extra money Joe needed was soon on its way.

Joe's mission was a time when the family was united, working to help each other. They learned that sacrifices brought them closer together. Joe arrived home somewhat unexpectedly on the morning of 5 July 1933. He called from the train station in the nearby city of Ogden saying, "I am home, come and get me." Dora (Sister Debora) piled all the nieces and nephews in her car so they could greet their Uncle Joe first. Adriana stayed home with her aging parents. Her little girl Ruth was worried her Uncle Joe, whom she only knew from his pictures, wouldn't like her because she had freckles. When he saw her he picked her up and gave her a big hug and said, "I love little girls with freckles." Needless to say, Uncle Joe was the big thing in her life after that. The family was completely happy and grateful to have Joe home once again—after nearly a three-year absence.

CHAPTER FOUR

MORMON MISSIONARY

SWISS GERMAN MISSION
THE CHURCH OF JESUS CHRIST OF LATTER-DAY SAINTS
1930-1933

In the words of Dr. Janse, written in December, 1984:

Characteristic of all Mormon youth in a typical Mormon community, I attended church regularly and progressively was ordained a Deacon, a Teacher, a Priest and then an Elder. It was fully understood by all of us in the family that upon completion of my two years in college I was to go on a mission. The Stake President (Stake equal to a Diocese) had been the President of the Swiss-German Mission and he insisted that I accept a call to that mission.

On October 8th, 1930, I and two of my personal friends and boyhood chums [Glenn Hall and Dilworth Jensen] left for Cologne, Germany by train and steamer. All in all, there were about 20 in the group. We landed

Janse Family, *(l to r)* Debora and Adriana sitting, Adrian, Pieter, Geertje and Joseph standing, 1930

in Hamburg and fortunately a regional church conference was scheduled so we had occasion to attend and be exposed to a typical event of the mission. The mission president, Fred Tadje, and his wife had come up from the mission headquarters in Basel, Switzerland. He met with us newcomers in a brief introductory session, which was most rewarding and encouraging.

After the conference, we left by train to Cologne via Bremen. Upon arriving in Cologne, we were met by a Brother Webb. He took us to a small apartment and advised us that for the next two

Dilworth Jensen *(l)*, Joseph Janse *(r)*, enroute to mission field, 1930

weeks he would instruct us in the basics of the German language. This was quite an experience. I was rather fortunate that I did know something about the Dutch language and there were similarities between it and the German language that were helpful. Cologne with its narrow streets, its cathedral (famous all over Europe), its shops and its location adjoining the Rhine with its almost innumerable boats was beautiful. It was a fascinating experience for a young farm boy, who was somewhat homesick and who like most missionaries had left a girl friend behind at home and for whom he longed. In my case, she was the belle of the town and the only daughter of a comparatively well-to-do merchant and of course I considered myself most fortunate. No, the romance did not last. Usually absence does not make the heart grow fonder. Upon my return home, she had become engaged to someone else whom she married and certainly found happiness. They had a son; both passed away rather early.

After the two weeks of language schooling in the German, I was assigned to begin my missionary activities in the fairly nearby tri-city complex of Wupperthal, so named because the Wupper River coursed

48

Elder Janse in the mission field, 1931

through this complex. Actually, there were three city complexes. We were stationed in the central one called Elberfeld and immediately joining was the city of Barmen to the North and West and Solingen to the South and East. Solingen of course is known practically all over the world as a major site in the manufacture of the tableware of knives, forks, spoons, etc. Wupperthal is of course prominently known for the "Schwabe-Bahn" (hanging railway). This unique communicating system between the three principalities consisted of a steel frame suspension system over this river and from which the cars were suspended by wheels that were electrically brought into movement. For us as missionaries, it was the quickest way to communicate between the three principalities.

There was a small branch in Elberfeld. Meetings were held in a rented room of a local schoolhouse. Barmen had a larger branch and was headed by a dear noble local brother who had converted his son-in-law and who later was called on a mission to Basel and served in the mission home as supervisor of the mission's financial affairs.

My first mission companion was a wonderful, grand person, Elder Morgenegg, from Idaho. His parents had emigrated from the German-speaking part of Switzerland. He was modest in his disposition but very exacting in the fulfillment of the relating duties. He spoke German fluently and that was such a help. Unfortunately for me, he was my senior companion for only three and a half months and then was transferred. While we functioned together we did convert and baptize some eight wonderful people. Two of the eight, husband and wife, were Jewish and I understand they were caught in the Nazi take-over and were thrown into concentration camps.

Wupperthal was primarily industrial and the site of the world-known Krug Fabricken, but practically inactive. People stood in food lines for hours. Attitudes were tense and suspicious of foreign influences. It made our missionary endeavors difficult and at times did result in unpleasant encounters. Adolph Hitler had begun his lectures and assertions that the German people had been taken advantage of and deprived by the other countries, especially France, Great Britain and the United States.

My senior companion, Elder Morgenegg had a bad cold and concluded that he could not go tracting [door knocking]. I had been on my mission but four months and still some what naive as to the circumstances at hand. So against the counsel of my senior companion, I concluded to go tracting alone and try out what German I had learned. The tract that I had to distribute was entitled, *"Mann Braucht Gott Zu Kennen"*, *"Man Needs To Know God"*. Essentially, the city residential area was arranged in four to five story tenement houses that had a central staircase and door leading to small apartments on either side of each landing.

It was in the forenoon around 10:00 A.M. I had gone to the top floor to work my way down. I knocked on a door. A tall burly man opened and scowled at me. In broken German I gave my little speech, "Ich mochte ihnen ein blattchen geben. Es ist frei und sie werder sich nicht verpflichten, bitte nehmen sie es und lesen sie es. Es ist eine wunderbahre aufgabe fur sie und ihre familie"

He looked at me and listening to my broken German he shouted at me, "Du bist ein verdammter Amerikaner". He grabbed me by the shoulder and pulled me into a small combination living and bedroom, pointed to a women in bed with injected [sunken] cheeks and eye grounds [sockets] and two children huddling against her. He laughingly read the title of the tract "Man Needs Too Know God". He crumbled it, threw it in my face and in a screaming voice said, "Tell your God to feed them," pointing to the woman and the children. Then he whistled and another burley German came out of the door across the landing and the two picked me up on the nap of the neck and seat of the pants and threw me down the staircase. My Dutch temper welled, unwisely I staggered back up and received a sound thrashing in the name of "Heil Hitler."

My second senior companion, although a fine person did not evidence the interest and the drive that my first companion did. He had a tendency to procrastinate so it wasn't long before I more or less had the responsibility of conducting the affairs of the Elberfeld Branch and relate to the leaders of the Barmen Branch.

After serving seven months in the Wupperthal area, I was called to go to the Northwestern part of the mission, namely Kiel, the capitol of

Elder Janse, 1932

the Schleswig-Holstein area that bordered with Denmark. By now I was senior companion and I sought to set a strong example for my junior associates.

I served in Kiel nearly seven months. It was in Kiel that I had my first primary exposure to the developing Nazi influence. I was branch president, my first counselor was a former Navy man who (against his will) was re-inducted as an officer in the submarine corps. Goering came to Kiel and held a series of lectures on the New Order.

At Thanksgiving, four missionaries from nearby Denmark came down to spend the day with us. Eight of us in all rented a small motorboat and went to a nearby island and had a picnic (food prepared by the sisters of the branch). On the way back we began foolishly to take pictures of a couple of battleships (Bismarck and Prince Eugene) in the Kiel harbor. The sound of a siren, a patrol boat and uniformed men confiscated the cameras and we were very exactingly told never, but never to make that indiscretion again. After two days in jail, our release was negotiated by the mission president. Eight frightened, repentant Mormon missionaries had encountered the rising tide of suspicion to all foreigners who did not declare the totalitarian philosophy of the Nazi regime.

51

After nearly seven months in Kiel, the new mission president, Francis Salzner, requested that I go to the small city of Flensburg, right against the Danish border, to see whether the branch could be re-activated. My junior companion [at this time] was a big husky loveable person from Southern Utah. He had found it most difficult to handle the language, but his pleasing, encompassing personality had a most positive influence. On several occasions, we were graced by visits of the president of the Danish Mission. Although I was in Flensburg only six months, the branch was actively re-established with a local brother as branch president. In addition, we opened a small subsidiary branch in the ancient little city of Husum, among the farm element of the Schleswig-Holstein area. All in all, the eleven months spent in this part of the mission were most rewarding. One of the families in Kiel came to the U.S. and settled in the Green River area of Wyoming. All during the subsequent war, these branches struggled to retain their identity and the basic principles of the Gospel.

As I served in Germany for well around twenty months, I noted the marked amount of unemployment especially in such industrial

Elders Hawks, Janse and Eldridge on their bicycles, 1932

cities as Cologne, Wupperthal, Dusseldorf, Bremen, Hamburg and Kiel. Young people were standing in lines for hours to obtain a few marks of unemployment compensation. Elderly people waited equally long for food handouts. Unrest was so markedly obvious even among some of our own church members.

While in Flensburg, I received a phone call from the mission president requesting that I come to Switzerland and be appointed president of the largest branch in the mission, namely Zurich. There had been problems among the local brethren and he felt that I might be able to help straighten things out. So I was transferred to Zurich. It was a commanding yet rewarding experience. My counselors were two local brethren, one an aggressive determined businessman with an ever-thoughtful wife and a large family. Eventually, some of their young people emigrated to Utah. The other, a gentle, diplomatic person who helped so much in setting straight the affairs of concern. The branch president had been a fine elderly person who simply lost control of authority and supervision. He was the printer of etchings of some of the most important artists in Switzerland. His daughter was very active and had an exceptional, beautiful voice. She married a fine young man recently converted and they moved to Salt Lake City and for years she was a prominent member of the Mormon Tabernacle Choir. One of the branch members was an exciting personality, an Armenian, very successful in sales abroad. He was married to a most gracious Swiss woman and their lovely daughter also emigrated to Utah. The fine Armenian brother, after I left my mission, was called upon by the

Elder Janse and the Zurich Branch Presidency, 1932-33

church leadership to open the Armenian Mission, which, however, has not survived. [Since this writing, the Armenian Mission has been re-opened.]

Dr. John A. Widtsoe (Ph.D.) was at that time, President of the European Mission and we of the Zurich Branch were called on to host President Widtsoe, President and Mrs Salzner of the mission, who incidentally had three lovely daughters, who served part time in the mission headquarters and attended some classes at the University of Basel. We also hosted brother and sister May Zimmer, who over the years had served so effectively in the mission headquarters as editor of the Mission Quarterly, as well as translator of many of the addresses of the General Authorities and a goodly number of the hymns out of the Deseret Song Book.

I served in Zurich with occasional visits to other branches such as Basel, St. Galen, Lucerne and Bern for some fourteen months and was released with special commendations. Upon being released, a close friend of mine who had served as district leader in the Zurich area, Elder Leo Hawks from Preston, Idaho and I by train and bus journeyed into Italy and visited such cities as Milan, Venice, Rome,

Missionaries in Switzerland, Elder Janse top left, 1933

Genoa and Naples. Then we traveled up to Paris and eventually boarded ship in Plymouth, England for the states.

In those days, the average missionary lived on $35.00 to $45.00 a month. While in Switzerland, I had been able to save a little because of the generous goodness of the saints and my hunch-back brother Adriaan (post master in Huntsville) had sent me a $100.00 extra. Yes, it was Adriaan who had practically kept me on my mission with money earned from raising chickens. The two sisters and their husbands also gave support and Pieter took on extra chores, working day and night to support my mission.

So there it is. I returned home July 5, 1933 grateful for the sentient privilege that had been mine. No, I will never forget or disclaim it. When I came to Chicago, I remained most active in both the old Logan Square Ward as well as the North Shore Ward, serving as Sunday School and Priesthood teacher, in the Presidency of the Seventies Quorum and both Sister Janse and I in the Northern States Mission Sunday School Superintendency and for three years in the North Shore Ward Bishopric. Then the overload of the Lombard campus developments and too many out-of-town conventions here and abroad, commanded too much of my time, causing neglect of family and in times of discouragement and sharp issues on campus, induced a digression of LDS principles which I am now seeking to overcome and find forgiveness for.

◆

CHAPTER FIVE

GLORIA'S STORY

Written by Gloria, May 1992

Joe Janse and I [then Gloria Schade] began our courtship in December of 1934. Joe was home from school at the University of Utah, for the Christmas holidays. We happened to meet on a snow skiing hill in the Huntsville foothills. In those days, there were no ski lifts so everyone carried their skis to the top of the hill before they could ski down.

We had always known each other because we both grew up in Huntsville and attended the same school [Weber High School; Joe 1927, Gloria 1931]. The kids from Huntsville would ride the electric trolley from Huntsville to Ogden to attend school. Often the train would jump the tracks and the kids (25-30) walked to their destination. Joe was four and half years older so he was out of high school and in college before I entered high school. At the time I was just a "kid" and he was a "sophisticated college dude."

Joe attended Weber Academy, [now Weber State University] in Ogden, Utah where he graduated valedictorian from a two-year program. Joe and his three best friends Don Engstrom, Dillworth Jensen and Carlye Doman were known as, 'The four horsemen of Huntsville.' Joe, always known as a sharp dresser, was at the head of the class and published short stories in the yearbook. I worked in the cafeteria at Weber State College and my father provided turkey for the cafeteria to pay for my tuition.

Joe served three-years in the Swiss-German mission (1930-33). Joe dated Edris Jessperson before his mission and she married while he was still serving. When he returned from his mission, he entered the University of Utah where he attended for about two quarters[1] before he left to go to National College of Chiropractic in Chicago. He had a difficult time adjusting to life in Huntsville after his mission. Academia was never a problem. He decided to be a chiropractor because of the dramatic effect chiropractic care had on his mother's headaches. He liked National College but not Palmer School of Chiropractic. President McKay [Member of the Quorum of Twelve Apostles in the Mormon church at the time and later became President of the Mormon church] wrote a letter to Joe telling him not to become a chiropractor. Many local friends also disapproved.

I was no longer considered a kid and the afternoon we met on the ski hill Joe asked me to go to the New Year's Eve Ball held in the dance hall above Peterson's general store. It was the big event of the year and a highlight in my life to be asked for a date with the one and only Joe Janse. All my friends were jealous.

We seemed to go together from that time on. Our courtship was mostly through letters and short vacation periods when there was a

Joe and Gloria hunting.

Joe milking a cow on the family farm, circa 1936

school break while Joe attend National College in Chicago. On one trip home Joe had purchased a BB gun and accidentally shot me in the leg. Joe always helped around the house when he was home. He was good at milking the family cow. His father always called him "Joepy." We used to ride horses a lot in the South Fork Canyon above Huntsville.

All the girls and guys my age picked peas and beans and cucumbers or whatever was ready for market. Our pay was one/fourth cent per pound for beans and peas

Gloria holding the horses for her and Joe, circa 1936

59

and you had to work hard and long to make two dollars per day. Neither Joe nor I were very affluent so we didn't see each other very often, but we remained in love and made a commitment to each other. In fact, Joe proposed marriage via a letter and he purchased from a family friend two rings, a diamond engagement and a wedding band and mailed them both to me. My aunt Elizabeth Laney gave me money to attend Joe's graduation held in the Sherman Hotel in Chicago. I wore my engagement ring to Joe's graduation. When Joe's mother died on the 16th of August, 1937 he didn't have enough money to come home for the funeral.

Before we were married we borrowed Adriaan's car to drive to Ogden to obtain a marriage license. The roads around the Pine View reservoir dam were clay and slippery, the dam being under construction. A poorly negotiated turn resulted in the car going off the road into the hillside. Joe went through the window and was knocked out. After he was bandaged up and on crutches, we went on to get the marriage license.

Two years later on June 24, 1938, we were married in the Salt Lake Temple by the temple president. My sweet mother made my beautiful wedding dress and the wedding cake. My family gave us a

Joe on crutches after accident in Ogden Canyon, 1938

reception held in the church recreation room. We had no honeymoon since we couldn't afford one. The 'Depression' was still hurting most every one in our little valley and so no one was expected to bring wedding gifts. People just could not afford such a luxury. It was enough to have a cake and punch and all our wonderful friends to give us a thrilling send off into 'matrimonial bliss'.

On the big night of the reception, the highlight was a live band and singer my parents had arranged for. We stood in the reception line for hours it seemed and the band never showed up. I was so embarrassed and hurt at the time. Now I look back and I can laugh at the situation.

Wedding cake made by Gloria's mother

My cousin was an accomplished pianist. She went to the piano and started playing all the popular songs of the day. We all danced to music after all. The next day we found out the band had been offered more money to play somewhere else and had taken another job without bothering to notify my parents. Money was so tight in those days I guess I couldn't really blame them.

So Joe and I started married life on a 'shoe string'. In fact, we didn't quite have enough for our train ride to Chicago where Joe had accepted a teaching position at National College of Chiropractic. My uncle Alma Peterson had just returned from a mission as mission president in Denmark and he bought our tickets with his clergy discount card.

We arrived in Chicago the latter part of June 1938 and lived in a one-room apartment in the New Ogden Hotel located at Madison and Washington [Ogden & Ashland by another account]. Our kitchen consisted of a hot plate and our living room by day became our bedroom by night with its pull down bed. We shared the bathroom with

other tenants. The roof sloped outside our window. Once while Joe was
gone a man tried to enter through the
window and I slammed the window
down on his fingers. We even entertained in our humble apartment.
There was also a bar and dance floor
below us and a basement full of slot
machines called "Little Bit of Sweden." Eller's Cafe and Wiebolts were
across the street as was National College.

Joe and Gloria, circa 1938

School and classes didn't begin
until September so Joe gave massage
and treatments for tips only until
school started. I used to walk to the
Loop almost every day seeking work.
I first worked for a court agency,
bought butter and stored it. I felt very
lucky to find a job in a typing pool in
the Union Railroad station cutting stencils for $60.00 a week com-
pared to the $60.00 a month I was making in Utah. The train fare
was only seven cents but I had to save money so I walked to and
from work in good weather.

Our first holiday together as a married couple was the Fourth of
July and we had enough money between us to ride one way to the
zoo. So we set out and decided to ride there and walk home which
we did. Believe me, we were a tired couple when we finally arrived
home. But we had a wonderfully happy day that I shall always cherish and never forget.

We decided to move into an apartment in the National College
school building and stayed about one year. We lived above the dissection lab and the smell was terrible. There were no private baths
only shower rooms for faculty and students. We had a small kitchen
with an ice-box. Parties and dinners at special holidays were held in
the halls. There was a gym and an outside pool in the park near by

[Washington & Warren]. Dances were held every Saturday night at the republican and democratic halls. Most students were not married and there were a lot of female students.

When school started and Joe had a salary, we thought we were millionaires. We saved every penny we could spare and finally on our second anniversary we purchased our first car. We paid less than $1,000 for our brand new Chevrolet. No heater, no radio, just a beautiful car that would take us home to Utah to visit family and friends for Christmas in 1940. No one can imagine how cold a person can be in the winter with no heater in the car. We stopped many times to go into a restaurant or gas station to warm up. But we made the trip and celebrated the Christmas holiday driving, partying and skiing, what a glorious time. On one trip in our new Chevrolet, Joe stopped to give a single Indian woman a ride. When stopped, a large group came out of the culvert. We fed them and gave them a ride. Their clothes were decorated with silver coins.

Early in his career Joe started lecturing every now and then, mostly at clubs, sororities, lodges, local conventions, etc. He definitely had

Gloria with Indian hitch hikers decorated in silver coins

Joe buried in the sand at the beach, 1940

a way with words and was a gifted orator and was soon recognized as an eloquent speaker placing him in great demand to speak at conventions. It wasn't long until he was traveling throughout the states and foreign countries as a guest lecturer.

After our first year living in the college building we moved to an apartment on 6118 Winthrop for which we had to buy all the furniture.

World War II interrupted foreign travel and limited state side travel but Joe kept busy. He taught first aid classes in the evenings, after classes at National College and on Saturday and Sunday afternoons.

In April 1943, I learned I was pregnant and would deliver in December. I continued working because it seemed

Joe and Gloria on the beach, 1940

64

Joe and Gloria in sleigh in Utah, 1943

Joe was never home and we couldn't afford for me to travel to the conventions with him. I went home to Utah in November 1943 to give birth to our first child, Jan Peter Janse, born December 13, 1943, Ogden, Utah, Dee Memorial Hospital. My mom and dad and brothers and sisters were with me, Joe was off in northern Idaho lecturing and didn't make it back until Jan was two days old. He took me for a ride in a sleigh that day. After Jan's birth, Joe stayed for 7-8 days and then returned to Chicago. I came later on a troop train where the soldiers were sleeping in hammocks. Joe met me and his new son, Jan, at the train station and rushed us directly to a colleague's wedding breakfast.

Joe holding Jan Peter Janse, circa 1944

Our lives seemed to take separate direction from there for a long time. I was home raising children and Joe was gone so much of the time. Joe did most of his traveling in the early days by car or train. As air travel improved I used to haul the kids to Midway Airport, about a twenty-five mile trip from our

65

Jan Peter, Gloria and Joe celebrating Joe's birthday, August 1947

four-room apartment on the North side of Chicago, to get Joe to or from a plane trip. We often spent hours waiting for him when a flight was delayed. We tried to make the most of the time when Daddy was between conventions. Sundays and most holidays Joe belonged to us and we always planned special events for the family.

Jan was two and half when Julie Ann was born in Chicago, a wonder of wonders. Joe was home with us for this blessed event. Our third and last child, Gloria Jo, was expected in June of 1948. The war had ended and Joe was never home anymore so I took Jan and Julie and traveled back to Utah to be with family because Joe again would be traveling to some convention. He was expected to come as soon as he got word of Joey's birth but he was delayed and my parents were on a vacation in Yellowstone so I was all alone this time. I nearly died from hemorrhage associated with the delivery and not resting properly. Joey was a week old before her Daddy saw his little blonde 'bomb shell'.

When Joey was in second or third grade I started working at a job inspecting bananas. Joey was verbally abused by her fourth grade

Dr. Janse and Gloria celebrating their 25th wedding anniversary at the dedication of the Lombard Campus, 27 June 1963

teacher because her father was a chiropractor. At Joey's high school graduation Joe was called to visit a chiropractor from out of town and graduation was missed in the shuffle. We even celebrated our Silver Wedding Anniversary conducting the Lombard campus building dedication.

Our small apartment seemed to grow smaller with each child and so on weekends Joe and I started looking for a house, a permanent home where we could set down roots and be a real family. We finally settled on our dream house on Chase Avenue in Lincolnwood, Illinois, about twenty miles from National College in downtown Chicago. We moved into our new home in the late summer of 1949. As the children were growing, Joe would take them down to his little office in the basement of this home (where he typed many of his personal letters) and talked (lectured) to the kids for hours. Jan was never disrespectful but grew weary of this experience. Dr. Al States and his family lived in the basement of our home for a short period of time when he first started teaching at the college.

67

I worked four blocks from home at Culligan Water for twenty years. I started part-time so I could be home with the children after school. When our children were ready for high school I went to work full-time so that on occasions I could afford to travel with Joe. It seemed as though Joe always placed the needs of the school above the needs of the family. The kids couldn't take private lessons or attend summer camps because of a lack of funds. Joe was never available for any of Jan's scouting activities.

During the college years the kids worked during the summer to earn money for tuition and they made a lot of their own clothes. Joe did buy a car for Jan and one for the girls at college.

Jan ran away from home once while in high school because of grades. He left a note under his pillow but no one ever found it. He left with a friend with only $7.00 in his pocket. Jan idealized Gloria's brother Fenno in Utah and the two boys were found in a motel working their way to Utah. Jan was on the swim team in high school. Their coach chaperoned a trip to Florida for the team. Upon returning, Jan took Roy Jespperson back to Florida without permission. They were found in Florida and Jan was returned on an airplane.

(l to r) Julie, Joey, Gloria, Joe and Jan on family trip, circa 1959

Jan went to school at the University of Arizona in Tucson. He tried to use his money for school to get to Hawaii. He then went to Weber State College and lived with Fenno. He served his [church] mission in New York but had wanted to go to Holland. He went to BYU after his mission and met Brenda who became his first wife. Jan was informed after the marriage that Brenda was a lesbian. She was the daughter of a former mission president and received counsel from Mormon Church General Authorities to help her resolve the problem. No General Authorities ever counseled with Jan. The marriage was annulled.

Jan's second wife was already pregnant when they married. She wanted an abortion but Jan was willing to adopt even though the baby was not his. She refused to keep the baby and the marriage never lasted. Jan has since married a girl from Bermuda and they have one little girl. They currently reside in Orlando, Florida.

When our oldest daughter Julie started her family it seemed like she had a child every year. She had ten children in fifteen years, all single births and so every time a new child was born I would travel to Santa Barbara, California, sometimes for a month at a time. Julie's health created a need for help and with Joey away at college Joe was left at home alone. When Joey graduated from BYU she returned home and worked. She cooked for and looked after her father when I was away in California helping Julie.

We attended church at the Logan Square Ward, North Shore I & II Wards and Chicago Inner City First Ward, a ward of culture and color. Joe served in the Wilmette First Ward bishopric [an assistant to the Bishop] and I was the Mutual Improvement Association President of the young women [local church organization for young women between 12 and 18 years old]. We were both in charge of the young adult firesides held every Sunday evening following Sacrament meeting [Mormon Sunday Service]. This was a calling we thoroughly loved, working together with the youth. Joe also served on the Mission Sunday School Board. I also served as the Jr. Sunday School Coordinator and on the Jr. Sunday School Mission Board [Sunday School for children 2 to 11 years old].

Joe always wanted to move to Nebraska to practice. He had many chiropractic friends there. He never really tried to go to Utah to practice. He always talked about it and eventually did get a Utah license. [Dr. Janse did obtain a Utah Naturopathic License but not a Utah Chiropractic License—See the Achiever Chapter for more details.]

Joe used to treat Merrill Meggs [VP of Hearst Corporation in Chicago] and more often his wife in our home. A common friend was Chick Evans. Joe treated David Kennedy of Continental Bank, Secretary of Treasury in the Nixon Administration and Special International Envoy for the Mormon church. Joe also treated gangsters at the school including Al Capone. A judge he treated would pay by giving him tickets to special events. Joe was never active in politics but he did speak to community lodges.

Even though Joe traveled extensively, the school never paid for any travel expenses for me or the kids to accompany him and Joe never accepted gratuities. The school did offer to build a house or condo close to the school on the campus in Lombard and offered to pay the taxes but Joe refused. The first concession Joe ever accepted from the school was a car. At his retirement party the alumni association promised us a vacation trip and the school did likewise. The one from the college never happened.

Joe would refuse to accept raises offered by the college. An IRA account was started for Joe when the college moved to Lombard in 1963-4. The account was kept in the college's general fund and interest was never added to the basic account but went back into the college general fund. NCC promised to keep up the value of Joe's life insurance. NCC was to pay half of the premium and Joe the other on a decreasing term policy. The college failed to pay their share of the premium. NCC also failed to convert Joe's health insurance at his death into a policy for me and refused to do so when requested. Rather they tried to put me as a dependant on Joey's health insurance since she was employed by the college but realized that wasn't allowed by the insurance company. Now I have no health insurance except Medicare.[2]

Even though finances were tight I did begin to travel a lot with Joe after the kids were away at college. We grew back together with a stronger bond than ever and Joe planned his conventions more carefully. We found time to travel together to Europe, to England, Germany, Netherlands, Paris, Belgium and to the Scandinavian countries, home of my ancestors. On one trip to Holland we visited one of Joe's ninety-seven year old aunts and many of his relatives. We also went through the little house where he was born and lived until he came to America as a child.

We traveled to South Africa on three different occasions and stayed in a compound in the middle of the game reserve. It was the 'honeymoon' we couldn't afford when we were first married. We hiked and explored and acted like teenagers, so we were told. We went to Japan and Hawaii and the Philippines for a month. Then another time we went with friends to China.

In 1982-83 Joe started having some prostate [bladder] problems but he was always too busy to really take care of himself and get help. He refused to see a medical doctor saying he would soon feel better. He continued his traveling and lecturing, even in poor health. It was in the fall of 1985 he took on an assignment to go to Australia and go on a lecture tour for a month's time. He was in a weakened state, his health being very poor but he decided to go anyway, because he wanted me to see Australia. We went and were treated royally. Joe's lectures were some of the best he ever gave. But I could see it was taking a great toll and finally he realized it was too much. We changed our plans and came home ten days earlier than planned. Joe paid for his last trip to Australia as Emeritus President and gave the money donated by the Australian chiropractors back to the National College.

Joe went down hill very fast after our return. He was operated on but it was too late, the cancer was too advanced and even though some days he was his old self and even went to work, he was constantly going down hill.

He always said he didn't want to go back into the hospital. He wanted to die at home. But when a loved one is so sick, you do everything you can, thinking a miracle will happen and when he stopped eating we took Joe back to the hospital where he could be fed intravenously. He didn't last too long. Julie and Jan arrived in time to see their Dad and hold his hand and tell him of their love. Jan

71

had spent the night with his father and Joey and I arrived early in the morning to relieve Jan. Joey stood on one side of the bed holding one hand, I stood on the opposite side holding the other hand. Joe opened his eyes and smiled and expressed his love to us. He shut his eyes and was gone. It was like he was just waiting to say good-bye.

After Joe died in December of 1985, Joey and I stayed in the home in Lincolnwood until the summer of 1992. We still own the home, but seldom go back. Some day we will have to go back and either live there or sell the home. [Home was eventually sold in 1999.] It is so hard to give up the place where happiness and love and wonderful memories were experienced.

One of his last requests was that he would be buried in the little hometown graveyard in Huntsville, Utah — his boyhood home. We honored this request. Joe was buried in the family plot next to his mother, father and brother, a beautiful spot on a green hill over looking Pine View Lake. We know he is waiting to receive us with open arms.

Head stone for Joseph Janse, Huntsville, Utah. Pine trees in the background are probably descendants of those originally planted by Joe and Adriaan as boys

1   Official Transcripts from the University of Utah. Janse Collection. NUHS Archives.

2   At the October, 1977 Board of Trustees meeting, a contract was presented to Dr. Janse that allowed for continued compensation for Gloria after his demise. The contract was modified a few years later but the section related to Gloria was unaffected. Unsigned versions of the contracts are in the Janse Collection in the NUHS Archives. The section specific to Gloria states:

> At the time of full retirement of Dr. Janse, a retirement package of a net income equal to his salary as President for the 1976-77 fiscal year, such income to be derived from the sum of Social Security, the College Pension Fund Plan, and a special Janse Retirement Fund established by the College, and that in the event of Dr. Janse's demise 50% of this amount shall be paid annually to his wife for the rest of her life.

In personal communication (6 February 2006) with Dr. Winterstein, the College/University has continued to meet this contractual agreement with Ms. Janse in the amount of an Annual premium on a Medicare Supplement Policy - $3,041.20 and a Pension payment of $799.17 per month. Personal communication with undisclosed individuals who would have had access to such information indicate Pension payment was reinstated in 1999 and were unaware how long the payments had not been made. Board minutes were not available for review.

73

CHAPTER SIX

INTRODUCTION TO CHIROPRACTIC

Dr. Ross McCune, a chiropractor from Ogden, Utah, treated Geertje Janse for several years, relieving her of excruciating head pains. Dr. McCune invited Joe to a chiropractic convention at the Hotel Utah in Salt Lake City. Joe was very impressed with the lectures and discussion, especially with the President of National College of Chiropractic, Dr. William Schultze. That is when he decided to become a doctor of chiropractic and go to National College in Chicago for training.

When Joe decided to become a doctor of chiropractic many of the learned towns people tried to dissuade him of that decision saying, "Joe, you are too smart and intelligent for a quack profession like that. You should be a medical doctor." Apostle David O. McKay was one of these highly respected community and church leaders who tried to dissuade him from his decision. But Joe was determined that being a doctor of chiropractic was what he wanted to do. Bishop Joseph L. Petersen was almost the only one in Huntsville who encouraged Joe in his decision to become a doctor of chiropractic. He was always interested in the progress Joe had made in his chosen profession and proud of him.

The following is an interview I had with Dr. McCune on 19 October 1983 (two years before Dr. Janse's death), regarding his memory of leading Dr. Janse into chiropractic.

McCune: Dr. Janse filled a mission in Europe, I think it was Switzerland and when he came home he was wondering about what kind of work he could do. At that time I was adjusting his mother who lived in Huntsville and she suffered with severe headaches and I adjusted her so she would be down once every week or ten days and she got a lot of relief. When Dr. Janse came home, I thought, well here's a man that's got a professional attitude, I think he would make a good chiropractor. So, I took him to Salt Lake to see Dr. Palmer, B.J. Palmer, and he had an interview and he was not very impressed. Later on when the Utah Chiropractors met down there again and they had the National School here teaching—I think his name was Schultze and I took him down and let him have an interview with him and he was sold and that was the reason he went back to study chiropractic because of the results his mother had and because of his interview, he was impressed with Dr. Schultze. So, he went back and instead of going to the Palmer College he went to the National. After he graduated, he became active there and later the head of the school. Dr. Janse is a fine man. He is clean cut and he's got very definite opinions and he can deliver the English language like nobody else.

Phillips: Did you ever treat Dr. Janse as a patient?

McCune: No, I never did. I adjusted his mother a lot.

Phillips: Did he ever watch you treat her?

McCune: No, I adjusted his mother before he came home and the results that she had and the fact that he was interested in chiropractic ideas was the reason he went back and enrolled in school. It was principally the influence of what his mother had gone through more than what he really knew about chiropractic.

Phillips: Did he ever visit you on his visits home from school?

McCune: No, not at that time. No. He always announced at the Utah Chiropractors meeting that I was the one who talked him into going to school.

Phillips: That makes you a pretty important person, you know that don't you?

McCune: To me it's remarkable how he can handle the English language and he has good balance on his talks too. That is my acquaintance with Dr. Joseph Janse.

Phillips: How old are you?

McCune: 96.

Phillips: How many years have you been practicing?

McCune: Since 1918. I closed my office and Dr. Wheeler has invited me to come up here and use his office while they're out. So, I had two today and adjusted three yesterday. I have a number of calls. I think that is pretty good for my age.

Phillips: Where did you go to school?

McCune: Palmer.

Phillips: Did you graduate in 1918?

McCune: Yes, 1918. I opened an office in Ogden [Utah] and I just closed my office a year ago [1982].

Phillips: Were you disappointed that Dr. Janse decided to go to National instead of Palmer?

McCune: Well, I wanted him to go to Palmer—that's where I came from. At that time I thought Palmer was farther ahead than National. But anyway, naturally I was pushing for Palmer because that is where I came from.

Phillips: Didn't Dr. Janse try to come back here and get a license and practice when he graduated?

McCune: I don't ever remember him trying to get a license.

Phillips: You should invite him to come out and practice with you.

McCune: Well, I think he would have made a big splash. I don't know how much practice he does back at school but he's a good student.

Phillips: Yes, he has a bright mind.

McCune: But anyway, I've always marveled at the way he could use public relations no matter where he was.

Phillips: Why did you decide to be a chiropractor?

McCune: Well, my grandfather was a doctor, my mother was a doctor, my brother was a doctor—a graduate of Bellview in New York and I didn't like the idea of a drug, I didn't like the idea of the knife and I wanted to do something different in the health game. I got some books and at that time I decided to go study osteopathy in Los Angeles but when I read B. J.'s book, I decided that there was more science to it [chiropractic] than there was osteopathy. And that was the thing that persuaded me to go into chiropractic.

Janse and the Palmer's of Chiropractic

Dr. Janse and B.J. Palmer were contemporaries throughout much of their professional lives. B.J. Palmer passed in 1961, sixteen years after Janse had been named President of the National College. In all of Dr. Janse's personal correspondence, I never found a derogatory comment about B.J. Palmer, in spite of his continuous opposition to the educational standards set by the Council on Education of the NCA, to which Janse served as an officer for over ten years.

I did find a comment regarding D.D. Palmer:

"D.D. Palmer was great—because he possessed the unique and admirable quality of being a person capable of combining biological concepts, philosophical wisdom and spiritual realizations into fundamentals of life interpretation that are both remarkable and invigorating."[1]

Janse's Wisdom on Choosing a Career

In a talk given to the young people of his church [undated], Dr. Janse lays out quite meticulously, as he is want to do, the process of choosing a career. In making his decision to become a chiropractor, he probably employed much of what he shared with the youth. His advice is germane even today.

> This matter of choosing a career appears at times to be so frighteningly immense and complicated, and surrounded by the quandary of indefiniteness and indecision. Yet in careful, objective study one will find that there is a formula that is unfailing and has proven itself in all instances when properly applied. May I briefly detail the main points of this formula:
>
> 1. Advice should be sought from one who knows us best and who is the greatest authority, namely our Heavenly Father. Certainly there is no one whose advice is better. In James, Chapter 1, verse five we read: "If any of you lack wisdom let

him ask of God, that giveth to all men liberally and upbraideth not; and it shall be given him."

2. The second step is self-analysis and evaluation. Everyone of us as young people should step back and look inside ourselves and ask the frank question, "What is it that I would like to do as a life's work?" This question must be approached and answered in all sincerity and seriousness and with maturity. It must not experience a playboy approach or with the attitude of idle dreaming and wishful thinking. Each of us must conclude in what area of human endeavor our talents, and interests find their primary definition. What is it that fills us with an inner glow and prompting, what is it that lends satisfaction and contentment? Whatever it is that we should follow.

3. After concluding what it is to be, then we must go about determining 'how it is to be.' Yes we must become acquainted with what is involved in the career that we seek. It is important to know such things as - the related academic and scholastic requirements. The stipulations as to length, depth, and quality of training must be comprehended. We must have a concise understanding of the requirements. To desire is one thing, to qualify for the fulfillment of that desire is another.

4. With an understanding of the qualifications must now come the self-honestly of determining whether we are willing and able to fulfill the requisites. No career, no future, or success is without the need for hard work, persistence, sacrifice, diligence and perseverance. The question now is, 'Are we ready and willing to pay the price?' Procrastination, indifference, and neglect have no place in the pattern.

5. Now we are ready to turn to our loved ones, and friends for advice, and guidance. Our parents should be consulted. Certainly they wish nothing but the best for us. If their counsel and interest are incorporated in the planning of a career, it will

represent the warmth and the brightness of it being a family project, surrounded by love and consideration.

> Amongst our friends and acquaintances there are always those who have attained success and happiness in the occupation that we wish to follow as a career. To these people we should turn and seek counsel. Some one once said, "Seek to associate with people who in worthiness, have become successful in line of endeavors that are akin to your own aspirations."

6. After all this has been initiated and is being concluded, attention, should then be directed in seeking to fulfill the dream. This necessitates setting up a plan, which among other things should include:
    a. A program of saving for one's education
    b. Choosing a college or university or avenue of training at which the subject of one's occupation or profession represents a major.
    c. Setting up a schedule and a set of datelines, that will lend progress to the program. There must be a plan because without a plan effort becomes chaotic.

7. Finally the whole conclusion and decision and effort must be surrounded by;
    a. Willingness to work
    b. Readiness to make sacrifices
    c. A wholesome capacity of modest self-denial and self-discipline
    d. A determination to stand on one's own feet, and to be prevailed upon by those who would procrastinate.
    e. To be punctual and prompt and ready to fulfill obligation and discharge responsibility when they arise and not delay.

    f.   To be friendly, humble and prayerful.

    g. To dream and aspire, valiantly, to think big but humbly. To want to be good and noble, true and honest, worthy and respectful.[2]

---

1 From a talk (undated) by Janse. Janse Collection. NUHS Archives.
2 From a talk (undated) by Janse. Janse Collection. NUHS Archives.

CHAPTER SEVEN

THE ACHIEVER

Thank God a man can grow
He is not bound with earthward gaze to creep along the ground
Tho his beginnings be but poor and low
Thank God a man can grow!

The fire upon his altars may burn dim,
The torch he lighted may in darkness fail,
And nothing to rekindle it avail...
Yet high beyond his dull horizon's rim,
Arcturus and the Pleiades beckon him.

Florence Earle Coates

Joseph Janse was many things to many people but he also had a self-imposed drive that at times appeared to move him beyond human capacity. His achievements suggest he was never satisfied with less than being the best, and he expected the same from others. Perhaps his personal expectations were more than could ever be measured. He continuously encouraged all of his acquaintances and colleagues to greater heights whenever we were in his presence.

Joseph Janse was an achiever in every capacity or endeavor. Whether selling the entire wagonload of watermelons in one day or planting hundreds of pine trees in the city park, Joseph did more than his share and prompted others to do likewise. For example, to be considered the smartest, best-dressed, eligible young man in Huntsville was no small achievement.

Early Schooling

Joseph was an above-average student during his three years attending Weber County High School in Huntsville as evidenced by his official transcripts.[1]

As mentioned earlier, in the Spring of 1930, a Miss Abbot and Joe tied for first honor at Weber State College. A drawing from the hat allowed Miss Abbott first place making Joe second place. Beaten by "the luck of the draw" he remained the best that Weber College had to offer as demonstrated by his official transcripts:[2]

1928-29

Freshman

English 1, 2	A, B	Composition & Rhetoric
Geology 1	A	Physical Geology
History 4, 5, 6	A, A, A	American History
Sacred Literature	B, A, A	Doctrine & Covenants
Phys. Ed.	A, B, A	Activities & Personal Hygiene
Economics 1	A	Prin. Of Economics
Geology 3	A	Historical Geology
Physics 3	A	Meteorology

1929-30

Sophomore

History 1	A	European
Zoology 1, 2	A, A	General Zoology
Chemistry 1, 2	A, A	General Chemistry
Sacred Literature	A, A, A	Book of Mormon
Zoology 3	A	Genetics & Eugenics
Physics 5	A	Adv. Physics
English 44	A	Modern British Literature
Botany 6	A	Taxonomy

Missionary Leader

As a missionary for his church, the Janse drive for excellence was demonstrated. After serving only seven months in the thirty-three month assignment, hardly time to become proficient in a new language, Janse was assigned to the city of Kiel as the "Branch President" according to his own account. In the Mormon church a branch is a geographical gathering of local members organized into a small functioning unit, where the membership is sparsely scattered.

It is not uncommon for missionaries to assume this leadership role in a developing area, as Kiel no doubt

Mission Picture, circa 1932

was at the time. However, such leadership responsibility would have been more common for a seasoned missionary, in command of the language and able to counsel with people struggling with problems of poverty or unemployment in pre-war Germany, broken marriages, or banishment from family circles because of their conversion to the message of the missionaries.

At the 24-month mark Janse was summoned to Zurich to serve again as the "Branch President" but at this time Zurich was the largest and most well-developed branch in the entire mission. His many duties strained as well as enhanced his leadership abilities. In his own words, "I served in Zurich with occasional visits to other branches such as Basel, St. Galen, Lucerne and Bern for some fourteen months and was released with special commendations."

Student at the University of Utah

There was a brief interlude between the time Janse returned from his missionary service and before he enrolled as a student at National College of Chiropractic. During this time he attended The University of Utah undetermined where his future might lead him. A transfer of credits from Weber State College placed Janse as a junior at the University of Utah as he entered the Fall Quarter of 1933-34. He got straight A's in six difficult classes.[3] During the Winter Quarter he withdrew, presumably for responsibilities at home and the need to prepare for his sojourn to Chicago and National College.

Student at National

While Janse carried on a correspondence-based relationship with his future wife, Gloria, he steeped his energies into his studies at National. Comments found in the *Mirror*, National's Yearbook, during the years he was a student (1935-38) indicate that he was involved, respected and admired.

1936   Janse is pictured as a junior and as a member of the Delta-Tau-Alpha Honorary Fraternity.

1937   Janse is pictured as a member of the senior class with the following caption next to his picture..." *'What the hell (o).' From Salt Lake City, Utah, and will return there. Joe has a hobby of teaching, but who wouldn't if one asked so many questions?"* Next to his name are the initials D.D.T. indicating he was going to be the recipient of the Doctor of Drugless Therapy degree. The class prophet made this statement about Janse, *"J. Janse—Puts physio-therapy on a real paying basis by the installation of an automatic therapy outfit. The patient starts in on a belt at one end and emerges in the same fashion at the other end, having received all the modalities by mere manipulation of a button."* The closing section of this year's book predicted individual's possible futures and Janse was noted as follows: *"Janse—We find Joe located in a little town in Utah spending his spare time away from his office working a small piece of land trying to successfully cross a grapefruit and a golf ball and get a crab apple."* There should be no doubt from the above comments that Janse had every intention to return to his beloved Utah upon the completion of his education.

86

1938   While Janse is not pictured in this year's edition, in the commentary section the following is noted: *"Joseph Janse— Sojourned to Utah; collected his license there and is again back in the Health Clinic. We suppose he will be leaving to establish a practice in Utah soon."* Here is more evidence of his plans to return to Utah but it is likely that his license referenced in this comment was a Naturopathic license and not a DC license. Further discussion on this point will be explored later in this chapter.

Grades may have been given at National College but official transcripts only confirm dates of attendance, subject matter and class hours and degree conferred. From his personal records an official transcript (22 December 1948) and an official letter (5 April 1949) from the National College of Chiropractic and an official letter (22 December 1948) from the National College of Drugless Physicians confirm the following:

Dates of Attendance:

April 1, 1935	to	Sept. 27, 1935
Oct. 7, 1935	to	June 19, 1936
July 6, 1936	to	June 18, 1937
Oct. 4, 1937	to	June 17, 1938

Subjects and hours:

Anatomy, including Dissection	792
Histology and Embryology	192
Chemistry and Toxicology	336
Physiology	360
Pathology	216
Bacteriology	72
Hygiene and Sanitation	48
Chiropractic Theory and Technic	591
Obstetrics and Gynecology	480
Diagnosis: Palpation, Symptomatology, X-ray, Physical, Clinical, Laboratory Diagnosis & Spinography	1032 (798 for DDT)

Eye, Ear, Nose and Throat	48	
Dermatology	72	(108 for DDT)
Orthopedics	48	
Pediatrics	72	
First-Aid (& minor surgery for DDT)	72	(198 for DDT)
Chiropractic Practice		
(Naturopathic Theory\DDT)	404	
Dietetics	72	
Abnormal Psychology	108	
Clinic	2456	
Total Hours	**7471**	– 45-minute hours

Degrees Conferred:

Doctor of Naturopathy	June 17, 1938
Doctor of Chiropractic Cum Laude	June 17, 1938

Note: The date of "1961" on the official transcripts from Weber College and the University of Utah are probably related to Janse enrolling in North Park College and Theological Seminary in 1961, most likely in pursuit of a bachelor's degree. It was during this period of time that accreditation of chiropractic colleges was on the agenda of the Council on Education of the NCA and part of the plan was to increase the number of faculty at the colleges who held academic degrees as well as their DC degree. While North Park accepted 67 hours of transfer credits from the University of Utah (Weber College) and ten hours of elective credits from National College (credit from chiropractic colleges typically was not recognized by universities at this time)[4] Janse apparently only completed one course in psychology in which he received the grade of "A".[5] Most likely the press of the building campaign, presidential demands, professional duties and travel precluded him from completing the bachelor program at North Park.

Professional Chiropractor

It is believed that failure to obtain licensure in Utah after graduation prompted the newlyweds to settle in Chicago and assume a

Joe and Gloria in the first year of their marriage, 1939

teaching role at National. Working for tips in the college clinic before school opened in 1938 to becoming a Dean of the Junior Class in 1940 to becoming the President in 1945 was nothing short of meteoric achievement. There was no greater official title National could bestow upon him, but the chiropractic profession recognition processes was another matter.

Licensure in Utah

As previously indicated in remarks found in the college yearbooks, Janse had made known his intention to return to Utah to practice. In fact, in a letter dated 25 June 1937 addressed to a Mr. Golding in the Department of Registration in Salt Lake City, Ms. DeVoto, National College Registrar certified, "...that Joseph Janse has been in regular attendance in the NATIONAL COLLEGE OF CHIROPRACTIC from April 1, 1935 to the present date. He will complete the Cum Laude course (32 months) of instruction on November 26, 1937, but is anxious to take the next examination given by your Board. Mr.

Janse has the required hours and time to take the Board at the present time. We are accordingly filling out his application and writing this letter in lieu of his diploma"

It is only speculation, supported by a comment in the minutes of the Council on Education meeting held in Chicago on February 1-3, 1950, that Janse was refused the opportunity to take the Utah Board examination for political reasons since he appeared to have met the academic qualifications. In the minutes it states, "...the example of the State of Utah, where the State Board of Examiners refused to recognize any of the colleges that taught physiotherapy."[6] Quite an irony given the fact that National's founder, J.F.A. Howard was a native son of Utah.[7] One can only wonder how the future of chiropractic education would have developed had Joseph Janse settled into private practice in Utah.

But the Utah saga does not end in 1937. Janse obtained his license to practice Naturopathy in Utah on 9 May 1939.[8] Apparently he applied for his Utah Chiropractic license again as we have record of a response from Dr. A.B. Kesler, Secretary for the Utah Board, whose grandson (Stephen Kesler) and grand nephew (Chris Kesler) both graduated from National College.[9] In part the letter reads:

Dear Dr. Janse:

At a meeting of the Department of Registration and the Chiropractic Committee held two days ago, your letter of May 24, 1949 to Dr. Wm. W. Seare and your letter dated June 2, 1949 addressed to Mr. McEntire, were discussed at some length and I was asked to give you the results of our discussion.

As you suggest, Chiropractic affairs in Utah are largely under control of the Chiropractors themselves. The majority of the practitioners have created the situation as it now exists and there is not much that we can do about it. However, if at some future time, when you have given up your school duties and are ready to enter the field of practice in your native Utah, we suggest that you then take this matter up. It may surprise you how many friends you have here.[10]

In an 8 January 1948 letter to Mr. William R. McIntire, Head of the Utah State Department of Business Regulation, Dr. Janse takes up the Utah situation in behalf of an unnamed student from National College who was going to seek licensure in Utah but was told the College was not recognized by the Department of Regulation. Mr. McIntire happened to not only be the head of the Department but had also been a Mormon Bishop in Huntsville and was a close friend to the Janse family. Janse makes positive comments about how he was received as a speaker at the Utah Chiropractic Society meeting the previous spring. He points out to Mr. McIntire that not many students apply to National from Utah. "In the twelve years that I have been affiliated with the college as a student and an officer three have been; only three, and I was one of them." Janse seeks help from his old friend.[11]

On this same 8 January 1948 Dr. Janse also writes to Dr. A.B. Kesler about the same lack of recognition. He expressed concern that Utah only recognized two schools, Palmer and Lincoln. [12] Kesler shot back a quick reply on 14 January 1948 claiming to have never made "said" statement to the unnamed student from National. He further advises Dr. Janse that National College has never applied for recognition by the State of Utah and he recommended they do so.[13]

The following June Dr. Janse again writes Mr. McIntire. Utah had just released a list of approved schools and those schools teaching physiotherapy in their curriculum were not included. Janse points out that the schools left off the list, Los Angeles College of Chiropractic, Western States College of Chiropractic and National College of Chiropractic must seek to qualify students for many states, several of which require training in physiotherapy including Utah's neighboring states of Idaho, Colorado and Wyoming. He then goes to the heart of the matter:

> The chiropractic personnel in Utah is, of course, predominantly of the Palmer school of thought, and that, incidentally, is perfectly fine, yet it seems rather incorrect to compel all applicants for licensure to fit within the category of this ideology of chiropractic therapy.[14]

91

George F. Parker, President of the Utah Chiropractic Association, informs Dr. Janse in a 14 November 1950 letter, that discussions regarding the recognition of National College in the State of Utah are taking place and such recognition will be based on the quality of the program provided by National. He offers hope by stating, "I feel confident that a favorable conclusion will be reached." He then asks for verification that National College no longer offers naturopathic instruction to which Dr. Janse affirmed in a follow-up letter.[15, 16]

In a 23 October 1952 letter[17] to Dr. A.B. Kesler, who was still serving as the Secretary to the Utah Board of Chiropractic Examiners, Dr. Janse once again seeks to obtain his Utah Chiropractic License, this time by reciprocity. Having no official response available it is assumed his application was again denied. Janse's letter reads in part:

> Dr. Dr. Kesler:
>
> Herewith, I am sending in my State Board Application. I think that you will observe that everything is in order and I hope that it may experience an understanding consideration from the Board.
>
> I am also enclosing a statement from Dr. H.E. Carrick, Secretary, Tennessee State Board of Chiropractic Examiners verifying my having taken this Board and I was wondering if the Boards decision is favorable to my application whether it would be possible to seek licensure via reciprocity with Tennessee. I am certain that you understand the severe involvement of my time and it would be a great asset to me if I did not have to make a special trip to Utah to write the Board. However, as I told you in your office I am at the full disposal of the Board. Ordinarily, in the summer I do take my vacation in Utah and would be happy to appear before the board at that time. May I seek your deference in my behalf and with every good wish I beg to remain,...

In a letter of 18 June 1960[18] Janse again receives a denial from Sidney C. Birdsley, D.C., Chairman of the Utah State Chiropractic Examining Committee and who a few years later became one of the leaders in the movement to amalgamate the ICA (of which Dr. Birdsley was an officer) with the NCA to form the new American Chiropractic Association (ACA). Dr. Birdsley's son Galen, became a graduate of National in the 1970's.[19] The letter reads:

> Dear Doctor Janse:
>
> Yours of June 17 received this date.
>
> Naturally I have not had time to discuss you[r] letter with the other two board members, but I would like to tell you I have not forgotten our discussion a year ago.
>
> It would give me pleasure to be able to give you the answer you desire and deserve. All I can say is we have had a number of meetings during the past year and we haven't reached a workable solution in regards to accepting a number of schools. And you are aware that the problem is not in your qualifications but in the individual schools.
>
> My personal feelings have differed a little with the other two members of the board at times in our discussions but not to the extent that I would be willing to cause friction by taking a definite stand. I do wish we could arrive at a better solution to the problem than the present ruling as it stands.
>
> At the present time we are undertaking a study on the possibility of reciprocity with a number of states. I do not know what will come of this effort, but if it should benefit you I shall inform you at the first opportunity.
>
> Thank you for your letter. I shall keep your desires in mind and inform you if I can help.

A 23 June 1966 letter from F.W. McGinn, Director of the Department of Registration·of the State of Utah, informs Dr. Janse,

"...following the recommendation of Dr. Phil L. Aiken and the other members of the Chiropractic Examining Committee, as of this date [they will] hereby accept applicants from your school for licensure as a Chiropractor in the State of Utah."[20]

In a personal phone conversation with the Department of Professional Licensing of the State of Utah on 21 March 2006, receipt of a Utah Chiropractic License for Joseph Janse could not be confirmed.

Licensure in Other States

As another mark of Janse's achievements, he obtained licensure and passed basic science examinations in numerous other states in spite of his difficulty with chiropractic licensure in his home state of Utah. The following is a listing of those accomplishments:

Arizona	Basic Science	No. 2783	Certificate	30 Apr 1952
Colorado	Basic Science	No 10881	Certificate (Waiver)	7 Mar 1974
Idaho	Chiropractic	No C-211	License (Ave 98)	12 Jan 1951
Illinois	Chiropractic	No 2405	License	24 Aug 1942
Illinois	Chiropractic		License	Jun 1942
Indiana	Chiropractic	No 211	License	19 Nov 1958
Montana	Chiropractic	No. 9	Renewal	1 Sep 1964
Montana	Chiropractic	No. 172	Renewal	9 Oct 1981
Nebraska	Application only			
Nevada	Basic Science	No 6043	Certificate (Waiver)	15 Aug 1974
North Dakota	Chiropractic	No. 254	License	9 Jan 1951
North Dakota	Chiropractic	No. 53	Renewal	1 Sep 1973
Ohio	Letter of Inquiry only			
Oregon	Chiropractic		License (Reciprocity)	Dec 1973
Oregon	Chiropractic	No. 1196	Renewal (Inactive)	30 Jun 1983
South Carolina	Naturopathic	No 422	License	17 Sep 1946
Tennessee	Chiropractic	No. 727	License	1 Jan 1964
Tennessee	Chiropractic	No. 727	Renewal	1 Jan 1972
Tennessee	Chiropractic	No. 727	Renewal	1 Jan 1973
Tennessee	Chiropractic	No. 727	Renewal	1 Jan 1974
Utah	Letter to Dept Registration verifying attendance			25 Jun 1937
Utah	Application to Chiropractic Board			25 Jun 1937
Utah	Naturopathic Physician		License No 23	9 May 1939
Utah	Naturopathic		License	1 Apr 1957
Utah	Naturopathic Physician		Renewal	13 Dec 1982
Utah	Naturopathic Physician		Renewal	26 Nov 1984

On 14 Jan 1976, Janse was granted status, by eminence, by the Canadian Chiropractic Examining Board. Other than Canada, it

cannot be determined if Janse held licensure in other international jurisdictions. Nothing in his personal records supports more licensures.

Academic Achievements

Diplomate in Radiology

While Janse was instrumental, directly or indirectly in his role on the Council of Education in the formation of several "Councils" sponsored by either the NCA or its successor the ACA, he took particular interest in the growth and development of training in the field of X-ray.

The use and study of X-ray had early beginnings in chiropractic. The Spinographic Society formed at the Palmer Lyceum in 1923 was the first organization dedicated to the specialty of radiology. This society was later merged with the Neurocalometer Society but was urged to disband by B.J. Palmer in 1924 due to friction between the two groups. In 1932 under the auspices of the NCA, the Board of Counselors of Chiropractic Spinographers and X-ray Operators formed (1932) later to be called the National Council on Chiropractic Roentgenology (NCCR). With the 1963 merger of the ICA and the NCA a new name was given to the NCCR—the Council on Roentgenology of the American Chiropractic Association.[21]

With all the interest in X-ray, much discussion occurred during the 1950's regarding the certification of those who had taken extensive training through their military experience. "On September 14 & 15, 1957, a committee composed of Edward Kropf, president of the Council [NCCR], Waldo Poehner, Fred Barer, Leonard Van Dusen, secretary, Joseph Janse, representing the Council on Education, and I [Michael Giammarino] met at the Morrison Hotel in Chicago to formulate plans for a certification program."[22]

The proposed rule and requirements and the proposed members of the *National Board of Chiropractic Roentgenologists* was approved by the National Council on Education on 20 January 1958. When the NCA became the ACA [1963] the name was changed to the *American Board of Chiropractic Roentgenologists* and then *Roentgenologists* was changed to *Roentgenology* and then *Roentgenology* was changed to be *Radiology.*[23]

The first examination for certification held 1 March 1958 by a Board consisting of Michael Giammarino, Leo Wunsch and Duane Smith examined 15 doctors. Three passed: Joseph Janse, Lester Rehberger and Earl Rich. A second exam held in May of 1958 in response to a request from a group of doctors who had completed an intensified course at National College, resulted in three more passing: Ron Watkins, Leonard Richie (a partner of Waldo Poehner), and Roland Kissinger, head of radiology at National.[24] Those who passed the examination were referred to as "Certified Chiropractic Roentgenologists" (CCR).

Requirements to sit the Board exam in 1958 required 200 hours of organized lecture and five years of X-ray use in practice. These hours had grown to 250 by 1966 and to 300 by 1967. Earl Rich

Members of the American Chiropractic College of Radiology, circa 1970, Janse seated on the left

96

Radiology Department at National College, circa 1970. *(l to r)* **Drs. Don Tomkins, Joseph Janse, Len Richie and James Winterstein.**

started an on-campus residency at Lincoln College that began in the senior term of the undergraduate training and ended with the 250-hour postgraduate training. Northwestern started a similar program in 1966 and in 1967 under the urgings of Dr. Leonard Richie, National followed suit. However, the National program was the first to require 2,000 hours (2 years) of postgraduate training.[25] In a letter written by James Winterstein, D.C., D.A.C.B.R. (President of the National University of Health Sciences, who was a student of Dr. Richie's at the time), he states the initial proposal made in 1966 was for 2200 hours but it was not accepted until a second proposal made a year later for 4400 hours was accepted by the American College of Chiropractic Radiology (ACCR). This body was formed by those who had passed the certification exam. In this same letter, Winterstein notes that it was Janse who motivated the College to change their name to the American Chiropractic College of Radiology, resulting in a more proper use of the adjective "Chiropractic."[26]

97

ACCR Workshop, Atlanta, Georgia, 1983. *(l to r)* Drs. Larry Pyzick, Terry Yochum, Len Richie, James Winterstein, Joseph Janse, Reed Phillips and Andrew Jackson.

Note: before all these certification and examinations-in the late 50's-doctors would send X-rays to the National College for interpretation. Many X-rays were sent from states surrounding Illinois but some came as far away as British Columbia. A review of copies of reports generated during this time frame demonstrates a complete radiographic interpretation over the signature of Roland Kissinger, D.C. after which, on the same report, was a brief recommendation on therapeutic measures to be employed over the signature of Joseph Janse. At times Janse would even send a separate letter to referring doctors if the X-ray report had been sent out while he was traveling. A fee of $2.00 was charged for the X-ray report and an additional $1.00 for the therapeutic consultation.[27]

Speeches and Presentations

Starting with his first chiropractic, off-campus lecture in Dodge City, Kansas in 1940, Dr. Janse traveled the world speaking to governments, medical professions, research bodies, and of course to

Dr. Janse delivering a lecture, circa 1970

Dr. Janse delivering a lecture, circa 1975

Pennsylvania Black Lung Conference *(l to r)*: Dr. Leonard Fay, Mrs. Evelyn Richie, Governor Milton J. Schapp, Drs. Janse, Louis Sportelli and Earl Liss, 1976.

members of the chiropractic profession. His use of the English (and sometimes German) language left many thumbing through their dictionaries trying to find words they had never heard before. His style of delivery was forceful yet entreating, confident yet humble, motivational, and aggressive.

It would be an impossibility to list all of the places and groups to whom he delivered his powerful message. Perhaps, a crowning achievement was the invitation to offer the introductory presentation on chiropractic to the workshop

Dr. Murray Goldstein (NINCDS) speaking at National College, circa 1976

on The Research Status of Spinal Manipulative Therapy.[28] He was one of four who were asked to give an historical perspective. It is interesting to note that at the conclusion of his paper in the Monograph just noted, Dr. Janse listed 505 references. His counterparts, notables from medicine, osteopathy and history listed a total of 66 references between them. He was always prepared.

Honorary Degrees and Awards

Los Angeles College of Chiropractic (LACC)

In the Spring of 1971, at the graduation exercises of the Los Angeles College of Chiropractic (LACC), Janse was awarded an Honorary Degree of Doctor of Laws. This was an esteemed honor, rarely granted by LACC, to honor, "...his long years of service to the chiropractic profession. Forty-eight candidates were awarded their Doctor of Chiropractic degrees and 16 their bachelor's degrees. People gathered to Glendale from seven states to honor Dr. Janse. Among them were:

Dr. J. Simons	President-Elect, ACA
Dr. John Fisher	Director Of Education, ACA
Dr. R. Martin	Governor, ACA
Dr. John Hemauer	President, CCA
Mrs. G. Olson	President, CCA Auxiliary
Dr. N. Hardy	Ethics Chr., Calif. Chiropractic Assoc.
Dr. G. Goodfellow	Regent, LACC
Dr. E. Homewood	Asst. Adm. Dean, LACC
Dr. M. Lipe	Graduate Dean, LACC
Dr. G. Poe	Trustee, FCER
Dr. R. Simon	President, Lincoln College
Dr. R. Hastings	Ex. Sec., Council of State Exam. Boards
Dr. J. deHeres	President, Calif. Examining Board
Dr. V. Kersey	President, Calif. Chiropractic Colleges
Dr. G. Haynes	Adm. Dean, LACC
Dr. K. Drengler	President, LACC Alumni Assoc.
Dr. T. Horton	President, Grad. Class 1971
Dr. J. Kirby	Toastmaster[29]

Texas College of Chiropractic (TCC)

Near the very end of his distinguished career, the Texas College of Chiropractic enshrined Dr. Janse into their Texas Chiropractic Hall of Honor on 27 July 1984.

> The Regents seek to enshrine chiropractic pioneers with dignity and honor for posterity. Only eleven chiropractors have been so honored for their many personal sacrifices made in behalf of the chiropractic profession.

There was an unveiling of a bust and on the plaque beneath the bust was inscribed the following:

> In recognition of his 46 years of dedication to the upgrading of chiropractic education, not only at National College of Chiropractic, his alma mater, but nationally and internationally through

101

his membership in the Council on Chiropractic Education, and his support of the development of chiropractic worldwide. This, and for his unsurpassed abilities as a lecturer, author and educator, has earned his enshrinement in this hallowed Hall of Honor.[30]

Officier des Palmes Academiques

In personal communication between Dr. Terry Yochum and Dr. Jean-Dominique Leullier, the following explanation regarding this award from the French Government was shared:

> Before I graduated in 1970, I noticed that Dr. Janse was proudly wearing a French ribbon that made him a Chevalier in the Order of the Palmes Academiques. At the time, my wife Pat, was working as the secretary to the French Cultural Attaché in Chicago and I asked her to find out how he was bestowed the honor. It turned out that a prior French student had proposed to nominate Dr. Janse for his many efforts in educating French students.

> As I personally knew Mr. Jean Digras, the French Cultural Attaché, I asked him if it was possible to have Dr. Janse nominated to the grade of Officer. Since it was indeed possible, we filled out all the paperwork and when the news came that it was accepted, I asked if it was possible to bestow the honor during the Graduation Ceremony in May 1970.[31]

The Palmes Academiques was founded in 1808 by Napoleon the 1st to honor the members of Universities. The modalities of attribution were extended in 1866 to non-teaching persons who rendered distinguished services to education. The decree of October 4th, 1955 (signed by President Rene Coty), has instituted the Order of the Palmes Academiques, comprising the grades of CHEVALIER, OFFICIER and COMMANDEUR. The Palmes Academiques can be bestowed to foreigners and to French people living abroad who actively contribute to the expansion of the French culture around the world.

From a Scrapbook kept by the Janse Family this typed entry was found.

President of N.C.A. Accredited College is Awarded Distinct Honor by French Government.

In a setting both exclusive and prompting, the Annual Commencement Banquet of the National College of Chiropractic held 11 May 1970, in the Gold Room of the Pick Congress Hotel, Dr. Joseph Janse, President of the National College was awarded the "Chevalier dams l'Ordre des Palmes Academiques, of the Republic of France." The award was made by M. Jean Bellard, Consul-General of France of the mid-west area. The origin of this award dates back to the Napoleonic era. It is granted to those who have made significant contributions in the Sciences and Arts. It is issued by the Ministry of Culture and Academics. It represents an honor exclusive to important men and women of Science and Letters. It is sought after with great diligence by the heads of

Chevalier dams l'Ordre des Palmes Academiques, of the Republic of France, 1970

103

world-renowned institutions of learning, culture and scholastics that is limited to a select and chosen group. Dr. Janse received the award on the basis of his writings and his work in the field of clinical biology.

M. Jean Bellard, the Consul-General of France is a man of purport and affluence. During World War II he was attached to the General Staff of General De Gaulle. His war record as a French Intelligence Agent is inscribed with valor and heroism far beyond the call of duty. When General De Gaulle visited the United States and met with then President Eisenhower, in the Spring of 1960, Mr. Bellard was called to Washington to serve as official interpreter.

Attending Mr. Bellard at the event was Rear-Admiral Haskins of the United States Navy, and now retired. Admiral Haskins earned the everlasting indebtedness of the American people by his gallant service in submarine warfare in the Atlantic during World War II. He and the Consul-General became acquainted when he served as a military attaché in Paris after the War. Both gentlemen in their remarks spoke with deference about chiropractic and its significant role in the healing world.[32]

Conclusion

To rehearse the many academic and personal triumphs of Joseph Janse is beyond the scope of this book. A focus on some of his more significant achievements has given a modest insight into his great-ness as a student, a missionary, a teacher, a college president and as a person. How appropriate to close with his oft-quoted stanza:

> The heights by great men reached and kept,
> Were not attained by sudden flight;
> But they, while their companions slept,
> Were toiling upwards in the night.
> William Wadsworth Longfellow

1 Official transcript cards issued to students from Weber County High School.

1925-26	**Sophomore**	
	English	A-
	History	A-
	Biology	B+
	Geometry	A
1926-27	**Junior**	
	English 11	B+
	Algebra I	B+
	Chemistry	A-
	Gym	B-
	Farm Mechanics	B
	Trigonometry	B+
1927-28	**Senior**	
	English 12	A
	Biology	A
	American History	A
	Physics	A
	Economics	A+

2 Official transcript issued 14 June 1961 by the Assistant Registrar of Weber College.

3 Official transcript issued June 1961 by the Registrars office at the University of Utah.

1933-34	**Autumn Quarter**		
	Zoology	I	Animal Phylogeny
	Zoology	A	General Entomology
	Zoology	A	Entomology Lab
	Botany	A	General
	Biology	A	Seminar
	German	A	Third Year
	Winter Quarter		
	Zoology	W	Economic Entomology
	Botany	W	General
	Biology	W	Seminar
	Psychology	W	Introductory Psychology
	Botany	W	Geographic

Note: The date of "1961" on the official transcripts from Weber College and the University of Utah are probably related to Janse enrolling in North Park College and Theological Seminary in 1961, most likely in pursuit of a bachelor's degree. It was during this period of time that accreditation of chiropractic colleges was on the agenda of the Council on Education of the NCA and part of the plan was to increase the number of faculty at the colleges who held academic degrees as well as their DC degree. While North Park accepted 67 hours of transfer credits from the University of Utah (Weber College) and ten hours of elective credits from National College (credit from chiropractic colleges typically was not recognized by universities at this time)[4] Janse apparently only completed one course in psychology in which he received the grade of "A".[5] Most likely the press of the building campaign, presidential demands, professional duties and travel precluded him from completing the bachelor program at North Park.

4 Letter from North Park College dated 2 June 1961.

105

5   Official transcript issued by North Park College and Theological Seminary 12 June 1961.

6   Minutes, Council on Education of the NCA. Feb 1-6, 1950.

7   Beideman, R., *In The Making of a Profession: The National College of Chiropractic 1906-1981.* National College of Chiropractic, 1995, pg. 17.

8   Original license on file in the Janse Collection. National University of Health Sciences (NUHS) Archives.

9   Personal communication. The author practiced with Stephen Kesler and author's son, Ryan Phillips practiced with Chris Kesler.

10 Letter on file in the Janse Collection. NUHS Archives.

11 Letter on file in the Janse Collection. NUHS Archives.

12 Letter on file in the Janse Collection. NUHS Archives.

13 Letter on file in the Janse Collection. NUHS Archives.

14 Letter on file in the Janse Collection. NUHS Archives.

15 Letter on file in the Janse Collection. NUHS Archives.

16 Letter on file in the Janse Collection. NUHS Archives.

17 Letter on file in the Janse Collection. NUHS Archives.

18 Letter on file in the Janse Collection. NUHS Archives.

19 Author attended National College of Chiropractic with now Dr. Galen Birdsley.

20 Letter on file in the Janse Collection. NUHS Archives.

21 Peterson, D., Wiese, G. *Chiropractic: an Illustrated History.* Mosby, St. Louis,1995, pg. 307-8.

22 Ibid. pg. 312.

23 Ibid, pg, 313.

24 Ibid. pg. 315.

25 Ibid. pg. 314.

26 Personal letter from Winterstein to Linaker, 19 May 2004, National University of Health Sciences Archives.

27 Letters and X-ray reports are on file in the Janse Collection. NUHS Archives.

28 NINCDS Monograph No. 15. *The Research Status of Spinal Manipulative Therapy.* DHEW, Feb. 2-4, 1975, pgs. 25-42.

29 The Chirogram, Los Angeles College of Chiropractic. Vol. 38, No. 7. July, 1971, pgs. 15-17.

30 The National College of Chiropractic News Bulletin, Sept. 1984.

31 Message transferred by e-mail and a hard copy has been placed in the Janse Collection. NUHS Archives.

32 Family scrapbook is in the possession of Dr. Joey Janse, Heber City, Utah.

CHAPTER EIGHT

THE RESEARCHER

Dr. Janse's keen intellect and insatiable drive led to the pursuit of research very early in his career. Coupled with his fluent knowledge of the German language and familiarity with the customs and geography of Switzerland, from his missionary experiences, it was only natural that he should become associated with Dr. Fred Illi and his work.

Dr. Fred W. Illi, 1927 graduate of the Universal College of Chiropractic (Pittsburgh), was an ardent student of spinal function and a successful practitioner in Geneva, Switzerland. He established the Institute for the Study of the Mechanics, Statics and Dynamics of the Human Body.

In the 1940's he installed an X-ray machine equipped with six 200 milliampere tubes, which by means of a time device automatically shifted the tubes into position so that anteroposterior and lateral full-spine radiographs could be obtained at a distance of 15 to 18 feet. As an attempt to overcome

Dr. Fred W. Illi, Geneva Switzerland

projectional distortion of radiographic images as well as to reduce entrance dosages, this was an invention well in advance of its time. X-rays of the spine were obtained in all positions including walking and bending to learn the exact position of the vertebrae in each type of motion. There was a special interest in the role of the sacro-iliac articulation and its relationship to spinal function and spinal balance. Illi believed the sacro-iliac joint to be a freely moveable joint, contrary to current medical thought.

Dr. Illi came to the National College in 1940, 1942 and 1949 to conduct dissection experiments on cadavers, not available to him in Switzerland. A thorough study of 25 cadavers in 1940 resulted in significant conclusions about spinal movement and the related movements of the dural sheath and the dorsal nerve root ganglions. In his later scholarly excursions, each of which lasted several months, relationships of spinal length to spinal motion were worked out. It was clearly demonstrated that fixated segments such as wiring C1 to C2 resulted in spinal cord tension when rotation occurred, and fixation of the sacro-iliac joints with metal pins resulted in spinal lengthening when movement occurred.

The story of the Janse-Illi team unfolds in Dr. Janse's own words:

...[Illi] traveled to the States [in 1940] and spent three extended and arduous months in the dissecting (gross anatomy) laboratory of the National College of Chiropractic. As the Director of the Department of Anatomy at the College it was my privilege to serve as an assistant to Dr. Illi. The spines and pelvises of some 25 cadavers were carefully dissected with special attention directed to the sacroiliac joints. These three months involved long and tiring hours each day but resulted in most revealing and astonishing information, which were published in a special issue of the National College Journal, January 1940, entitled, "Sacroiliac Mechanism, Keystone To Spinal Balance and Locomotion." Considered by many as a classic not only in the chiropractic profession but also the other clinical groups. In 1942 Dr. Illi returned to the States for another two months research effort in anatomical laboratory of the National College. This time his studies penetrated still further and

108

were primarily centered about the effort to imitate normal sacro-iliac movements in the pelvises of young fresh cadavers. The methods employed were too extended and involved to permit description in this writing. Let it suffice to say that the results permitted conclusions of tremendous significance in describing the exact movement and function of the sacroiliac mechanism. This second trip [In another writing it was stated the third trip in 1949 resulted in the translation[1]] to the States precipitated the writing and translating into the English of the revealing text, *The Vertebral Column, Life Line of the Body*, published by the National College of Chiropractic.

Therefore it was with a fraternal sense of awareness and appreciation for Dr. Illi's keen mind and talent that I went to Geneva [circa 1958]. Furthermore, having followed Illi's research almost since its primary inception I am compelled to frankly and honestly state that neither in the chiropractic or medical professions has anyone ever presented a more concise, thorough, and exacting description of the structure, statics and dynamics of the spine and sacroiliac mechanism. It cannot and must not be denied that Illi's works are monumental and classical constituting by far the most brilliant single contribution in chiropractic research and representing a clinical premise of tremendous significance. Furthermore, it should be remembered that Illi's work is that more remarkable when it is considered that he penetrated an almost totally new and unknown field. Certainly the profession must stand in respect for the brilliance of his mind and the inestimable value of his work.[2]

Janse proceeds to elaborate nine specific conclusions he reached after his studies and investigations at the Institute established by Illi. They are:

(1) Full knowledge of the exact structure, nature of movement and function of the sacroiliac mechanism as an ever accommodating base for the upright, weight-bearing, mobile spine.

(2) A concise and detailed description of the structure and mechanics

109

of the spine, both in the static (resting) and dynamic (in motion) states; with full description of the nature of movement of all the vertebral segments, individually and collectively; describing the location and extent of all radii and axes of movement.

(3) A description of the precise manner in which the pull of gravity and the force of weight-bearing shift are altered in the daily activities of man the biped.

(4) The manners in which the intricate mechanism of the spine and pelvis may become disturbed and compromised through the strain and stress imposed upon them in the efforts of daily life.

(5) Within the Institute have been developed and evolved most exacting instruments and methods for the analysis of possible spinal and pelvic, distortions as well as the extent and degree of these distortions. Nowhere can they be duplicated and represent the most comprehensive procedure in the study of the structure, statics and dynamics of the human mechanism, ever conceived by anyone to date. Some of the major instruments and procedures include:

(a) An X-ray plant equaled by none other, designed to reveal the structure of the spine and pelvis in every detail and permitting by means of miniature films to carefully study the progress that is being made as the patient is under management.

(b) A unit of scales enables the clinician to estimate the degree of distortion the spine and pelvis have been caused to experience; the extent of compensation that nature has initiated; the extent of compensation that the spine and pelvis will permit; as well as the degree of compensatory capacity these structures have lost and must be restored through management.

(c) This unit of scales permits the clinician to determine to which side the spinal and pelvic distortion has shunted the force of weight bearing and gravity; the extent of this shift and the amount or propensity of this shift in terms of units of weight.

110

(d) Another device enables the clinician to correctly estimate how severely the spine is "off-centered," and what effect the treatments and shoe corrections have had in bringing the spine back to its center of rotation and movement.

(6) Therefore, not only is the clinician provided with a thorough understanding of the structure of the spine and pelvis but the nature and disposition of the mechanics contained within that structure as well as the dynamics of function that the combined structure and mechanics portray. This is a science of body engineering heretofore never thought possible.

(7) The research thus performed has revealed the cardinal fact that the function of the spine is dependent upon the normalcy of the sacroiliac mechanism; and when this mechanism is disturbed by faults of movement and incompetence in the dynamics of locomotion the entire spine must suffer with far reaching results, which because of the intimacy of neurological mediation extend not only onto the muscles and joints of the body but also into the conduct of the internal organs.

(8) Another rather remarkable clinical feature developed at the Institute is that method that permits the clinician to determine whether the spinal distortion is the consequence of a fault in structure, mechanics or dynamics or whether it is primarily the result of some disturbance within an internal organ that is giving reflex expression through a contraction of the deep spinal muscles and causing the vertebral segment to become mal-aligned.

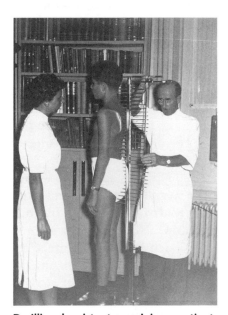

Dr. Illi and assistant examining a patient

111

(9) As one of the public health benefits that this research has assured is the fact that, to a noticeable degree, scoliotic deformities of the spine can be prevented and corrected if detected early enough according to the principles of mechanics and function evolved through this research.

Aside from the publication *The Vertebral Column: Life-Line of the Body*[3], three articles published in the National College Journal of Chiropractic in 1940[4], 1944[5], and 1956[6], Illi also published a monograph titled, *High Lights of 45 Years of Experience and 35 Years of Research.*[7] Not only prolific for their times, the concepts discovered during this association formed the foundation of Janse's teachings and lectures for the remainder of his life. "Man the Biped, a Biological Phenomena" is mirrored repeatedly in the extant recordings and writings of Janse. This concept grew out of his relationship with Illi.

Janse attempted to promote and preserve the work of Illi by encouraging NCA's Executive Director, Dr. Loran M. Rogers to fund a request from Illi to develop a movie of the movements of the spine using X-ray cineradiographic technology. Illi requested $40,000 USD[8] but in a follow-up letter from Janse to Rogers, Janse suggests the project could probably be done for $15,000 USD[9]. No record of any further discussion on this request is available so we may presume it was never funded; nor was a film ever created by the NCA or National at that time. Illi did produce his own cineradiographic movies and Janse often used them in his personal lectures.[10]

There was also an exchange of correspondence between Janse, Illi and representatives from Los Angeles College of Chiropractic in 1962 attempting to establish a residency of some duration (6 to 18 months) wherein a competent student, fluent in French, could go to Geneva and work with Dr. Illi in his Institute.[11] Other correspondence between Ronald G. Nikolich (Palmer student), and with Dr. George Haynes at LACC demonstrate continued discussion regarding some form of internship sponsored by an American School for training at Illi's Institute.[12] There is no evidence to confirm this idea ever bore fruit.

Janse never gave up on his determination to enshrine the concepts of Illi. While serving as a resident in radiology at the National

College of Chiropractic under the direction of Dr. Joseph W. Howe (1974-76) I worked as an assistant in the Anatomy lab with Dr. Janse. During this time we recreated models similar to those used by Illi that demonstrated the coupled movement of rotation and lateral bending. Janse had a four-quadrant scale produced like the one used by Illi. Numerous dissections of cadaveric spines were used to demonstrate the relationship of the lower spinal canal to movement of the cervical spine. Stretching of the dura mater surrounding the spinal cord by flexing, extending or rotating

Illi's four-quadrant scale for measuring body balance

the cervical spine created enough tension at the exposed lower (L4-5) levels of the cord that an actual indentation of a cot filled with water could be seen.

One of my major tasks as a resident was to produce two 16mm movies, much like what Illi had proposed over a decade before. Starting with a live model, movement of the cervical and lumbar spine in flexion, extension, rotation and lateral bending were filmed. Dissected cadavers were then filmed replicating the same dynamic movements with various levels of the musculature and eventually the exposed spine. Next, static radiographs were taken at the extreme ranges or end range of movement demonstrated by the live model. Finally, cineradiographic views of the cervical and lumbar spine were obtained using a new cineradiographic machine acquired by National College. These dynamic views demonstrated the actual movement of the vertebral segments confirming what had been demonstrated in the static end-range X-rays.

113

Because of the large size of the two movies produced (12 inch reels) they were difficult to transport and so Dr. Janse had them cut apart and only selected portions were preserved. There whereabouts or any resultant video or digitized remains have not been identified.

Nevertheless, through the writings of Illi and Janse, the principles espoused have been preserved and have been inculcated into the fabric and culture of today's chiropractic thinking. With the upsurge of new technology and the many superbly trained engineers and biomechanists in chiropractic, there may be a time when the works of Illi and Janse can be re-evaluated, re-confirmed and re-distributed for future generations of practitioners.

Janse never gave up his desire to expand the scope and depth of research in the profession. In his later years he wrote often in various publications on the importance of research and clinical examination into the principles and practice of chiropractic. The following is one example of his many attempts to spur the profession and the faculty at National College to engage in such activities.

In a cover letter to the faculty and clinic staff of National College dated 15 Aug 1977, Dr. Janse attached the following document regarding research.[13]

> Relevant to investigatory and research needs in the chiropractic profession may I ask the following questions—
>
> 1. Is there need and value to the attempt to competently develop a program of computer data banking as to the common type of cases handled in the College clinics with an over view of such factors as age, sex, ethnic grouping, occupation, economic status, complaint, diagnosis, X-ray findings, lab findings, type of treatment, frequency, response, and post-therapy findings?
>
> 2. Would there be investigatory and instructional value to a well prepared computer graphics film portraying the normal motor conduct at the atlanto-occipital, atlanto-axial, cervico-brachial, thoraco-lumbar, lumbo-sacral and sacro-iliac spinal levels?

114

3. In the discipline of applied clinical spinal biomechanics is there any further teaching value to additional competently edited cinema radiographic films? Would the reinstallation of the cinema radiographic unit serve any useful further investigatory purpose?

4. In the discipline of applied clinical biomechanics would it be of value to thoroughly investigate the Illi-Janse principles, namely:
    a. Spinal and pelvic segments deviate into distortion more readily than out of the distortion pattern?
    b. In lateral bending and in scoliotic deviation there, normally, is attending segmental compensatory rotation otherwise there is an undue disc compression, dural root sleeve traction, and extension of the vertebral column?

5. Would it be of any further investigatory value to expand upon the work done originally by Illi-Janse and attempted in repeat by Phillips-Eddington in investigating the seeming phenomenon that segmental fixation places undue traction upon the radices, dural root sleeves and cauda equina?

6. Is the project now in process in the anatomy department of debriding spines, suspending the spinal nerves? Permitting dehydration by simple air exposure drying in the attempt to demonstrate the possibility of the existence of IVF microtraumatic adhesions of any relevant value—the Sunderland nerve root entrapment concept?

7. Does the original work done by Awad (now continuing at the U. of Maryland Medical School) on inducing (without too much interventive surgical trauma) segmental derangement in the spines of laboratory animals have any pertinence?

8. Should this project be continued by Lin (who maintains that he has perfected a more competent method) and introduce phase two by simply determining the gross vascular and myological reactions upon the visceral beds?

115

9. Might the Awad-Lin vertebral derangement technic in the spines of laboratory animals lead to the possibility of monitoring the vascular, myological, neurological, endocrine and chemical changes that might be affected, and do we have the personnel on campus who might be interested and possess the ability to make the attempt?

10. Have we been sufficiently thorough in investigating (by means of the synchronized four-scale instrumentation) of the Illi-Janse concept that more weight is carried on the side of the "anatomical short leg"?

11. Is it at all probable that by means of image intensification radiologically (on regular clinic patients) we can determine the effect of a vertebral adjustment at a select spinal level upon visceral conduct?

12. Would such instrumentations as electromyography and physiography lend themselves to the investigation of the effect of:
    a. Discogenic spondylosis and pathological subluxation upon the neurological element?
    b. A chiropractic connection at this segmental level upon the somatic and visceral neurological elements?

13. Is there any clinical value and investigatory interest to the investigation of the effect upon head and neck posture by optometric prism changes?

14 Two types of major scoliotic deformities are defined—(1) congenital – characterized by asymmetrical segmental developments and (2) idiopathic—characterized by a collapsing of the spine into scoliotic deformity without apparent cause—is there any value in seeking to determine whether chiropractic care and controlled supervised kinesiological assignments have meaningful corrective value?

116

15. Does anyone on campus have the interest and the ability to create a method whereby it might be possible to determine the effect of subluxation (in a total broad concept) and a specific spinal dynamic mobilization upon the chemical atmospheres of the nervous system?

16. Is there any interest in the helping to set up and supervise a program that would progressively help to determine whether chiropractic care has any value in the care of the autistic child?

17. Would it be of any significance in fully investigating the effects of controlled fasting and the dieting in the management of rheumatoid arthritic conditions (the investigation of the principles of nature cure)?

18. Would anyone dare to assume the responsibility of determining whether the Illi-Janse concept of sacro-iliac mechanism function is correct or wrong?

19. Is there any validity to the claim the spinal manipulations are helpful to those with chronic respiratory ailments whether asthmatoid, emphyasemetous, bronchiectasis, etc.?

20. Is there any merit to a careful investigation of the effect of sole and heel lifts, heel drops and foot levelers upon spinal balance as determined by synchronized four-scale evaluation?

21. Is there any worthwhileness in the epidemiological determination as to whether the low back syndrome, the radiating sciatic neuralgia syndrome has or has not a higher incidence in a-basic pelvic distortion, pseudo-sacralization, lumbarization, pars defect, facet asymmetry, facet override due to lumbosacral hyperextension?

22. Is there any value to and any instrumentation methodology to determine the tension-spasm of head-neck-spinal musculature

in over-wrought, emotionally tense individuals?

23. How do we go about determining the effect upon the spinal musculature of fatigue?

24. Would it be of any epidemiological value to carefully obtain and review the medical and surgical history of all patients that come to the College clinics with complaint of head, neck, back, low back and sacro-iliac pain with probable attending radiating neuralgia? And determine why they sought chiropractic care?

25. Would it be of any value to staff and students to make a thorough literature search to determine, within all the health care professions the concepts of:
    a. vertebral and sacro-iliac subluxation?
    b. Nature of nerve root compression and irritation at exit from the vertebral canal?
    c. The surmised effects upon the functional conduct of the neurological element and the possible symptoms that may result?

26. Could the classical method designed by Fregerio and Stowe to demonstrate "bone-torsion in vivo" be applied to a study of vertebral body compression and zygapophyseal torque associated with such common biomechanical derangements as scoliosis, hyper-extension, cervical kyphosis, subluxation, etc.?

27. Would it be of any clinical significance to demonstrate by means of roentgen studies the effects of reverse gravitational ankle suspension upon the lumbar and lumbosacral spine areas?

28. Would it be of epidemiological significance to differentiate one to 200 cases of high blood pressure; submit them to three weeks of chiropractic adjustments and manipulation (all in similar manner) to a total of 15 treatments and then revaluate the pressure?

118

29. Most chiropractic colleges in their student health care programs maintain a set of spinal roentgengrams of each student. Would it be of any value to have these roentgengrams studied to determine the incidence of lumbosacral developmental defect and whether there is any correlation with the incidence of low back problems at this relative early age?

30. Could and should methods be devised to rather thoroughly investigate the clinical basis and effectiveness of some of the major clinical concepts and methods so vigorously propounded by the entrepreneurs?

1   Janse, J., "The Concepts and Research of Dr. Fred W. Illi." National College Journal of Chiropractic, Vol. 28, No 1, June 1956. pg. 14,

2   Illi File, Personal writing of J. Janse, National University of Health Sciences Achieves.

3   Illi, F.W., *The Vertebral Column: Life-Line of the Body.* National College of Chiropractic, 1951.

4   National College Journal of Chiropractic, Vol. 13, No. 4, Dec. 1940.

5   Janse, J. "The Spine is the Life Line." National College Journal of Chiropractic, Aug. 1944, pgs. 11-14, 52.

6   Janse, J. "The Concepts and Research of Dr. Fred W. Illi." National College Journal of Chiropractic, Vol. 28, No. 1, June, 1956, pgs. 10-35.

7   Illi, F.W., *High Lights of 45 Years of Experience and 35 Years of Research.* Presentation at the E.C.U. Convention in Norway, May 1971.

8   Letter to NCA from Illi, 1 July 1960, Illi file, National University of Health Sciences (NUHS) Archives.

9   Letter to Rogers from Janse, 29 July 1960, Illi file, NUHS Archives.

10 Letter to Illi from Janse, 30 June 1965., NUHS Archives.

11 Letters between Illi, Janse, Haynes and Hastings, Illi file, NUHS Archives.

12 Letters between Illi, Janse, Nikolich in 1965, NUHS Archives.

13 Letter to NCC Faculty, 1977. Illi file, NUHS Archives.

CHAPTER NINE

THE EDUCATOR

THE ROLE AND INFLUENCE OF JOSEPH JANSE ON CHIROPRACTIC EDUCATION AND ACCREDITATION

By most respected accounts, Joseph Janse was clearly in a socially unacceptable profession. Undaunted, his inherent drive for truth and excellence, coupled with his missionary zeal, fueled uncanny passion towards his efforts to help chiropractic take its place among other health care providers. The following is the educational evolution of the "Apostle of Chiropractic Education."

Early Struggles

The concern for quality in chiropractic education had beginnings early in the history of the profession. An excellent and detailed historical account of educational development and accreditation can be found in Keating, et al., *A History of Chiropractic Education in North America.*[1] As is typical of chiropractic, the history of educational advancement is bifurcated around issues related to philosophical underpinnings and scope of practice. This account will deal with a cross-section of these issues, only as they are germane to the role and influence of Dr. Janse.

When he enrolled at the National College of Chiropractic in 1935, the country was deeply involved in an economic depression. There was also deep division within chiropractic over the required length of schooling to train chiropractors and to prepare them to successfully pass an increasing number of Basic Science Boards (nine in 1936[2]) required to obtain licensure.

At the 1935 National Chiropractic Association's (NCA) annual convention held in August, in Hollywood, C.O. Watkins, D.C. introduced a resolution to create the Committee on Education and was made its first chair.[3] Later, (1939) Gordon Goodfellow, D.C. replaced Watkins who moved to the Board of Directors of the NCA. Goodfellow proceeded to combine the Committee on Education with the "...Joint Committee (of [State] Examining Boards and School Heads)[4] into the NCA Committee on Educational Standards.[5] Following the 23 July 1939 annual convention of the NCA in Dallas, Texas, the work of this committee was published as the "...official code of educational standards."[6] By 1941, John J. Nugent, D.C. (Palmer;1922) had been named the Director of Education for the NCA and published the "...first substantive educational accreditation guidelines for the chiropractic profession...*Chiropractic Education: Outline of a Standard Course.*"[7] This outline proscribed, "...a minimum of 'four years of eight months each,' involving not less than 3,600 hours of training," and, "...its preamble described the chiropractor as a 'physician...'"[8]

As a leader in chiropractic education, National College (1928), under Dr. W.A. Budden, dean, initiated the four-year (32 month) course known as the "Cum-Laude" course of 5,620, 45–minute hours. "Cum Laude graduates were issued the Doctor of Drugless therapy degree and the Doctor of Chiropractic degree...By 1939 no degrees were granted except after completion of a 4-1/2 year or 36 months' course which required 7,430 45–minute hours of resident attendance consisting of 5,760 hours of lecture and laboratory, and 1,670 clinic hours. It was at this time that the Doctor of Naturopathy (N.D.) and Doctor of Drugless Therapy (D.D.T.) degrees were issued in addition to the D.C. for certain unique state licensure purposes."[9]

As a student (1935-38), Joseph Janse experienced the impact of the NCA and the National College to increase the standards and quality of chiropractic education. He is pictured in the 1937 National College yearbook (*Mirror*) as a candidate for the Doctor of Drugless Therapy (D.D.T.) degree. He "...completed the requirements for the

Dr. Janse at his desk dictating to a secretary, circa late 1940's

D.C. and the N.D. degrees on June 17, 1938, following thirty-six months of full-time in-residence attendance at National."[10] Janse is pictured in the 1939 *Mirror* as a member of the faculty at National with a D.C. and D.D.T. degree to his credit. In the 1940 *Mirror* he is listed as the Dean of the Junior Class, one of four Deans (along with L. Tobison, B.F. Wells and I. Perlman). On 18 December 1944, Janse was officially employed as President by action of the Board of Trustees.[11] Throughout his 38-year tenure as President, he remained an active teacher in both the undergraduate and postgraduate programs of National College.

Janse's rise to prominence was not limited to his own institution. The minutes of the 1940 meeting of the Council of Chiropractic Schools held in Minneapolis designates Janse as the temporary secretary in the absence of Dr. Beatty. It was in this meeting where Janse listened to Carl S. Cleveland, President of Cleveland College, criticize the NCA for mandating a scholastic standard of not less than thirty-two months. Cleveland was also in attendance to address concerns the NCA Council might have regarding the "*Ultimatum*" presented to the NCA by the Allied Chiropractic Educational Institutions and the Chiropractic Health Bureau. Essentially, the "*Ultimatum*" stated,

> ...if physiotherapy, that is to say, instruction in the use of the modalities such as were heretofore pointed out and indicated, is to be given, that in order to do so, it will be necessary to establish a separate educational institution with a faculty that is ample and competent to teach each and all of the subjects of physical or physio-therapeutic...and such institution shall never employ Chiropractors as a part of its faculty...[12]

Thus, early in his professional career, Janse became involved with the internal disputes so prevalent within chiropractic. His influence was to be felt for the next forty plus years.

THE COUNCIL ON EDUCATION

1947

The House of Delegates of the NCA took action on 4 August 1947 following Nugent's program for improving educational standards by organizing the Council on Education. This body was formed by merging the Committee on Educational Standards and the National Council on Educational Institutions. This merger brought together the "...chief administrators (presidents or deans) of participating schools, the former members of the standards committee, plus Nugent as Director of Education."[13] Janse, having been appointed President of National College in December 1944 became a member of the Council on Education from its inception.

1948

From the minutes of the Council on Education meetings held 23-25 January 1948 (presumably the first formal meeting after the organization of the Council), the following attendees and their status with the Council are noted:

124

The Institute of Chiropractic of New York (accredited)
    Dr. Thure C. Peterson
The Lincoln College of Chiropractic (accredited)
    Drs. James Firth and Arthur Hendricks
Western States College of Chiropractic (accredited)
    Dr. W.A. Budden
The Los Angeles College of Chiropractic (accredited)
    Dr. Ralph J. Martin
The Canadian memorial College of Chiropractic (accredited)
    Drs. R.O. Mueller and S.F. Sommacal
National College of Chiropractic (accredited)
    Dr. Joseph Janse—Dr. R.C. King and
    Mr. O.J. Turek attended the Sunday session
Northwestern College of Chiropractic (provisionally accredited)
    Dr. John B. Wolfe
Carver College of Chiropractic (provisionally accredited)
    Dr. Paul Parr
Denver University of Natural Healing (non-accredited)
    Dr. H.C. Beatty
The Missouri College of Chiropractic (solicited provisional accrediting)
    Dr. H.C. Harring
The Logan Basic College of Chiropractic (solicited full accrediting)
    Drs. Fern M. Logan, Wm. M. Coggins, and Hedburg
Dr. John J. Nugent, Director of Education

Also in attendance were the following members of the Committee on the Accrediting of Chiropractic Colleges: Drs. Walter Wolf, E.H. Gardner, T.J. Boner, Dr. Justin Wood having sent in his excuse.[14]

There were six resolutions discussed at this meeting. A review provides insight into the early issues facing the Council. The first resolution required all accredited colleges to teach 240 hours of X-ray. The ensuing debate resulted in a modification emphasizing the importance of diagnostic studies in bone and soft tissue as well as spinography.

The second resolution of requiring physical therapy as part of the curriculum in approved colleges "...provoked rather extensive discussion especially by the delegates from California."[15] The California delegates were in favor of the resolution but ultimately it did not pass. It is interesting that more than 50 years later the same debate continues.

The third resolution to require dues for membership to the NCA to be extracted from student tuition dollars did not pass. Many schools accepted students referred by non-NCA members and felt this would hurt their enrollment.

The fourth resolution came from the Delaware Chiropractor's Association and requested a mandatory 200-hour course on psychology be implemented. The recommendation was not supported by the Council.

The fifth resolution offered by the National Council on Educational Institutions was designed to assist the recent graduate in establishing a successful practice. In addition to sending letters of encouragement, the schools should take the responsibility of placing new graduates in the offices of successful practitioners for at least one year to help them develop the necessary skills to run their own practices. The Council found favor with this recommendation but could see no way to implement it.

The sixth resolution related to establishing a chair of chiropractic in the University of Denver. The University of Denver had published a policy that it would sponsor any profession or trade as long as it was financed by the organization and not by the university. Janse queried if courses would be taught at the university? Beatty indicated courses would be taught at his University of Natural Healing Arts or at Spears Sanatorium. The school men feared the chiropractic inclusion would result in domination by either the medical profession or the hierarchy of the university. Nugent felt it was an ideal opportunity for chiropractic education.

Janse opined that the University of Denver would lose its standing with North Central if it brought in a chiropractic program. He then placed the proposal into a context that probably scuttled it:

> Furthermore, it was his [Janse] contention that if such a college were organized at the Denver University every member of that college faculty, whether they taught pre-clinical or clinical subjects, would have to possess an academic degree besides that of a Doctor of Chiropractic, if Denver University were to expect to retain its rating [with North Central Accrediting Agency]. This then, he maintained, would give us a chiropractic college all of whose faculty members possessed either Ph.D's, M.S. or B.S. de-

grees. He voiced the apprehension that this was setting a precedence toward which the medical exponents could make reference in their legislative battles against us and which may force upon all of the other accredited colleges the same stipulations. Dr. Janse questioned whether any of the other colleges at the present time would be able to comply with such a regulation or would even want to because he felt that in many of our chiropractic colleges were men who, although they did not possess an academic degree, but as the result of the training that they received at their colleges and as a result of their personal efforts, possessed teaching capacities and an understanding of their subject matter that placed them in the category of being extraordinarily capable and he felt that it would represent an abuse to have to sacrifice men of this caliber. It was his conviction that those graduating from our accredited colleges, were men whose degrees in every respect, were comparable in knowledge and information possessed of any master of science degree that a person could have obtained from a state university. He asserted that we should strive for higher educational standards and better qualification among our faculty members on the strength of our own attainments and educational procedures rather than to plagiarize the methods and efforts of others.[16]

While the majority of the Council concurred with Janse, Nugent and Martin were in favor of pursuing the proposed relationship. Nugent shared his reasons but finished by telling the Council that he intended to pursue the potential and that he was so instructed to do so by the Executive Board of the NCA. The Council in turn let it be known that they were opposed to any commitments being made by the NCA or the Chiropractic Research Foundation relative to professional or pre-professional requirements without Council consent. Subsequently, by assignment from the Council, Janse and Nugent each made presentations to the Executive Board of the NCA and differences dissipated.

Not three years into his presidency of National College, Janse was already designated as a spokesman for the Council on Education and co-presenter, with Nugent, the National Director of Education for the NCA.

The Attendees listed in the minutes of the Council at their mid-year meeting (June 18-July 3, 1948) in Portland, Oregon were as follows:

(A) Members of the Committee on Educational Standards

>Dr. John J. Nugent
>
>Dr. Edward H. Gardner
>
>Dr. Justin C. Wood
>
>Dr. Walter B. Wolf
>
>Dr. T.J. Boner

(B) Members of the Committee on Educational Institutions

>Dr. W.A. Budden, President, Western States College of Chiropractic
>
>Dr. Arthur Hendricks, Vice President, Lincoln College of Chiropractic
>
>Dr. Thure C. Peterson, Administrator, Chiropractic Institute of New York
>
>Dr. Raymond Houser, Dean, Los Angeles College of Chiropractic
>
>Dr. Ralph J. Martin, President of the Board of Directors of the Los Angles College of Chiropractic
>
>Dr. Lee H. Norcross, Dean of the Graduate School of the Los Angeles College of Chiropractic
>
>Dr. John B. Wolfe, President, Northwestern College of Chiropractic
>
>Dr. Paul O. Parr, President, Carver College of Chiropractic
>
>Dr. Homer C. Beatty, President, University of Natural Healing Arts
>
>Dr. Joseph Janse, President, National College of Chiropractic

(C) As a guest, Mr. C.P. Von Herzen, attorney of the California Chiropractic Association, present at several meetings.

It was at these meetings in Portland where the Council dealt with an angry Dr. Vinton Logan. The Council refused to list Logan Basic College of Chiropractic as one of the "NCA Approved" colleges. The

Kansas State College of Chiropractic, the University of Natural Healing in Denver, the Missouri College of Chiropractic and the Carver College of Chiropractic also remained on the "Un-approved" list. There had been discussion regarding the need to consolidate some schools and to reduce the overall number of schools because of the impending demise of the support for students from the GI Bill. Dr. Nugent had identified the Ross-O'Neil College in Ft. Wayne, the Bebout College in Indianapolis, the Brooklyn College in Brooklyn and the Ratledge College in Los Angeles as those institutions that should be closed.[17]

It was also at this meeting that Janse informed the Council on Education that the National Council of Chiropractic Examining Boards desired closer working relationship with the Council on Education. Janse was instructed (as Secretary for the Council) to write the executive members of the National Council of Chiropractic Examining Boards and invite them to a joint session with the Council on Education at the NCA convention next year.[18]

Janse also gave a report on his visit to the meetings of the National Society on Basic Science Boards held in Chicago the previous winter. He advised the council he had been well received and that chiropractic representation was invited to participate at their meetings again the next year. The Council selected Janse to establish a relationship and to attend the meetings of the National Society on Basic Science Boards the next year.

Dr. Lee H. Norcross, Dean of Los Angeles College of Chiropractic introduced the concept of graduate level training as a means of helping those practitioners who had received inadequate training in obtaining their DC degree. He further proposed that such graduate training would, "...allow the creation of chiropractic specialties such as X-ray, physio therapy, psychiatry, cardiology, etc."[19]

Finally, Janse brought forth a proposal from Dr. C.O. Watkins, now on the executive committee of the NCA regarding a standardized course for all approved schools, "...dealing with the orientation of the student in relation to the study of science, what it consists of, what its procedures are, what its methods of analysis represent, the manner it employs in the establishment of recognizable date, Dr. Watkins' contention being that by virtue of this program much of the inconsistency of scientific philosophic approach now existent in chiropractic and chiropractic education would be dissipated."[20]

Janse was instructed to prepare mimeographed reproductions of the Norcross and Watkins proposals to be distributed with the minutes of the meeting for further study by the Council and to be considered at their next meeting.

1949

In a closed session at their January meetings in Chicago, the Council placed the Logan Basic College of Chiropractic on the "approved" list after dropping the requirement that Logan be paid by any school teaching the Logan Basic Technique.[21] The minutes state Dr. Thure Peterson is the President, Dr. Joseph Janse, Secretary and that the Council is composed of the combination of the "Committee on Educational Standards and the Accrediting of Chiropractic Colleges" and the "Committee on Educational Institutions."[22]

It was in this meeting that the Watkins proposal to standardize the teaching of philosophy and science was given credence. As it was already partially implemented in some schools, all school leaders would be advised as to the value of implementing the proposed changes. No vote to require the changes was recorded.

Nugent's report recommended the addition of "applied physics" and better teaching in the biological sciences was badly needed at all the schools. He went on to recommend more research reading by students, a substantial library for every college, improved teaching capacity and ability, museums and collections, competent clinical training and the need to train students in clinical and physical diagnosis. He took issue with the Palmer School claiming they were, "...resorting to the falsification of their educational program to the extent where they are padding their curriculum ostensibly to represent a four-year course."[23]

Dr. Schreiber, Kansas State Chiropractic College, advocated a two-year liberal arts education in an accredited state college as a prerequisite requirement for entrance into chiropractic college. This was not passed because it was considered to be "premature." Dr. Martin from LACC advocated student screening to eliminate undesirable students. He reported that it had brought improvements to LACC's student body. His suggestion was not voted on.

It was reported by a Dr. Finn Christensen that the Denmark Chiropractic Association had organized a chiropractic college designed to teach the clinical subjects while pre-clinical work was to be obtained in the University of Copenhagen.

Nugent addressed two concerns at this meeting; 1) an approved college shall be incorporated as a 'non-profit' institution and 2) a college offering multiple degrees such as the naturopathic degree. National had made the change to a non-profit in the early 1940's but still offered multiple degrees. Janse's response to Nugent's concern about the naturopathic degree at National was very positive, "...in some respects at least it represented an incompetency that should be rectified..."[24]

In the July meetings of the Council, Janse and Nugent were put on notice of a full meeting of the House of Delegates to, "...consider and air the matter of the charges...by the International Chiropractors Association and the Palmer School of Chiropractic as they relate to the Iowa and Illinois situation."[25] The Council then called upon Janse to explain the position of the National College regarding these charges.

> Dr. Janse said that with reference to the Iowa matter the college had made no official declaration of attitude, but that under the auspices of the Student Council several telegrams were sent to the Iowa State Legislature recommending that the Iowa Basic Science Law for the time being be not repealed, for the simple reason that in Iowa the Chiropractic Law only required 18 months of resident training and that if the Basic Science Law were set aside it would flood the state with short-term graduates. Another reason why these students felt that the law should not be repealed at the present time was the objective fact that the Iowa Board, of all Basic Science Boards is the easiest and affords the most extensive reciprocal privileges. Consequently, students from all chiropractic colleges, as well as osteopathic and medical schools were using the [Iowa] Board as a springboard into more difficult states...

Then Dr. Janse proceeded to read a letter written to him by Dr. Ben H. Peterson, Secretary of the Iowa Basic Science Board, which in substance revealed that National College students were not the only chiropractic students that had sent in telegrams, that in fact, the students from the Palmer School had also sent in telegrams requesting the maintenance of the Basic Science Law in Iowa...The Illinois situation was then fully reviewed. Dr. Janse outlined the licensure situation in Illinois. Originally the chiropractor was licensed under the 'other practitioners act', which existed up to 1927. This act provided that all practitioners other than medical men should be examined by a board consisting of 2 osteopaths, 2 chiropractors, and 2 naprapaths, and that all schools of these respective professions teaching a course of a minimum of 32 resident months would have their graduates recognized. The 'other practitioners license' was a broad one even including the practice of obstetrics. However, even then in Illinois there were a goodly number of unlicensed short-term practitioners and they continued to endeavor to obtain an independent board of chiropractic examiners.

Because of this constant agitation for a license, the State Department of Education eventually had the Legislature revise the medical act to include the practice of chiropractic. The unlicensed practitioners were given the opportunity of qualifying by taking six months special training and taking a special board.

This of course did away with the 'other practitioners act' and included chiropractic under the medical act, ...

At this time a goodly number of the unlicensed practitioners proceeded to qualify, others refused to do so. Since this time they have yearly proposed a bill for the purpose of establishing an independent board of chiropractic examiners.

This effort in itself was most worthy, the only fault being that each bill was of a limited and low educational standard quality, attended by such liberal 'grandfather clause' privileges that it would not only have licensed the unlicensed practitioners but also given almost free entry for many people still in chiropractic colleges.

This year the efforts of the unlicensed group because of a large political pot took on rather a formidable disposition. As a result many of the licensed chiropractors began to ask why National College, being in Illinois, and the Illinois Chiropractic Society an N.C.A. affiliate, didn't do something about it.

Resultantly, careful considerations were made by the college administration, the board of directors of the Illinois Chiropractic Society, and also Dr. Nugent as Director of Education NCA. It was decided to withstand the House Bill #484 on the following reasons:

(1) That the total amount of 45 minute class hours required by the Bill were not commensurate with the minimum 60 minute class hour requirements of the NCA.

(2) The interpretation of chiropractic practice, especially the clause stating that scientific instruments could only be used for the analysis (rather than diagnosis) caused the licensed group to feel that the traditional practice of chiropractic in Illinois would be reduced and limited.

(3) The almost unlimited grandfather clause provision would not only grant licenses, on a bob-tail examination, to the unlicensed practitioners, but also to all students in chiropractic colleges regardless of the length of course of training. In fact, the bill gave the specific date of Dec. 31, 1950. It is quite obvious that this date gave leeway to hundreds of 18 month students.

(4) Furthermore, the bill in no way stipulates the amount of resident months that the ostensible 4500, 45-minute hours should cover.

It was further divulged that as the result of this pending legislation nearly all of the students in short-term colleges became residents of the State of Illinois within a week-end's notice.

133

Because of these primary reasons the Illinois Chiropractic Society and the Administration of the National College of Chiropractic saw fit to fight the passage of the bill. Unfortunately, these efforts were of course, subject to the criticism and displeasure of certain elements, who rather verbosely and vehemently conducted a program of severe criticism.[26]

Thus we see, early in his administrative career as President of National and as Secretary of the Council on Education, Janse was criticized for his firm stand on educational standards.

1951

Lest one assume that serving as the Secretary of the Council on Education was lucrative, the minutes of the 22-27 July 1951 meeting contain remarks regarding a $10.00 assessment to each of the accredited colleges to defray the expenses of both Dr. Janse and Dr. Peterson. Dr. Janse reported, "...that he had spent some $48.01 leaving a sum of $31.99 to cover Dr. Peterson's expenses.[27]

1952

The main issue in the 16-18 January 1952 meeting held in Indianapolis was the call by Dr. Parr [Carver College of Chiropractic] to hold a meeting of just school heads to debate the request from the field (ICA) and from non-accredited schools to create an accrediting body void of any ties to a national political association. Those members of "approved schools" decided not to support such a movement.[28]

Point No. 10 of this meeting was a proposal to establish a committee on graduate study and research within the Council. "The majority of the Council members, however, concluded that inasmuch as graduate and specialty education had not been established to any noticeable degree at any of the colleges...it might be best to refrain from organizing such an elaborate program until the objective need for one actually existed. Therefore the matter was tabled until further necessity arose.[29]

Point No. 14 raised by Nugent dealt with the inadequacies of the graduates of the colleges as found by members of examining boards. To his concerns Janse responded, "...the process of education at chiropractic colleges was charged with responsibilities and difficulties that did not reside in other professional colleges, especially medicine for the simple reason that in other professions pre-professional requirements brought into the professional colleges students who are fully conditioned in attitude and standardized in background and hence as a group other professional student bodies were more homogeneous."[30]

Point No. 16 was further discussion regarding the subject matter being taught at the Los Angeles College Graduate School in anticipation of a broadening of the law through a current bill being proposed. Nugent pointed out that the accrediting committee was against, "...teaching of any subject that related to standard medical and surgical procedures...especially emphasized such subjects as pharmacology, aperture surgery and the usage of the antibiotics."[31]

"Dr. Janse expressed the opinion that some of the difficulty was arising out of the fact that chiropractic practice does not lend itself to a great deal of specialization, simply because the basis of the chiropractic concept is that of systemic correction. Therefore, as soon as a great deal of specialization is indulged in it will lead to an over lapping onto other fields."[32] For one who six years later sat and passed the first certifying exam in the specialty of chiropractic roentgenology, this was an interesting position to take.

1954

While the issue of pre-professional college training had been a topic for discussion for several years, it was in the 11-13 February 1954 meeting of the Council that a motion made by Dr. Budden, "...namely that the Council re-endorse the recommendation of two years of pre-professional requirement and that all of the accredited colleges not having instituted this program begin making definite preparations to institute such a program."[33]

Los Angeles College of Chiropractic had already instituted the two year requirement and Dr. Haynes reported at this meeting that, "...it had cut down the enrollment quite noticeably and it had represented a definite economic compromise."[34] Nugent had proposed establishing contact with undergraduate colleges in the city of domicile with the intent of having students, "...take a goodly number of their pre-clinical subjects at these colleges."[35] Both Peterson and Janse, "...expressed opinion that in the instance of the respective colleges they represented this would not be desirable or practical."[36]

Speaking to Dr. Budden's motion, "Dr. Janse insisted that the motion was unnecessary because all of the colleges were well aware of the ever increasing tendency of the various states to introduce the [pre-professional] requirement and hence the colleges would automatically have to devise mechanisms of adaptation."[37] Dr. Budden withdrew his motion and the matter was set aside for some future meeting.

1955

Apparently Janse had responded on behalf of the Council to meet with representatives of the Council on Medical Education and Hospitals, a Dr. Wiggins and Dr. Turner, secretary of the Council (25 November 1954). Janse addressed concerns as to the intent of the meeting and the desire of the Medical Council to inspect chiropractic colleges. He was assured there were no sinister motives but a real intent to gain better understanding. The meeting concluded with the agreement to report to their respective bodies and if future meetings were desired that they could be scheduled.

In a letter to Dr. Janse dated 22 December 1954, Dr. Turner wrote that any future meetings should be conducted "on an informal basis" and that he and Dr. Wiggins would be happy to meet with him again if so desired.

At the 9-11 February 1955 Council meeting, discussions focused on numerous events in many states where medical activity was attempting to control or eliminate chiropractic. The Council through Janse responded to Dr. Turner stating, "They are willing to accept your [Turner's] suggestion for further informal conferences to continue the discussion originally initiated by your body if in your opinion such conferences are desired."[38] There was no report of any further meetings.

It was also in this February meeting that the issue of "United Medical Practice Acts" was being proposed wherein all health care practitioners would be placed under a single composite healing arts board that was controlled by medicine.

The issue of pre-professional requirement was on the agenda because thirteen states and the District of Columbia had already implemented some form of requirement and eleven more states were contemplating doing likewise. Janse, Wolfe, Peterson and Hendricks were assigned to "...draw up statements of policy and explanation of the Council in relation to the issue and to submit their efforts for survey and approval by the Council before the termination of the meetings."[39]

The committee reported their recommendations based on their survey of members at the meeting;

1. The National Council on Education of the National Chiropractic Association on several occasions has announced its policy in relation to the program of extra or pre-professional education now so commonly considered throughout the profession. In substance this policy may be stated as follows:

(a) The Council on Education is not opposed to the institution of extra-professional college requirements but is concerned with the mechanism by which this program might be instituted and operated. Therefore, the following recommendations are offered to guide and advise state organizations and examining boards who may be contemplating the adoption of such requirements.

(1) There should be no stipulation of required subjects except that the course taken must lead to a baccalaureate degree.

(2) That the maximum supplemental educational requirements not be in excess of two years.

(3) That this extra-professional college education for the present not be made a matriculation requirement but rather licensure.

(4) That at least six years elapse between its enactment date and the date of enforcement.

(5) If by virtue of state requirements it becomes necessary

> to stipulate content we recommend that they not ex-
> ceed the ordinary requirement which is necessary in
> the pursuance of the first two years of the course lead-
> ing to a baccalaureate degree.[40]

In the 4-8 July 1955 meeting of the Council it was decided to place the resolution on pre-professional educational requirements in the various publications of the profession. It was also decided to print a brochure that not only contained the resolution but also explained the reason behind the resolution to the various state boards who were promulgating these kinds of changes, "...as a vehicle of public impression in order to obtain added licensure privileges or added public relations recognition, or even to reduce the number of new entrees into the state." According to Janse, these requirements were creating a hardship on all the schools.[41]

On 7 July 1955, the Council held a joint meeting with the National Council of Chiropractic Examining Boards. Of the many concerns between the two groups, Janse addressed the issue of complaints regarding the average chiropractic examinee, "...that he often was too brief in his answers, that he frequently failed to interpret the questions, and that often he neglected the importance of proper conjugation of sentences and spelling." He suggested this poor performance was related to the pressure of taking the board and felt that, "...a little friendly talk before the examination..." by a board member would be helpful.[42]

In a closed session of just the Council on Education, Dr. Ralph J. Martin, Chairman of the Accrediting Committee raised the concern of Mr. Otto J. Turek, Chairman of the Board of Trustees of the National College of Chiropractic. Mr Turek had refused to meet with the Accrediting Committee unless they were willing to come to Chicago. Dr. Janse assured the Council that Mr. Turek would indeed meet with them and that he avoided coming to Atlantic City to avoid further squabbling.[43]

They also expressed concern regarding Mr. Turek's role as Chairman of the Board and also as the Administrative Officer of the college. However, Mr. Turek had a concern with Dr. Nugent and his attitude toward National College. In a letter from Mr. Turek he states, "Another incident occurred last year at the NCA Convention in St. Louis that I consider indicative of Dr. Nugent's animosity toward us. He severely humiliated Dr. Janse, ...both in public and in Council meetings by making inordinate accusations such as 'Dr. Janse being nothing but a puppet fully subservient to my stipulations,' and by divulging personal confidences far beyond his prerogatives."[44]

Mr. Otto J. Turek, Chairman of the Board of Trustees and Administrative Officer of National College, circa 1955

1956

The 15-17 February meetings of the Council were held in Toronto, Canada. Many of the issues discussed and voted upon give insight on Janse's position and perspective. For example, Western States College was again admonished to discontinue teaching a course in naturopathy following the example already set by the Los Angeles College and National College.[45]

Another issue was the graduate courses taught in Michigan by the Specialty Societies of the California Chiropractic association and accredited by the Los Angeles College of Chiropractic. Dr. Haynes had advised the Michigan group to have National teach the program but Janse told the Council that, "...when he found out the nature of work they were primarily interested in he had to advise them that the National College could not be interested in considering their request...That essentially the local group had procured the services of doctors in osteopathy, medicine, and psychology to conduct the classes. That although good and informative work in certain phases of diagnosis had been taught, there had also been classes in fundamental pharmacology, proctology, ambulant minor surgery and other borderline subjects. It was Dr. Janse's opinion that such procedure constituted a hazard and danger that would provoke division of professional concept in Michigan..."[46]

Janse also reported on a visit (1956) with a Dr. Pyott [ND?] of Salt Lake City, Utah. Dr. Pyott was the secretary of the American Institute of Manipulative Surgery. This group was seeking accreditation as a specialist organization in graduate education to further enhance their public image and strengthen their marketing. Dr. Pyott had stated that his organization started in 1948 and defined manipulative surgery as, "A specific manipulative technic designed to accomplish the detachment of adhesions, existing between fascial and muscle planes, and the walls of internal organs." The Council denied their application.[47]

It was at this meeting that a resolution regarding Mr. Turek was reached.

> Following were the mutual agreements attained:
> a. That a doctor of chiropractic will be placed on the Board of Trustees of the National College of Chiropractic. That this person will be a leading personality in the profession and the National College alumni faculty.
> b. That the accrediting committee is to receive annually a statement of the net worth of the college.
> c. That the National College in fulfilling these agreements would then fully conform to the educational code of the committee and experience all the consideration and deference's that related thereto.[48]

In deliberating the Turek issue, Nugent felt the accrediting committee and the council, "...had been more than patient with the situation and that Mr. Turek in his hesitancies to conform had necessitated added work and sacrifice on the part of certain council members." Mr. Miller, VP for National, expressed satisfaction in the understanding but also, "...expressed the hope that the accrediting committee would instruct the Director of Education to refrain from talking about the intimate details and problems of one school to repre-

140

sentatives of another school or to the field in general and to refrain from being unduly hypercritical of any school when in conversation with students or the alumni of that school."[49] Thus it would appear the compromise did little to improve the relationship between Nugent and Turek even though National College would now be in full compliance with the Council's standards.

It was also at this meeting that Dr. Hendricks from Lincoln College replaced Dr. Peterson as the President of the Council and Dr. Janse was elected to remain as Secretary.

At the 1-6 July meetings in Chicago, an issue relating to the changing format of Basic Science Examinations from an essay type answer to more multiple choice answers was deliberated upon. Nugent favored the change since in chiropractic examinees, "...one of their primary deficiencies is in the proper writing of discussion answers because of their incompetence in grammar." To this Janse responded, "That it was fundamentally impossible to expect the average chiropractic student to fully parallel the academic capacities of medical students, because of the latter's pre-professional background and because the medical student in all instances represents a hand picked scholastic personality. The fact cannot be avoided that in many instances we are asking our chiropractic students to measure up to the talents of the medical student in every respect when neither his background or the depth of his education has privileged him to acquire these abilities."[50]

1958

On 2 June 1958, Hendricks, President of the Council on Education circulated a *"Preliminary Report—Committee on Economic Support for Chiropractic Colleges."* This report was to be a point of discussion at the up-coming meeting in Miami Beach.

From the report we learn that when the NCA initiated its plan for standardization of chiropractic education in 1938 they forgot to consider the economic costs. When the plan was finally put into place in 1944 requiring the schools to "...make large capital expenditures for physical plant, increased budgets for administration and teaching staffs, the profession was fortunate that all of the schools became the

141

beneficiaries of a large percentage of government subsidies in the form of training of veteran students...the first phase of building the chiropractic schools to the proper academic level was completed with a minimum of economic hardship."[51]

By 1957 with the absence of qualifying veterans, inflation and rising costs of running the schools in the second phase of the plan "...an economic plateau had been reached." The dependence upon student tuition income would no longer support the third phase of the plan of "...development of the program for the establishment of national accreditation and the achievement of social prestige through academic accomplishments.... None of the schools have been able to accumulate actual reserves for depreciation...if the program of continued advances in chiropractic education is to be consummated, the accredited colleges will need economic support from sources not now available."[52]

The proposed plan was the formation of a National Fund for Chiropractic Education under the control of a Board of Trustees comprised of:

1. A representative of the Executive Board of the NCA
2. The director of education
3. A representative of the accredited schools [rotating person]
4. Three prominent laymen who have had experience in the business world in administrative capacities

The fund would be initiated by increasing dues by $5.00/quarter resulting in about $100,000/yr. With evidence of supporting this initiative, the schools could then seek additional support from foundations.

"This fund would then be dispersed as required to individual accredited colleges according to demonstrated need substantiated by proper investigation and only after each of the schools have also demonstrated that they are operating without any wasteful expenditures or inefficiency of administration. Such part of the fund that may not be needed each year should accumulate against future requirements."[53] It was expected that student tuition would cover costs

142

for faculty and administration while this fund would cover the cost of a plant and its maintenance.

The plan first had to be sold to the Executive Board of the NCA. Next it had to be endorsed by the House of Delegates after which it was expected to be an easy sell to the profession. The Committee recommended this not be a voluntary program but mandatory.

Timing:
1. June 1958—presentation to the Council on Education and then a meeting combined with the Executive Board of the NCA in Miami.
2. General presentation to the House of Delegates in Miami about the needs of the colleges.
3. Further discussion at the mid-year meeting with the Executive Board.
4. Presentation to the House of Delegates at the 1959 convention in Dallas.
5. Letters to members of the NCA between the Miami and Dallas meetings.

The plan was not to be discussed outside the Committee and Council. They also recommended talk of mergers cease since there would be a need for all the schools to provide new life into the profession. The letter was signed by the Committee responsible for the *Preliminary Report*, Drs. Thure C. Peterson, Chair, George H. Haynes, John B. Wolfe.

A breakdown of the costs of operation typical of a NCA accredited school in the 50's was included in this plan:

25%	Faculty Salaries
25%	Plant Operations, Rent, Taxes, Mortgage, Custodian, Light, Heat, etc
12.5%	Office Salaries
5%	Administration Salaries
10%	Office Expenses
5%	Advertising + Conventions

2.5% Library
2.5% Insurance and legal
2.5% Clinic
5%   Books
5%   Hospitalization and Social Security

There is no budget allocation for depreciation, for general reserves or capital outlay.[54]

The first issue on the 15-18 June meeting of the Council held in Miami Beach, Florida was the subject of financial aid from the NCA to assist school men to advance their educational training towards bachelor's, master's and doctoral degrees. While this was positive for the respective NCA-approved schools, the NCA also felt there were too many schools and there should be efforts to consolidate to reduce the amount of funding needed. Janse feared amalgamation might drive some students into ICA schools and also provide fertile ground for new ICA schools to spring up in areas where NCA schools had closed. The Council proposed to the Board of Directors of the NCA that monies be allocated equally among the NCA-accredited schools and only after an investigation had, "…demonstrated that it was operating without any wasteful expenditures, or inefficiency of administration."[55] Janse was in support of a definite need for all of the present accredited colleges.

Dr. M.A. Giammarino, Executive Secretary of the National Examining Board of Chiropractic Roentgenologists advised the Council that the first examination had been held in Omaha and that three of the twenty applicants [which included Dr. Janse] had successfully passed the exam. A second exam was held in May at the Illinois Chiropractic Society in whom five new and three repeaters took the exam. One new and one repeater passed. Janse spoke highly of the exam he had taken in Omaha. Giammarino advised that to date five had been certified by examination

L.P. Rehberger
Earl Rich
Leonard Richie

Ronald Watkins
Joseph Janse

Three were certified by waiver;

Clifford B. Eacret
Chas. A. Moran
James O. Empringham

Three were certified as original members of the Board

Leo E. Wunsch, Sr.
Duane Smith
M.A. Giammarino.[56]

1959

It was at the Dallas, Texas meetings held 3-6 January that the legal battle shaping up in Louisiana was first noted in the minutes of the Council. The fact that the Louisiana delegation revealed, "...their intent to submit their case on the basis of the typical limited ICA definition and interpretation of diagnostic and practice scope... [and]...that these people had been misinformed about the status of chiropractic practice under the medical acts of such states as Illinois, New Jersey and Indiana...provoked concern and caution in the minds of the Council members and the counsel of the NCA as well as the Executive Board."[57] It was finally approved to provide, "...both financial aid and documentary assistance to the Louisiana group under the stipulation of certain reservations."[58]

A review of the Executive Board of the NCA's plan to fund chiropractic education referred to as the Foundation for Accredited Chiropractic Education (FACE) became a major matter of concern within the Council. Apparently the recommendations from the Council regarding the organization of FACE had been sidestepped and the monies promised were nothing more than "figures on paper."[59] In a joint meeting with the Council and the Executive Board it was

145

requested that a separate Board of Trustees be established to induce the flow of monies and that this Board include prominent lay members as well as representatives from the Council and the Executive Board. It was further requested that funds be derived from a dues increase of NCA members and that monies provided to the colleges be used to support the operating fund and student procurement needs and not be dedicated totally to research. The NCA Executive Board was surprised at the dismay displayed by the Council and indicated the difficulty associated with a dues increase when the California Association had just disaffiliated itself with the NCA causing a large drop in membership. Before the meeting ended the Council had taken the position to not accept financial aid from the NCA unless some changes were made in the working mechanism of FACE.[60]

Final deliberations of the meeting involved an issue in Utah. "The Utah situation came in for a brief discussion. Comment being made that sooner or later NCA representation would have to seek to establish contact with the agencies concerned. At present the Utah Board of Chiropractic Examiners would not accept the applications of graduates from schools teaching physiotherapy."[61] This would explain the difficulty of Janse obtaining his Utah license to practice chiropractic.

It was also at this January meeting that Dr. Janse was elected as Chairman of the Council replacing Dr. Hendricks and Dr. John B. Wolfe was elected to be Secretary. Dr. Janse had served as Secretary of the Council from 1948 to the beginning of 1959, essentially a decade.

The issue regarding the organization of FACE and the distribution of funds was yet unsettled at the 6-9 July meeting of the Council in Chicago. A motion was passed to have the FACE Liaison Committee meet with the Executive Board to present to them recommendations from the Council.[62] In a memo to the Executive Board from Nugent following the meeting, the recommendations were repeated with an emphasis on where authority lies with respect to chiropractic education:

The Council asks the Board to consider:
1. Recommends FACE Trustees consist of 1 elected by Executive. Board, 1 by HOD, the Executive Secretary of NCA, the

146

Director of Education from Council on Education, and three laymen.

2. Council will recommend an equitable plan for distribution of funds.

3. Council encourages an immediate grant of $4,800 to all accredited schools for student procurement.

4. "The Council asserts that it has been given authority by the House of Delegates over all matters concerning education; that the Council is the only body which can add or remove a school from the list of accredited institutions; that upon re-examination of the situation of the Western States College it has unanimously agreed to retain the school on its accredited list, and that, therefore, the Western States is entitled to benefits from the funds available on the same basis as the other schools.[63]

The final assertion was a bold stand taken by the Council over which Janse now presided. Always a peacemaker, his clear position on this matter is revealed in a personal letter to Dr. L.M. Rogers, Executive Director of the NCA on 20 August 1959.

Janse first compliments Dr. Rogers on the accomplishments made at headquarters after his visit. He makes reference to a confidential meeting in Dr. Roger's office while there. Janse is trying to avoid a confrontation between the Council on Education and the Board of Directors in front of the House of Delegates.

I wish with all my heart that the 'personalization' of issues, the 'pitting' of one group against the other, and the 'jockeying' for position and authority by some could be avoided.[64]

He then expresses concern over the conflict between Nugent and the Board of Directors.

To me personally it appears most regrettable that a common denominator of understanding can't be reached without the hazzle [sic] of colored expressions and attitudes of resistance. When FACE was first organized and the idea of eventually asking for a raise in dues was evolved it never occurred to me to question who should

147

be the administrative personnel of the same. And frankly I honestly still wonder as to what right the Council or any member of the Council has in challenging the conclusions of the Board.

The Board submitted to the House the recommendation that the dues be increased. The House unanimously accepted this recommendation, then certainly the administration of these extra funds is a matter between the Board and the House.

There has been much talk about 'slicing a melon.' Yet it is my firm conviction that if equal yet carefully supervised benefit is not afforded the various schools there will result much feeling and dissension, especially among the alumni groups who make up the bulk of NCA membership.

I can honestly say that at the National there is no desire to 'feather a nest' nor to be benefited more than anyone else. There is no grudge nor resentment. We are seeking to do a job that is worthy. We are not out of the woods by a long ways. There are many things that we must and plan to do to 'up-grade' and it would harm us severely to be subject to functions of bias and prejudice.

In closing may I make the personal and confidential recommendation. First, that the Board itself concisely conclude what is to be done about the FACE policy...

Dr. L. M. I am going to ask that you consider this as a personal confidential communication. If I were to be quoted and if as the result of these honestly submitted evaluations, 'pressure' detriment were to be experienced by the college, I would then feel obligated to resign my position at the college, because no person is of any value to an institution or organization if all that he does is not in support and safe-guarding of the same.[65]

While Janse is trying to keep the peace with the Executive Board of the NCA, Nugent continues to embroil himself in controversy. In a report Nugent makes to the Council on 26 August 1959 regarding his appearance before the Executive Board on 12 July he feels he was insulted by both Dr. Cecil Martin and Dr. Rogers.[66]

Janse turns to Dr. Walter Wolf, Chairman of the National Committee on Chiropractic Educational Standards for solace:

> Walt, the appearance of Dr. Nugent before the Board after the Council meetings has resulted in a tremendous volume of bitterness amongst the Board members. I have been criticized for not seeing to it that some member of your committee as well as myself did not accompany him.

> This is confidential Walt, but might I sincerely determine just what interpretation you place on all this.

> It seems that the Board was left with the impression that the school men had threatened to carry the matter of what personnel is to constitute the Board of Trustees of FACE to the floor of the House of Delegates and of course the Board resents this very much.[67]

Wolf's response brings calm to the issue:

> With reference to Dr. Nugent's appearance before the Ex. Board., I have not heard of any confusion or bitterness. I doubt that we have any reason to get excited about anything that we might hear, certainly, we are aware of the fact that Nugent and several members of the Board just do not hitch, consequently every time they have a session the fur will fly. My experience with the Ex. Board is that they must be kept on the defensive, if they are allowed to carry the ball they always come up with the wrong play, we have seen that happen to often. I am certain that John's tactics are to threaten them with the thought that if they do not perform their duties, as Trustee's of FACE, we do have an alternative by going to the House of Delegates. Although I agree that it might not have been the most diplomatic procedure, I sincerely believe that this strategy will put the members of the Ex. Board in a mood

149

to consult with our council before they make any drastic decision.

As far as your position is concerned Dr. Janse, I suggest that you just sit tight and let the waters about you bubble a bit. Defer any promises or decisions until our next meetings, by then many problems will have solved themselves.[68]

A long delayed discussion regarding the recognition of chiropractic education by the federal government was reignited by a letter to the Council on Education from Nugent on 12 September 1959. He made reference to discussions he had been having with a Mr. Goldthorp in the Division of Higher Education. Mr. Goldthorp had not previously been favorable to entertaining discussions on chiropractic education because there were three different parties (NCA,

Drs. Joseph Janse and Walter Wolf at the dedication of the Ortman Clinic in South Dakota, 1971

ICA, California Group) seeking recognition from the same profession.

In his letter Nugent now informs the Council Mr. Goldthorp is ready to listen, "Well, I guess you are the people who are doing things, so let us get on with your application. Mind you,' he added, 'the Committee will not accept any 'paper set-ups' and it's going to be tough, long and expensive." He then lists those items that changed Mr. Goldthorp's mind:

1. The collapse of the Norcross agency.
2. The fact that the ICA was a creature or captive agency of the Palmer School; that all the schools on its list were rejected by our Council; some of these already defunct or about to close and its obvious attempt at deception.
3. The fact that the Council on Education was organized after the pattern of accrediting agencies in other professions.
4. The close parallel of the pattern which we used in building our schools to that followed by Dr. Abraham Flexner in building the medical schools.
5. The concurrent program in the states to raise educational requirements for license, especially the two years of pre-professional college. Our accomplishments here brought praise.
6. The affiliation of the Texas School with the San Antonio College with the approval of the University of Texas.
7. The recognition by Lewis & Clark and other Oregon universities of credits earned at Western States College.
8. The prechiropractic courses in Oregon and Southern California junior colleges inspired by our schools.
9. The ownership by our schools of their own plants. The new $300,000 plant of the Lincoln, and the $500,000 building program of the National. The raising of $212,000 in California for the Los Angeles school and other donations for schools elsewhere.
10. The scholarships available to students.
11. A fact considered most important—The support of our schools by a large segment of the profession as evidenced by the fact

151

that the NCA had accepted the recommendations of the Council on Education and had provided for (1) graduate instruction for faculty members to upgrade instruction, (2) had appropriated $50,000 for operating expenses in 1959 and $50,000 for research and (3) had allocated $100,000 or more annually to be available for our schools beginning in 1960.[69]

It would be another fifteen years before federal recognition of a chiropractic accrediting agency would be achieved.

1960

At the Council meeting, presided over now by Dr. Haynes, in Minneapolis, 3-7 July, resolutions and recommendations between the Council and the Executive Board were still being discussed. The use of funds had moved more towards upgrading the schools and were to be based on actual expenditures. There was also a recommendation that Dr. Nugent be retained as the Director of Education, "...until the present phase of gaining accreditation is accomplished." Later in the meeting a proposal on the allocation of FACE funds was approved to be submitted to the Executive Board. The figures were based on the mortgage purchase needs that had been submitted by the various schools. LACC, National, New York and Lincoln each were to receive 18%; Northwestern and Texas received 14% and Western States was to receive a special allocation.[70]

The Executive Board received the recommendations conveyed by the FACE Liaison committee of the Council, of which Janse was a member, and after deliberation moved to accept them with some modifications which the Council did finally approve. The main change was removal of any reference to the employment of Dr. Nugent.

It appears that Janse now stepped down from the leadership of the Council being replaced by Dr. George Haynes from LACC, while Dr. Wolfe remained as Secretary.

1961

The issue of employment of Dr. Nugent as the Director of Education was a significant item at the 11-17 June meeting of the Council in Las Vegas. The application for recognition by the Council to the Department of Education was not accepted. The letter of non-acceptance listed the deficiencies of the Council and their schools but the school men were not discouraged and concluded that, "...with concentrated effort and sufficient funds these deficiencies could be eliminated in a reasonable time..." Based on this hope the Council submitted to the Executive Board that Dr. Nugent be retained for a sufficient amount of time to complete the process. There was no action by the Executive Board regarding this recommendation reported in the June minutes of the Council.[71]

Dr. Nugent shared a denial letter from the U.S. Office of Education (26 May 1961) with the Council on their application for recognition. There was a revision of the NCA Committee on Education component of the Council. The new committee was named the Committee on Accreditation and the NCA Director of Education was no longer retained as a member. The new committee consisted of four doctors of chiropractic who held other academic degrees and each inspection team was to include two persons with a Ph.D. (Drs. Dewey Anderson and Gregg Evans).[72]

1962

This year the Council on Education initiated the drafting of the 6th revision of its *Educational Standards for Chiropractic Colleges*. The Council also undertook the effort to revise its Constitution and Bylaws under the leadership of Dr. Haynes.[73]

The debate over pre-professional requirements took on a new spirit. Resistance from the institutional members, now twenty years running, based on the fear of lowered enrollments and dire economic consequences, remained. [74]

1963

Dewey Anderson, Ph.D., consultant to the Council on Education in a letter of 17 December 1963, brought the pre-professional requirement into sharp focus:

> Chiropractic cannot afford to carry the burden of inferiority in
> its educational standards. Nor can the colleges pitch their offerings

153

at a professional level of learning if forced to teach recent high school graduates whose courses of study have not been of the mind required for college entrance. Finally, these colleges cannot be expected to produce professionally trained chiropractors of high quality if they continue to accept high school graduation or its equivalent as sufficient for matriculation.[75]

It was at the 19-24 January meeting in Los Angeles that the Council voted unanimously to accept the recommendation from the Executive Board to pass the authority to accredit an institution exclusively to the Committee on Accreditation, a difficult task for the institutional people to relinquish such authority all done in the effort to gain recognition with the U.S. Office of Education.[76]

1964

The biggest political event of the year was the merger between the National Chiropractic Association and the International Chiropractic Association to form the American Chiropractic Association. Twenty-three states had incorporated mandatory pre-professional educational requirements, five more were pending and the House of Delegates of the ACA passed a resolution encouraging all other states to do the same. While appearing harsh, it appears the political motivation was to prevent substandard schools from finding a place for their graduates to practice.

1965

At the 16-21 January meeting in Des Moines, the Council finally passed a motion to "...approve in principle the phasing of the two-year pre-professional requirement for matriculation to be instituted on September 30, 1968 by institution, if possible, a one year pre-professional requirement by September 30, 1967 or before."[77]

Dr. John Fisher replaced Dewey Anderson, Ph.D. as the Director of Education for the ACA.

1966

Dr. Janse's role in the Council was less apparent as the format of the minutes became more concise in the early 1960's. In the 18-22 January minutes Janse is noted as making a motion to not accept, "...the proposed definition or scope of practice proposed by the Unification Committee of the ACA." Three items later in the agenda, the Council approves the "Foreword" for the booklet, *Educational Standards for Chiropractic Colleges* to be amended to read, "A Doctor of Chiropractic is a physician concerned with the health needs of the public...The purpose of his professional education is to prepare the doctor of chiropractic to diagnose, treat or refer to other physicians..."[78]

It was also in 1966 that the Council implemented the use of "self-studies" as a part of the process of achieving accreditation. Both National and Lincoln Colleges were successful in being granted accredited status by the Committee on Accreditation of the Council.

From 1967 through 1972, Dr. Janse and Dr. Lenard Fay from National College worked on a committee chaired by Dr. Haynes to gather data and prepare an application for recognition to be submitted to the U.S. Office of Education in the Department of Health, Education and Welfare. In July of 1974, the Commission on Accreditation of the Council on Chiropractic Education was recognized by the Commissioner of Education of the U.S. Office of Education.

Approvals and Accreditations

National had a tradition of academic excellence started by its founder, Dr. John F. Howard and pursued vigorously by Dr. William Schultz, National's second president. Thus, in 1941 when the Committee on Educational Standards of the NCA "published their first list of twelve 'provisionally approved' chiropractic colleges..." National was on the list, never to be removed.[79]

The new Committee on Accreditation of the Council on Chiropractic Education in 1966 did their first site inspections and granted accredited status to the Lincoln College of Chiropractic and the National College. That same year National, "...was certified by the advisory Council on Degree Granting Institutions of the State of Illinois Office of the Superintendent of Public Instruction (OSPI) to confer a bachelor of science degree in human biology."[80]

(l to r) Hooded in academic regalia, Drs. Joseph Janse, Paul Silverman, Norman Frigerio, Andreis Kleynhans and Mohammad Awad, circa 1974

The New York State Education Department approved National College's professional educational program making it the first chiropractic institution to be recognized and approved by the State of New York.[81]

National College was first denied recognition by the North Central Association of Colleges and Secondary Schools (NCACSS) but with the aid of Paul Silverman, Ph.D., obtained the status of "candidate for accreditation" in March 1974. Dr. Silverman remained a close friend of Dr. Janse and exchanged letters regarding personal matters.[82]

It was in this year of 1974 that U.S. Office of Education in the Department of Health, Education and Welfare granted recognition to the Council on Chiropractic Education — a battle Dr. Janse had been a part of from the beginning.

After several more site visits, North Central granted to National "initial accreditation" on 28 October 1981[83] thus removing the final stigma he faced as a witness in the Louisiana trial in 1965. It was at this "England Trial" that Dr. Janse was challenged by the fact that his degree was spurious since it came from a school that had no accreditation of any kind and that, in 1965 the absence of an accredited school in chiropractic education remained. Dr. Janse, "...vowed that he 'would correct this fault...or leave the profession.'"[84] Being a man of his word, he stayed and corrected the problem becoming **"The Apostle of Chiropractic Education."**

1   Keating, Callender & Cleveland, *A History of Chiropractic Education in North America.* Association for the History of Chiropractic, 1998.

2   Ibid., pg. 83.

3   Ibid., pg. 85.

4   Ibid., pg 87.

5   Ibid., pg. 89.

6   National College of Chiropractic J., "National Chiropractic Association Adopts Educational Standards Code." Vol. 12, No 4, Dec. 1939, pg. 15

7   Keating, Callender & Cleveland, *A History of Chiropractic Education in North America.* Association for the History of Chiropractic, 1998. , pg. 89.

8   Ibid., pg. 89.

9   Beideman, R.P. "Seeking the Rational Alternative: The National College of Chiropractic from 1906 to 1982." Chiropractic History, Vol. 3, No 1, 1983, pg. 19.

10 Beideman, R.P. *In The Making of a Profession: The National College of Chiropractic 1906-1981.* National College, 1965, pg. 86.

11 Ibid. pg. 75.

12 Minutes of the Meetings held by the Council on Chiropractic Schools, 28 July 1940, Minneapolis, Minn.

13 Keating, Callender & Cleveland, *A History of Chiropractic Education in North America.* Association for the History of Chiropractic, 1998. pg. 113.

14 Keating, Callender & Cleveland, *A History of Chiropractic Education in North America.* Association for the History of Chiropractic, 1998, Minutes, Council on Education of the NCA, 23-25 Jan. 1948, pg. 251.

15 Ibid. pg. 252.

16 Ibid. pg. 255.

17 Keating, Callender & Cleveland, *A History of Chiropractic Education in North America.* Association for the History of Chiropractic, 1998 Minutes, Council on Education of the NCA, 18 June—3 July, 1948, pg. 263.

18 Ibid. pg. 265.

19 Ibid. pg. 266.

20 Ibid. pg. 266.

21 Keating, Callender & Cleveland, *A History of Chiropractic Education in North America*. Association for the History of Chiropractic, 1998 Minutes, Council on Education of the NCA, 5-7 Jan. 1949, pg. 267.

22 Ibid. pg. 267.

23 Ibid. pg. 270

24 Ibid. pg. 272

25 Keating, Callender & Cleveland, *A History of Chiropractic Education in North America*. Association for the History of Chiropractic, 1998, Minutes, Council on Education of the NCA, 25-29 July, 1949, pg. 277.

26 Ibid. pg. 277.

27 Keating, Callender & Cleveland, *A History of Chiropractic Education in North America*. Association for the History of Chiropractic, 1998, Minutes, Council on Education of the NCA, 22-27 July, 1951, pg. 307.

28 Keating, Callender & Cleveland, *A History of Chiropractic Education in North America*. Association for the History of Chiropractic, 1998, Minutes, Council on Education of the NCA 16-18 Jan. 1952, pg. 313.

29 Ibid. pg. 317.

30 Ibid. pg. 319.

31 Ibid. pg. 319.

32 Ibid. pg. 320.

33 Keating, Callender & Cleveland, *A History of Chiropractic Education in North America*. Association for the History of Chiropractic, 1998, Minutes, Council on Education of the NCA. 11-13 Feb. 1954, pg. 338..

34 Ibid. pg. 338.

35 Ibid. pg. 338.

36 Ibid. pg. 338.

37 Ibid. pg. 339.

38 Keating & Cleveland. *Appendix B: Minutes of the NCA/ACA Council on Education*. Unpublished Manuscript, Minutes, Council on Education of the NCA. 9-11 Feb. 1955, pg. 97.

39 Ibid. pg. 104.

40 Ibid. pg. 105.

41 Keating, Callender & Cleveland, *A History of Chiropractic Education in North America*. Association for the History of Chiropractic, 1998, Minutes, Council on Education of the NCA. 4-8 July, 1955, pg. 356.

42 Ibid. pg. 360.

43 Ibid. pg. 360.

44 Personal letter from Turek, 15 June 1955, NUHS Archives.

45 Keating, Callender & Cleveland, *A History of Chiropractic Education in North America*. Association for the History of Chiropractic, 1998, Minutes, Council on Education of the NCA, 15-17 Feb., 1956, pg. 362.

46 Ibid. pg. 363.

47 Ibid. pg. 365.

48 Ibid. pg. 372.

49 Ibid. pg. 372

50 Keating, Callender & Cleveland, *A History of Chiropractic Education in North America*. Association for the History of Chiropractic, 1998, Minutes, Council on Education of the NCA, 1-6 July 1956, pg. 374.

51 Letter to the Council on Education from Hendricks, 2 June1958, NUHS Archives.

52 Ibid. 1958.

53 Ibid. 1958.

54 Ibid. 1958.

55 Keating, Callender & Cleveland, *A History of Chiropractic Education in North America*. Association for the History of Chiropractic, 1998, Minutes, Council on Education of the NCA, 15-18 June 1958, pg. 392.

56 Ibid. pg. 396.

57 Keating, Callender & Cleveland, *A History of Chiropractic Education in North America*. Association for the History of Chiropractic, 1998, Minutes, Council on Education of the NCA, 3-6 Jan. 1959, pg. 400.

58 Ibid. pg. 402.

59 Ibid. pg. 402.

60 Ibid. pg. 405.

61 Ibid. pg. 405.

62 Keating, Callender & Cleveland, *A History of Chiropractic Education in North America*. Association for the History of Chiropractic, 1998, Minutes, Council on Education of the NCA, 6-9 July 1959, pg. 406.

63 Memo, to NCA Executive Board from Nugent, 9 July 1959, NUHS Archives.

64 Letter from Janse to Rogers, 20 Aug. 1959, NUHS Archives

65 Ibid. 1959.

66 Report to the Council on Education from Nugent 26 Aug 1959, NUHS Archives.

67 Letter to Wolf from Janse, 2 Sep 1959, NUHS Achieves.

68 Letter to Janse from Wolf, 4 Sep 1959, NUHS Archieves.

69 Letter to the Council on Education from Nugent, 12 Sep 1959, NUHS Archives.

70 Keating, Callender & Cleveland, *A History of Chiropractic Education in North America*. Association for the History of Chiropractic, 1998, Minutes, Council on Education, 3-7 July 1960, pg. 408.

71 Keating, Callender & Cleveland, *A History of Chiropractic Education in North America*. Association for the History of Chiropractic, 1998, Minutes, Council on Education 11-17 June 1961, pg. 413.

72 Hidde, O. Historical Perspective CCE & COA. Unpublished manuscript. Pg. 2.

73 Ibid. pg. 2.

74 Ibid. pg. 2.

75 Ibid. pg. 3.

76 Keating, Callender & Cleveland, *A History of Chiropractic Education in North America.* Association for the History of Chiropractic, 1998, Minutes, Council on Education, 19-24 Jan. 1963, pg. 425.

77 Keating, Callender & Cleveland, *A History of Chiropractic Education in North America.* Association for the History of Chiropractic, 1998, Minutes, Council on Education, 16-21 January 1965, pg. 438.

78 Minutes, Council on Education, of the ACA, 18-22 January 1966

79 Beideman, R. *In The Making of a Profession: The National College of Chiropractic, 1906-1981.* National College, Lombard, IL, 1995, pg. 257.

80 Ibid. pg. 262.

81 Ibid. pg. 264.

82 Personal letters between Dr. Janse and Dr. Silverman. Janse Collection. NUHS Archives.

83 It should be noted that North Central Accreditation has remained with National with its most recent positive reaffirmation coming shortly before the publication of this book in 2006. Personal Communication with Dr. Winterstein, President of NUHS.

84 Ibid. pg. 260.

Chapter Ten

THE DEFENDER

Young Jozias ("Joe" in English) was inherently a scrapper. as detailed in Chapter Three. You will recall that he and his older brother went to their first day of school in their new Huntsville, Utah home decked out in their finest "Dutch Duds"—making quite a spectacle. When they returned home, dirty and torn, mother Geertje learned how Joe had stuck up for his brother, himself, and their heritage. Joe made it quite clear, however, that they would never attend school again in their traditional clothing.

Later, as a missionary under the widening shadow of the Third Reich, then "Elder" (missionary) Janse spent three years defending his faith in the Mormon church in Germany and Switzerland. As was typical, missionaries often held "street meetings" in which they would stand elevated on a box at a busy street corner and shout out to those passing, their purpose and their message. Times were difficult, unemployment was high and likely there were many who had nothing more to do than heckle the young boys from America. This no doubt was a character building experience for young Joseph, teaching him to defend his beliefs.

According to Gloria's story (Chapter Five) Joe's decision to enter chiropractic school was not well received. David O McKay, then (1930) a member of the Quorum of Twelve Apostles (one of the highest councils in the Mormon church and who later became president of the church), wrote a personal letter to Joe advising against becoming a chiropractor. Many local long-time friends also disapproved. Once again Joe had to defend his decisions and his beliefs against rather significant public opinion.

The brief quip adjacent to Dr. Janse's picture in the 1937 Yearbook, *The Mirror*, states, "Joe has a hobby of teaching, but who wouldn't if one asked so many questions?" Such tenacity in his schooling prepared him well for a life-time of defending the profession he had adopted.

On a more humorous note, during a trip to Tucson, Arizona, in the 1950's, it appears Dr. Janse was forced to defend himself from a rather heavily armed reception party at the airport (imagine this happening today!). Apparently, as seen in the next photo, he managed to procure his own weaponry and was able to defend himself against the ruffians at the airport.

It was also during the late '50's (February, 1957) that Dr. Janse was a guest on the T.V. show "Night Beat" hosted by Mike Wallace. At this time, legislation attempting to legalize the practice of chiro-

Dr. Janse arrested by a posse (of self-appointed chiropractors) at the Tucson, Arizona airport, circa late 1950's

162

Dr. Janse enjoys the party now that he is fully armed

practic in the state of New York was under consideration and condemnation by the medical profession, so Dr. Janse was invited to the program to "defend" chiropractic against a pretty vicious attack by Mr. Wallace. (*An audio reproduction on DVD accompanies this book.*) This is an example of Joseph Janse's decorum and intellect at its finest, as he withstood the repeated verbal attacks made upon chiropractic by Mr. Wallace.

Numerous pages could be filled with accounts of the many governmental dignitaries from local, state, federal and international jurisdictions; the many site teams from numerous state board of examiners and accrediting agencies; and representatives of the various types of media over the years looking for a story—a sensational, controversial story—that would draw attention to their work. One particular instance preserved on tape was an interview Dr. Janse had with a Mr. Jack Righeimer, host of the show *"Consultation"* sponsored by the University of Illinois Medical Center in Chicago, Illinois. (*Complete interview is contained on DVD accompanying this book.*) Again, in a most erudite fashion, Dr. Janse explained chiropractic and chiropractic

163

education to the moderator and the audience, making them more friend than foe.

Of the many instances where Dr. Janse has been called upon to defend chiropractic, perhaps none had more dramatic effect on him than the legal battle for recognition of chiropractic in the State of Louisiana, more commonly known as the England case.

THE ENGLAND CASE

The State of Louisiana was the last state in the United States to pass a law regulating the licensure and practice of chiropractic.

Dr. Janse and Mike Wallace on New York T.V. show, "Night Beat", 1957

The law was signed by Governor Edwin Edwards in 1974. The story of licensure in Louisiana began some twenty years prior and was known as the "England Case" named after Jerry R. England, D.C. (Palmer, 1951).

Dr. England returned to Louisiana, his home state, to practice chiropractic in spite of the recommendations by faculty at Palmer College to go to a state where chiropractic was licensed. The Medical Practice Act of Louisiana, written in 1928, precluded the legal practice of chiropractic. In fact, Drs. James Drain (President of Texas Chiropractic College) and Parker (Dean at TCC) were summoned to court in Louisiana in 1949 to defend a group of doctors of chiropractic being accused of "practicing medicine without a license."[1] The five chiropractors were "...permanently enjoined...from practicing medicine...[and] assessed a fine of $150.00...each"[2] More legal actions were to follow. A new law would need to be enacted to make the practice of chiropractic legal. Actions to create new legislation began as early as 1949-50[3] and were repeated in 1952, 1954 and 1956, each time ending in failure to pass.

While legislative activity continued, it was decided to pursue legal action in 1957. The lawsuit was named *England Jerry R., et. al. vs. the Louisiana Medical Association.* Dr. England was the president of the organization filing the lawsuit on behalf of the chiropractors, thus the suit carried his name. The following is a summary of the nine-year court battle that ended in 1966. This battle eventually captured the attention of the chiropractic profession throughout the country, Dr. Janse being a significant player. The England Case also played a pivotal role in Dr. Janse's life and his commitment to quality chiropractic education.

Early Interactions

William S. Boyd, D.C., President of the Louisiana Chiropractic Association, sent a letter (circa 1956) to, "My Fellow Chiropractors" requesting financial help to support legislative activity in Louisiana to gain recognition and licensure. In a handwritten "p.s.," Dr. Boyd made a personal request to Dr. Janse to take up a collection in the classroom.[4]

The times were difficult in Louisiana. Doctors of Chiropractic were not allowed to advertise, even with their name in the phone book; many were being put in jail.[5] New legislative language was badly needed. Success in the legislature seemed quite distant at that time.

An alternate approach was to file a legal action. In 1957, forty doctors of chiropractic filed an action attacking the constitutionality of the Louisiana Medical Practice Act and its administration by the State Board of Medical Examiners. The case was filed in the United States District Court but the judge threw the case out because of "no jurisdiction" and "no cause for action." The group of forty appealed to the Fifth Circuit Court of Appeals and it was remanded back to the District Court on 9 September 1958 for trial. The Fifth Circuit Court of Appeals also interjected the opinion that chiropractors should not be prohibited from practicing a "useful profession" and the Court also recognized the "individual's reasonable choice of a method for the treatment of his ills."[6]

An excerpt of the opinion follows:

We are not called on at this time to say whether chiropractors should be admitted to practice in Louisiana but the question is whether they are entitled to an opportunity to prove that the State's denial of their claimed right to practice an allegedly useful profession is so arbitrary and unreasonable as to amount to a denial of due process or of the equal protection of the laws under the Fourteenth Amendment.

...It would certainly be arbitrary to exclude some, if not all, of the following classes which Louisiana does admit to practice: dentists, osteopaths, nurses, chiropodists, optometrists, pharmacists and midwives. Just where is the dividing line? Under all of the cases, we think it is that the State cannot deny to any individual the right to exercise a REASONABLE choice in the method of treatment of his ills, nor the correlative right of practitioners to engage in the practice of a useful profession.

...It is not denied that the state may regulate, within reasonable bounds, the practice of chiropractic for the protection of the public health; but it is claimed that the requirements of a diploma from a college approved by the American Medical Association and a knowledge of surgery and material medical bear no reasonable relation to the practice of chiropractic. Without hearing the evidence, we cannot say that those claims are untrue, or that a reasonable man might not intelligently choose a chiropractor for the treatment of some particular ailment. We hold simply that the plaintiffs are entitled to a day in court, to an opportunity to prove their case.[7]

By sending the action back to the District Court for trial and interjecting the opinions noted, the Fifth Circuit Court catapulted a local licensing action into a national concern. A Federal Court was now in position to render an opinion on the "usefulness of chiropractic" and the "individual's right" to the method of choice for health care. The England case in 1958 had become the opportunity for chiropractic to establish under federal recognition its distinct and separate existence from medicine or be put under an even darker cloud than heretofore experienced.

In a letter from J. Minos Simon, Chief attorney for the Louisiana Chiropractic Group filing the law suit, to Mr. Hugh E. Chance, General Counsel for the International Chiropractic Association, we learn many details of the legal strategy to be employed. A copy of this letter reached Dr. Janse and probably all other educational leaders in the profession.

The burden of proof on the chiropractors may be subdivided into four general categories, the first one being of paramount importance over all of them. The plaintiffs must prove:

1. The science of chiropractic is a useful profession.
2. The science of chiropractic has progressed impressively over the past thirty years, and as part evidence thereof a demonstration that the courses of study in chiropractic are comparable in length and equal in quality to the medical colleges.
3. That the requirement of a diploma from a college approved by the American Medical Association bears no reasonable relation to the practice of chiropractic.
4. That knowledge of or an examination in surgery and materia medica bears no reasonable relation to the practice of chiropractic.

The evidence in support of the summary judgment motion must be in affidavit form. These must be comprehensively drawn, and time is of the essence. Each person signing an affidavit should, in the inception thereof, detail his qualifications, showing his academic attainment and his experiences, qualifying him to attest to the facts mentioned in his affidavit. Treating the issues in globo, properly drawn affidavits on the following basic issues should be obtained:

1. The theoretical basis of chiropractic.
2. The anatomical basis of chiropractic.

3. The physiological basis of chiropractic.
4. The physical basis of chiropractic.
5. The clinical basis of chiropractic.
   a. How adjustments act to cure ailments.
6. The neurological basis of chiropractic.
7. Actual case histories, demonstrating the usefulness of the science of chiropractic.
   a. Diagnosis upon entry; mode of treatment, and reason therefore.
   b. Results of treatment.
   c. Affidavits from outstandingly prominent patients who received benefits of chiropractic treatment. (I am told President Eisenhower received chiropractic treatment. An affidavit from him as to the benefits he received from it would be tremendous in establishing the usefulness of chiropractic.)
8. Affidavits comprehensively explanatory of the reasons assignable that demonstrate that a knowledge of surgery and *materia medica* bears no reasonable relation to the practice of chiropractic.
   a. Similar affidavits demonstrating that the requirement that chiropractors produce a diploma from a college approved by the American Medical Association bears no reasonable relation to the practice of chiropractic.
9. Affidavits attesting to the curricular or prescribed course of studies in the various chiropractic schools, and pertinent explanatory statements, annexing the official schedules thereof.
10. Affidavits attesting to the existence of the many chiropractic hospitals, the equipment, facilities, number of rooms, qualifications of staff members, etc.
11. Comprehensive statements of the history of chiropractic demonstrating the progress made, i.e., advancement in scholarship and academic requirements, advancement in practical application of chiropractic principle, etc., to demonstrate that chiropractic is more entitled to recognition today than it was thirty odd years ago (when the Fife case was decided.)[8]

It is interesting that while attorney Simon is discussing legal strategy with chief legal counsel Chance of the International Chiropractic Association, Robert D. Johns, legal counsel for the National Chiropractic Association renders an opinion of no interest in the England Case. "...it is apparent that a decision by the United States Circuit Court of Appeals or the United States Supreme Court, that chiropractic was not a useful profession and that no reasonable man would choose chiropractic care, would be of inestimable injury from a practical and psychological aspect throughout the country. It would not, however, have any legal significance insofar as the various state statutes are concerned."[9]

Mr. Johns informed Mr. Simon that the National Chiropractic Association (NCA) would render financial assistance up to $5,000 for litigation in the District Court. The NCA urged the Louisiana Chiropractic Association to pursue legislative relief and that the NCA would not support the England Case beyond the District Court level. Furthermore, the NCA was reluctant to give a general call to its membership for financial support.[10]

A Day In Court

The Fifth Circuit Court of Appeals remanded the *Jerry R. England, et al. vs. Louisiana State Board of Medical Examiners, et al.* to the District Court of the Eastern District of Louisiana (case no 16920) on 23 January 1959. The legal strategy of the Legal Action Committee and legal counsel of the Louisiana Chiropractic Association was to produce so much evidence attested to by affidavit that the judge would have no option but to render a summary judgment in favor of the Louisiana chiropractors.

An all out effort was mounted to gain the needed information with appropriate affidavits. Dr. J. J. Nugent was Director of Education for the NCA and through his office urgent requests were sent to all leading educators in the profession for help. Dr. Janse responded with information on how the curriculum at National College of Chiropractic had improved in the last thirty years, along with other pertinent information.

There were 307 affidavits submitted for evidence to support the request for a summary judgment of the case. "Our affidavits cover the scientific basis of chiropractic and its value as proven by research and application, both here and abroad. Such outstanding educators as Weiant, Janse, Pharoah, and Quigley have contributed to the wealth of the material."[11] The total number of hours spent in gathering this material must have been quite significant.

In an editor's note found in the Journal of the National Chiropractic Association, Dr. Weiant makes the following statement:

> Your brief is one of the greatest surprises in the history of chiropractic. We of the other states have long thought of Louisiana as the darkest spot on the chiropractic map, the home of a hopelessly submerged handful of chiropractors foolhardy enough to think they could succeed under utterly impossible conditions. Yet it is you who have come up with the most imposing assemblage of data—scientific, legal, economic, sociological, and political—bearing upon matters of chiropractic, ever seen...You, the 'lowly chiropractors' of Louisiana, have shown us how to attack, how to thrust without mercy at the most vulnerable spots in the armor of the enemy. Let chiropractors throughout the world salute you for your courage and recognize the enormous debt they owe you for your sacrifices and matchless service.[12]

In October, 1959 an appeal went out to all chiropractors asking for financial support. It stipulated that the ICA and the NCA had contributed $5,000 each. It noted that the "four thousand members of the Louisiana Medical Society had been assessed $100 each" accumulating a war chest near a half million dollars to support thirty to forty lawyers. Mr. Simon had not charged the chiropractors a fee. Trial date was set for 13 November 1959.[13]

In a surprising response, the District Court rendered an opinion on 5 January 1960 (notice from the Clerk of the Court was released on 29 January 1960). In effect the three-judge court said, "We have decided not to render a decision at this time. We have jurisdiction and, therefore, the power and right to render a decision, but under the circumstances of this case, we believe we should extend the State of Louisiana the opportunity of having its courts decide this case."[14]

Mr. Simon declared a victory for chiropractic. "If we abide by the decision, it simply means we have the opportunity for two hearings. If we are not satisfied with the state courts decision, we shall apply to the three-judge court for a determination of the issues presented. If we are satisfied with the state courts decision, it will mean we have achieved complete victory."[15] The next course of action was to file the same lawsuit in a state court.

The Battle Continues

It came as no surprise when in 1960 the state courts ruled against the plaintiffs, arguing their constitutional right to require individuals who purported to be doctors and treat patients acquire training as stated in the Louisiana Medical Practice Act.[16] Expecting the state to rule against them, Mr. Simon was already prepared with an appeal to the First Circuit Court of Appeal of Louisiana. However, the plaintiffs were discouraged in 1960 when the appeals court affirmed the action of the state court and the Supreme Court of Louisiana denied an application for a writ of certiorari.[17] The appeals court then (1961) dismissed the complaint for the second time on the ground that it was without authority to review the state court action.[18] The only recourse now was the U.S. Supreme Court.

The District Court and the Circuit Court of Appeals would not rule on the constitutionality of the Louisiana Medical Practices Act on the basis of "Abstention" claiming it was the duty of the State to determine the constitutionality of a state law. In mid-1961 the District Court ruling was appealed to the U.S. Supreme Court. On 12 January 1964, the Supreme Court handed down its eight to one decision, "We reverse and remand to the District Court for decision on the merits of appellants' Fourteenth Amendment claims."[19]

A Day In Court – Finally

In 1965 (March 22-24) the England Case finally came to trial. A Mr. LeCorgne, legal counsel for the Louisiana Medical Association was vociferous in his interrogation of Dr. Janse. Mr. LeCorgne attacked Dr. Janse and chiropractic on points of vulnerability while Dr. Janse countered with academic illustrations beyond Mr. LeCorgne and the judges' ability to understand and beyond their willingness to listen. I will cite few examples from the actual transcript[20]

Accreditation, Research and Quality Chiropractic Education

LeCornge: Is the National College of Chiropractic accredited by any nationally recognized accrediting body?

Janse: The National College of Chiropractic has been, already been recognized by the Board of Education and Registration of the state of Illinois...

LeCornge: Is it [National] recognized by the Department of Education, Health and Welfare?

Janse: At the present time it is not.

LeCornge: Has it applied for accreditation?

Janse: The committee on Accreditation of the American Chiropractic Association is preparing for recognition of the schools...

LeCornge: Was the National College of Chiropractic accredited by this group by the time you graduated, in 1938 I presume it was?

Janse: At that time there was no committee on accreditation within the American Chiropractic Association.

LeCornge: Then your answer is no, there was no accrediting body.

Janse: That's right because there was no accrediting body.[21]

LeCornge: Now, you say that chiropractic is accredited, or, I mean the schools, particularly the one with which you are associated, the National College of Chiropractic, is accredited by the American Chiropractic Association?

Janse: We are under the auspices of the accrediting program of the committee on accreditation of the American Chiropractic Association, yes.

LeCornge: What does that mean?

Janse: It simply means that we are seeking to fulfill the criteria as laid down by this committee.

LeCornge: You are not accredited?

Janse: We have the accreditation, we have their acknowledgement, and they, in turn, are going to seek to approach the HEW.

LeCornge: Let me ask it this way, because I can't make it any plainer than—well, is the National College of Chiropractic accredited by the committee of the American Chiropractic Association on Education?

Janse: The National College of Chiropractic is associated in the accrediting program, as all of the other schools are.

THE COURT: (JUDGE JONES) You can't answer his question?

Janse: I can't answer it any clearer than that.

LeCornge: Could you answer it yes or no, and then explain your answer?

Janse: The National College of Chiropractic is accredited by the committee on accreditation, professionally, as all of the other chiropractic colleges are because in their efforts of expanding our educational facilities, there is a certain criteria and one of these is the pre-professional stipulation that I mentioned.

LeCornge: You don't plan to do that until 1968?

Janse: Yes, we do; one year pre-professional by '67, and two years pre-professional by '68.

THE COURT: (JUDGE CHRISTENBERRY) I must confess that I am at a loss here because I understood you earlier to say, I think, that there were tremendous efforts being made to secure accreditation. And you later said that all of the colleges are either accredited by the American Association or the International association, and I was wondering what these strenuous efforts were to secure accreditation? But now you say that just your school is accredited? Or is it not?

Janse: There is no school in chiropractic that is totally accredited by the accrediting agencies within the chiropractic. We are all seeking to fulfill the criteria laid down by these committees on accreditation. We have been assured by the officers in HEW that when these criteria are filled, we again may make the approach for federal recognition.

LeCornge: Well, then, no chiropractic college that you know of is recognized or is accredited by any recognized accrediting institution, is that correct?

173

Janse: Not totally.

LeCornge: Name one?

Janse: I said not totally.

LeCornge: Do you consider the American Chiropractic Association a recognized accrediting agency?

Janse: Just as much as I consider the committee on Medical Education and Hospitals as a recognized accrediting agency.

LeCornge: But it meets the requirements and is approved by the office of Education of the Department of Health, Education and Welfare?

Janse: There was a time when probably it wasn't; and there was a time when optometrists were not, and there was a time when osteopaths were not, but yet they have an accrediting committee.

LeCornge: Well, I wish you would try to answer the question and then you can explain it all you want?

Janse: I am trying to answer.

LeCornge: Who recognizes the American Chiropractic Association as an accrediting agency?

Janse: At the present time, outside of the professional chiropractic, no agency.

LeCornge: Do you agree with his [Dewey Anderson] conclusions that one of the primary difficulties with chiropractic schools is that there are too many part-time instructors, and too few giving their major professional time as fully employed faculty members engaged in instruction, administration and research and too many instructors teaching the basic science without having had any advanced or graduate training in these sciences resulting in slavish devotion to textbook teaching and instruction considerably below the level of post-college professional education?

Janse: I don't totally agree with that – I can't. But certainly it is an atmosphere of responsibility that confronts all of our educational systems.

LeCornge: And then he says on page 3: "Teaching loads of those who do give full time to their schools are usually too heavy to allow much needed outside preparation or research. Membership and participation in professional, scientific or learned societies is almost non-existent. Nor is there any substantial program of faculty-student research which forms the lifeblood and growth of other professions." Do you agree with that?

Janse: Not entirely.

LeCornge: What do you disagree with?

Janse: Because I believe that in many of these atmospheres alteration and upgrading and improvement has been made, and very definitely, and very consistently. ...

LeCornge: Do you agree or disagree with this statement: "Nor is there any substantial program of faculty-student research which forms the lifeblood and growth of other professions."?

Janse: I would take issue with that.

LeCornge: You would say that in the chiropractic schools there is a substantial program of research?

Janse: I would say there is a definite effort to establish a substantial program.

LeCornge: In other words, right now there is none?

Janse: Right now there is a beginning of research effort, and a reputable beginning.

LeCornge: Then, in the past, there has been none?

Janse: No. Up to a certain point, and, again, determining or asking the question: What is research?

LeCornge: You are the president of a college and you don't know what research is?

Janse: In your terms? I know what research is in my terms.

LeCornge: You mean there is a different concept of research in all fields of science except in chiropractic?

Janse: The heterogeneity of research is many-fold – you know this as well as I.[22]

LeCornge: Have you done any research?

Janse: I had the occasion to be in Switzerland in 1948 and also in 1956 and primarily I had worked with Doctor Fred Illi of Switzerland on cinemaroentgenology in chiropractic, yes, sir. I have the original film that we evolved years ago...

LeCornge: Have you published any papers in connection with your work?

Janse: Yes.

LeCornge: Where were they published?

Janse: They were published by the National College of Chiro-practic...[23]

Disease Processes & Procedures

In explaining the reflex phenomena between viscera of the body and the structural components (visceral-somatic) Dr. Janse was asked to explain the rationale for the chiropractic treatment of tonsillitis[24], infected gall bladder[25], psychiatry[26], tetanus[27], cancer[28], polio, diph-theria, meningitis and immunizations[29], and typhoid fever;

> **Janse:** We must always keep in mind, you see, that the degree of infection, the hazard of the infection, and the hazard of the disease process is always surrounded by this qualification: What is the status of the vital tissues, the tissue vitality within that organism at the time of the invasion and at the time of the disease process.
>
> **LeCornge:** You would say that the bacillus is the primary cause of typhoid fever?
>
> **Janse:** I would say that the bacillus, superimposed upon devi-talized mucosa of the alimentary canal, yes, is the provocative and precipitating agent.
>
> **LeCornge:** It is a primary cause then?
>
> **Janse:** It is a primary – it is the precipitating and provocative cause superimposed upon a tissue that has experienced a lowering of its vital threshold.
>
> **LeCornge:** Could you answer this yes or no, and then explain it all you want? Is the typhus bacilli, or bacillus, the primary cause of typhoid fever?
>
> **Janse:** Of the infection, yes.
>
> **LeCornge:** Well, typhoid fever is an infection?
>
> **Janse:** Yes, but the typhoid fever is a complexity of reactions of the tissues to an infection when the tissues' vitalities, resistance is low. And that is true of tuberculosis, and in many instances that is true of many of the infections. And infections are just not infec-

tions; certainly micro organisms have a greater virulence and intensity of detriment than other organisms.[30]

Chiropractic Dissension

At two points medical counsel tried to belittle chiropractic by reference to "straight vs. mixer" division and specifically to a Dr. L.W. Rutherford, president of the ICA[31], and later he was queried on the concepts and theories of B.J. Palmer.[32]

The Decision

"The Three-Judge District Court, Judges Wright, Jones and Christenberry, held that it is not irrational and unreasonable for Louisiana Legislature to require chiropractors to comply with licensing provisions of Louisiana Medical Practice Act before being allowed to practice their profession in Louisiana.

"**Injunction denied and complaint dismissed.**"[33] [emphasis added]

Judge Wright argued that the Medical Practices Act defined the practice of medicine to include "...the holding out of one's self to the public as being engaged in the business of diagnosing, treating, curing, or relieving any bodily or mental disease, condition, infirmity, deformity, defect, ailment or injury..."[34] He further argued that the Act defined the requirement of receiving a diploma from an approved school and passing a licensing exam and that certain specialties (dentistry, optometry, homeopathy, etc.) were exempted from the Act and chiropractic was not included in the specialty list.

Judge Wright described the duality of the profession as represented by the International Chiropractic Association—one cause (subluxation) and one cure (manipulation) of disease; and the American Chiropractic Association—chiropractic is a complete and independent healing art which not only can prevent disease, but can cure disease if the manipulation of the spine begins in time.[35]

Recognizing the difficulty of the legislative process, Judge Wright noted that the medical lobby may be strong enough to prevent chiropractic from passing favorable legislation. However, he added, "It may also be true that, since chiropractic claims to be a complete and independent healing art capable of curing almost all kinds of disease, the Legislature may have felt that the requirement of a foundation in *materia medica* and surgery, even for chiropractors, would be a protection to the public. Perhaps also the Legislature concluded that knowledge of these subjects would assist chiropractors in diagnosing disease and determining in specific cases whether or not the disease was too far advanced for successful treatment by chiropractic ministrations."[36]

The final blow of Judge Wright's argument hit a vulnerable point.

> The legislature may also have been impressed by the fact that there is no school in the United States accredited to teach chiropractic, even by the accrediting committee of the American Chiropractic Association. In fact, the Director of Education of the American Chiropractic Association states:
>
> 'None of the ACA colleges is fully 'Accredited' as yet. For none meets all of the standards...
>
> 'The Accreditation Committee [of the American Chiropractic Association] has been guided not only by its strict interpretation of the Standards, but by what is required for accreditation of schools of podiatry, optometry, nursing and osteopathy. All of these kindred or associated fields in the healing arts have had their accrediting agencies accepted by the U.S. Office of Education,...'
>
> If the education obtained in chiropractic schools does not meet the standards of the American Chiropractic Association and the United States Office of Education, it may well be that the legislature of Louisiana felt that in the public interest a diploma from an approved medical school should be required of a chiropractor before he is allowed to treat all the human ailments chiropractors contend can be cured by manipulation of the spine.[37]

Paul J. Adams, D.C. of Lafayette, Louisiana wrote of the trial,

Dr. Janse was our chief witness and occupied the stand most of Monday. His forthrightness and obvious sincerity coupled with his knowledge were most impressive. There was no evidence of evasiveness in his answers on cross examination. Some of the questions related to statements on principles, practice and concepts made by authors during the past twenty-five years. Accreditation of colleges prompted several questions. Etiology, diagnosis and treatment of most every disease problem came into the picture. Specific emphasis was placed on infectious and fatal disease processes, particularly those of great notoriety and fear-instilling quality, e.g., tetanus, polio, typhoid, cancer, etc. The subject of immunization was not ignored. Through all of the cross examination Dr. Janse maintained his composure, forthrightness and dignity.[38]

Fellow witness in this three-day ordeal, W.D. Harper, D.C., Dean of Texas Chiropractic College and author of *Anything Can Cause Anything*, wrote a tribute to Dr. Janse's contribution.

You may well individually stand just a little bit taller today because of the presentation he made and because of his influence on the presiding judges. He definitely influenced their thinking and they were impressed with his moral honesty and with the sincerity with which he spoke about the science of chiropractic.

Dr. Joe Janse is such a man, as he very convincingly demonstrated in the five-hour period that he was on the stand. His years of experience and all that he knew were focused in the direct answers that he gave, and he may well be proud of the contribution that he has made to this profession in spite of the emotional stress that he experienced as a result of the responsibility placed upon him to speak for all of this profession.[39]

The Aftermath

In spite of the discouragement resulting from the defeat in District Court, the chiropractors continued to pursue the legislative route. On 24 June 1974, a former friend of chiropractic and then Governor of Louisiana, Edwin Edwards signed a chiropractic bill into law.[40]

In 1967, Dr. England and his wife left Louisiana in the middle of the night to avoid going to jail. They relocated in Alabama where Dr. England practiced for the next 27 years.[41]

Dr. Robert Jackson, former member of the Board of Governors of the ACA relates that Dr. Janse was,

> ...raked over the coals so badly by the Med. Attorney's over the issue that no DC college had any accreditation status with USOE or any Regional Accred. Agencies, that our education was therefore in fact inferior to Medical schools and that we were all a bunch of uneducated so-and-so's. J.J. was so stimulated by his handling, he became the driving force, along with Geo. Haynes of LACC, to get an Accred. Agency for the Prof., and we know what happened. J.J. then went for Reg. Accred. And I believe was first to receive this type of status.[42]

Indeed, while the England Case was felt to be a failure since it did not obtain its original goal, it did become the nucleus for the educational accreditation movement and the formation of the Council on Chiropractic Education. The chiropractic profession was strengthened as a result of this monumental effort against insurmountable odds.

In a graduation speech in 1985, Janse offered his own personal reflection:

> 1965, the year of reckoning for Dr. Janse—The England Case Trial—Unanswered Questions.

> Question No. 1—"You, Mr. Janse, claim to hold the Doctorate in Chiropractic as issued upon your graduation from the institution of which you are now president—by what authority did the National College of Chiropractic issue this degree?" There was dead silence as there was no answer. "It would seem to me, Mr. Janse, that the D.C. degree is a spurious degree."

> Question No. 2—"You, Mr. Janse, have maintained that the college of which you are president is accredited by the Council on

Chiropractic Education. May I ask, has the Division of Higher and Professional Education of the U.S. Office of Education granted approval to the standards of your council on education?" Again no answer and an awkward silence.

Question No. 3—"Mr. Janse, if a student at the National College of Chiropractic after having ably concluded two years of study but decides that he does not wish to continue, are his credits acquired at your college transferable into a regionally accredited college or university?" A stutter, an attempt at an answer, a facetious smile on the counsel's face, turned to the Judge with the snide expression, "there you are, your honor." Mr. Janse, alias Dr. Janse, went to his hotel room a beaten man. According to Beidman, "He vowed that he 'would correct this fault...or leave the profession.'"[43]

Since then, and by dint of undeniable and unqualified input from the N.C.C. administration, the chiropractic profession has realized the following:

1. The official authority as stipulated by the Commission on Degree Granting of the Illinois Department of Higher Education to issue the Bachelor of Science (B.S.) in Human Biology and the Doctor of Chiropractic (D.C.).
2. The Standards and Commission of Accreditation of the Council on Chiropractic Education have been fully approved by the U.S. Office of Education and today resultantly chiropractic is listed with medicine, dentistry, and osteopathy as a first primary profession.
3. The regional North-Central Association of Colleges and Secondary Schools has awarded N.C.C. full accreditation status, and is now an absolute must to the administration of all C.C.E. affiliated colleges.

At times our apparent failures become [the impetus for] some of our greatest victories.[44]

1   TCC News Letter, Issue No. 89, pg. 5, 1949.

2   J. National Chiropractic Association 20(6) pp 54, 56, 1950.

3   J. National Chiropractic Association, 20(5) pg. 50, 1950.

4   Letter from Dr. Boyd (circa 1956) in the Janse Collection, NUHS Archives.

5   ICA Review. Vol. 8 (6), pp 7, 31, 1953 (Dec).

6   Letter from Adams & Colins to Dr. Watkinson, 1958, in the Janse Collection, NUHS Archives.

7   ICA International Review of Chiropractic. 13(4), pg. 27, 1958 (Oct.)

8   Letter from J Minow Simon to Hugh E. Chance, 1958, in the Janse Collection, NUHS Archives.

9   Letter from Robert Johns to Dr. Frank Ploudre, 1959, in the Janse Collection, NUHS Archives.

10 Letter from Robert Johns to J. Minos Simon, 1959, in the Janse Collection, NUHS Archives.

11 Adams, PJ. "The Brief for Chiropractic in the England Case Is Available." J. NCA, 1959. Pg 9,10,36.

12 J. National Chiropractic Association 29(12), pg 9, 1959 (Dec.).

13 Letter from Adams & Collins to all chiropractors, 1959, in the Janse Collection, NUHS Archives.

14 Civil Action No. 9292, 29 Jan. 1960, in the Janse Collection, NUHS Archives.

15 Letter from Mr. Simon to Plaintiffs, 30 Jan 1960, in the Janse Collection, NUHS Archives.

16 England v. Louisiana State Board of Medical Examiners, E.D. La., 180 F. Supp. 121 (1960).

17 England v. Louisiana State Board of Medical Examiners, La. App., 126 So.2d 51 (1960).

18 England v. Louisiana State Board of Medical Examiners, E.D.La., 194 F. Supp. 521 (1961).

19 Simon, JM. "U.S. Supreme Court Remands England Case to District Court for Decision." JACA pg. 9, 1964.

20 England Trail Transcript, 1965. Janse Collection, NUHS Archives.

21 Ibid. pg. 88-89.

22 Ibid. pg. 150-155.

23 Ibid. pg. 90-91.

24 Ibid. pg. 94.

25 Ibid. pg. 96.

26 Ibid. pg. 159-160.

27 Ibid. pg. 174-187. In this discussion, counsel referenced *Chiropractic Practice, Volume I, Infectious Diseases.* By B.F. Wells, D.O., D.C., Joseph Janse, D.C. as a basis for challenging Dr. Janse on the chiropractic method of treating an infectious disease such as tetanus. Janse claimed having only assisted Dr. Wells as a fledgling faculty member on the anatomical referencing and that he could not be held responsible for some of the therapeutic claims made in the text. Dr. James Winterstein claims in personal communication that Janse cautioned him as a young faculty member never to put your name on something you didn't write and referred to the testimony of the England Trial.

28 Ibid. pg. 189-197. It is interesting to note that in the reference to the chiropractic management of cancer, specific reference was made of "bladder cancer" to which Dr Janse gave a very conservative approach to a disease not easily diagnosed by any means in 1965. Ironically, it was cancer of the bladder that Dr. Janse finally succumbed to some twenty-years later.

29 Ibid. 213-226

30 Ibid. pg. 204-205.

31 Ibid. pg. 169-171.

32 Ibid. pg. 199-201.

33 England v. Louisiana State Board of Medical Examiners, 246 F.Supp. 993 (1965).

34 Ibid. pg. 994.

35 Ibid. pg. 995.

36 Ibid. pg. 996.

37 Ibid. pg. 997.

38 Adams, PJ. "Trial of The England Case." JACA May, 1965. Pg. 13.

39 Harper, WD. "In Tribute to Dr. Joseph J. Janse." JACA, May, 1965. Pg. 18.

40 England, JR. "The England Case: A Battle for Licensure." Today's Chiropractic. Nov/Dec 1995. Pg. 88.

41 Letter from Dr. E. Long to the Chiropractic Profession. October, 1997. Janse Collection, NUHS Archives.

42 Letter from Dr. R. Jackson to Dr. J. Keating. 25 Feb. 1993. Janse Collection, NUHS Archives.

43 Beideman, R. *In The Making of a Profession: The National College of Chiropractic 1906-1981*. National College, Lombard, IL, 1995, pg. 260.

44 Ibid. pg. 261.

Chapter Eleven

THE BUILDER

20 North Ashland—Chicago

When Joseph Janse entered the National College of Chiropractic in 1935, the school was located at 20 North Ashland in Chicago. The building was erected in 1899 and had been the Chicago Theological Seminary building. Dr. Schultz purchased the building to accommodate rising enrollment, to extend curriculum, and to increase clinic space for patients. National occupied the building on 1 December 1919.[1]

The building was large and spacious, accommodating, "...large, light, airy classrooms and lecture halls, laboratories, offices, parlors, library, museum, gymnasium, and living rooms for two hundred students."[2] Gloria's recollections of her and Joe having lived in the school suggests that faculty as well as students resided in the upper floors of the school.

Mr. Otto J. Turek, businessman and grateful patient, joined the staff at National in 1924. Soon thereafter the clinic was renovated and enlarged and the Chicago General Health Services (CGHS) was established as a "corporation not for pecuniary profit" in 1927 with its own Board of Directors, including Mr. Turek.[3] Mr. Turek eventually became the Chairman of the Board of Trustees of the College and its Chief Administrative Officer (an arrangement that became a problem in seeking accreditation with the NCA) and purchased $100,000 of the schools indebtedness when it transitioned to a not-for-profit institution. That was a huge sum in the 1942.[4]

National College of Chiropractic at 20 North Ashland Blvd., Chicago, circa1930

According to Beideman, plans to build a thirteen-story hospital, "...adjacent to the west side of the main building on the college property with its entrance facing Warren Boulevard..." never materialized due to the effects of the Depression and World War II. "...a framed architect's rendering entitled: 'A view of National College and New Hospital as it Will appear When Completed'...hung in the front office until the college moved to Lombard."[5]

When Dr. Janse stepped into the Office of President in 1945, the building occupied by National was already 46 years old. For the next 18 years every effort was made to maintain and improve the facility. The January 1953 issue of the *National College Journal of* Chiropractic ran an article announcing the completion of a new clinical laboratory, "...the third new laboratory to be built at National College of Chiropractic since the war."[6] In the end, the City of Chicago threatened to fine the College because the building, still being used as a dormitory in the early '60's, was no longer compliant with existing building codes. Expansion of the medical complex surrounding Cook County Hospital failed to expand northward to encompass the college. Rather, "skid row" moved westward from the inner city and the area deteriorated becoming inhospitable for students and patients alike. The need to relocate the College, rested squarely on an ever-so-busy president.

200 East Roosevelt Road—Lombard

The College purchased twenty acres of unincorporated farmland adjacent to the Village of Lombard in the center of DuPage County, Illinois in 1957. They intended to build but the DuPage County Medical Society mobilized themselves for the 1957-1958 "Battle of Lombard." They "...propagandized their patients, made appearances before civic groups, distributed circulars in the village accompanied by an unsigned pamphlet...[they] protested in writing and testified in person before several meetings of the Lombard Village Board of Trustees and the Lombard Planning Commission in their effort to block first the annexation of NCC's property to Lombard and then the re-zoning..." Opponents created, "...racial innuendo to be used against the college, if only because NCC had ten black students in 1958."[7]

A four-hour public hearing held by the Lombard Planning Commission on 11 February 1958 was attended by 300 people, mostly opposed to the chiropractic school plan. A petition signed by 600 residents opposed the proposed rezoning plan. Beideman gave this first-hand accounting of National's chief witness, Joseph Janse.

> In his own inimitable way he represented the college and his profession in a most enchanting, exacting way. There was no pomposity nor arrogance within his testimony. He defended as well as represented his people sincerely, modestly, and factually, and he ably rebutted a number of untruths, half-truths and innuendos that had been uttered by the opposing faction in Lombard during the preceding several months.[8]

On 13 February 1958, the *Lombard Spectator* newspaper reported a unanimous decision by the Planning Commission in favor of the proposed rezoning changes for the National College. Dr. Janse had carried the day, the first of many battles associated with building a school while at the same time building a profession.

If all that was needed was a new building to be built, life would have been much easier, but someone had to cover the costs of the building project. Janse had to establish a nation-wide capital fund raising campaign under the diverse leadership of the Trustees, corporate members, a board of professional consultants, the alumni association and the administration of the college.

In actuality, Janse was well-advanced in his planning for the relocation. A building program was announced by National in a publication noting their 50th anniversary in 1956.[9] In addition to architectural renderings of the proposed new facility, the organization of the fund-raising effort was presented.

The campaign to raise funds started with the Trustees of the college. In addition to Otto. J. Turek as Chair of the Board, three additional Trustees were listed:

Edward S. Scheffler, Member, Board of Education, City of Chicago, Chief Justice, Municipal Court of Chicago, Retired Director, Welfare Council, City of Chicago.

William C.DeVry, Chairman of the board, DeVry Technical Institute, Director, Paromel Electronics Corporation, Director, Continental Electric Company.

Dr. Ralph C. King, Director, Illinois Chiropractic Society, Editor, Illinois Chiropractic News, Former Chief of Staff, National College clinic.

The second group of prominence in fund raising efforts was the Board of Professional Consultants consisting of:

Dr. J. Dutton	Rushville, Illinois
Dr. Wray Hughes Hopkins	Ardmore, Pennsylvania
Dr. Herbert W. Ortman	Canistota, South Dakota
Dr. Arnold R. Tolley	Chevy Chase, Maryland
Dr. Mark Van Wagoner	Oxford, Michigan

188

There was also a Building Fund Executive Committee.

Dr. L.J. Darr, Chair	Oak Harbor, Ohio
Dr. E.H. Bubar	Bangor, Maine
Dr. George E. Hariman	Grand Forks, North Dakota
Dr. Gordon L. Holman	Cheyenne, Wyoming
Dr. J.W. Lawrence	Lebanon, Tennessee
Dr. Earl G. Liss	Detroit, Michigan
Dr. Norman E. Osborne	Hagerstown, Maryland

Dr. Martin R. Stone, Special Gift Chair, Chicago, Illinois
Mr. Charles A. Miller, Executive Secretary, Chicago, Illinois

A state representative was identified in each of the forty-eight states (Hawaii and Alaska excluded). The key to making this elaborate organization function, of course, was Dr. Janse.

In this same publication, an elaborate Building Fund Plan was also presented.

BUILDING FUND PLAN

I. The basic plan is to have each Doctor of Chiropractic pledge himself to a payment of $10.00 per month for thirty-six months, or $120.00 per year for three years, or give $360.00 now.

II. The National College of Chiropractic will purchase and pay for the real estate for the new campus which will be located in suburban Chicago. The college will also pay for all public relations costs, printing and other related expense so that every dollar collected will go into the Building Fund. Negotiations for the real estate are near completion and a very suitable site will grace the new National College of Chiropractic.

III. The collected monies will be held in escrow and can only be taken out under the signature of a majority of the members of the Building Fund Executive Committee.

IV. The present physical plant of the National College will be retained as income property to serve as an endowment for the new college.

189

V.   Being a non-profit corporation, donations to the National College of Chiropractic-Building Fund are an allowable federal income tax deduction.

VI.   The entire program will involve five years, and extensive plans have been formulated to effect its realization.

VII. The present National College is completely solvent, debt-free, and sustains a competent reserve all of which will serve as a fitting legacy for the new college.

VIII. The signing of the pledge card is not the formation of a legal binding contract, but will merely serve the Building Fund Executive Committee in formulating its future plans. Some will wish to give more than the basic pledge of $360.00, others will prefer to pay on a weekly, or yearly basis. Use the method most convenient for you, or devise a plan of your own.

IX.   The pledge card can be found on the last page of this brochure.

X.   The success of chiropractic, the success of your profession – rests with you.[10]

In the April, 1959 issue of the *National College Journal of Chiropractic* the college published a thermometer showing more than $282,000 in hand toward the needed $500,000 to build the first unit—the college and administration building. Ground breaking ceremonies were scheduled in conjunction with National's Postgraduate Course and Homecoming was held the first four days of July in 1959. Dr. Janse was a main speaker at these events as well as being in charge of the ground breaking ceremony.[11]

It will be recalled that in an effort to have the NCA Schools recognized by the U.S. Office of Education of the Department of Health, Welfare and Education, it was necessary to upgrade the schools. The NCA had agreed to fund school needs through the establishment of the Foundation for Accreditation of Chiropractic Education (FACE). Essentially FACE offered a 2 to 1 matching grant to the NCA-approved schools up to a certain amount that varied each year. Monies were to be used to procure students, build infrastructure and improve facilities. Much of the fund raising done by Dr. Janse was acquiring the college's portion of the 2 to 1 matching program with FACE.

In 1961 the *Journal* published more thermometers with the estimated building costs for the first unit, the college, clinic and administration adjusted to $700,000. Pledges and reserve funds were just over $500,000, however. Dr. Darr reported that building contracts had been awarded (4 April 1960) and plans to hold classes in the new building by September, 1961 would be fulfilled. The plans called for a one-story (with basement) building of approximately 33,000 square feet on each level. Initially no basement was planned but when the soil conditions forced excavation to a depth of 12 feet to reach solid ground for the foundation, it was decided to add a basement. In his detailed description of the building, Dr. Darr placed a heavy emphasis on the number of windows and amount of lighting along with the spaciousness of the new building. Apparently, the 20 North Ashland building lacked sufficient numbers of either. [12]

Although construction got underway in 1960, due to insufficient funds, construction activities ceased for about a year. Dr. Janse, once again stepped in to save the day.

> Soon after activity at the Lombard construction site was interrupted, Dr. Janse single handedly conducted what might be called a phonothon today and sold thousands of dollars of debenture notes to individual alumni and friends of the college. These were not pledges. They were loan dollars that enabled the college to acquire mortgage money sufficient to complete construction of the first building erected on the Lombard campus. [13]

In the December, 1961 issue of the *National College Journal of Chiropractic*, Dr. Janse gave a thorough accounting of the building fund status—perhaps in response to the dire need to raise funds for completion of a project with walls and no roof. Perhaps, however, it was in response to the (so rumor has stated[14]) departure of Mr. Miller, the Executive Secretary to the Building Fund Committee, and the loss of funds.

The following is what Dr. Janse provided regarding the financial commitments and circumstances of the Building Project. He hoped to raise $155,000.00 in the sale of Corporate notes:

1. Contractual commitments to architects and contractors:
   a. Total Commitments including architect's fees,
      contractors, water, sewers, and basic landscaping. $879,485.00
   b. Total paid as of above date (Dec, 1961) $410,461.00
   c. Total yet to be paid $469,024.00

2. Financing arrangement for total yet to be paid:
   a. A 2 year mortgage with the Harris Trust and Savings
      Bank with option to renew or transfer into a 15 year
      mortgage, at 6.5% interest $250,000.00
   b. A commercial loan from Harrris Trust and Savings
      Bank for 90 days with the privilege of renewal up to
      two years $100,000.00
   c. Cash deposited with Harris Trust and Savings Bank
      by National College as obtained from following resources
      1. Corporate note sale, on hand $95,000.00
      2. Building Fund collections, on hand $11,000.00
      3. NCC Reserve Fund, on hand allocated to
         Construction $14,000.00
          $120,000.00
          $470,000.00

3. Funds still needed for following purposes:
   a. To retire Commercial loan (2 b. above) $100,000.00
   b. For moving costs $25,000.00
   c. For furniture, fixtures, miscellaneous equipment
      needed in the new building $30,000.00

4. CORPORATE NOTE PROGRAM
   a. A total of $250,000.00 to be raised at 5% interest annually. Of this
      amount $95,000.00* has already been raised, leaving balance of
      $155,000.00 bill to collect, per 3 above.
   b. Certificates are in denominations of $100.00, $500.00 and $1,000.00
      for tenures of 5, 6, 7, 8, 9, and 10 years. Yearly issue not to exceed
      $35,000.00.
   c. Beginning September 1961, the college has and will continue to set
      aside $2,200.00 dollars a month in a special Corporate Note Savings
      Account at the Harris Trust and Savings Bank to assure full coverage of
      interest on notes as well as repayment of principal.

5. The $250,000.00 mortgage and interest will be paid as follows:
    a. Proceeds still remaining and to be collected on Building
        Fund Pledges (see footnote No. 3) $75,000.00
    b. Sale of 20 N. Ashland Blvd. building $150,000.00
    c. Balance $75,000.00

To be secured through:
    1. Increase in tuition fee effective September 18, 1961 from $180.00 to
        $200.00 per semester. Estimated $12,000.00 annually or $30,000.00
        2.5 years.
    2. $45,000.00 from NCC general fund over a period of 2.5 years.[15]

From various letters between Dr. Janse and members of those helping in the fund raising efforts it was evident the bulk of the asking was on the shoulders of Dr. Janse. No possibility was overlooked. For example the women's auxiliaries were collecting S&H green stamps to trade for a school automobile (they came up 400 books short[16]). Each state association was tasked to raise funds to decorate individual offices or the foyer of the main building. Personally engraved brass acknowledgement plates were stuck to everything that had a flat surface.

In an exchange of letters, between Dr. Janse and W.F. Marquardt, V.P. sales, Anabolic Inc., January to April of 1962, Dr. Janse was able to retain the $4,000 dollar pledge from Anabolic while allowing National out of the exclusivity agreement to only use Anabolic products in the school clinics. This allowed National to court additional support from other venders. Dr. Janse was initially brought into this exchange of correspondence to apologize for Dr. Darr's comments regarding Anabolic's exclusive hold on National College, Dr. Darr being the Chair of the Building Fund Executive Committee.[17]

In a letter dated 6 Oct 1962, Dr. Janse wrote to Dr. Margaret D. Evans, Miami, FL. Her brother made bronze plaques at a company in Chicago, and the college needed a plaque for front entrance. Janse tells Dr. Evans they want the plaque for free.[18]

Dr. Janse was literally speaking every weekend at state conventions, postgraduate seminars and national conventions. He would return from a speaking engagement with $120 in cash, take out $5.00 for personal expenses and put the rest in the Building Fund.

The treatment-of-the-month and the Century Club were all started as part of this massive fund raising effort.[19]

Colleagues have shared personal stories, that on more than one occasion when Janse would arrive at a certain hotel on Friday evening in preparation for his speaking engagement on Saturday morning. The hosting chiropractic group would give him the keys to a hotel room and trusted he would be comfortable until morning. When one from the host group happened to arrive a little early they would either find Dr. Janse freshening up in the public rest room of the hotel lobby; or, if they came early enough, they might even find him still sleeping on the stage or on a bench in the lecture hall. He would tell them that he had forgone the expense of the room and hoped the group would put that cost towards the school building fund.

Dr. George A. Smyrl, NCA Delegate from Massachusetts indicated in his 15 April 1960 report to the NCA that Dr. Janse never got any sleep on the plane flying to their convention, nor did he eat any lunch, for his time was consumed with meetings. He did get a check however to be put towards the new classroom building at NCC. But, "We never heard Dr. Janse when he was better. Here is a speaker who improves with age. With just a classroom blackboard and some chalk Dr. Janse spent five hours lecturing and everyone was awake and alert every minute."[20]

Classes started in the new building on 13 May 1963. On 27 June 1963 the new campus building was dedicated. This happened to fall on the 25th wedding anniversary of Joseph and Gloria, so the couple was presented a silver candelabra. The Lombard Chiropractic Clinic occupying 8,000 square feet in the basement of the new building opened for patient care in September 1963. The first student housing facility to open was Tiezen Hall in September 1963. It had space for 100 single male students and 16 single females or married couples.[21]

In 1965 National College constructed a new two-story building on property at 20 North Ashland and shortly thereafter demolished the old National building, having never sold it. They had attempted to lease it but in the end more was required to renovate than the building was worth. The new building became the new Chicago

General Health Services (CGHS) and continues to serve the University today. Additional married student housing was constructed on the Lombard campus with Buccholz Hall being occupied in 1968, Turek Hall in 1970 and Lincoln Hall in 1972. Construction and remodeling in the basement and on top of the main building started in 1974 resulting in the operations of the Radiological Learning Lab, the Earl A. Rich Cineroentgenology Lab, the Interdepartmental Research lab and the Sordoini-Burich learning Resource Center. In 1975 two additional satellite clinics were established in addition to the Lombard clinic and CGHS. By 1976 construction of a new student center was started and in 1981, the Diamond Jubilee seventy-fifth anniversary year, "The National College of Chiropractic opened a completely new seven million dollar, 52,000 square foot Patient and Research Center...it was opened without any long-term debt whatsoever."[22]

What a fitting finale for the continual, extra-ordinary efforts of Dr. Janse to raise funds for the building campaign on campus. It is to be remembered that in the midst of a building program from the

Lombard Campus, main building with second level addition, circa 1975

195

(l to r) Architects for new Student Center (3); Drs. Janse; Earl Liss, Board Chair; Herbert Ortman, Board Member; Leonard Fay, Executive Vice-President, 1976

Ground Breaking for the Patient and Research Center, Dr. Janse with shovel

196

date of announcement, 1956 to the completion of the Patient and Research Center, Dr. Janse occupied other responsible positions, traveled extensively, taught postgraduate and for awhile undergraduate courses, remained prominent on the national and international scene, and carried out all his other duties and a member of his church and as the father of his family. To his regret, and by his own admission, the latter two responsibilities were often neglected simply because there was not enough time in his clock.

There were many who worked with Dr. Janse during these demanding times—Jacob Fisher, Ph.D., Dean of Faculty; Dr. Arnold Houser, Alumni Association President; Dr. Chester Stowell, Dean of Students; Ms. Marge Neely, Office Manager then Executive Director of the Alumni Association and Ms. Beth Herza, Secretary to the President.

Two in particular are worthy of additional mention. Dr. Earl Liss, elected to the Board of Trustees 28 October 1961, served as the Chair of the Board for the next 21 years.[23] Dr. Leonard Fay,

(l to r) Drs. Jacob Fisher, Janse and Fay, circa 1975

(l to r) Ms. Marge Neely, Drs. Janse, Chester Stowell and Arnold Houser

Board and Administration, *(l to r)* Drs. Frank Hoffman, Ed Mauer, Mark Van Wagoner, Mr. Otto Turek, Drs. Janse, Earl Liss, Herbert Ortman, Len Fay, Chester Stowell, and L. J. Darr, circa 1975.

faculty member, clinician, and long time administrator, was Dr Janse's Executive Vice President. A plethora of daily correspondence (often self-typed, in the days of carbon copies and manual typewriters) flowed between these three men during the building years in Lombard. Gazing through memos and letters provided by the preservation of much of this correspondence—gives a glimpse of the intensity of the times. The summaries and excerpts which follow are from minutes, letters, and documents preserved in the Janse Archives at the National University of Health Sciences. The material has been abbreviated for ease of reading and indexing of salient points.

Correspondence between Drs. Janse and Liss and others, during the building years (1959 to 1967)[24]

3 May 1959—Letter from Janse to Senator Andrew J. Sordoni of Pennsylvania.
Summary of current progress with new building plans.
Janse indicates that he has been on the road for the last ten weekends straight.

13 June 1959—Letter from Janse to Sordoni.
Invitation to attend and speak at the ground breaking and dedication ceremony slated for July 4th

27 July 1962—Letters from Leonard E. Fay, D.C. to various state groups, raising funds
Leroy Kohlhorst, Ohio—raising money for the new clinic
Frederick Smidell, Minn.—raising money for the office of the Dean
Herbert Ortman, S.D.—raising money for the Board of Trustees room
Clarence H. Laue, MI—raising money to furnish the main lobby
S. Wallace Westre, WI—raising money to pay for furnishings

5 Oct 62—Letter from Fay to Gerald Rodgers, DC
Contact publishers to see if they will donate texts to the new library.

1 July 1962—Letter from Liss to Janse
A "brainstorming" letter in relation to FACE's offer of 2:1 fund matching for up-grading.

Source of matching funds	$10K
Sordoni Library	$2.5K
Ortman Chem Lab	$2.3K
Eliminate $600 dream boat emblem in lobby	
Only panel one wall in Pres Office save $400	
Direct Appeal	$4.2K

What to do with $20K to upgrade faculty next year?
1. Sec/Stenographer/shorthand, Dictaphone $3K
2. Administrative Dean $3K
3. Faculty raises

Dean Parker	$300 [JJ-$200]
Full Time Instructors 5@$100 ea	$500
Part Time Kissinger & others	
hourly increase	$300 [JJ-total cost]
Librarian @ Lombard	$2.5K
Research Director (Tyska's D.O.)	$6.5K
Clinic Director @ Lombard Part-time	$4.4K

8 July 1962—Letter from Liss to Janse
Related to current budget concerns
1. Consummate immediate sale of Corporate Notes to NCA for $50K
2. Don't mention $8K X-ray proposal
3. Following are essential positions for accreditation
   a. Administrative Dean $7.5–$8K
   b. Academic Dean $3K
   c. Office Secretary $3.2K
4. Following are not essential for accreditation but worthy of consideration
   a. New Clinic Director and part-time staff
   b. Librarian

    c. Research Director part-time

    d. Caretaker, janitor, utility man with student help

    e. Utility tractor for grass cutting, weeds and snow

    f. Increase in salary for department heads with degrees, staff and hourly for part time

    g. $10K for physiology lab

    h. Dean of Admissions and Dean of Student Affairs can be tacked to faculty who are not too involved.

9 July 1962—Letter from Janse to Liss

1. Readied a note to Trustees on Corporate Note sale and FACE proposition.
2. $9K in bank now for FACE matching money.
3. Asked Penn. Group if OK to reallocate their funds from faculty lounge to physiology lab.
4. Will ask Ortman if can do the same, transfer funds from chem. lab to physiology lab
5. Will ask same of Ohio, from clinic reception to clinic lab.
6. Clinic plans have been sent out for bid.
7. Difficult to find outfits to bid on fill, grading and road bed.
8. Sewer matter not concluded. Village can't make a decision.
9. Hired local for night watchman.
10. Fearful of attendance at PG seminar. Wished we had cancelled.

16 July 1962—Letter from Janse to Liss

Observations

1. Directors of the CGHS – Turek, Janse, DeVoto
    a. Turek receives of his total salary from CGHS
    b. Suggest CGHS be retained as separate corporation for malpractice purposes yet as an ancillary to the NCC.
2. Auditors changing book keeping system and fiscal year to start 1 Sept.
3. $50K notes sent to NCA
4. Letter of acceptance to FACE today.
5. Dr. Keim to remain part-time for undetermined length, his choice.

6. Darr coming on Wednesday, Jackson and Parker to meet on academics.
7. PG course is a moot question.
8. Planning vacation last week of Aug, first week of Sept.
9. Decorators are set to start laying tile in the new building.

18 July 1962—Letter from Liss to Janse
1. Elated with news of the Darr and Moser Note purchases.
2. Happy with the August issue of the Newsletter.
3. Liss' wife, Eva, rushed to hospital for blood transfusions and surgery and had a 14 cm fibroid removed, non malignant.
4. Need to get Fay on faculty or in the clinic.

23 July 1962—Letter from Janse to Liss
1. NCA purchase of Notes was on the understanding there would be a fully functional school by NCA convention in Chicago in June. This necessitates moving forward with decorating, fill and grading, construction of the clinic with sidewalks and furnishings. If this is more can handle will have to return $50K to NCA.
2. FACE money will tie up some money that would have been used differently. Have $11k on hand toward the $20.5.
3. Have $66K on hand but not enough for all to be done. Hope to raise more from State alumni chapters, extra on the sewer connection, another 5-8 K in notes.
4. Fay and Trustees think we will move in Jan.
5. 42 students set for Sept but hope to get 70. Several have deferred due to neighborhood.
6. Cannot speak to Turek about his pledge. Feels he has done a great deal by turning over the dormitory. Likely to retire once moved to Lombard.
7. Going through with PG on 8 Aug.

24 July 1962—Letter from Liss to Janse
1. Working with Cliff, Gus and Pisarek on school newsletter.
2. Tells JJ to take a weekend off.
3. Says NCA Notes and FACE money are big relief.

4. Coming to Chicago soon, wants to review Clinic Plans and bids.
5. Set January as a target date. He knows full well that will never make it.
6. Reviewing catalogs form Osteopathy, Podiatry and Optometry for designation of officers in adm.
7. Thanks Mrs. Darr for S&H College Courtesy Car program.

12 Mar 1963—Letter from Ben J. Hill of Hill Laboratories to HC Gustavson
Offers to donate one Anatomotor to the College.

1 Feb 1964—Letter from Liss to Janse
Disappointment in Jan enrollment of 17 students. Encourages JJ to get Beideman to improve the program and to report back to him the progress.

1 Feb 1964—Letter from Liss to Janse
1. Criticizes JJ for planning Homecoming and Seminars for six days without consulting with Alumni and in opposition to Liss's recommendation. Sets out a plan to make it work…by comparing costs and length of programs with other schools, increase fees and hope that Illi draws a crowd, promote the program.
2. Get a professional printing job done rather than using the schools mimeograph machine ("We at National have NOT produced a single piece of conventional printing with photos except catalog) for the past four years.") [This is an example of Janse's frugality running counter to Liss's extravagance and apparent meddling.]

23 Feb 1964—Memo from Liss to Fay
Issues in need of attention obvious to an outsider
1. Lack of clothes hooks in rest rooms and dressing rooms all over campus
2. Lack of waste paper receptacles in same rooms.
3. Need standing clothes tree in front office reception area.

4. Purchase an electric sander and GOOD grade of paint spray gun and keep under lock and key in boiler room.
5. Renovation of the OLD lockers under supervision of Mr. Rich by student to be paid by piece work.
6. Set up a spray booth in boiler room to do lockers and file cabinets
7. Use some of the old desks from Ashland for faculty needs.
8. Start spraying the downstairs so can be done by Homecoming.

27 Feb 1964—Letter from Liss to Janse and Fay
1. Responding to request to spend $5,000 to put kitchen and dining facility into men's dorm. Requesting more study and then present to Trustees.
2. Expresses opinion that problem is teenagers rejection of authority. Notes that 50% of enrollment was recent high school graduates.
3. Recommends considering the need to feed faculty and other students.
4. Suggests the need to address specific questions from Trustees before exploring feeding problem followed by a list of questions about how many students actually live in the dorm, live off campus, what happened to the idea of putting a food service in the basement...

28 Feb 1964—Letter from Fay to Liss
Concerns that are being addressed;
1. Residents in dorm object to curfew, restriction on alcohol, no female rule, no cooking facilities. Ashland dorm was an open house.
2. Fraternities renting nearby homes and drawing students out of the dorms. Some students in rooms in homes were using dorm facilities to wash clothes and take showers.
3. Clothes hooks, trash cans and clothes tree all addressed.
4. Purchased a spray gun to repaint old lockers, walls in the lower level. Lights (fluorescent) from Ashland have been trans-

204

ferred to Lombard. Old desks still need to be refinished. Looking at getting some from war surplus store. Have already purchased from the war surplus store 2 typewriters and a microscope for $7.00, "...not the best but they work..."

14 Mar 1964—Memo from Liss to Janse
1. Comments on Liss's wedding anniversary of Friday 13th. Appreciated JJs phone call the night before.
2. Says he will get Fay going on the kitchen and classroom issues downstairs.
3. Favors holding onto 20 N. Ashland for awhile. If we had no firm offer to buy we could offer to the city that we would rehabilitate the property and meet codes. Could agree to make improvements not to exceed $3-5 million. If sold later would just improve the value of the property. If a deal is in the making, could placate the judge and the litigants.
4. When you go to court, don't send Haber. "Don't send a boy to do a man's job. You and Turek go and you will get the deal closed."

18 Mar 1964—Memo from Liss to Janse
1. Encourages a conference with Chicago City Alderman to show the school will make TOKEN arrangements to take to court to show that something is being done. Examples are repairing the toilets and showers on the second floor.
2. The idea is to demonstrate token compliance to allow retention over a period of time (at least until Lombard debt is reduced).

18 Mar 1964—Letter from Janse to Liss
1. States that great effort put forward to meet all expectations, Directory was bigger job than expected.
2. States Dr. Haber needs a chance to explain the problems he is coping with, "At present he is a very disturbed person because, notwithstanding, he is an extremely conscientious and sincere person."

3. Fay with the school for little over a year finding all kinds of unexpected problems.

Pressing matters within the next month:
1. Teaching two hours every day
2. Reading 80% of the outside films from the field. Dr. Kissinger asked to be relieved. By my doing it makes the school more money but takes time.
3. X-ray seminar in Topeka, KS Mar 21-22
4. ACA Roentgenological Council seminar in Cincinnati, Apr 4-5. Five hours on totally new subject, The Orthopedics of the Cervico-Brachial Area...cannot say no to the ACA
5. Regional ACA seminar in New Jersey, Apr 25-26, another new assignment -Spino-Visceral Syndromes
6. Turek and I have a court date on Apr 2nd
7. Meeting with you on Mar 11-12—will have complete format for Century Club, Alumni Directory and Homecoming.
8. Ashland Ave property utilization
9. Plans for Standard Oil to buy or lease 20 N. Ashland, plans for new clinic and city codes we have to meet
10. FACE report due Apr 1. Fay will have all the plans for the lower level ready.
11. 33 old adjusting tables are being reupholstered by father of a student
12. Junior ACA Day 29th of Mar with Hidde and Berner. Apr 18-19 lecture at the Illinois Convention on Traction. Going to a convention in Philadelphia for the Licensed Chiropractor Physicians Association, "of which Michael Giammarino is the strong arm."
13. National graduation May 7-8. Leaving on 8th for Oklahoma, 12-13 in Michigan and then to Tucson the following weekend.
14. Summer registration will be upon us. Fifteen signed up so far, hope to get 18.

Comments on the leadership set by National that has caused the ACA to move and has served as an incentive for NWCC, Lincoln,

LACC, NYCC, TCC, Logan and Columbia to follow NCC's example.

So, if perchance, there is a stumble along the way, may I hope that you will not be too disappointed. We have to keep the thing on the move. Let down one day, one weekend and you experience inundation.

Things are very tight now. The more we accomplish the more is expected. It just can't be any other way. I shall fret and stew and blow my top. People around here believe that I am worse than an ogre, yet it has to be. The pathetic thing is that we do not have the monies necessary to employ the help necessary, so we do our best on the strength of compulsion, an honest prayer and a dedication.

Now let us all stand together. If mistakes have been made they should be acknowledged, but not become a mitigating issue. My ever-existing sense of appreciation. When I anger, when I bite, it is primarily because I have failed to fulfill my expectations.

p.s. Dr. Walter Canton paid full membership for Treatment-A-Month and put National in his will to receive the profit from his farm —$1500/yr. Pictures of the college allowed Swiss DCs to gain full Work Comp privileges. A contingent of Michigan legislators coming next month.

29 Mar 1964—Memo from Liss to Janse
1. Expresses support for Janse's decisions on Homecoming.
2. Expresses concern again regarding a $35 fee rather than $50.
3. Also concerned that lady friends come free.
4. Takes issue of cheap charges for dorm rooms in Lombard $3.00 per day and recommends going to $5 for single and $7 for double or just leave them empty. Says these charges belong to the 1930s at Ashland.
5. Also recommends charging more for catered meals so school can make a little there as well.

Undated Memo on 20 North Ashland Property
1. Turek and Judge Scheffler appear in court April 2, had $1,000 fine rescinded and got a five month postponement of all infractions. [Ashland Property]

2. Bids for repairs

Electrical	$31,000
Staircases, boiler rooms, partitions	$37,000
Related plumbing and sprinkler system	$60,000
Additional work in lavatories	$25,000
Total $153,000	

3. Kate Maremont Foundation, Salvation Army and Walgreen Drugs rejected offer to purchase Ashland property.
4. State Welfare and Rehab inspected building but showed no interest.
5. Standard Oil Division of American Oil Company interested.
6. Thirty to 32 residents in building earning $800 to $1,000 per month rent. Hold on until August.
7. Clinic practice is down due to fear building will be torn down.
8. Buildings in surrounding area are being torn down.
9. Exploring rental @$1,200/month of clinic space in People's National Bank adjoining Pixley and Ehlers.
10. Renovating costs exceed potential rental income.
11. Explored new land in Humbolt Park area to relocate CGHS but costs and loss of income too great.
12. Options
   a. Sell Ashland and move clinic personnel to Lombard—net 120 to 130 K.
   b. Sell or lease and preserve some land to build new CGHS
   c. Keep land, demolish old building piece meal and build new CGHS
13. Turek, Janse, Blackmore, Fay and others recommend CGHS be retained at present site and build new facilities.

20 April 1964—Letter from Liss to Janse

1. Feels Turek is stuck in the past with desire to turn Ashland property into a dormitory for 300 and bus students to Lombard.
2. Concerned for Van Wagoner's ability to run alumni association in Michigan because he is tied up in Michigan activities and gives in too easily to the militant "Palmerites." Recom-

mends Dr. Ruchalla who just lost re-election to Michigan Society.

3. Concerns about set back requirements under lease with Standard Oil.
4. Concerned about layout of new clinic, does not want Blackmore and Gus involved after how they "garbled" the plans for the new Lombard clinic.

4 May 1964—Letter from Janse to Liss

Response to many questions and concerns

1. Does not know when ACA accrediting Committee is coming
2. Not concluded on Greene but feels he lacks executive initiative and creative capacity
3. Cut down on janitorial help in Chicago.
4. Met with Blackmore, Piontkowski and Rabe, to stimulate their determination to be a little more alert and progressive.
5. Happy Birthday letter to JJ helped pay off $1200 to Williams Mfg.
6. Cost $565 to have 32 old tables re-upholstered. One was stolen from basement, new locks on the building.
7. Spent Saturday looking for new Chicago clinic site.
8. Still recommends lease to Standard Oil with clinic in the back of the lot.
9. Rain has prevented reseeding and landscaping.
10. Work with Van Wagoner on pledge cards
11. Tullio and Quirk letter to alumni for century club ready.
12. Visited NY Institute and sees NCC having much more
13. ACA to raise one million to be used to create a single school in NY
14. Recommends completing the additional technic room
15. License plate for '56 Chevy to be used by Beideman, DeVoto and Cohn for transportation to Lombard rather then pay any more taxi fees.

p.s. – Dr. Rinehart is thinking of amalgamating with Logan

(l to r) **Drs. Francis Quirk, Paul Tullio and William Dallas who later became President of the ACA and Western States Chiropractic College, circa 1970s**

5 May 1964—Letter from Liss to Janse Re: Mr. T. Kiley

1. Mr. Kiley has been the representative for Anabolic Foods and has just lost his job as they are closing down the Chicago office. Liss suggests to Janse the need to consider this person as an administrative assistant at a starting salary of $7,500 to $7,800 with time off to complete his PhD. At which time he could be offered a salary of $8,000 or up to $9,000 tops.
2. With his background Liss proposes that he could help with publications, serve as a substitute teacher in basic sciences, fill in on extra administrative duties and replace Dean Greene over admissions.
3. Liss takes it upon himself to invite Mr. Kiley to send his resume to JJ and call for an interview.

14 May 1964—Letter from Janse to Liss

1. Positive comment about the Michigan convention, includes a check $[?] for expenses and apologizes that Liss got stuck

for them.

2. Apologizes for his vigor regarding the 20 N Ashland property, received a lecture honorarium of $75 of which he put $50 into his Century Club dues.

3. Received $300 from Russ Erhardt and three new Century Club memberships and concludes with another apology stating that nothing will be done without Liss's approval.

23 May 1964—Letter from Liss to Janse

1. Wants Janse's schedule for June thru Sept.

2. Raises concern over JJs offer to Mr. Kiley of only $6500. An offer of $7000 is $200 less than what he is receiving now and $500 less than the person he is to replace.

3. Would rather an offer not be made than one so cheap.

5 Jun 1964—Letter from Janse to Holman

Apologizes for Quirks letter, "He is young, he is cocky and appears to be very aggressive. Yet, behind it all resides genuine honesty and goodness."

5 Jun 64—Letter from Liss to Fay

1. Completion of the technic and projection rooms

2. Kitchen project is yet to be decided. Currently paying electric and heat and no return.

3. Registration for Homecoming expected to pick up. Regular copy of "Alumnus" is out.

4. Insurance retirement plans. Asks for simplified version for Trustees to be offered without the college making a contribution.

5. Advises against using cinders as fill for roadway. May have to limit project to curbing and drive. Suggests we get broken brick and concrete from demolition of Ashland property.

6. Advises setting a fee schedule for JJ at $200 to $250 for one day and $300 to $350 for two days. Says BJ once asked for $2000 from Michigan society but would have gotten $500 had he accepted the invitation. Need to save Dr. Janse for the big audiences.

7. Wants financial report on CGHS for last three years.

8 Jul 1964—Letter from Liss to Fay
1. Rode on train from Denver next to Frank Hoffman.
2. Has a contact with ready-mix drivers who are looking for a place to dump excess concrete.
3. Thought it would be a good place to get concrete for future sidewalks on campus.
4. Need to organize students to be ready to level and spread when ever a truck shows up.
5. Has similar contacts for cold asphalt for filling holes in driveway.

Dr. Frank Hoffman, circa 1970

12 Jul 64—Letter from Liss to Janse & Fay
Results of FACE allocations most likely to occur:

LACC, Capital Loan for bldg	$50K
Chiro NY Columbia Capital Loan	$50K
Matching Funds for all others	$200K

Likely disbursement to the Colleges	
National	$70K
Lincoln	$68
LACC	$68
CINY	$40
Logan	$10
Texas	$8
NWCC	$8

14 Jul 1964—Letter from Janse to Liss
1. Mr Kiley declined the offer.
2. Lowell Dunham plans to return to Osteopathic College but willing to help set up physiology lab and be listed in school catalog

212

3. Letter going out to all alumni requesting funds for college
4. Dempsy-Tegeler ready to provide money for construction of CGHS. Mr. Schubert to finalize re-zoning and permits
5. Quick Cafeteria proposes to provide two meals a day for 100 students at $2 per day per student.
6. Went to West Suburban Bank for another $15K secured by personal government bonds. If FACE comes through and enrollments are up we will be all right.
7. Eleven applications have been rejected because of poor high school records.
8. May not get FACE $75K until we raise our $35K
9. Dean Parker tasked to find new faculty but not to make any commitments until FACE money is in hand.
10. Have $7500 in FACE fund currently.

At times the ambivalence of circumstances just about drives me out of my mind. The sophistication of expectation everyone confronts us with and with a financial tongue in cheek [that] is a pretty doggone difficult problem to find a solution for...So you see the press is on. Whom can I turn to? What areas of support have been untapped? Are we twisting too many arms? Yet, what else can we do? How much can we expect from our people? How far dare we go? What will be the demands of the Accreditation Committee in the future? What stipulations will we have to fulfill to be considered by H.E.W.? How many students will our Alumni feed us? All these questions are a carousel of concern. With these reasons, I humbly seek a continuation of the support of the entire College family.

30 Jul 1964—Letter from Janse to Liss
Schedule:
Scottsbluff, NB Sep 5,6;
Cape Cod, MA Sep 12, 13;
Pueblo, CO Sep 25, 26;
Laconia, NH Oct 17, 18;
FACE approved NCC for $68K at a 1:2 ratio.

213

Advised that Herbert A. Jackson, BS, MS, PhD, and DC retiring from the faculty of Valparaiso University, will become an educational consultant working on campus 8-10 days a month.

31 July 1964—Letter from Janse to Liss
Feels good about Dr. Jackson. His duties will be:
1. Build collaborative relationships with local small colleges.
2. Supervise entrance testing and on-campus evaluations
3. Serve as campus statistician.
4. Work on student-faculty ratio issues.
5. Re-vamp college bulletin
6. Correlate credit system into semester credit hour system.
7. Review forms and student records.
8. Help identify new qualified faculty

To be paid $100 a month plus per diem and travel when on campus. Will stay in the dorm.

8 Jan 1965—Letter from Janse to Liss
1. Concern over apparent excessive billing from Metzdorf, charging for every phone call. Expressed the need to limit the need to call on his services and even limit his time serving as the Secretary of the Board of Trustees.
2. Notes Gloria underwent surgery yesterday and not only had her gall bladder removed but had to have the duodenum opened and irrigated.

13 Jan 1965—Letter from Janse to Liss
1. Gloria in the hospital until 20th. Will farm out Jo so he can attend mid-year meetings in Des Moines.
2. DeVoto and Norris to follow-up on Treatment of the month Club.
3. Stone doing the newsletter.
4. Cafeteria service being worked-out.

22 Jan 1965—Report from Janse to the Boards of NCC
Report on mid-year ACA meetings in Des Moines.
1. Complimentary on the new ACA offices.
2. Report to the Committee on Accreditation and the Application to FACE well received.
3. Everybody under ACA umbrella happy with NCC.
4. Conclusions of the Committee on Accreditation and Council on Education
   a. In 1965 NCC must seek full accreditation with the Committee on Accreditation. Dr. John Fischer, Director of Education will spend a week on NCC to assist.
   b. Committee is convinced HEW recognition will not be obtained until pre-professional requirements are set in place.
      1) No high school graduate with less than a C average can be accepted.
      2) Sept. 1967 all matriculates must have one year pre-professional college.
      3) Sept 1968 all matriculates must have two years pre-professional college leading to a baccalaureate either in liberal arts or science.
   c. Council on Accreditation recognizes the financial burden that will result and has recommended the following.
      1) A larger FACE subsidy to the colleges.
      2) College alumni are to be called upon to expand support.
      3) A Foundation will be formed to contact Foundations and Industry for support.
      4) Stepping up recruitment in colleges rather than high schools
      5) Getting Alumni to help with student recruitment.
5. All schools are being asked to make mandatory the taking of part one (basic sciences) of the National Board. They have made arrangements to offer a special exam for NCC students in addition to exams at Los Angeles, Davenport and New York in March.

6. Fay stayed an extra day to work with Haynes, Fischer and Wolf to determine the feasibility to establish with ACA Washington representative Mr. Koller a stronger presence for the ACA and the Colleges.
7. Contacted by European Chiropractic Union to see if NCC would offer an external degree to graduates of the newly formed AECC.
8. Fay to continue to serve as the Chair of the Committee of the annual Seminar of the Clinic Directors of the ACA. And also chair of the Committee on Ethics in Advertising. JJ will remain Chair of the Committee on the Standardization of Chiropractic Principles and the Committee on Public Health.
9. Accreditation issue is faculty quality. Interviewing a person with a BS and DO who has taught at the DO school for 12 years. Offering an annual salary of $10K
10. Nineteen new students and six drop outs registered for the Jan. class. Paid back West Suburban Bank $40K borrowed last summer.

3 Feb 1965—Memo from Liss to Fay
Advises Fay to follow his example and slow down and not take on so much administrative pressure.
Adds suggestions for indoor winter projects for students
1. Building an indoor stage or platform for Homecoming and lectures.
2. Painting of ceiling and walls
3. Podium for stage.
4. Ever get a snow blower for the Hoffman tractor?
5. Look for riding tractor or jeep, cement mixer, 100 folding chairs from salvage dept.

4 Feb 1965—Letter from Janse to Liss
1. Unfortunate circumstances with Dr. Workman that need to be corrected.
2. Cold weather, clinics down, heating bill up.
3. Gloria is home after extended stay in hospital.

4. Overhead is killing us.
5. Not pleased with the cafeteria service wishing the college had taken it on themselves. Paying all the expenses while the cook gets all the profit.
6. National Boards on campus soon. Providing review courses charging students $1 to pay instructors.

(Notes in the margin from Liss asks DeVoto to summarize electric bills Jan thru Dec for '63 and '64. Tells JJ to assign someone to go around to all the rooms and turn down the "heat convectors" after 4pm and not turn them back on until 6am. Also told to stop using "room" coffee pots, they burn 15 amps and 100 rooms really adds to your bill. Stop it.")

13 Feb 1965—Letter from Janse to Liss
1. Lee Arnold spent three days lecturing on ethics and economics.
2. Wed. in Boston on legislative hearings representing the ACA.
3. Tues. in Lansing and had lunch with Mrs. Romney (Gov. wife) in their home.
4. Dr. John Fisher on campus Mon. thru Sat.
5. Meeting on Fri. with Dr. Kowalek, Dean of Arts and Sciences of Roosevelt U.
6. Lecturing in PG Ortho course in Philadelphia on 20-21 – will earn $150 for college.
7. This Sat. eve Gus and JJ working on personnel for state alumni chapters.
8. Tullio and Quirk decided to keep Stone on for one more issue with Quirk's help.

Dr. Lee Arnold and wife "Bubbs", circa 1965

9. Having trouble with students in the dormitory, especially the foreign students.
10. Heuser will lecture six hours.
11. Netted generously from Anabolic contracts.

4 Mar 1965—Letter from Janse to Liss
Leaving for Portland for the weekend with a stop on Monday in Utah to see wife, daughter; and a brother and his wife who he hasn't seen in three years. Issues:
1. Dr. Lysne to get 40 railroad ties for road and parking area
2. Dr. Rabe resigned—personality conflict with Dr. Piontowski
3. National Board on campus for the next three days
4. Turek still working on zoning issue.
5. Stone, Quirk and JJ worked on Alumnus yesterday
6. Homecoming program nearly finalized
7. Amalgamation between the Missouri College and Logan not going well
8. Drs. Parker and Jackson working on new catalog.
9. Dr. Lawrence of Lebanon, TN exploring credit transfer with local universities.

9 Mar 1965—Letter from Liss to Janse
Comments:
1. Have railroad ties taken to the basement and whitewashed by students with cheap grade of paint.
2. Will bow out of giving input on the Alumnus and function more like a Board member.
3. Suggests including Australia in an upcoming trip down under.

19 Apr 1965—Letter from Janse to Liss
1. As a result of England Case ACA plans meeting with Harper, Homewood, Weiant and Bittner to discuss role of chiropractic as a profession, scientific basis of chiropractic and position in relation to management of infectious diseases and artificial immunizations. Will be in Des Moines from 26th to 30th.

218

2. From 31 to May 3rd travel to Wyoming and Montana. Not been there in 8 years.
3. May 1-2 Dr. Fay in Colorado
4. May 5-16 in Sacramento with one-day stopover in Utah to see Adriaan [brother] who is ill.
5. Turek had no trouble with the zoning board. Now to City Council.
6. Will know this week the effects of the shopping center being built next door on drainage.
7. PG seminar being supported by vitamin houses at $20 each for a display table.

29 Apr 1965—Letter from Janse to Liss

1. Dr. Fisher advised JJ that Dr. Louis Bierman is resigning as president of Lincoln and should be considered as Academic Dean at National.
2. Spent Saturday with Hoffman and engineer. Roads can't be finished by PG. Will need to make do with painted railroad ties.
3. Saturday will have a man caulk all crevices in retaining walls to keep out water that might freeze.
4. Agreed to pay a gardener $120 to recondition lawns out front.
5. Discussed with Hoffman your idea of cement apron leading into clinic. Hoffman donated four trees worth $300.
6. No word on zoning.
7. In Des Moines end of May for Standardization of Chiropractic Principles.

Must close, classes to teach.

7 May 1965—Letter from Janse to Alumni

Letter written at the request of the Officers of the Alumni Association. Is a request to join the Century Club to help achieve matching funds for FACE.

11 May 1965—Letter from Liss to Janse
1. With approval of zoning changes soon to happen, concern of adding debt to pave Lombard road ways and build new CGHS.
2. Why do we need two clinics? Is the $150K investment worth training 8 interns who now service the old CGHS?
3. Can we do roadways piece-meal with a pay as you go plan?
4. Are we behind in the amortization of the Corporate Notes?

27 May 1965—Letter from Liss to Janse
Making college aware of a 1952 Farnall Cub Tractor available through Van Wagoner patient for $850. Maybe Mark could haul it down when he comes for Homecoming?

28 May 1965—Letter from Liss to Janse
1952 Farnall Cub Tractor, new tires, motor overhauled with multiple attachments for weeds, grass and snow removal. Comes with trailer but trailer needs new tires. From a patient of Dr. VanWagoner. Challenge is to transfer to Lombard from MI (300 miles).

6 Jul 1965—Letter from Liss to Janse
List of 36 names of senior doctors who should be added to the mailing list for Dr. Janses' personalized letters.

8 Jul 1965—Memo from Liss to Janse

1. List of four more senior doctors from Michigan to be added to the list.
2. Hopeful that Bierman and Parker can run the school so Janse can start doing more fund raising among the rich lay people of the world. Need to visit Mr. West of Martin Oil.

Dr. Mark Van Wagoner, circa 1970

220

Dr. George T. Parker, Dean of Faculty, circa 1970.

17 Jul 1965—Letter from Janse to Liss

1. Copy of letter to Dr. Clothier
2. Letters to Drs. Smith, Radford, Bucknell building relationship with former Metropolitan College in Cleveland.
3. Dr. Schroeder brought in a $1,000 check from one of his patients.
4. Engineer estimates more than $30k to do roads.
5. Monday meeting with architect of CGHS
6. Finalizing brochure on "Who's Rocking the Boat at National."
7. Copy of the Alumnus.
8. News Letter ready to be mailed.
9. FACE contribution will not be available until after first of the year.

18 Jul 1965—Letter from Liss to Janse
1. Reviews Florida happenings
2. Schierholz resigned as a Director to become Assistant Sec-Treas of NCIC and Liss elected to replace Schierholz for remainder of unexpired term of one year.
3. Inman elected chair of Board of Governors.
4. Looking for a house for JJ and Gloria at Central and Hammerschmidt.

23 Jul 1965—Letter from Janse to Liss
1. Approved Grossmans plans and advised Mr. Gross to obtain bids for roadways.
3. Jewel Tea market opening next door.
4. Gloria busy in her job.
5. Dr. Schroeder's patients are Mr. and Mrs Buchholz who contributed another $1,000.
6. Graduating class of '65 just gave $1,000

23 Jan 1966—Letter from Liss to Metzdorf
Regarding establishment of an endowment fund. Asked for guidance on limits, spending policies, use of interest, management of the fund and investment of monies. Goal of reaching $1 million.

12 Feb 1966—Letter from Liss to Janse, Fay & Haber
1. Need to address parking problem, 195 spaces and 340 persons on campus.
2. Need to expand into areas by dumping large rock and then finer gravel for the next five years. Need to expand dormitory parking. 116 residents and 20 parking places.
3. Enclosed a chart for final plans with extra parking where Lake Janse now exists.

9 Mar 1966—Letter from Janse to Liss and Van Wagoner
1. Apparently Cliff Woolard was dropped from the Board of Members but never informed. JJ fixed it. "With Miss. DeVoto leaving as well as Dr. Burgess and the constant press of an

222

ever increasing administrative and organizational bureaucracy has left the portfolio of my desk in total overload."

2. Reception for DeVoto tonight. Turek giving her a check and $100 collected from staff.

3. Plan to shut down Ashland bldg on 15th of April.

4. Sordoni giving another $500 to the Library.

5. Donations from patients of Dr. C. Zaplicki, Dr. Benz and Dr. Schroeder.

6. Doing clinical anatomy seminar on campus this weekend and in Virginia next weekend.

Mrs. Evelyn Buccholz Richie presenting a check to Dr. Janse, circa 1980

7. ACA self study near finished.

8. Tomorrow meet with Dept. of Public Instruction to become degree-granting institution for B.S. degree.

20 Apr 1966—Letter from Liss to Janse

RE: April 16th Mid-year meeting of the Ex. Comm of Trustees Larson, Ortman, Liss: Agenda

1. Purchase of new Multilith unit and training an operator

2. Preparation of a pictorial supplement to catalog.

Ms. Minette DeVoto between Dr. and Gloria Janse, circa 1966

223

3. Revision of 1947 edition of Chiropractic Principles to be done by JJ with additional compensation for extra time.
4. Approval of Beideman to become Registrar.
5. Approval of purchase of water-softener on two year payment plan
6. Contract with Lee Arnold to do clinic orientation for staff at Lombard and CGHS
7. Plans for library downstairs and cafeteria. Identify funds before committing.
8. Approval of special Committee on Development and Endowment
9. Development of "articulate" alumni to work with Junior College Counselors.
10. Consideration of new studio apartments for married students be delayed until Blackmore bldg (CGHS), Ashland building demo, new library are near complete.
11. Happy with PG-Homecoming.

1 Jun 1966—Liss report to the Board of Trustees and Members
1. Reports on visitation and that Dr. Jackson was also present.
2. Summer brings lower tuition and lower rental from dorms.
3. Strike by construction workers as stopped work on parking lots and on shopping center next door. In agreement on the creation of an Advisory Committee on Endowment.

14 Jul 1966—Letter from Liss to Gov. George Romney
Expresses disappointment for his veto of bill that would upgrade the law on chiropractic in Michigan. Accuses him of bowing to medical prejudice.

25 Jul 1966—Letter from Janse to Liss
1. Hopes the rest of the summer will slow down because "old man Janse is getting tired" and now he must cut out his vacation. Can't leave campus for two whole weeks.
2. $18K now in the demolition account.
3. Tremendous pressure coming from IL Med. Soc. Regarding Dept. of Public Instruction granting us the right to issue a BS degree.

4. Two applications from South Africa and Rhodesia result of last falls trip.

4 Aug 1966—Letter from Janse to Liss

Because of accreditation by the Illinois State Teachers Certification Board, the Veterans Administration has reclassified us from a nonaccredited institution with approval to an accredited institution with approval.

"Again I say that we have accomplished so much, that the irritations and the rankle of the everyday become so insignificant and our people should be riding on cloud nine."

18 Aug 1966—Report from Liss to Board Trustees, Members & Alumni Officers

1. Construction of spillway and curbs and finishing touches to grounds near completion
2. Conclusion on additional parking at rear of dormitories and in East area.
3. Bids for construction for new Library downstairs are out. May be slow response due to backlog from strike.
4. Visit to CGHS found bldg. enclosed with finishing work in progress. Occupancy probably end of Sept.
5. Negotiations in progress for apartment complex next to CGHS on Warren.
6. First time in long time able to function through summer without borrowing from bank or reserve funds.
7. Loss of valuable office employees attracted to other places by higher salaries.
8. Water softener in place in college building. Not yet in dorm.
9. New Advisory Committee on Endowment includes all Trustees and Members.
10. Account report shows we are close to budget. Beideman reports 100 students accepted for Sept.
11. Need more members to the Treatment of the month club.
12. JJ travel very heavy for Sep and Oct.

8 Sep 1966—Letter from Liss to Janse
1. Don't be too concerned about [Skosbergh] burglarizing. Recommend a reduced charge in exchange for time and fine. Removing the felony will preserve their license. Wonder if they stole the adjusting table last year.

9 Sep 1966—Letter from Janse to Liss
1. Assembly is great idea.
2. Concerned for how Gustavson will take the release of duties.
3. Any plans for the Annual meeting beyond the agenda? Concern for Dr Tieszen.
4. Requests 15 minutes to speak to combined Trustees, Members, Alumni Officers and CGHS Board members. [Wishes to express many concerns associated with growth].
5. Janse overloaded and is taking a vacation and requests no more deadlines or tasks beyond what is already on the table.
6. Lunched with past president of Elmhurst College
7. In Burlington, Iowa for orthopedics class
8. Skosbergh problem serious. Could lose his license.
8. Haber without custodial help. Many visitors on campus.
9. Sending Gloria and girls out west. They need to get away from me.
10. $19.4K in Donation account.
11. Going to CGHS to talk to Michalec who can't get along with Dr. Karlheim while Piontkowski is on vacation. May have to run clinic myself.
12. Fisher coming again next week to work on ability to transfer credits
13. Bldg Fund account for Aug. enclosed.

"If you need to talk with me I am usually home after 10:00 pm."

15 Oct 1966—Memo from Liss to Fay
1. Any progress in getting modern equipment in recording and transcribing? If not then will need to take notes at meetings.
2. Concerned about air conditioning needs for next year. Now is the time to find something used and cheap.

20 Oct 1966—Letter from Janse to Liss
1. Home from Atlanta. Quite an experience. The ICA influence down there is very strong, and encountered this personality, "Sid Williams."
2. Enclosed article from 1942 College Journal Article.
3. Alumni meeting in Detroit on the 27th. Had a chat with Inman. Very difficult to figure out.
4. In Akron, Toledo and Vermont rest of week.

30 Nov 1966—Letter from Janse to Liss
1. Letter to Ege enclosed.
2. Day in court, got the Skogsbergh-Haitt case dismissed.
3. Dr Parker had third heart attack last week.
4. Beideman's wife on critical list for a week with Addison's disease.
5. Move to CGHS done.

16 Dec 1966—Letter from Janse to Liss
1. Regarding parking – "I become as irritated as you about the parking and I suppose the only thing that I can do is to go out every morning and stand by the highway and direct traffic and if it has to come to that, it is perfectly alright with me."
2. Pleasure to meet Ms. Hidebrand
3. "I have run into a severe fatigue syndrome the last two or three days and somehow I am going to have to ease off for awhile…"

27 Dec 1966—Letter from Liss to Janse
Acknowledges Janse's fatigue syndrome and recommends time off for him.

21 Jan 1967—Letter from Liss to Fay
1. Instructions to clean out Ashland building of lockers, fluorescent lights, X-ray film, mail-box section, clocks, two McManus tables and old documents from the basement.

2. Need to install heating shutoff values in the front offices to assure proper heating relief.

3. Have Turek clean away any junk around building in preparation for a Feb. 15th demolition date.

1 Beideman, R., *In The Making of a Profession: The National College of Chiropractic 1906-1981*, pg.189-90.

2 Ibid. pg. 190.

3 Ibid. pg. 190.

4 Ibid. pg. 79. (The purchase of $100,000 was noted in the Building Program Announcement published in 1956, pg. 2.)

5 Ibid. pg. 191.

6 *The National College Journal of Chiropractic.* Vol. 25, No. 1, Jan. 1953. pg. 12.

7 Beideman, R., *In The Making of a Profession: The National College of Chiropractic 1906-1981,* pg. 193.

8 Ibid. pg. 194.

9 National College of Chiropractic Building Program. *Fifty Years of Progress – Now A Dynamic Plan for the Future.* Golden Anniversary 1906-1956.

10 Ibid. pg. 26.

11 *The National College Journal of Chiropractic.* Vol. 31., No. 1, April, 1959.

12 *The National College Journal of Chiropractic.* Vol. 32. No. 1, September, 1960.

13 Beideman, R., *In The Making of a Profession: The National College of Chiropractic 1906-1981*, pg.195.

14 Personal communication with Dr. Winterstein, Feb. 2006.

15 *The National College Journal of Chiropractic.* Vol. 33, No. 1, December, 1961.

16 Comment found in personal notes of Janse for 1963 Dedication. Janse Collection, NUHS Archive.

17 Correspondence in the Janse Collection, NUHS Archives.

18 Correspondence in the Janse Collection, NUHS Archives

19 Correspondence in the Janse Collection, NUHS Archives.

20 NCA Delegate Report by George A. Smyrl, 15 April 1960, Janse Collection, NUHS Archives.

21 Beideman, R., *In The Making of a Profession: The National College of Chiropractic 1906-1981*, pg.196-197.

22 Ibid. pg. 200-204.

23 Ibid. pg. 81

24 Personal letters. Janse Collection. NUHS Archives.

Chapter Twelve

The Ambassador

An ambassador is an official messenger with a special errand, or "an authorized representative of the highest rank."[1] Dr. Janse certainly fits the qualification, but he didn't start out that way. His first trip across the mighty Atlantic Ocean started on 16 December 1916[2] when he immigrated with his family to America. He was seven years old at the time. On 24 October 1930[3], some 14 years later, he arrived in Hamburg, Germany to begin his church missionary service. He had returned across the mighty Atlantic Ocean in the opposite direction of his first trip. For three years he was an ambassador for The Church of Jesus Christ of Latter-day Saints and traveled through much of Germany and Switzerland, returning to the United States, 21 June 1933.[4]

A contemporary of Dr. Janse, also a world traveler, was B.J. Palmer (son of the original founder of chiropractic). He was well-known for his world-wide travels wherein he became quite the collector of a variety of interesting objects. B.J. was also well known as one who would spread the "word" about chiropractic. Consequently, there were many from foreign lands who sought and obtained entrée to the United States and Palmer School of Chiropractic. B.J.'s generosity to needy foreign students enabled many from foreign lands to come to Palmer, gain a chiropractic education and return to their homeland as future disciples of the "chiropractic word." Thus, in many countries, the Palmer tradition of chiropractic became firmly rooted.

In Europe

Dr. Janse's next trip east, across the Atlantic Ocean occurred in August of 1955. It appears he took four days to visit family and friends in Holland and an additional two days to visit friends in his German mission field.[5]

Dr. Janse's influence was felt in Europe even when he was not present. During the years of 1958-59, while he was serving as the Secretary and then the Chair of the Council on Education of the NCA, he was called upon to help the chiropractors in France. Dr. Edward J. Antoine shared with Dr. Janse the dilemma of chiropractors being fined and put in jail for practicing medicine without a license. The medical profession had determined that chiropractic was a part of medical practice. Dr. Antoine requested Dr. Janse write a letter (a document) to then President-Elect, Charles de Gaulle and the Ministre de la Sante Publique in Paris, "...earnestly protest[ing] against such measures of prejudice and injustice." Dr. Janse, after having the entire Council on Education review his response, submitted a beautifully detailed document supporting the value of chiropractic.[6]

In an undated document, Dr. Janse reports on his first formal trip to Germany and Switzerland as an ambassador for the college and the profession. His passport indicates this trip was between 5 June and 10 July 1958.[7] He was officially invited by Dr. Henri Langnar, President of the Swiss Chiropractic Association to, "...appear on the program of the special postgraduate convention to be sponsored by the association and to be held in Geneva... ." [8]

His first stop was a visit with "...two leading chiropractors in Germany, namely Dr. Peper of Hamburg and Dr. Bielefeldt of Frankfort."[9] He also conversed with potential students and two medical practitioners who had an interest in chiropractic. The war had isolated the few chiropractors practicing in Germany. This isolation coupled with hard economic times lead a few of these chiropractors to teach their skills to their medical counterparts, who were quite numerous in post-war Germany. Several Scandinavian chiropractors had also engaged in similar teaching situations. As a result, he found a very high level of interest in chiropractic in Germany among the medical community and the physical therapy community to the extent they had formed the Gorschungs Und Arbeitsgemeindshaft Chiropractische Tatiger Aerzte (Research and Clinical Society of Practicing Chiropractic Physicians). One physical therapy school even listed chiropractic courses in their catalog. Members of this society were voracious readers of chiropractic literature published by the NCA and the ICA, as many of their publications were found in individual offices visited. Janse then listed the names and positions of eight prominent physicians in Germany who were active members of the Society.[10]

Dr. Janse on a stroll in Europe, circa 1958

Dr. Janse's solution to the challenge was to have a European Chiropractic College that would produce more practicing doctors of chiropractic as well as sending more European students to chiropractic colleges in America. He was not in favor of collaborating with the medical profession however:

> From time to time someone ventures the idea that the solution might be found in collaborating with the medical profession. Let us not be deceived; equality is never attained through collaboration. Subjugation, and loss of professional identity and self-respect is all that we will ever gain through collaboration. It is and always will be the philosophy of medicine that all other schools of healing should be and eventually must be under its control and authority.[11]

It was on this same trip that Dr. Janse spent time with Dr. Illi in his laboratory in Geneva, Switzerland (see Chapter Eight).

231

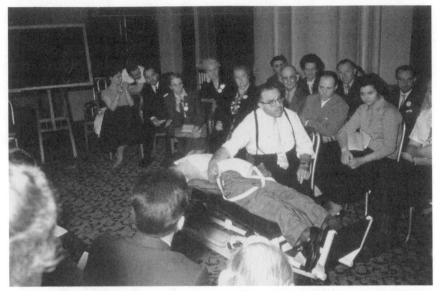

Dr. Janse teaching technique at the 1958 European Union Conference in London

During the early years (1964-65) of the Anglo-European College of Chiropractic in England (AECC), correspondence between Dr. Robert Beach, Secretary of the school, and Dr. Janse, explored the feasibility of National offering "external doctorates" to AECC graduates from Switzerland to meet their requirements for licensure. This option was explored thoroughly with the Council on Education of the ACA and it was recommended the AECC join the ACA Accreditation program and seek to qualify at a level equivalent to National College.[12]

Dr. Janse and Dr. Gross from Paris, 1964

It was not until the early 1980's that National College Alumni Association started their "Hands Across the Ocean" tours. A report of the first tour to Belgium, France, Switzerland, Luxemburg

232

Dr. Janse with Dr. Genevieve Bergien, European Coordinator of Alumni Affairs, 1981

and Germany occurred in October 1981. It was labeled as, "National's first European Homecoming."[13] The Second Annual European Tour sponsored by the Alumni Association traveled in September 1982, through Denmark, Norway and Sweden. Dr. Janse and Gloria traveled together on this trip along with the President of the Alumni Association, Dr. Harry Trestrail and his wife Sue.[14]

The third alumni-sponsored "Hands Across the Ocean" tour to Europe was in the later part of May and the forepart of June, 1983. This trip focused on Italy, where Dr. Janse relates his oft-told story of having the Pope recognize their tour group as he

Dr. Janse outside the office of Dr. Erwin Lorez, 1981, Dr. Lorez was a cousin of Dr. Illi and an NCC Graduate. He made the original translation of Illi's *The Vertebral Column* from French to English.

233

spoke to the crowds in St. Peter's Square (see DVD). He also stood near where the Pope passed by and was within an arm's length of His Holiness.

Australia

Dr. Janse's first trip to Australia and New Zealand was in the fall of 1965.[15] He was planning a trip to South Africa and Dr. Liss, Chair of the Board told him that as long as he was that far away, he might as well keep on going.[16] In response to the encouragement of Dr. Liss, he not only visited Australia and New

Dr. Janse lecturing at the first European Homecoming, 1981

Zealand after leaving South Africa, but saw Japan before returning home. He was gone the entire month of October 1965.

Drs. Janse and Trestrail see Pope John Paul II, Rome, 1983

Shortly after his departure, Dr. Stanley M. Martin responded to Dr. Janse's visit with letters each dated 7 November 1965.[17] In the first letter he asked for copies of notes used by Dr. Janse. He hoped to reproduce them and distribute them among the chiropractors in Australia. He also thanked Dr. Janse for his wise counsel to Pat and Dick Leahy, "…just your few words completely changed the marital relationship…"

In a letter to Dick Leahy of 3 December 1965, Dr. Janse expressed frustration in getting appropriate papers for Dick and family to come to the United States to attend National College.[18]

The second letter addressed potential student recruitment in Australia. Dr. Stanley Martin said Australia is largely made up of Palmer graduates and that Palmer offers two full, four-year scholarships every year to students from Australia. He said the Canadian school (CMCC) is also gaining in popularity because of the ease in migration from Australia to Canada, and that CMCC offered one full scholarship for every six full-paying students.

The last of the three letters addressed the chiropractic situation in Australia. Dr Martin said chiropractic was an unregulated profession and was dominated by "…the prejudices you might expect a senior student at the Palmer College of Chiropractic to have." He concluded there were about 100 to 110 chiropractors in Australia who received their D.C. degrees from the United States or Canada of which only one was a National graduate. He also indicated about 200 other people who were masseurs, athletic trainers or something else were calling themselves chiropractors under "The Common Law." Chiropractic was well accepted by the public but

(l to r) **Drs. Joseph Janse, Stanley Bolton and Jim Maxwell, Sydney, 1970**

235

not by the medical profession or insurance industry. A treatment was only $2.50 (Australian dollars) but an income of $15,000 resulted in one paying $7,500 in taxes.

In 1970 Dr Janse returned to Australia and Japan. He spoke on the subject of *The Clinical Basis of the Practice of Chiropractic*. In five separate lectures he applied this theme to each part of the human spine from the Occiput to the Sacrum. The Conference was held at the Gazebo Motel in Kings Cross, Sydney. [19]

Dr. Janse was again in Australia and New Zealand from 30 April to 14 May 1977.[20] As a visiting scholar he gave the annual Philip Law Lecture at the Preston Institute of Technology that housed the International College of Chiropractic, Dr. Andries Kleynhans serving serving as principal.

Probably the most significant contribution to Australia and New Zealand was Dr. Janse's influence on the introduction of chiropractic within the government-funded and accredited higher education system. Dr. Janse's influence on the thinking, particularly relating to education standards, of Dr. Andries Kleynhans who guided chiropractic educational developments in the late seventies in Australia, was immense. Dr. Kleynhans regards Dr. Janse as his chief mentor who shaped his understanding of the educational and scientific needs of chiropractic. He writes:

Dr. Andries Kleynhans, Principal, International College of Chiropractic, circa 1975

Dr. Janse provided benchmarks and a point of

236

Dr. Terry Yochum, faculty at the International College of Chiropractic in Australia, along with his wife Inge, children Kimberly and Philip and Aunt Franzi *on right*

reference not only for the design of the chiropractic program at Phillip Institute of Technology (now part of RMIT University in Melbourne) but also influenced, through Dr. Kleynhans, the redesign of the Australian Chiropractors Association's Committee on Chiropractic Education in 1975 into the Australasian Council on Chiropractic Education that ultimately gained recognition from the U.S. Council on Chiropractic Education.[21]

During the late 1970's, the Australasian Council on Chiropractic Education (ACCE) was seeking a reciprocal agreement with the U.S. Council on Chiropractic Education (CCE). Dr. Janse was serving as the Chair of the CCE Committee on International Relations in Education. As such, his visit to Australia in 1977 probably included an evaluation of the educational situation and the potential for local accreditation. At the June 1979 meeting of the CCE, a resolution presented by Dr. Orville Hidde, Chair of the Commission on Accreditation, resolved that the ACCE had completed "Phase I" of the reciprocal agreement process and should work with the Committee on International Relations to begin "Phase II.[22]

In 1982 Dr. Janse attended the Pacific Regional Conference in Manila which was concurrent with the AGM of the Australian Chiropractors Association. He is reported to have spoken, "… dynamically on 'Contributions of chiropractic in the fields of clinical neurology, orthopaedics, anatomy and biomechanics"[23]

As President Emeritus of National College, Dr. Janse [and Gloria] was invited to fulfill a visiting fellowship, "…for a period of no less than six weeks and that you will be available on campus for the major portion of the period of time involved." The School of Chiropractic at the now Phillip Institute of Technology, under the leadership of Dr. Andries Kleynhans, former faculty member at National College, would grant a sum of $4,000 to cover his costs. The visit was planned for the end of May and the forepart of June 1985.[24]

In a 17 April 1985 response to Dr. Foster, Dr. Janse warns him he is bringing, "…a large variety of audio-visual materials in the form of 16 mm. films and almost innumerable 35 mm. slides…work has always been my primary pleasure and so I would simply say no one needs to fret about the amount of hours that I will have occasion to expend." In this same letter he also indicates that Gloria and Joey will be traveling with him.[25]

It is surprising that Dr. Janse would so clearly state his desire to work and work hard when on the same 17 April he writes to Dr. Kleynhans to advise him of his health, "The neutron radiations have helped and next week I go in to have the urologist, by means of cystoscopic penetration and dilation, go in and crumble and aspirate the debris that the radiation has left."[26]

As Gloria explained [Chapter Five] the extended lecture tour took its toll on Dr. Janse and due to his weakening condition they cut their trip short by ten days to return home. He never fully regained his strength.

Japan

The land of the "Rising Sun" was one of many areas of the world that for Dr. Janse held a special interest. It was a culture where health was an inner quality of the soul, as much as an external expression of symptoms. Manual approaches to health care extant in Japan were not dissimilar to concepts and procedures in chiropractic. An affinity between Dr. Janse and chiropractic and the traditional Japanese healers was a natural.

The condition of health care in Japan was described in a 31 January 1979 letter from Dr. Kazuyoshi Takeyachi to Drs. Janse and Fay. This letter came in response to discussions regarding National College's involvement in postgraduate education courses in Japan.

In 1945, General MacArthur was the ruling authority in postwar Japan. He banned all non-medical practitioners practicing unorthodox healing arts. Over the next several years the acupuncturists, bone-setters and masseurs battled for and won legal recognition and survival. Many thousands of "healers" using a variety of methods including light, heat, electricity, stimulation and manipulation (not included in the legislative mandate) joined to form the All Natural Therapist Association. This group, in excess of 10,000, continued a battle to achieve two modest steps towards legal recognition.

The first step in 1960 was a Supreme Court decision that anyone could practice their healing art as long as the therapy was harmless. With this decision, the Department of Health could not restrain those practicing natural therapies. The second step, in 1964, grandfathered all those practicing natural therapies but did not allow new practitioners the same recognition. Thus, the recognized members of the All Natural Therapy Association that had legal recognition would eventually pass and no new members would be allowed to replace them.

Dr. Takeyachi, the son of a natural healer and the first student of the Takeyachi family to attend National College summarized the situation by describing four scenarios under which chiropractic could be practiced in Japan. First, a member of the All Natural Therapy Association who had received lifetime recognition could practice chiropractic unencumbered by legal sanction. This person could legally be called a chiropractor. Second, persons using natural therapies could include chiropractic procedures but could not receive a license nor call themselves chiropractors. Third, U.S.-trained chiropractors, even those who had passed national boards, could not be recognized by the Japanese authorities, although, because of their education they were not likely to be bothered as they practiced. Finally, legally licensed bone-setters, masseur-pressure therapists and acupuncturists could practice chiropractic but could not call themselves chiropractors because such designation had not received legal recognition.[27,28]

Chiropractic was first introduced into Japan in 1915 by Dr. Saburo Kawaguchi, one of about a dozen American-trained Japanese chiropractors in the early days. Chiropractic was easily accepted into a culture where manipulation was a traditional form of therapy. In some areas it was regulated by the local police department. Drs. Osawa and Kodaira taught chiropractic extensively and translated texts from English. Dr. Shigeru Matsumoto was a noted student. In 1945, during the U.S. occupation of Japan, spinal manipulation was banned as unscientific, along with many other healing arts.[29]

In 1947 the Zenkoku Ryojutsushi Kyokai (All Japan Natural Therapists Association) organized and lobbied for governmental recognition that was finally achieved in 1964. Since no American-trained chiropractors returned to Japan after 1935, no systematized education existed and chiropractic was almost absorbed by many of the traditional manipulative arts. Dr. S. Matsumoto (Chief Director of the All Japan Natural Therapists Association (ZRK) and Dr. Yoneo Takeyachi, neither of whom had a formal education in chiropractic, fought for their identity and taught chiropractic to various groups. In 1961, these two and several other smaller groups joined to form the Japanese Chiropractic Association. Dr. R. Itoh was the first president, Dr. T. Kusanagi the second and Dr. Y. Takeyachi the third. Dr. Yoneo Takeyachi's second son, Kazuyoshi, was later trained at National College of Chiropractic and returned to Japan in 1969—the first to return in 34 years.[30]

The Takeyachi Family

The development of chiropractic in Japan is closely tied to the Takeyachi family and their relationship to Dr. Janse and National College. Thus some necessary background on the Takeyachi family.

Yoneo Takeyachi was born in 1906 in the city of Tokyo. At the age of seventeen (1923) he obtained his Master level in the art of

240

Dr. Janse ready to lecture in Japan, 1965

Judo. He pursued a career as a police officer in 1930 and married Masako in 1936. With a black belt in Judo, Yoneo had an inborn ability in his hands. Though never formally educated as a chiropractor in America, he studied the art, science and philosophy of chiropractic where ever possible and opened an office in 1946 at the age of forty. During his years in practice he corresponded with many notable leaders in the profession including Drs. Janse, Clarence Weiant and Ernest Napolitano.[31]

In 1961, Yoneo made a world-wide pilgrimage and visited several chiropractic colleges. While at National, he was hosted by Dr. George Parker due to Dr. Janse's absence. However, he corresponded with Dr. Janse for many years. This trip instilled in him an appreciation for a formal chiropractic education and the importance of introducing chiropractic as a science in Japan.[32]

In 1964, Kazuyoshi Takeyachi, second son of Yoneo, left Japan to enroll at National College of Chiropractic. The following year (1965) Yoneo invited Dr. Janse to lecture in Japan. This marked the first time a senior educator from the United States came to Japan to

241

Dr. Janse with Kasu Takeyachi and fiancée Toshiko

lecture on chiropractic. More than three hundred practitioners attended the conference.[33]

Yoneo introduced chiropractic to Japan over television in 1966 and became the third president of the Japanese Chiropractic Association (JCA). A coalition of seven chiropractic associations originally founded the JCA in 1961. Yoneo was a prolific writer publishing several books on chiropractic, a monthly newsletter and translating the text, *Chiropractic Principles and Technique,*" Dr. Janse being a co-author.[34]

In 1973, Nobuyoshi, third son of Yoneo, enrolled at National College of Chiropractic and in 1974 Hiroaki, first son of Yoneo and an orthopedic surgeon of ten years, also enrolled at National College. All three sons went to National College because of their father's influence. Yoneo passed away at the age of 68 (1975) due to stomach cancer.[35]

Dr. Kasuyoshi Takeyachi's two sons have also pursed chiropractic training. Yasunobu enrolled at National after completing his medical degree at Jikei University (2000) and will graduate in August 2006 as the valedictorian of his class. Yoshiaki graduated with a medical degree from Tokyo Medical and Dental School (1997) and completed his

Ph.D. at Fukushima University School of Medicine in 2003. He is now taking classes and teaching at RMIT Tokyo chiropractic program.[36]

The Growth of Chiropractic in Japan

In 1961, leaders of six chiropractic organizations got together to seek unity and the Japanese Chiropractic Association (JCA) was formed. Since the ZRK remained the recognized body for nonmedical practitioners, the JCA served as a gathering of chiropractic leaders for study seminars.

Dr. Janse's first trip to Japan was October 29-31, 1965. He met with the leaders of the chiropractic associations and was instrumental in encouraging them to form a unified profession. Kazuyoshi Takeyachi, (NCC, 1969) was elected president of the JCA in 1970. Following the influence of Dr. Janse, he proposed to the JCA a change in organizational structure from a loose coalition to a formal organization based on individual membership. While some defected from this new organization, within a year it boasted a membership of 100. By 1972 membership reached 170 although most members were not formally trained D.C.'s but came from other traditional healing arts.[37] In 1974, the JCA re-elected Dr. Kazu Takeyachi as president and he selected two young practitioners as members of his executive committee, Koichi Wada and Tsugio Muramatsu. Their average age was thirty — rather unusual considering that a great part of the membership of the JCA remained older practitioners.[38]

On November 14-15, 1970, Dr. Janse returned again to Japan. On this particular trip he was privileged to have an audience with the former Minister of Health of Japan, Mr. Uchida.

In 1975 big plans were afloat for a large contingent of NCC alumni to make an around-the-world trip. Japan was to be a major stopping place. However, as the year toiled onward, pressing demands forced Dr. Janse to withdraw from the trip. The large group dissipated to a seminar group consisting of Drs. Lee Arnold, Bud Grove, Len Richie and Everett Pope. Dr. Pope, and Dr. Richie's wife (the former Evelyn Buchholz), were members of the College's Board.

In a December 14, 1976 letter to Dr. Kazu Takeyachi, Dr. Janse congratulated him on the graduation of his younger brother

Nobuyoshi from NCC. Dr. Janse also informed Dr. Kazu of a potential trip to Australia and offered to make a trip to Japan for a three-day seminar as part of the same trip. In their exchange of letters, Dr. Janse planned to bring a 16mm movie of combined views of cadaveric specimens, X-rays and actual living models. The trip occurred September 22-25, 1977.[39,40]

The JCA formed an Education Committee in 1977 to begin a systematic educational program for certification of members of the association. Dr. Janse granted this committee use of all NCC copyright-protected material. They only taught members of the group and successful completion merited a certificate of completion (Certified Chiropractor). National College provided anatomy instruction by dissection for the JCA in the 1980's. National College provided many lectures for the certificate program and treated the certified chiropractors as NCC alumni. A listing of these presenters is presented in Table 1. These programs ended when Royal Melbourne Institute of Technology-Japan (RMIT-Japan) started in 1995.[41]

TABLE 1[42]

National College of Chiropractic presenters in Japan

Year	Presenter(s)
1965	Dr. Janse
1967	Drs. Pennel & Houser
1969	Drs. Pennel & Houser
1970	Dr. Janse
1971	Dr. Gillet
1975	Drs. Arnold & Grove
1977	Dr. Janse
1979	Dr. States
1980	Drs. Arnold & Grove
1981	Dr. Mazion
1982	Drs. Janse & Richie
1983	Dr. Swenson
1984	Dr. Janse & Arnold
1986	Dr. States

1988	Dr. Lawrence
1989	Dr. Triano
1990	Dr. Cox
1991	Drs. Arnold & Phillips
1992	Drs. Cleveland & Skogsburg
1993	Dr. Kleynhans
1994	Dr. Ames

The correspondence between Dr. Janse and Dr. Kazu Takeyachi was frequent and meaningful. During the years of 1978-1980 their exchange of letters addressed the need for unification of the profession in Japan, the need to prevent substandard schools and programs from starting and developing the process to bring NCC Postgraduate programs to Japan. Correspondence in 1980-82 created the joint research program between Dr. Akio Sato and Dr. Rand Swenson. It was also during this same period that Dr. Janse's trip in November, 1982 to Japan with Gloria and Dr. Len and Evelyn Richie was arranged. While in Japan he met with the former Minister of Health and Welfare, Mr. Nemoto.

Dr. Janse lecturing in Japan, 1984

Dr. Janse and Gloria in Japan, 1984

On Dr. Janse's final trip to Japan, traveling with Gloria and Dr. and Mrs. Arnold, 15-17 September 1984, he was not feeling well so Dr. Arnold made most of the official visits.

Janse's correspondence between 1982 and 1985 dealt with a group of Japanese chiropractors coming to an NCC Homecoming, plans for an alumni trip to Japan and China, Dr. Janse's transition to emeritus status and finally his health. The following are samples of this correspondence:

> Since I had the pleasure and privilege of being with you in Narita, much has happened. I am now wearing a pace-maker for my heart. Upon returning home it was found to be most irregular and inconsistent.
>
> A carefully cystoscopic examination, supplemented with X-rays and scans show me having a tumor of the urinary bladder and prostate about the size of an apple. Biopsy indicates a low-grade cancer.
>
> After much thought I have decided not [to] have the bladder

246

and prostate taken out and seek to function with an artificial outlet. I am going to take some controlled radiations and see what
happens.[43]

The last letter received by Dr. Takeyachi was dated 29 October
1985.

Some personal experiences from the pen of Dr. Kazu Takeyachi
are quite revealing of Dr. Janse's character.

> Dr. Janse was always concerned about us not spending too
> much for the lecturer. When I gave an honorarium to him after the
> seminar, he said to me 'Kazu' I am being paid a salary while I am
> here, so you do not need to do this. I will just take your hearts. He
> would not receive it. So at the time of departure, I gave him a letter
> asking him to read on the plane at the airport and money was en-
> closed in the envelope. Dr. Janse gave a letter upon return thank-
> ing and saying that the money will be donated to the College.
>
> At the time of his visit in 1977, I was thinking of resigning
> Presidency of the JCA for I was under such a stress from politics.
> This is a personal matter and I did not tell anything about this to
> Dr. Janse. However, he said suddenly to me at the hotel front door,
> 'Kazu' the easiest thing in the world is to give up. I was surprised
> how he read my mind. Ever since I kept his words and continued
> my Presidency for 19 years until 1988 when I thought I found a
> successor.
>
> Dr. Janse always thought of our position, our situation and
> never told us what to do but gave us encouragement, gave us hope
> and emphasized the importance of sincere efforts for the good cause.
> Everyone in Japan was touched by his approach and greatly influ-
> enced by him. He was the single most influential person in this era
> to promote chiropractic in Japan.
>
> The JCA has demonstrated their affection for Dr. Janse through
> their check books. They donated $3,697 for appreciation at the
> time of Dr. Janse becoming emeritus position in 1983, donated
> $14,666 for Dr. Janse memorial gift in 1986 and $10,000 for NCC
> Capital campaign in 1992. Total of $28,363 was donated to NCC

Drs. Janse and Takeyachi at National College, circa 1980s

as of today. I personally donated $20,000 as of today and my brothers several thousand dollars.

My relationship with Dr. Janse was one of the greatest memories in life. He was a great leader of the profession and to me my personal mentor. Our profession was very fortunate to have him at the time of great need, a developing stage. He was not born in America and having gone through hardship in his youth, he was very understanding of overseas situations. His thought was universal for he captured the minds of oriental Japanese immediately. He was a man of action as well as a man of words. He said and did everything for the good of others with his own sacrifice. He knew exactly what people wanted and needed instinctually for having rich experiences in hardship. Without doubt his leadership contributed immensely to today's chiropractic in Japan.[44]

While chiropractic remains chaotic in Japan, the RMIT Tokyo chiropractic program, an outgrowth of the Janse—Takeyachi connection was granted accredited status by the Australasian Council on Chiropractic Education in 2006.[45]

South Africa

Dr. Janse left an extensive account of his visit to South Africa in 1959.[46, 47] He was enthralled with the beauty and grandeur of this most exotic land. He had been invited by the Pan-African Chiropractic Association (PACA), and current President Dr. William Sligting, to speak at their educational conference. He indicated that some 45 of the 70 chiropractors in South Africa were in attendance, several having traveled over 1,000 miles. The PACA was a successor of the South African Manipulative Society and was only four years old. This new body had, "...primarily used NCA concepts, policies and standards as a glossary of function."[48]

Johannesburg Mayor Maltz hosted the group and spoke highly of chiropractic in the presence of many respected city officials. Political recognition was critical as chiropractic was seeking legislation granting recognition and the usual negative press was prevalent. In addition to his lectures to the doctors, a public lecture was planned and more than 600 people attended.

It was on this trip that Dr. Janse experienced the wild game of Africa spending several days in the Kruger National Park in company with a Dr. Taylor. He was overwhelmed with the majesty of the animals both large and not so large. He was also very descriptive in his report regarding the beautiful flowers seen everywhere. Gloria was not with him on this trip.

In a letter to Dr. Janse from Dr. Lennox Fisher, Secretary of the PACA in 1962, he reviews the continuing struggles for recognition of chiropractic in South Africa and extends an invitation to Dr. Janse to spend a week in a game park. He talks about referring students to National and comments that since Dr. Janse had been to South Africa twice to participate in postgraduate lectures it was alright for the Secretary of the Association to show some partiality. [49, 50]

In 1965, Dr. Janse took Gloria and Joey to South African with him.[51] They traveled through Zambia, Mozambique, Rhodesia and South Africa. In a report written for his church newsletter he talks of attending Sunday School in Salisbury, Johannesburg, and Durban. Again he is overwhelmed by the beauty of the flowers and the majesty of the animals. As with previous trips, he lectured at the educational conference, interacted with the media and politicians, and encouraged unity (recognition had not yet be obtained).[52]

According to available passports, Dr. Janse traveled to South Africa from the 31 July to the 28 August, 1970, and again from the 19 August to 25 August, 1972.[53]

In 1982, the NCC Alumni Association sponsored yet another

Dr. Len Fisher and Dr. Janse, 1965

(l to r) **Dr. Ron Bidieman (seated), Dr. Len Fisher from South Africa, Dr. Janse and Mrs. Evelyn Richie, 1976**

250

"Hands Across the Ocean" experience, taking a party of 30 people to South Africa. The highlights recounted in Janse's report included, "...the welcoming reception by the Mayor's Office of Pretoria [Mr. Charl Van Heerden], the annual three-day conference of the Chiropractic Association of South Africa (CASA, formerly PACA), the presentations by Dr. Dennis Ray Skogsberg and myself, the illustrated lecture presented by South African, Dr. Willem H. Boshoff and the special questions and answers forum..." Dr. Janse honored Dr. Lennox Fisher of Johannesburg by conferring upon him the degree of Doctor of Laws from National. Dr. Fisher had served as the Secretary of the PACA/CASA for almost 30 years and had been Dr. Janse's personal host each time he traveled to South Africa.[54]

In June 1985, the Chiropractic Association of South Africa circulated a confidential Presidential Communication from Dr. Reg Engelbrecht to which Dr. Janse received a copy. "On Friday evening the 7th of June, minutes after the Amendment to Act 63 of 1982 had finally been approved, I received a phone call from Dr. Veldman in Parliament, advising me of this moment that our profession had waited for so long. It now only remains for the State President to sign the document making it an Act of Parliament."[55]

This meant that chiropractic had gained legal recognition in South Africa. But equally if not more important, there was only ONE association of chiropractors in South Africa. Finally, his many trips and undaunted efforts had borne fruit. In all the places he had traveled throughout the world, there was always a division of the profession. Elements of the "tribal divisiveness" he so often condemned existed in South Africa but out of the need to avoid extinction, they came together.

Unity within the profession had obviously been a dream and a desire of Dr. Janse's as one considers a comment he made in his report of his 1965 Africa trip:

> As we went about meeting people of all walks of life; the leaders in government, the heads of state, the directors of industry and the stewards of the law, as well as the Bantu in the Kraal and the native settlements; as we estimated these variations of humanity

251

and the contrasts of background they displayed we could not but
help sense the fact that only through the patience of tolerance,
understanding and reciprocal respect will interracial
[intraprofessional], ethnic and relating social and economic issues
ever find solution.

Janse achieved his dream of harmony in South Africa with official notification of their unified legal recognition, only shortly before
his passing in December.

Another world traveler, and alumnus of National College (1972),
Dr. Terry R. Yochum, postulates why Joseph Janse may have loved
South Africa so much in this poignant story:

DR. JOSEPH JANSE'S CAMELOT

What enters your mind when you hear the word "Camelot?"
Literally, it refers to King Arthur's famous castle in Southern England. The very place, where legend has it, he met with the Knights
of the Round Table and began the Quest for the Holy Grail. In the
famous musical "Camelot," Robert Goulet, Julie Andrews and Richard Burton, metaphorically refer to this perfect world as a Utopian society of prosperity and harmony. So perhaps, "Camelot,"
although a fantasy on the stage, can be realistically viewed as a state
of mind or a reflection on a lost ideal. In the mind's eye of every
great leader, organizer or visionary there is a clear image borne of
the ideal, grounded by a firm sense of what ought to be. There is
much to be learned from examining the ideals or "Camelot Concepts" of great men. Dr. Janse was a man worthy of Arthurian Legend who created a personal and professional Camelot. So with that
in mind, what was Dr. Joseph Janse's Camelot and where was it?

During the years 1967-72, I was an eager young student entering the realm of chiropractic at the National College of Chiropractic in Lombard, Illinois. These were troubled times both in the
United States and the world. During my second year at National,
the anatomy professor quit with no advance notice. It was then
that our college president, Dr. Joseph Janse, became our new gross
anatomy instructor. Little did the class know how blessed we were

252

to receive instruction from a master anatomist, as well as someone who had mastered the science and philosophy of chiropractic. It was again our great fortune to have him the following year for classes on both the central and peripheral nervous systems. Despite his one-hour drive from Lincolnwood to Lombard, he taught us at 7:30 A.M., one hour earlier than all other classes. His lectures were superb, making the complexities of morbid anatomy come alive. He never used lecture notes and the few times he had Gray's Anatomy open, it usually displayed a page unrelated to the topic at hand. I vividly remember Dr. Janse, or "J.J." as he was sometimes known, drawing the descending tracts of the central nervous system in color using <u>both</u> hands simultaneously.

Scattered throughout his anatomy lectures were many motivational interludes, as well as some expressions of frustration regarding the state of disunion of the chiropractic profession. I could feel Dr. Janse's stress build during his relentless attempts to unify the profession much like King Arthur felt as he tried to unite the many isolated kingdoms of England into one. He often referred to the foolishness of the profession trying to "homogenize" chiropractic and he would differentiate between unity and homogeneity by asking, "Have you ever heard Beethoven played by the masters exactly the same way?" He would inevitably reply to his own question. "Of course not but you certainly knew it was Beethoven, didn't you?" It was obvious the vociferous fringe element of the profession greatly frustrated him. He often referred to these zealots as the "lunatic fringe." They were "like the smallest child or smallest kidney stone, screaming the loudest, having a seemingly endless source of negative energy." It was these fanatical, religious zealots who Dr. Janse would refer to as "biotheologists" rather than true chiropractors.

Metaphorically, Dr. Janse envisioned chiropractic as an equilateral triangle. He recognized the need for an appropriate balance between the three essential components of the profession – philosophy, science and art. He conceptualized the problems arising within the profession, both internally and publicly, as an imbalance on one aspect of the triangle. Dr. Janse felt that the "fanatical" approach to chiropractic was fraught with danger, creating more problems than it would solve. His definition of a "fanatic" was classic: "Someone who triples their speed after they've lost their sense of direction." Dr. Janse's heart was greatly burdened by how frequently he encountered these wayward individuals at the state and national levels of professional organizations; even within the ranks of some chiropractic educators.

With all the responsibilities of the presidency at the National College of Chiropractic and his leadership role in the profession worldwide, Dr. Janse's moods would sometimes swing like a pendulum. We would observe this in the classroom, never being completely sure of the cause. As an ambassador of chiropractic, Dr. Janse traveled the world over for the profession, fighting its battles on both local and global fronts. Between 1959 and 1982, he made many trips to South Africa. These trips required two grueling air flights and Dr. Janse would be gone for a week to ten days at a time. Surprisingly, he would always return in high spirits, a reaction which was not usually observed when he would return from any other foreign country (and there were many), nor from any of the many state association meetings he attended. The reason he was so happy and motivated following his trips to South Africa was a mystery. I wondered at that time if it was his great love for animals and safaris. How wrong I was! It wasn't until February 1994, when I visited South Africa myself, that I finally discovered why Dr. Janse's spirits were uplifted by these trips.

On my South African lecture tour, I took occasion to show some images of Dr. Janse. Many local chiropractors responded with how much they appreciated the tribute. While in Johannesburg, we were invited to the home of the local chiropractic association president for a traditional South African braaivleis (barbecue). A dozen or more chiropractors attended, representing a spectrum of educational backgrounds from colleges all over the world.

After dinner, we all gathered around a large bonfire, sharing life experiences, exchanging jokes and relating stories about the various places where we had lived and traveled. The fellowship that evening was delightful. As we were sitting around the bonfire, I posed a question to the group and asked, "Who here interacted with Joseph Janse when he visited?" Surprisingly, there were many that remembered him and they spoke of considerable interactions with him. I shared with them how uplifted in spirit he would be each time he returned to the United States and wondered if it was due to the natural beauty of the country and the wildlife?

I'll never forget the response from Dr. Len Fisher, an elderly statesman-like chiropractor who graduated from Lincoln Chiropractic College. "Dr. Yochum, I think I can answer that question for you." He recounted how Dr. Janse had been approached to help with a huge problem they had with the South African government. He explained that the "tribal divisiveness" and bickering between the various chiropractic factions had reached a frenzied level and the South African government decided that it would no longer register or license chiropractors as of 1974. The chiropractors had been given their final ultimatum — if they could not agree among themselves, their profession would be denied registration and licensure. Dr. Fisher continued, "I do believe as a result of Dr. Janse's extensive efforts and his multiple visits to South Africa to meet with us, the members of the profession finally decided to set aside all personal egos and political agendas for the best interests of chiropractic." It took the threat of complete extinction of the chiropractic profession in South Africa before the various factions of chiropractors could become one unified profession.

Having heard this, I clearly sensed that Dr. Janse had faced a once-in-a-lifetime "Arthurian" opportunity in South Africa; to unify a group of chiropractors—helping them to set aside all political, professional and personal differences—allowing the profession to survive. Years later, it was apparent these differences remained minimized among these South African chiropractors. Their "round table" focus on the "bigger vision of a united profession" ultimately guaranteed their survival and future success. It became obvious; the opportunity to foster a united attitude in the profession and see it prevail is what caused Joseph Janse to be uplifted by his South African trips. This was undoubtedly Dr. Janse's private Camelot!

This chiropractic harmony created in South Africa was the very model our leader wanted to bring back to the United States. Uniting the profession in South Africa for one central important cause was one of Dr. Janse's greatest accomplishments. As elated as he was when he returned from these trips with great hope, he would inevitably be gripped by despair and frustration as he realized the chiropractic profession in his own country was being guided by many ego-driven, self-centered individuals, who could only focus on philosophical and political differences instead of the true needs of the profession. Dr. Janse strived to create a similar Camelot in the United States, but suffered great disappointment because his vision wasn't embraced in this country.

A memorable quote by an unknown author could be a fitting epitaph. "You are not remembered for those things which you begin, but only for those things you begin and finish." Dr. Janse finished his work in South Africa and hoped to start and conclude the same work in the United States. Alas, the political machinery between the "straights" and "mixers" was too divided, and even Dr. Joseph Janse fell short in his meritorious vision.

I am sure Dr. Janse often embraced his Camelot experience in South Africa and longed to create the same in his own country. Should the threat of "total extinction" of a profession be necessary before chiropractors join in spirit to unite? The profession today continues to be philosophically separated and if Dr. Janse were still with us, he would certainly be frustrated, but not surprised, at our continued "tribal divisiveness." Perhaps the time will come when chiropractors in the United States will set aside their differences, work together, and honor Dr. Joseph Janse's memory by creating the unified ideal of his dreams – a chiropractic Camelot.

Few words can describe Dr. Janse, however, many superlatives come to mind such as: a prolific writer, a charismatic speaker, a superb anatomist, a person of great stewardship, an incredibly unselfish, distinguished College President, the leader of the profession and exceptional father and husband. If I were asked to label this great man, I feel he would be best described with only one word, the very same word, described in the theme in a song sung by the late Nat "King" Cole – "Unforgettable."

Dr. Janse was the most unforgettable human being I have ever met. He is often remembered for his eloquent public speaking ability but perhaps his most memorable, oft-repeated quote is from Rudyard Kipling, which speaks of the great kindred spirit of understanding and fellowship Dr. Janse held for his chiropractic colleagues:

> Here's to the men [and women] of my own breed,
> Good or bitter bad, as though they may be,
> At least they hear the things I hear,
> And see the things I see.

Thank you, Dr. Joseph Janse, for all you gave to the thousands of your students, the National College of Chiropractic, the profession of chiropractic worldwide and to me personally. You truly were the visionary architect of our dream of Camelot. May your legacy live forever.[53]

(l to r) Drs. Lawrence Rosenbaum, Joseph Janse, Ken Yochum, Terry Yochum, circa late 1970

1 Stein, Jess, Editor in Chief. *The Random House Dictionary of the English Language*. 1968, Random House, New York, pg. 41.

2 Immigration Papers for the Janse family. Janse Collection, NUHS Archives

3 Passport, Book 1, No. 314474, Janse Collection, NUHS Archives.

4 Ibid.

5 Passport, Book 2, No. 577672. Janse Collection, NUHS Archives.

6 Personal Correspondence between Dr. Antoine and Dr. Janse. Janse Collection. NUHS Archives.

7 Ibid.

8 Undated Report on European trip by Dr. Janse. Janse Collection, NUHS Archives.

9 Ibid.

10 Ibid.

11 Ibid.

12 Personal Correspondence between Dr. Beach and Dr. Janse, 1964-65, Janse Collection, NUHS Archives.

13 National College Alumnus, Dec., 1981.

14 National College Alumnus, Dec., 1982.

15 Passport, Book 4, No. F299175.

16 Janse/Liss Correspondence. Janse Collection, NUHS Archives.

17 Personal Correspondence. Janse Collection. NUHS Archives.

18 Personal Correspondence. Janse Collection. NUHS Archives.

19 J Aust Chiropr Assoc 1970;4(3)(August-October):7.

20 Passport. Book 6 No. F938135. Janse Collection. NUHS Archives.

21 Personal Communication with Dr. Kleynhans. April. 2006.

22 Copy of the Resolution in the Janse Collection. NUHS Archives.

23 Hinwood JA. Report on the Pacific Regional Conference, Manila, Philippines, November, 1982. J Aust Chiropr Assoc 1982;12(5):4-7.

24 Letter from Leo Foster to Dr. Janse. 4 April 1985. Janse Collection. NUHS Archives.

25 Letter from Dr. Janse to Leo Foster, 17 April 1985. Janse Collection. NUHS Archives.

26 Letter from Dr. Janse to Dr. Kleynhans. 17 April 1985. Janse Collection. NUHS. Archives.

27 Letter from Kazuyoshi Takeyachi to Dr. Len Fay, 31 Jan 1979, Janse Collection, NUHS Archives..

28 Takeyachi, K. "Chiropractic Status in Japan: Slow But Steady Progress in the Land of the Rising Sun." JACA, Feb, 1985, pg. 22.

29 Ibid, pg. 23.

30 Ibid. pg. 23.

31 Letter from Kazuyoshi Takeyachi to Reed Phillips, 1 Sep 1999, Janse Collection, NUHS Archives.

32 Ibid.

33 Ibid.

34 Ibid.

35 Ibid.

36 Personal Communication. Kasuyoshi Takeyachi. April 2006.

37 Takeyachi, Kasuyoshi. History of Japanese Chiropractic, JCA J. of Chiropractic, No. 173, 1995, pg.31.

38 Ibid. pg. 33.

39 Letters from Dr. Janse to Dr. Takeyachi, Dec., 1976 to Sept., 1977, Janse Collection, NUHS Archives.

40 Janse, J. Dr. Janse's Observations of Japan. ACA J. Chiro., Dec., 1977, pg. 27-29.

41 Letter from Dr. Takeyachi to Dr. Phillips, Sept., 1999, Janse Collection, NUHS Archives.

42 Ibid., pg. 4.

43 Letter from Dr. Janse to Dr. Takeyachi, Nov. 9, 1984, Janse Collection, NUHS Archives.

44 Letter from Dr. Takeyachi to Dr. Phillips, Sept. 1999, Janse Collection, NUHS Archives.

45 Personal communication with Dr. K. Takeyachi.

46 Passport Book 3, No. 1669380, 30 October 1959.

47 Janse. "Observations in South Africa." Janse Collection. NUHS Achieves.

48 Ibid. pg. 7.

49 Passport Book 3, No. 1669380, 22 Septembrer1960

50 Letter to Janse from L. Fisher, 4 Dec 1962. Janse Collection. NUHS Archives.

51 Passport. Book 4 No. F299175. 30 September to 19 October 1965.

52 A page labeled "Observations in Africa" by Brother Janse. Janse Collection. NUHS Archives.

53 Passport. Book 5, No. A1095495

54 *The Alumnus.* Vol. 16, No. 5. December, 1983, pg. 8-9.

55 Letter to the Chiropractic Association of South Africa. June 1985. Janse Collection. NUHS Archives.

53 Terry R. Yochum, DC, DACBR, Fellow, ACCR., with special thanks to "Dr.'s Michael S. Barry, Chad J. Maola, and Jeffrey R. Thompson for their review of the story; and to Mr. Daniel J. Weikle, Denver, CO., for his literary critique."

Chapter Thirteen

The Emeritus President
1983–1985

The passage of power and influence, gained after many years of leadership, is never an easy or simple process. As the heavy mantle of the presidency bore down upon his aging shoulders, Dr. Janse struggled in many ways. A complex series of events took place in this transition process, each of which can be described from multiple viewpoints. Every attempt to maintain objectivity and/or to provide differing perspectives has been made. Historical evidence may well explain a seemingly appropriate and logical sequences of events; however, the reader alone must conclude of virtues or vices at play.

The Transition Plan

At the 23 October 1977 Annual meeting of the Board of Trustees, the following resolution was unanimously approved:

> WHEREAS, Dr. Joseph Janse has devoted over 40 years to the development and progress of THE NATIONAL COLLEGE OF CHIROPRACTIC, and to the chiropractic profession in his endeavors, and,

> WHEREAS, Dr. Janse has made great personal and family sacrifices, and is a national and international leader in the chiropractic profession.

THEREFORE, BE IT RESOLVED, the Board of Trustees does hereby adopt the following program for Dr. Joseph Janse and does hereby authorize and instruct the Executive Vice President to execute such program, to wit:

1. The 1977-78 fiscal year salary to be increased twenty-five percent (25%)
2. There shall be annual salary increments of six percent (6%) minimum, thereafter, so long as he remains President.
3. At the time of assuming title of President Emeritus, the time to be decided upon by the Board and such title is automatic upon relinquishing the title of President, and with such status shall act as a representative of the College either on campus or off campus at a compensation equal to the last salary as President.
4. At the time of full retirement of Dr. Janse, a retirement package of a net income equal to his salary as President for the 1976-77 fiscal year, such income to be derived from the sum of Social Security, the College Pension Fund Plan, and a special Janse Retirement Fund established by the College, and that in the event of Dr. Janse's demise 50% of this amount shall be paid annually to his wife for the rest of her life.

IT IS FURTHER RESOLVED, the Executive Vice President is hereby authorized and directed to immediately execute this program with the necessary funding and to transmit the executed program to Dr. Janse, such program not to be dependent or contingent upon acceptance by Dr. Janse.[1]

The charge to the Executive Vice President, Dr. Len Fay was to assure the necessary funding was in place but Dr. Janse argued the decision to become "Emeritus' should be something he and the Board jointly agree upon when such a change should be enacted.

This same employment agreement between the College and Dr. Janse, relinquishing the Office of President to become President Emeritus was repeated (December, 1980) although Dr. Janse had successfully modified the agreement to say the transition would be jointly decided upon by the Board and Dr. Janse and not be made unilaterally by the Board. His salary for the 1980-81 fiscal year was $47,640.64 with a guaranteed six percent increase for each year that he remained president. Upon acceptance of Emeritus status, Dr. Janse's salary would be, "...in the same amount as the salary paid to him as President by the College at the time his emeritus status is declared by the Board of Trustees."[2]

Finally, a memorandum of agreement was signed by Dr. Janse on 8 December 1982 confirming an action taken by the Board of Trustees at the 30-31 October 1982 meeting to retire Dr. Janse as President and make him President Emeritus on 31 August 1983, according to previous resolutions.[3] Present at this meeting were Drs. E. Liss, Chair, J. Dintenfass, R. Reimer, E. Pope, P. Tullio, H. Ulrich, W. Barnes, H. Trestrail, Mrs. E. Richie and Mr. E. Metzdorf, general counsel for the Corporation. Dr. Trestrail had just been elected to replace Dr. H. Ahrenholz and Dr. Liss and Dr. Barnes and been re-elected to fill another three-year term. The decision to retire Dr. Janse was unanimously agreed upon by this body.[4]

This change of status that was to occur was announced in the November, 1982 *NCC News Bulletin*. In this same bulletin, an announcement was also made of Dr. Earl Liss stepping down as Chairman of the Board, and being replaced by Dr. Paul Tullio.[5]

Thus, the Board of Trustees and Dr. Janse concluded upon an action that had been under consideration for the last five years. What follows is an attempt to understand why this transition resulted in a flurry of recitals and allegations from so many individuals.[7]

The Facts Of The Transition

The transition moved forward without a problem, in the public eye. In March, 1983, Dr. Janse published a list of twelve actions he wanted to accomplish as an Emeritus President. His objectives were:

1. I would like to do some undergraduate teaching, primarily in Chiropractic Principles and Practice and Related Aspects of Clinical Anatomy, Neurology, Orthopedics and Roentgenology.
2. I would like to augment in every dimension in my field contacts at convention participations, special clinical seminars,

public and service club addresses on chiropractic, legislative conferences and appearances in behalf of chiropractic, etc., etc., etc.

3. I would like to continue the worldwide outreach for NCC that I have sought to establish over the years, not with the intent of imposing NCC upon our overseas associates, but with the intent of placing NCC as an accredited, primary health care institution at the service of the profession throughout the world.

4. I would like to stand, but only by invitation, in advisory to the Administration, Faculty and Clinic Staffs, the Corporate Members, Board of Trustees and Alumni Association at all levels, if desired.

5. I would find reward and pleasure in rendering similar service to State Associations, National Associations, Specialty Councils, the Council on Chiropractic Education, as well as the federation of State Chiropractic Boards, etc.

6. I would like, through the amenity of "gentle persuasion," to prevail upon all Alumni to become active members of the Alumni Association. An institution is no stronger than the sharing interest and support of its Alumni Family.

7. I would like to assist in augmenting the current programs and help design new programs of fund raising. As long as we are practically totally without state or federal support, these imperatives cannot be escaped.

8. I would like to classify and index some of my recent papers and, yes, do some writing. I feel that the classical biological principles underlying the practice of chiropractic need to be expounded, and emphasized and more effectively brought to the attention of the clinical world.

9. I would like to sit in active advisory to the College's Department of Research. Presumptuous as it may seem, I feel that I can make some significant contributions.

10. I would like to be an advisor to the personnel of the Patient and Research Center and the satellite Clinics and emphasize the exciting satisfaction of effective chiropractic health care.

11. I would, somehow, like to help enhance the quality of teaching at both an undergraduate and postgraduate level, as well as help design a more fulfilling internship and residency program.

12. I would so like to conclude my final, active on-campus years in an atmosphere of understanding, interaction and trust and confidence, interchange of ideas, abilities, talents and creative input. I would like to seek to index the meaning of the words "Goodness is its own reward and friendship, trustworthiness and sharing dedication still remain the primary elegance.[6]

The annual Homecoming in May 1983 was a dedication to Dr. Janse. With his announced retirement to an Emeritus status, the entire event was focused as a tribute to him. He was especially surprised when his entire family including grandchildren, were paraded onto the stage to pay honor to him. He had no idea they were in town. At

Dr. Janse in his office as President Emeritus

Dr. Janse cutting the ribbon at the dedication of the Patient Research Center, Janse Chiropractic Center

the conclusion of the Saturday afternoon festivities, the Patient and Research Center was dedicated as the Janse Chiropractic Center.[7]

The cover story of the NCC News Bulletin in the summer of 1983 announced the appointment of Dr. Tullio as the Acting President. The decision was reached by the Board of Trustees on 23 July and was to become effective 1 September 1983, when Dr. Janse assumed Emeritus status.[8] Dr. Tullio was to remain acting president until a new president was hired.

On 13 November 1983 two memos were released by Dr. Tullio, Acting President and Mrs. Richie, Chair of the Board of Trustees to the student body, faculty and staff of NCC. Both memos addressed the resignation of Dr. Tullio as Acting President. Dr. Tullio continued to be an active candidate for the permanent position as President. Dr. Leonard E. Fay, Executive Vice President was designated

Drs. Joseph Janse and Lee Arnold beside Ms. Evelyn Buccholz Richie. Construction of the Patient Research Center in the background.

by Mrs. Richie to conduct the affairs of the College.[9]

The NCC News Bulletin of Winter-Spring 1983-84 announced the appointment of Dr. Lee E. Arnold as President of NCC. He was to assume the office 15 February 1984.[10] The 1984 Summer issue of the NCC News Bulletin announced the selection of Dr. Stephen E. Owens as the new Chairman of the Board of Trustees. This decision was made at the, "...mid-year meeting in November." Dr. Robert Gwynn and Mr. Park Livingston were also appointed as new members of the Board at this same time.[11]

With the selection of Dr. Arnold as the new president, Dr. Tullio would relinquish his title of "Acting President." It is interesting to note that he was not invited to return to the Board of Trustees; rather, two new persons were selected to fill empty chairs.

THE STORY BEHIND THE FACTS OF THE TRANSITION

The Patient and Research Center (PRC)/Janse Chiropractic Center (JCC)

There was a natural uneasiness with the passing of a 38-year mantle of leadership. Intertwined in this melee of musical chairs previously described were issues emanating from the Patient and Research Center (completed in 1981) that was renamed Janse Chiropractic Center at Homecoming (1983).

In October, 1983, a letter (name withheld by request) was directed to the President (Dr. Tullio at that time), alleging inappropriate patient care in the Patient Research Center (PRC). Allegations included excessive charges, unnecessary tests and ignoring patient requests to the point of bordering on patient abandonment.

A memo of 28 October 1983 to the Trustees, Corporate Board and the Officers of the Alumni Association, Dr. Bill Waln addressed what he felt was his unwarranted termination on 1 September 1983, (the first day of Dr. Tullio's administration). He claimed his termination was because he, "...refused to become part of or support a certain group which practices poor quality health care delivery, advocates unethical practices, frightens patients without clinical support, and diverts college resources into personal use."[12]

On 2 November 1983, Dr. Janse released a memo to the Trustees, Corporate Board and Officers of the Alumni Association. This memo was a catharsis of problems emanating from the transition.

> At occasion of the 1982 Board of Trustees Meeting I was in Florida attending the state convention and lecturing. Upon my return, the final day of the Board Meeting, I was advised that in an official action of the Board, that it had been concluded that I should resign as president of the college, and assume the title and position of president emeritus [contrary to previous agreement between Janse and the Board since Janse had not been consulted before the decision was made]. True it shocked me, as I had not been consulted by anyone. However, I sensed the fact that it had to happen sooner

268

or later, and so I accepted the decision without issue.

Subsequently I have been told that it was the opinion of the Board that I had done very little the last year or so as an administrator and that I had permitted the Executive-Vice-President to run the show.

My tenure as president was to conclude the end of August 1983. Long before that date there were dismissals of personnel, the assignment of new personnel, the change of position of personnel, without any consultation with my portfolio.

Title changes have been precipitated at rank excess. Concessions are being made to those who stand in favor and authorities are licensed far beyond the description of certain portfolios. Mistakes of some have been converted into immensities and by others snow jobbed into nothing and all done under the designation, 'The New Order.'

I am frank in my concern as to whether there aren't those who, inadvertently, are seeking to imitate a medical facility, in process of operating the PRC.

As well meaning as it might have been (and for this I am most appreciative) designating the PRC the Janse Chiropractic Center is an anomaly and an embarrassment. I shall insist that my name be taken down.

When all this eventuated I was asked whether I would support those appointed on an acting basis. This I have sought to do honestly and honorably but unfortunately on the one hand I have been patronized and on the other used for image and P.R. emphasis. There has been an almost total by-pass as far as primary matters were concerned.[13]

Another memo was addressed to the same three administrative bodies by Patricia Julison, a registered nurse working in the Janse Chiropractic Center. The 5 November 1983 memo stated the reason for her termination was, "...incompatibility with the establishment." Ms. Julison then provided a list of twelve (12) incidents reflective of inappropriate patient care, excessive charges and rude behavior.[14]

Other accusations from field practitioners, postgraduate faculty and students filtered back to the Board of Trustees. In *The Synapse*, a student run campus paper, a lead article talked of students meeting with the Board.

> The presentation very nearly did not occur. Previous to the meetings, Ivan Kelley asked the then Acting President, Dr. Tullio, to make it possible for the students to make a presentation to the Board. Dr. Tullio agreed to place the presentation on the agenda of the Sunday Board of Trustees meeting. Ivan refused this procedure, as the students wished to make the presentation at Friday's joint meeting. Later, Dr. Tullio personally offered to present the students' concerns to the Boards on Friday, but this was not acceptable and as such they contacted the Board members who might help them. And they did. Board members physically escorted the student representatives into the meeting.[15]

The students requested an investigation of the Janse Chiropractic Center practices and suggested a format for an ongoing evaluation system.

Accusations were rampant. In a 14 November 1983 letter to Dr. Janse, Dr. James Winterstein wrote, "It was reported to me on the telephone this morning that a member of the Post-Graduate faculty at National College, who is an M.D., made the statement that Dr. Fay is embezzling funds from the school for the purpose of building his new home."[16]

In a letter to Evelyn Bucholtz Richie, Chair of the Board of Trustees, on 18 November 1983, Dr. Leonard Chinnici wrote:

> Please allow me the opportunity to express my dismay at hearing that the Board of Trustees of the National College of Chiropractic has appointed Dr. Leonard Fay acting president and is actually considering making this appointment permanent.
>
> I feel that the appointment of Dr. Fay has been a slap in the face for the National College of Chiropractic. What we need is a strong progressive leader as Dr. Tullio, but not one whom is dis-

liked and distrusted.[17]

An awareness of campus discontent spread when a letter was sent on 21 November 1983 to the alumni by the "Committee of Concerned National College Graduates." The letter signed by Drs. J. Kellenberger, D. Mammano and J. Filberth as officers of the committee listed the following eight concerns:

1. We are concerned that Dr. Leonard E. Fay was elected to be in complete administrative control of the National College of Chiropractic as of November 13, 1983.

2. We are concerned that there is an imbalance in the composition of the Board of Trustees at the National College of Chiropractic. At the present time there are only two National College of Chiropractic graduates on the Board out of nine members.

3. We are concerned that the Corporate Members, for apparent political purposes, elected three non-National College of Chiropractic graduates to the Board of Trustees, one of which was not even a dues paying member of the National College of Chiropractic Alumni Association.

4. The Corporate Members rejected as nominees to the Board of Trustees three loyal National College of Chiropractic graduates who were supportive dues paying members.

5. We are concerned that the Corporate Members, again for apparent political reasons, rejected for membership a representative of the Alumni Board. This is the first time in twenty years that your Alumni Association does not have representation on the Corporate Board.

6. We are concerned that, after interviewing candidates in making recommendations to the Board of Trustees, the Search Committee of the National College of Chiropractic make a proper decision in recommending the right person to be permanent president of the National College of Chiropractic.

7. We are concerned that Dr. Paul M. Tullio saw fit to resign as acting president of the College, effective November 13, 1983.

> This action we understand was taken for numerous valid reasons. Fortunately, Dr. Tullio is actively seeking the permanent position of president.
>
> 8. We are concerned that the morale and attitude of students, faculty and staff are now at an all time low.[18]

Bringing the Alumni into the discord on campus appeared to Dr. Janse as a political move to strengthen Tullio's bid for the presidency. At that point, Janse apparently felt obligated to go public as well. A letter to the President's Cabinet dated 24 November 1983 outlined many of the same complaints and concerns noted in his memo to the Board of Trustees earlier in the month.[19]

Letters began to flow in from around the country. Many were saddened by the tenor of the "Committee of Concerned National College Graduates." Some were supportive of Dr. Tullio and his actions on campus.

Feeling responsible to the alumni regarding campus actions, Janse felt compelled once again to share with them his own perspective. A letter dated 11 December 1983 was mailed to all alumni. This was Dr. Janse's attempt to clarify issues and restore confidence in the College. Some excerpts:

> Within me there is a reluctance and hesitancy. I wish that I did not have to write this letter, yet there is a need to do so.
>
> Subsequently, [to Dr. Janse's acceptance of his required retirement as president to become president emeritus] in personal conversation in my office, the then Chairman of the Board (Dr. Tullio) advised me of the primary following reasons for the Board's decision: (1) my age (then 73, now 74), (2) loss of my administration, (3) weakness in leadership, unbecoming faults and personal habits, (4) that it was time for a 'new order.' Of course, I was hurt.
>
> Then, by the seeming need for an immediate replacement, the Board accepted the offer by the Board Chairman (Dr. Tullio) that he stood ready to assume the position of Acting President of the College and would resign as Chairman of the Board. This proposition, so readily acknowledged and accepted by the Board, enabled

272

the Board to avoid the need to designate the Executive Vice-President (Dr. Fay) as the interim head administrator of College affairs according to the Corporate Bylaws. It is a well known fact that the Executive Vice-President did not, and does not, stand in favor with the then majority of the Board membership.

I was to retire as President September 1, 1983. Long before that, the appointed pending Acting President proceeded to take over and establish the 'new order.' Flattering changes in administrative titles, as well as new appointments of committees with self-styled authority, were organized. Hirings and firings eventuated without any consultation with my portfolio. The Acting President functioned on a part time basis, two and one-half days a week with his office being at the PRC. Soon 'two campuses' developed; the west campus of the National College proper and the east campus of the Patient and Research Center.

Special student assemblies were called and the students were advised of the intents of the New Order and were told that the shamble of thirty years or more of incompetence were over.

On Thursday, November 10th, the day before the joint Alumni-Corporate-Trustee Board meeting, the Acting President [Tullio] called a special meeting in the Board Room of the members of the President's Cabinet and the Chairman of the Department of Physiological Therapeutics. We were commanded not to take notes, yet he taped our discussion. In rather severe and accusing questionings he challenged our influences upon students and interns and upon Board or Corporate members. Each one of us was thus confronted except one, the Vice-President of Clinics and Health Facilities (Dr. Haber). In conclusion, he turned to me, questioned me thusly and succinctly stated, 'Come Monday I shall either be the President of NCC or I shall be the Chairman of the Board of Trustees', turning to the others he said, some of you will not be here.

On Friday morning of November 11, 1983, the day when the Corporate Members were to meet, the Acting President caused to be convened a special meeting with students. He alleged that nothing effective had been done at the College in over thirty years, and even went so far as to tell students that windows had not been washed in over twenty years. He turned the meeting into a political forum to further his bid for the presidency of the College. Everything about the College which the students complained about he disclaimed any responsibility for, however, he did not tell the students how long he had been a Trustee, Chairman of the Board of Trustees, and incidentally Chairman of the Executive Review Board – the body responsible for dealing with clinic problems (the most vociferous of the students' complaints).

On Saturday afternoon, November 12th, at my request, the Acting Chairperson of the Board of Trustees [Dr. Stephen Owens] granted me the privilege of addressing the combined assembly of the Board...I sought to articulate the concerns that beset me.

At the November 13th meeting of the Board (which I was not privy) the Acting President [Tullio] was questioned and in consequence he resigned, but submitted his name to the Presidential Search Committee...Concurrently, the Executive Vice-President...was instructed by the Board to conduct the daily affairs of the College...[20]

Janse also addressed the issue of the non-NCC alumni now serving on the Board. Dr. Wunsch, the non-dues paying member, from Colorado was noted by Dr. Janse for many outstanding achievements in the profession and that he was indeed an alumnus by virtue of his graduation from Lincoln College. The other non-NCC graduates on the Board were Chiropractic Institute of New York (CINY) or Lincoln graduates also.

Janse also notes having received a letter from Dr. Tullio wanting to bury the hatchet. Dr. Tullio stated in his 7 Dec. 1983 letter:

I am now sincerely appealing to you to join with me in calling together these persons who can put an end to the problems that now confront us. We must meet with one honest and meaningful objective in mind; that to place aside differences, cement relationships and work to preserve and protect our precious institution.

Our allies wait anxiously for this to happen, our adversaries wait in anticipation of our failure. We cannot fail. Dr. Janse, the

274

profession's future depends on us: Please let me hear from you.[21]

In Janse's 11 December letter to the Alumni, he responded to Dr. Tullio as follows:

> He asked me to join him in the effort of making peace with all who now stand in controversy. He acknowledges the detriment and problem that has resulted and the hurt it has inflicted upon the College. This is most laudable, if he means it. Now let him prove it. Let him hold thoughtful conference with those he or his supporters have belittled and derogated; let him and his supporters stop seeking to play politics with students, interns, alumni and faculty and clinic staffs; let him look himself in the mirror and simply find frank and honest answer to the question, "Why have I so intensely played the game of politics[22]

Janse closed this letter to the alumni with:

> 1984 is now in progress and I would so sincerely hope that it will enable us to design an honorable and proper solution to our concerns.
> P.S.   Note the date on this communication. Yes, I had hoped and prayed I would not find it necessary to add to it and release it.[23]

As expected, Janse's letter brought a massive response from alumni with expressions of concern, respect and love for Dr. Janse and all he had done for the College and the profession. W. B. Wolf quoted W.H. Budden's description of Dr. Janse made some twenty-five years earlier, that he was the "Great White Hope of Chiropractic."[24]

By his closing remarks, it is apparent that Dr. Janse did not release his 11 December letter to the Alumni until after the beginning of 1984. Perhaps the second general mailing to NCC graduates by the "Committee of Concerned National College Graduates" on 30 December 1983 was the motivating factor for Dr. Janse to go public. The letter contained many strong accusations and demands:

275

Our first mailing to approximately 8,000 National College Graduates initiated a tremendous world wide response... The responses <u>overwhelmingly</u> indicated the following:

1. That Dr. Leonard Fay must not continue in a position that would influence College affairs.
2. That it would be in the best interest of the College for Dr. Tullio to be elected as President. This response indicated a mandate from the Alumni.
3. That National College Graduates must have greater representation on the Governing Board of Trustees...

September 1—November 13, 1983—Dr. Tullio initiated a number of constructive programs designed to increase efficiency and also augmented positive programs concerned with students, faculty, staff, and alumni. Morale, harmony, and new encouragement was at an all time high.

November 11, 1983—Certain Administrative and Board of Trustee Members encouraged student unrest for political reasons designed to embarrass the new Administration and to gain control of the Board of Trustees.

November 12, 1983—Corporate Members, again for political reasons, rejected three loyal, supportive National Graduates and elected three non-National Graduates to the Board of Trustees. One of whom never personally supported the College; and one who chaired the important Presidential Search Committee for seven years, during which time he did not conduct one interview. This same Board Member had refused to be re-elected a couple of weeks earlier because he stated, in writing, he no longer had time to serve.

November 13, 1983—Dr. Tullio resigned as acting President so that he could actively pursue the permanent position of President. Dr. Tullio found it impossible to continue in the acting President position because of the existing politics within the College. (Four NCC employees were seeking the position of President, and two Board of Trustee Members (non-NCC Graduates) are openly and publicly campaigning against Dr. Tullio's bid for the Presidency. One of which is the Chairman of the Search Committee.)

November 13, 1983—Dr. Fay was placed in <u>full</u> control of the College. The college morale and Alumni support is now at an all time low. Dr. Tullio's programs came to a halt. "Smokescreen" investigations and firings take place, in inquisition style, while critical issues and concerns are ignored.

December 7, 1983—Presidential Search committee meets to interview the following: Dr. Leonard Fay, Dr. Orville Hidde, Jacob Fisher, Ph.D., Dr. Paul Tullio and a Mr. Prinze. The Presidential Search Committee members criticize their chairman, Dr. Julius Dintenfass for his biased and politically motivated interrogation of Dr. Tullio. Dr. Dintenfass delays decision and "seeks" out more candidates to interview in January, at a meeting to be held in Florida.[25]

The letter closed with a demand for Dr. Fay's resignation, the resignation of Drs. Owens, Wunsch and Dintenfass from the Board of Trustees to be replaced with <u>"Loyal National College Graduates"</u>, and the discontinuation of lifetime membership on the Board of Trustees.

While the first letter of this committee was signed by three members representing the executives, this letter carried names of the same three executives, Drs. Kellenberger, Filberth and Mammano and committee members; Drs. L. Chinnici, D. Doornkaat, T. Sircher, S. Connors, W. Wichert, A. Keller, D. Schneider, A. Paolucci, J. Chinnici, T. Patterson, R. Story, T. Suddeth, J. Battersby, T. Reiter and E. Long.[26]

The Appointment Of A New President

As indicated in the second letter from the "Committee of Concerned National College Graduates," a presidential search committee had been appointed by the Board of Trustees but had not been significantly active until the Board took action regarding Dr. Janse's change to emeritus status. In the 30 October 1982 Board of Trustees Meeting, the following report was given:

Dr. Tullio then requested a report from the Committee on Selection of a President. Dr. Dintenfass responded, saying the Committee had been active for the past six years. The problem involved selecting a man who could satisfy the alumni and the student body. He recommended to the Committee that it draft a questionnaire for submission to a candidate which would bring out what the candidate could do and what he has done. Dr. Tullio said the Committee should not only consist of Dr. Pope, Dr. Dintenfass, and Dr. Ulrich, but also a representative of the alumni. He added Dr. William F. Hynan for this purpose, and also Dr. Frank Hoffman as representing the members.[27]

Correspondence between Dr. Lee Arnold and Dr. Janse indicated that Dr. Arnold was a consideration for president. In a 16 November 1983 letter, Dr. Janse states the following:

> I know that you are in confrontation of having to make a decision. If you decide in the affirmative and if you are appointed by the Board on an interim basis I shall support you totally. In no way do you need to feel obligated to me. In no way do you have to feel that I should remain on campus if it is best that I quietly and properly leave.[28]

Dr. Tullio expressed to Board Chair, Mrs. Richie his dismay regarding his interview with the Presidential Search Committee. In a 7 December 1983 letter he writes:

> As a proven loyal, dedicated and supportive National College graduate, I resent the unprofessional and unethical manner in which Dr. Julius Dintenfass conducted his antagonistic and prejudicial 'interrogation' during my appearance before the committee.
>
> It was immediately apparent that I was not being interviewed with good intent, but, on the contrary, I was confronted with accusations, innuendoes and false statements. His attempts to embarrass and intimidate me were appalling under the circumstances. It was obvious that the chairman was not interested in what I had to say, but rather in what he had to say.[29]

278

A similar letter of complaint was sent to Mrs. Richie by Dr. Trestrail, new member of the Board of Trustees. In his letter of 6 December 1983 he listed several improprieties of the Presidential Search Committee by the Chairman, Dr. Dintenfass at their meetings of December 3rd and 4th. From a statement in a letter written by Dr. Trestrail he left the impression that no candidate had been selected, "The Chairman announced he had received the resumes of more candidates..."[30]

Ms. Richie, Chairperson of the Board of Trustees also received letters from Dr. Earl G. Liss, a member of the Board of Trustees. In his 27 December 1983 letter he chided Ms. Richie for conducting a meeting on 15 December 1983 wherein students were interrogated. His concern was the Board taking action without the full Board in attendance. He asked her to "defer" any further action until the Board meet on 21, 22 January 1984.[31]

On 1 January 1984 Dr. Liss sent a second letter to chairperson Richie restating concerns from Drs. Frank Hoffman and Harry Trestrail concerning the Presidential Search Committee. His concern was that the Presidential Search Committee was stacked by Dr. Tullio appointing Ms. Evelyn Richie and Drs. Frank Hoffman and Harry Trestrail to the committee. He pointed out that there was no record in the Board minutes by a majority of the Trustees to expand the committee as was required by their bylaws.[32]

Another letter from the "Committee of Concerned National College Graduates" on 11 January 1984 contained the following:

> We are most happy to inform you that the Presidential Search Committee of the Board of Trustees has endorsed Dr. Paul Tullio as the person most qualified to be the permanent President of the National College of Chiropractic...Dr. Tullio's name will now be submitted to the full board of Trustees, for their final consideration and vote, at a special meeting to be held in Lombard on January 21st and 22nd, 1984.
>
> ...we are concerned that certain Board of Trustee members may reject the choice and recommendation of the Search Committee and vote contrary to what has been concluded.[33]

279

A letter sent to the Board of Trustees by Dr. Jon Houser, President of the NCC Alumni Association asserted, "…we, the Board of Directors of the National College of Chiropractic Alumni Association, representing 8000 alumni, unanimously agree with the PRESIDENTIAL SEARCH COMMITTEE'S recommendation to elect Dr. Paul M. Tullio to be the President of the National College of Chiropractic."[34]

The Board of Trustees did not follow the recommendation of the Presidential Search Committee and selected Dr. Lee Arnold as President Designate at their special meeting of January 21st and 22nd. Dr. Arnold spoke to the President's Cabinet on 31 January asking everyone to submit major concerns in need of attention. Dr. Janse's response of the same date included the following:

1. Attention to certain working relations between the College and clinicians in the Patient and Research Center (PRC) established by the former acting president.
2. Giving the Alumni Association complete control of the Office of Development and Alumni.
3. The need for more custodial help and administrative support.
4. A need to review all salaries.
5. A review of all research projects.
6. The role of Dr. Haber and Dr. Henson.
7. The need for stronger faculty supervision and upgrading of the residency programs.
8. The need to talk with Dr. Wickes concerning attending osteopathic school.
9. Re-evaluation of the X-ray department.[35]

In response to the Board's action, "The Committee of Concerned National College Graduates" released another letter on 13 February 1984.

We are concerned that on January 21 and 22, 1984, a special meeting of the Board of Trustees was held to elect a new president. This was to be the most important meeting in the history of National College. It proved to be the most disgraceful. It was immediately obvious that the coup that occurred at the Annual Meeting

280

in November was to continue and grow. It was apparent that there was to be two voting blocks. The majority block consisted of the following:

Dr. Stephen Owens (CINY), Former Board Chairman of the Bankrupt Chiropractic Institute of New York. Dr. Julius Dintenfas (CINY), who chaired the Presidential Search Committee, then voted against its recommendation. Dr. Herman Ulrich (Lincoln), a member of the Search Committee, who also voted against its recommendation. Dr. Leo Wunsch (Lincoln), a member of two months. Dr. Earl Liss (NCC), a member of the Board for over 25 years.

The minority block consisting of Mrs. Evelyn Richie (Chairperson), Dr. Harry Trestrail (NCC), Dr. Everett Pope (Lincoln), and Dr. Waylan Barnes (Lincoln).

The facts are as follows:

1. The majority block rejected the Presidential Search Committee recommendation. This, after much deliberation and expense. Also, they ignored a resolution from the Alumni Association and an overwhelming response from the field supporting the recommendation of the Search Committee.

2. The majority block refused to allow a registered parliamentarian to attend the meeting in the Chairpersons attempt to see that the meeting was held in strict compliance with recognized rules of order.

3. The majority block voted to enter executive session for the entire two days of the meeting. This extremely unusual action raised great suspicion and doubt.

4. The majority block refused to allow Dr. Jon Houser, Alumni Association President and Dr. Frank Hoffman, Corporate Member Representative, their seats in observance of the meeting.

5. The majority block rejected a proposed change in the Bylaws which would allow an officer of your Alumni Association to occupy a seat on the Corporate Membership, (The Corporate members elect the Board of Trustees.)[36]

281

The signature on this letter was Dr. James Filberth, replacing Dr. Kellenberger as Chairman. The list of committee members had grown from 14 to 43 and the footnote indicated that these committee members had made a financial contribution to the committee.

President Arnold remained as the President Designate and the Board did not respond to the letters from the Committee of Concerned Graduates. In fact, under advisement of College legal counsel, Dr. Arnold issued a memo on 13 March 1984 instructing all College Personnel, "...to make no statements, comments or responses on matters raised by the group represented by Mr. Helfand," legal counsel for the Committee of Concerned Graduates.[37]

The Committee made a final attempt to have their concerns addressed when Dr. Filberth sent a letter to Chairperson Richie requesting audience before the Board of Trustees at their May, 1984 meeting. He requested the attendance of Dr. Tullio to render first-hand accounting of the events.[38]

Investigative Committee

Throughout the transition of power between Drs. Janse, Tullio and Arnold, there were numerous accusations of wrong doing from multiple sources. The concerns of students and patients captured the attention of the Board of Trustees sufficiently to organize an investigation. Rather than delve into the many allegations and personal testimonies, most of which have not been made available for public consumption, the final report of the Investigative Committee of 18 January 1984 will be provided.

**REPORT OF THE INVESTIGATIVE COMMITTEE
OF THE NATIONAL COLLEGE OF CHIROPRACTIC**

**REGARDING STUDENT CONCERNS
WITH RECOMMENDATIONS AND A QUESTION**

This committee, created by resolve of the Board of Trustees (11-12 Nov. 83), has been charged to "...investigate the concerns of the students stated to members of the Board of Trustees and corporate Members during November 11 and 12, 1983 and subsequently transmitted to the Vice-President for Student and Alumni Affairs;..."

Included within this charge is the expectation of a report of the committee's findings based on interviews and examination of appropriate records and documents.

The panel (composed of committee members and respective alternates) met for an organizational meeting on 18 December 1983 and discussed the concerns and procedural approach to our assignment. We listed individuals to be interviewed that would represent a cross section of people involved in the concerns submitted by the students.

The panel met again on 5, 6 and 7 January 1984, for the purpose of conducting interviews and examining material relevant to the concerns submitted. A conference call was conducted on 15 January 1984, to discuss findings.

Based upon facts obtained by this committee's investigation, it was the committee's opinion that a report with recommendations and a question should be prepared and presented to the Board of Trustees at their 21-22 January 84 meeting for consideration.

The student concerns and the investigation conducted by this committee have primarily focused upon the clinics of the National College and associated personnel. At no time has the committee made any charges or accusations nor has the committee intended to intimidate or harass any individual. Their intent was to determine if any valid cause for the student concerns existed.

It is our opinion, as your duly designated representatives, that our investigation thus far, has shown that there is more than sufficient substantiation to make the majority of the student concerns valid.

Of particular significance, are those concerns relating to:

a. Apparent questionable clinical judgment regarding incorrect, inadequate and/or inappropriate diagnoses that have led to care bordering upon if not outright malpractice.

b. Unethical and unprofessional conduct on behalf of individuals for purposes of personal gain at the expense of stu-

283

dents, patients and the college.

c.   Incomplete patient records.

The process of investigating the student concerns has also brought to light other problems relating to the administration of clinic responsibilities. The absence of protocols for patient confinement, patient management and clinical investigatory studies was grossly evident. Rules, regulations and standard operating procedures were either unknown or interpreted differently by individuals responsible for performance of clinic duties leading to an array of confusion, disorganization and demoralization of interns, patients and staff. In the midst of the confusion, the glaring problem of inefficient utilization of present staff became evident, overshadowing the chronic problem of understaffing. It is the committees understanding that problems of this nature have occurred before with no significant action resulting thus allowing these problems to perpetuate and intensify.

This committee would like to make the following recommendations to the Board of Trustees based on the data accumulated thus far:

a.   Further investigation be conducted.

b.   This investigation be under the auspices of a commission empowered by the Board of Trustees to go beyond fact finding and to cause specific administrative remedies to occur.

c.   Since certain problems carry legal implications, this committee should be protected with full legal counsel.

d.   Further consideration be given to establishing a permanent fully functioning grievance committee which will assure direct communication between students, staff and the Board of Trustees.

This committee would now pose the following question to the Board of Trustees: Have we as a committee provided sufficient information to you, the Board of Trustees, to empower such a commission as we have recommended, or do we need to further document the student concerns?

The members of this investigative panel deeply appreciate your confidence in us and for the opportunity to serve National College. We stand prepared to lend assistance to any future efforts applied to this issue.

Respectfully submitted,

David Snyder, D.C., Chm.
Linda L. Zange, D.C., Sec.
Holly M. Schultz, student member[39]

Conclusion

Should the investigative committee have looked at other allegations? What of the improprieties in the Postgraduate Division as suggested by the Committee of Concerned Graduates? Should there have been a complete financial audit at the time of leadership transfer? Were there really 8,000 supporters of the Committee of Concerned Graduates? Could Dr. Fay have been an adequate replacement for Dr. Janse? Would Dr. Arnold be successful in bringing peace and togetherness back to the campus? Could Dr. Janse really let go?

While much detail on the transition has been brought to light, it is rarely possible to reach final determination of people's motives and attitudes retrospectively, even though many of those mentioned in this chapter reviewed the material for accuracy of content. Final judgment on the correctness of what took place as Janse exited the presidency, interpretation of what was said, and whether another course of action should have resulted, is left to the reader.

1   Board of Trustees Annual Meeting Minutes, Exhibit "A", 23 October 1977.
2   Exhibit I, Employment Agreement between Dr. Janse and the College, 12 December 1980.
3   Memorandum of Agreement. 8 December 1982.
4   Minutes Annual Meeting of the Board of Regents, 30 Oct. 1982, Janse Collection. NUHS Archives.
5   NCC News Bulletin. Vol. 38, No. 5., November, 1982.
6   The Alumnus. Vol. 16, No. 2., March, 1983.
7   The Alumnus. Vol. 16. No. 3., August, 1983.
8   NCC News Bulletin. Vol. 39, No. 2., Summer 1983.

285

9   Memos from Dr. Tullio and Mrs. Richie dated 13 November 1983.

10 NCC News Bulletin. Vol. 39, No. 4., Winter/Spring 1983-84.

11 NCC News Bulletin. Vol. 40, No. 3., Summer 1984.

12 Personal memo to the Board of Trustees, Corporate Board, Alumni Association Officers. 28 Oct. 1983. Janse Collection. NUHS Archives.

13 Personal memo to the Board of Trustees, Corporate Board, Alumni Association Officers 2 Nov. 1983, Janse Collection. NUHS Archives.

14 Personal memo to the Board of Trustees, Corporate Board, Alumni Association Officers 5 Nov. 1983, Janse Collection. NUHS Archives.

15 The Synapse. Vol. IX, Issue IX. Dec. 1983, pg. 4.

16 Personal letter to Dr. Janse from Dr. Winterstein, 14 Nov 1983. Janse Collection. NUHS Archives.

17 Personal letter to Mrs. Richie from Dr. Chinnici, 18 Nov. 1983, Janse Collection. NUHS Archives.

18 Public letter to NCC Alumni by the "Committee of Concerned National College Graduates." 21 Nov. 1983, Janse Collection. NUHS Archives.

19 Letter to "Members of the President's Cabinet." 24 November 1983, Janse Collection. NUHS Archives.

20 Letter "To Our Alumni" 11 Dec. 1983. Janse Collection. NUHS Archives.

21 Personal letter to Dr. Janse from Dr. Tullio, 7 Dec. 1983, Janse Collection. NUHS Archives.

22 Letter "To Our Alumni" 11 Dec 1983, Janse Collection. NUHS Alumni.

23 Ibid.

24 Personal letter to Dr. Janse from Dr. Wolf, 11 Dec. 1983. Janse Collection. NUHS Archives.

25 Letter to National College Graduates from Committee of concerned National College Graduates, 30 Dec 1983. Janse Collection. NUHS Archives..

26 Ibid.

27 Minutes, Board of Trustees Meeting, 30 Oct 1982, Janse Collection. NUHS Archives.

28 Letter to Dr. Arnold from Dr. Janse, 16 Nov. 1983, Janse Collection. NUHS Archives.

29 Letter to Mrs. Richie, Board Chair from Dr. Paul Tullio, 7 Dec. 1983, Janse Collection. NUHS Archives.

30 Letter to Mrs. Richie, Board Chair from Dr. Harry Trestrail, 6 Dec 1983, Janse Collection. NUHS Archives..

31 Letter to Mrs. Richie, Board Chair from Dr. Earl Liss, 27 Dec 1983, Janse Collection. NUHS Archives..

32 Letter to Mrs. Richie, Board Chair from Dr. Earl Liss, 1 Jan 1984, Janse Collection. NUHS Archives.

33 Letter from Committee of Concerned National College Graduates, 11 Jan. 1984, Janse Collection. NUHS Archives.

34 Letter from Dr. J. Houser to Board of Trustees of NCC, 21 Jan 1984, Janse Collection. NUHS Archives..

35 Memo to Dr. Arnold from Dr. Janse, 31 Jan. 1984, Janse Collection. NUHS Archives.

36 Letter from Committee of Concerned National College Graduates, 13 Feb 1984, Janse Collection. NUHS Archives..

37 Memo from Dr. Arnold to All College Personnel, 13 Mar 1984, Janse Collection. NUHS Archives.

38 Letter from Dr. Filberth to Mrs. Richie, 28 Apr 1984, Janse Collection. NUHS Archives.

39 Report of the Investigative Committee to the Board of Regents, 18 Jan. 1984, Janse Collection. NUHS Archives.

CHAPTER FOURTEEN

AFTERWORD — THE LEGACY

I first met Joseph Janse while serving as a Mormon missionary in the windy city of Chicago. My only previous experience with a chiropractor was passing my Boy Scout First Aid merit badge from the local chiropractor. Neither he nor his kids (classmates of mine) had the greatest reputation in the neighborhood.

Brother Janse, as we referred to him in the church, cared for the missionaries who had health problems. I enjoyed taking my companions to his home for care. He would take us down into the basement and share volumes of wisdom while he rendered his chiropractic magic. I admit I was more impressed with the wisdom than the treatments. He also had a couple of attractive teenage daughters in the house, and his son Jan, was on his own mission in New York at that time.

Four years later I found myself in Chicago once again. This time I was with my wife. After my interview with Northwestern Dental School, we had some free time. I called National College. Dr. Janse remembered me well and invited us out for lunch and to see the new campus (1969). Stephen Kesler, Associated Student Body President and senior student at National, was summoned upon our arrival to give us an extended tour of the campus. Steve just happened to be from Salt Lake City, our home as well. I'm sure Janse's selection of this particular student guide was more than a coincidence.

We had lunch with Dr. Janse and he invited us to consider chiropractic as an alternative profession to dentistry. Given we already were blessed with the first of our eight children, my wife was immediately drawn to the open living space surrounding new dormitories —this in contrast to the confining, deteriorating, high-rise apartments available to dental students in the city. When we returned home, I became intrigued with the notion of switching health care fields enough to spend the next several months visiting offices, researching, and scrutinizing each of the specialties.

One year later, expectations were high as I entered National College as a beginning student. By the end of the first semester, I and three of my classmates, all with bachelor's degrees from a major university, were in Dr. Janse's office registering our disappointment in our teachers. He listened, he soothed, he encouraged and we all signed up for another semester. By the time I had completed six semesters he had me teaching and dissecting in the gross anatomy department under his tutelage. At the end of the program, Dr. Janse and Dr. Joseph Howe convinced me to become a resident in radiology following my chiropractic training.

During these six years, I had many opportunities to interact with Dr. Janse, whether in the anatomy lab over a cadaver, or in his office

1973 Graduation *(l to r)* **Dr. Joe and Dee Howe, Sandra and Dr. Reed Phillips, Gloria and Dr. Joseph Janse**

where he carefully shuffled stacks of papers from one side of his desk to the other and back again, as he shared his own problems. Although I admired him greatly, I assured my wife I would never become embroiled in politics, and I especially would never want to live the frenetic life of a college president. After completion of the radiology residency we returned to Utah, passed the necessary boards, and spent more than ten years in private practice in Salt Lake City.

My admiration for and close association with Joseph Janse led to a conversation about me writing his biography one day. The following letter suggests he didn't feel worthy to have anyone make such an effort. It was not known then just how little time he had left.

Personal letter from JJ to RB Phillips
28 March 1985

Dear Friend Reed:

Within me there is a great hesitancy and yes a chagrin. You and Sandra will never know how deeply and affectionately I have appreciated your efforts at doing a history on me.

However, you must be aware of certain facts that are most personal and private.

I could not ask Gloria to talk with you about our lives together. At present she is very disturbed about what has transpired with me at the college.

She feels that I have spent altogether too much time at the college and within the profession at sacrifice of our family life and the nearness that we should have had.

Resultantly, our family togetherness has been brought into compromise, and our closeness to the church etc. has become meager.

In the desperation of so much I have resorted to indulgences that were wrong. So indeed I question whether a writing about J. Janse is truly merited by J. Janse.

So often of late I confront myself with the question, All that I sought to do—was it ego or dedication. Frankly I do not know.

So about all that I am now trying to do is to conclude the time I have left in seeking to restore some of that which I once was, before the strut of ego and untoward image ambition took over.

You see Reed I wonder why our mutual noble friend Steve Kessler [sic] had to leave his family as it happened. [Steve had been killed in a plane accident]

I lecture in Africa and encounter the endless number of tribal blacks. I lecture in the Philippines and encounter the poverty of these handsome ever gracious people, and I go to China and am impressed with the shyness of the children.

About a month ago Gloria and I were in Santa Barbara and took care of Julie's eight [children] while she and her husband went to Japan where he served as the orthopedist for the U.S. Olympic skiers. And as I cuddled the smaller of the grandchildren I asked the question, why should they have so much and in Ethiopia children are starving?

Too often I am confronted by the question, where do I belong in all this?

Joey as you know graduated from National. She is currently working at the Brookfield Clinic but I think that she will resign and probably start a little practice of her own.

She is or was (I really do not know) engaged to Mitchell Weiss a classmate of hers. He is Jewish. Can they hack it if they get married? Should she become Hebrew religion- wise. I question whether he would become L.D.S.

Yet what people have more in common than the Jews and the Mormons? The Nazarene was a Jew.

For all this I have no answer and don't seem to be able to find one. So I kneel down in the total of my loneliness and ask Our Heavenly Father to give me Faith and some Peace of Mind.

Joey would give all to have a family. Now she bestows her affection upon her dog Mollie the Alaskan Malamute.

So [your] good friend J.J. simply wishes to express his love and respect, notwithstanding his own mishaps and mistakes.

Give my love to Sandi and your youngsters. Say a bit of a prayer for me.

Gratefully,
J.J.

How badly he wanted to please and be loved by his children and wife. I am sure his children loved their father very much, but his absence from their lives made expressing love difficult in both words and behavior. His transition to Emeritus President and all the associated disarray in his professional family brought further frustration and anxiety. Faltering health was but another aggravating factor.

Grandpa Janse embracing his son Jan while observing two of Julie's children, Homecoming, 1980

Here was a man, quite possibly the profession's most respected, perceiving himself to be living outside of his own family. He felt so many things had gone wrong; things he held himself responsible for and things that ate at

Dr. Janse with Adriana (his sister) on his right and Grace (Adriaan's wife) on his left, 1980

293

his soul. He had done so much for so precious little in return. In the end, the very things he sought most, such as love and some appreciation, seemed beyond his reach.

Inarguably, he was a man of astounding professional accomplishments. Heads shake in awe at his undertakings. What created his drive?

From his parentage, he learned respect for hard work, integrity, appreciation for meager material possessions, respect for authority and a fundamental faith in God.

From his childhood experiences he learned the meaning of sacrifice, sharing, humility and love for the underdog, such as his caring for his brother with a "crooked spine." When Adriaan was on his death bed, Dr. Janse spoke to him saying, "Hang in there Ad, you're gong to make it." Ad responded meekly, "I know I'm going Joe, but tell me this…when I get to heaven will God give me a straight back?" What a reunion it must have been at Joe's passing, for the scriptures they often shared assured him that, "The soul shall be restored to the body, and the body to the soul; yea, and every limb and joint shall be restored to its body; yea, even a hair of the head shall not be lost; but all things shall be restored to their proper and perfect frame." (Alma 40:23; Book of Mormon)

From his professional experiences Dr. Janse learned knowledge far in advance of most of his contemporaries. He learned tolerance yet never touted this attribute for he often said, "Beware of the intolerance of those who cry for tolerance."

He took time to show concern for all people as he shared cards, wedding and baby gifts, and countless letters. He showered them upon our family and hundreds of others who communicated with him.

He learned diligence to the extent that it became as he described it, "pathological," and amusingly described himself as a fanatic, i.e., "One who triples his speed after he has lost his direction." As he matured in his presidential duties, he acquired great wisdom and with that wisdom a vision for the necessary future of chiropractic. This wisdom fueled the unrelenting power behind such notable achievements as the accreditation of chiropractic education.

His charisma I suspect he inherited; but through perseverance he developed his style into a leadership characteristic that would influence millions world-wide. How many dozens or perhaps hundreds did he bring into the chiropractic profession as he did me?

He never claimed perfection. His influence was only used for what he believed to be right and true. He applied this influence by a process he learned from his religious beliefs…by persuasion, by long-suffering, by gentleness and meekness and by love unfeigned. (Doctrine and Covenants 121:41)

This book has briefly summarized a life, but it has also coalesced the attributes of a man that made a prodigious difference in the credibility of a fledgling profession. The edifice he built and paid for at 200 East Roosevelt Rd., Lombard, IL, is just one physical remainder of his achievements.

Joseph Janse left another legacy, one beyond bricks and motor. It is the "Spirit of the Soul." All that he was emanated with every word and deed. And his inspirational words continue to mold our

Janse Hall unveiled at the 2005 National Homecoming. Building "D" was the original structure dedicated in 1963.

thinking and direction even today. How grateful the chiropractic profession should be for all that he was, so that we might be.

It is my desire that his life will be remembered and celebrated. This book is a token of my appreciation for what he has done for the profession I am a part of.

And for all who knew the man Janse, may I close as he would have closed:

> Here's to the men [and women] of my own breed,
> Good or bitter bad as they might be.
> At least they hear the things I hear,
> And see the things I see.

—Reed B. Phillips

CHAPTER FIFTEEN

SELECTED PROFESSIONAL WRITINGS
OF JOSEPH JANSE, D.C.

To acquire and assimilate the works of such a prodigious writer is no meager task. From a fledgling faculty member to a pre-eminent president, Dr. Janse never let his typewriter gather dust. Class study aids, professional position papers, historical documents, motivational and instructional treatises and letters of varying lengths and for all purposes found their genesis on a manual Underwood. He must have utilized two of the clunky, clattering mechanical monsters for he wrote both at the college and in the quiet of his home basement office at Lincolnwood. It's not likely he carried the same one between home and college given the cumbersome task it would have been.

The re-creation of his works in their entirety would consume a volume of its own distinction.[1] A summarization of his philosophy and belief in his beloved profession coupled with the essence of his teaching follows. No written word will ever capture the charisma and strength of his delivery—they fall on fallow ground without the punctuation and the pause of his distinctive style of presentation. The use of another medium of communication is required to capture that uniqueness; thus, a DVD is included at the end of this text.

Direction of Thought and Development of Character

Advancing from a spring graduate to fall faculty member in 1938 offered a great challenge for Janse. He left no doubt in the minds of any that he was a teacher by nature. His early writings were a gelling of his lecture notes in the areas he taught. Anatomy, technic, biomechanics, roentgenology and physiological therapies were the mainstay of his curriculum. With increasing clinical experience, his writings expanded to include clinical application in his academic disciplines.

Assuming the chairmanship of the Department of Chiropractic and the Dean of the junior class in 1939, and the presidency in 1945, created additional responsibilities to an already burdensome teaching load. Several articles published through the 1940's and early 1950's identify Dr. Janse as a member of the NCA Committee on Public Health. This broadening of experience brought a new dimension to thinking and writing. Publications began to address problems related to public health as well as chiropractic. He addressed them from a profession-wide perspective. Greater philosophical thought and motivational quips were worked into the pedagogical works previously prepared for the classroom or the postgraduate seminar.

In all his works, Dr. Janse was organized. He clearly wanted the reader to learn from the experience of reading his words. But just learning was never adequate. Janse wanted learning to take on a motivational perspective. He desired that the reader do something with their new information. He always thought of the "person" and was constantly trying to lift them to higher ground. Ultimately, he strived to lift an entire profession to a higher level of excellence. No small task in any historical period.

The following categories represent the essence of his writings. These categories are my creation. I have drawn upon original documents, my own personal class notes, and from articles in the *National College Journal of Chiropractic, Journal of the National Chiropractic Association, Journal of the American Chiropractic Association, National College Alumni News*, and *Principles and Practice of Chiropractic* edited by R.W. Hildebrandt.

298

The wisdom and foresight of this giant in the chiropractic profession is laid before the reader. As you peruse his works, remember the context and historical time frame from which they were developed. Remember also, that below the surface there remains a humble Dutchman born and raised in poverty, taught in country schools but always one who searched for the greater good in his struggling world. His writings portray his love for his profession, his frustration with its shortcomings and his desire to lift and lead those whom he served — his colleagues in chiropractic.

Public Health Issues

Mental Disorders, the Mind and Psychology

Just three years after graduating Dr. Janse, as a member of the NCA Committee on Public Health, writes an article linking psychic disturbances to body balance, a very chiropractically oriented perspective.

> Thus through the cerebrospinal system we become acquainted with our world and make our responses to it. Through the autonomic system our various other systems are kept in orderly rhythms individually and collectively and are enabled to make such adjustments as may be needed, with sufficient energy to survive.
>
> ...we can readily see that there is no such thing as a purely psychic phenomenon, nor one singly physical. These factors are inseparable and interrelated because they both are initiated and expressed by means of nerve function.
>
> ...chiropractic, like all other forms of manipulation, intends primarily to do one essential thing, to relieve peripheral strain and stress so that the inflow of impulses from the sensorium will be normal.
>
> I contend emphatically that the minor irritations and unwonted stimulations of the nervous system as the result of muscular tensions and skeletal strains, do have far-reaching effects, not only upon visceral function, but also upon mental and emotional integrity.[2]

In a 1942 article, Dr. Janse relates the over-use of alcohol and drugs as a cause of mental disorders.

I frequently question whether the public ever gives thought to the possibility that their mental effectiveness and emotional stability may become insidiously undermined by certain promiscuous tendencies. In this day of pronounced medication and drug store elixirs the public finds itself exposed to a danger which already has and may assume still larger proportions in the problems of public health and especially in relation to mental and nervous disorders.

The ever increasing tendency for experimental medicine to blossom forth with a new medicinal preparation every little while, to which is attributed all the glamour and enthusiasm of being a probable "cure all" only to find later that its usage and benefits are pitifully limited, makes the average layman most vulnerable to the over dosaging by some general practitioner who is more gullible than scrutinizing in his consideration of the supposed powers of the new drug...many people are suffering from a chronic intoxication, which has led toward a general deterioration of their health, as well as subjecting man as a whole to a persistent irritation or benumbing of his psychic and emotional centers, thus reducing his capacities as a thinking and normally feeling being.[3]

The field of psychology had strong relevance to the general practitioner. In an article published in 1947 we read:

The realization that mindful and physical functions interrelate in the accomplishment of the full expression of man as a being has become such a pertinent clinical study that throughout the clinical world careful and conscientious attentions are being directed toward the study of the same.

No longer is the field of dynamic psychology considered the domain of the specialist. Rather, every general practitioner, regardless of what school of therapy he might pursue, is beginning to realize the need of personal counseling and psychological reconstruction.[4]

War Nerves & Emotions

As the United States entered World War II, Dr. Janse addressed the "war of nerves" being waged by the enemy through propaganda upon the citizens of the free world as part of their effort to win the war. This was a derivation from his usual subjects but certainly relevant for the times.

> Realizing this advantage, our opponents have and are conducting a vigorous campaign in the "War of Nerves", hoping therefore to wreck our morale and create a civilian chaos which will invariably throttle the effectiveness of our fighting forces.
>
> The war of nerves is an attack directed at the individual personally; if he can dissociate himself from the mass movement of a nation at war he may escape some of the effects. But then, from the point of view of an enemy he has become a casualty.[5]

Dr. Janse was a physician to the whole person and not to the presenting aches and pains. His article on the effects of emotion on well being, demonstrate his wisdom and insight.

> It should be an axiom of daily conduct that physical health is inseparable from mental and emotional health; that the physical is even more determinative than the physical environment; that the thought and action of the individuals who surround us in the everyday world are as determinative factors in our bodily conditions as physical hygiene, exercise, fresh air, sunshine and good food have ever been. Negative thought is as dangerous as bad meat and as malignant as cancer and as fully capable of producing toxic condition in the body. An overbearing, petulant companion can lower the vital tone of the body as a gloomy damp cellar…unhappy marriages have produced more gastric ulcers than dietary indiscretions ever did.[6]

Clinical Relevance and Application of Anatomical Principles

Chiropractic Theory

- Dr. Janse's theoretical explanation of chiropractic was deeply rooted in a neurological perspective welded tightly to the mechanics of posture and motion. As early as 1940 he gravitated from the typical vital life-giving force philosophy—that was so strongly advocated by many—to a more scientifically based explanation.

- What chiropractors formerly termed 'innate intelligence' and 'life force' now is called by physiologists neuro-trophism.

- The phenomena of neuro-trophism is now well-established. Throughout the world of scientific thought the fact is recognized that all body cells are dependent upon trophic impulses for the normal expression of their powers of assimilation and metabolism, and that the condition of 'Life' is no more or less than the bio-chemical response of all the body cells to these impulses.

- Keeping the foregoing facts in mind it is easy to realize that basically the integrative action of all body cells is a matter of normal innervation.

- …essentially, the health of all body cells is a matter of neuro-trophic expression.

- Thus all pathology is directly or indirectly the result of nervous dystrophy.

- Neuro-trophic perversions are the principal basis of all pathology! What a world of chiropractic truth![7]

This neuro-trophic approach to chiropractic theory and application was further amplified in the 1945 writings of Dr. Janse when he declared the chiropractic principles taught to incoming students at the National College.

> …the student is required in the first semester…to take a course in…the evolution of the neurological phenomenon in the vertebrate animal, up to and including its paramount influence upon

the coordinated function of all other systems and organs, as related to the health and disease processes within the human organism. Here the student is made acquainted with the fact that the neurological principle is the primary element that maintains normal bodily functions;

...the second progressive step is made. This consists of a careful study of the neuro-muscular mechanism, body mechanics, structure and form and how they relate to body health and discomfort. Here the student's attention is directed to the fact that joint fixations (subluxations) especially of the vertebral and pelvic segments, and undue tensions of muscles and ligaments, frequently serve as foci of nerve energy waste and reflex irritation...to produce dysfunction and eventual pathological change.

The student is taught...how the mechanics of the biped body in the erect position constantly are vying with the forces of gravity...the body often becomes mechanically distortioned, leading to an over-taxing of bodily energies and capacities. The intimate relation of the proprioceptive mechanism to normal neurological balance is carefully considered...the student is able to grasp the profound truth that undue stimulation of the proprioceptive sensorium will lead to the reflex contamination of important reflexes upon which health is dependent.

The fact that structure and form determine function is emphasized. Close study is made of structural anatomy...That the whole body is greater than the sum of its parts, and that there is no such thing as localization of effect...[8]

In a 1948 article, a definition of *The Science of Chiropractic* is located at the end and is presumed to be penned by Dr. Janse. It concisely states his theoretical premise of chiropractic.

Chiropractic science is founded on the premise that the neurological component is the primary element in maintaining normal bodily functions; that its influence penetrates and controls all tissue function, whether chemical, glandular, or muscular; and that if there is a disturbance of this neurological component, the ground-work is laid for dysfunction and eventual pathology. Disturbance of the neurological component constantly from joint fixations, or subluxations, especially of the vertebral and pelvic segments... These fixations, accompanied by undue tensions of muscles and ligaments, become foci of nerve energy waste and reflex irritation, the latter spilling over into visceral and mental pathways to produce dysfunction and eventual pathological change. The principle application of chiropractic science is to locate and release any joint fixations to the end that the neurological component may again restore and maintain normal bodily functions.[9]

Janse never openly discussed his religious beliefs in his professional writings even when he encountered what he thought to be conflicts between his religious views on the creation of man and the theories of evolution. He expressed a healthy respect for the evolutionary process as a part of his science-based world and spoke oft of "Man, The Biped" and the erect posture as a blessing and a curse.

Bipedism represented the physical necessity that led to human mental and spiritual realization. No other vertebrate is comparable to man in having attained the structural ability of maintaining the erect posture and as a result no other vertebrate possesses a nervous system as completely developed and as fully endowed with critical discrimination and response.

It requires but little insight into the science of physics to realize that man as a biped must possess a much more complex and integral neuromuscular mechanism of movement and posture than the quadruped, a neuromuscular mechanism that involves a great many more proprioceptive patterns whose correlations are so very essential to proper balance and locomotion yet which, because of their complexity of composition and the effects of gravity, are very vulnerable to abuse which frequently mirrors itself in the mental and visceral aspects.

Therefore, man the biped is confronted with the irrevocable necessity of constantly vying with the pulls of gravity. The chiropractor, a student of structural anatomy, is fully cognizant of this fact as it relates to the problems of health and ill health. His constant effort is toward maintenance and normalization of body mechanism. He is a bio-engineer and seeks to understand the intricate relation that exists between body balance and well-being.[10]

These fundamental principles remained the foundation of Dr. Janse's latter writings. He constantly would refer to the bipedal nature of man and its affects upon the neurological element, especially the proprioceptive nerve bed, as a basis for dysfunction, pain and eventually pathology. Though he garnered a vitalistic component in his belief system, his expressions were launched from the bedrock of science, a not-so-common occurrence in the chiropractic profession in the 1940's. Janse's vision was far beyond that of his contemporary professional colleagues.

Subluxation

In a non-published paper titled, *"Subluxation-An Interpretive Overview,"* the process of defining "subluxation" in chiropractic is placed in perspective:

> The word subluxation is being bandied about from pillar to post. Its reality as a component of biomechanics can no longer be denied or disrespected, but unfortunately it has become the 'scapegoat' of ideological chauvinism and prejudice and the semantic issue of group clinical postures. It might well be beneficial and proper to thoroughly explore the term from as many angles, levels and sources as possible and attempt to penetrate the biomechanical inferences and the clinical connotations. With this in mind, let us proceed frankly, honestly and without the debative rangle of possible group and ideological differences.

After listing fourteen definitions of subluxation (including three of his own), he provides the following definition:

> A vertebra is subluxated when the axis of bilateral symmetrical movement has deviated out of normal position with resultant

strained motoricity of entire segment, articular stress, proprioceptive insult and static compromise of the I.V.F.'s [intervertebral fo-
ramen].

A vertebra is subluxated when because of articular 'off-center-
ing' it is no longer capable of responding competently to the demand of integrated spinal movement.

Basically we may conclude, therefore, that a vertebral or sacro-
iliac subluxation is a segmental derangement of a spinal or pelvic
segment within its motor bed with resultant embarrassment of its
kinesiological conduct and with possible insult of the relating neurological and vascular elements.

Beyond this basic definition, Dr. Janse ties in additional dimen-
sions of the subluxation concept. For example,

> ...attending kinesiological embarrassment will to some degree
> extend the effect to the segment or segments above and below or
> adjoining. So indeed it should definitely be recognized that sub-
> luxation cannot biomechanically be exclusive to one segment but
> that the mechanically retarding, disturbing or deranging may ex-
> tend to varying degrees above, below and adjoining.

In his desire to avoid the "...exercise in segmentation and irrational compartmentalization..." he provides a descriptive classifica-
tion of the subluxation.

1. Uncomplicated spinal subluxation that may occur within the
    spines of children, youths and young adults in consequence to
    play, work, or any other asymmetrical activity.
2. Postural subluxation. Closely related to the foregoing but as-
    sociated with common postural inadequacies, pelvic tilts and
    inequality of leg length.
3. Reflex subluxation. ...visceral, optic disturbances, negative feed-
    back from neurological elements to spinal musculature.
4. Pathological subluxation. Such relates to the derangement of a
    vertebral segment within its motor bed in consequence to the

degenerative proliferative changes so commonly attending the
mechanical stress factors of every day life and aging.

Janse also included the related affects of a disturbance to the
neurological bed on the "...myological, syndesmological and vascular elements." His concept of the subluxation was broad and inclusive of multiple elements. This approach placed his definition above
the confining boundaries of a single ideological approach to chiropractic care.[11] [12]

Neurological Basis of Chiropractic Practice

The previous two sections touched upon Dr. Janse's appreciation for the nervous system and its effects on body functions. More
specific details pertaining to the neurological mechanisms as understood at the time follow.

In an article published in 1939, Dr. Janse provides a lengthy and
detailed description of the anatomical relationship between vertebrae and their surrounding soft tissue structures. He points to the
recurrent meningeal nerve as the controlling mechanism for the blood
and nutritional supply to the vertebral segment and the associated
disc. He points out that poorly functioning discs allow for improper
spinal balance that results in a vicious circle of segmental disturbances.

> This thinning of the disc, because of pathologic change, brings
> the vertebral bodies closer together, and the articulating processes
> encroach upon each other. This places the capsular ligament on a
> stretch with resultant reflex irritation by way of the meningeal re-
> current to set up painful segmental symptoms. If the articulations
> do slip past each other, the lumen of the intervertebral foramen is
> encroached upon with resultant spinal nerve irritation.
>
> It will be remembered that the statement was made that each
> spinal segment, by means of the meningeal recurrent nerve, is self-
> sustaining and governing, and that as long as the segment remains
> in normal position with the others this self-regulating function is
> carried out more or less as an involuntary activity. If, however, a
> subluxation or spinal imbalance exists, a stream of exaggerated im-

307

pulses is created and conveyed over the sensory filaments to the dorsal root ganglion.[13]

A concluding explanation of the interconnections within the dorsal root ganglion of the spinal nerve root is offered as an explanation for the, "...cause of the many vague spinal pains and irritations, so commonly existent in cases of spinal imbalance and yet not associated at the beginning with any definite pathological processes."[14] The interconnections of the dorsal root ganglion are also described as the basis of reflex symptoms derived from a mal-aligned segment.

The interrelatedness of the nervous system gave rise to multiple concepts associated with reflexes and their effects upon the structures innervated. Attempts to treat a variety of symptoms and conditions through a reflex process resulted in the technique of spondylotherapy advocated by a medical doctor named Abrams. Dr. Janse was eloquent in his description of the neurological element as shown in an unpublished paper titled, *"A Concept: The Neurological Element As It Relates To Clinical Chiropractic,"*

> The nerve impulse in its physiological affectivities effects cytological reactions and responses of much greater dimensions than the basic modalities of sensation and motor response, although these within themselves in depth are inexplicably intricate and variable. To this basic complexity must be added such protopathic yet totally significant terms as trophic effect, neuro-endocrinological interrelations, biochemical affinities, proprioceptive build-up, summation increments, patterns of facilitation, input of the ascending and descending reticular activating mechanism, genetic neurological diathesis, synaptic overlap, demoralization and disintegration of the synaptic threshold, the neurological spread and build-up, reflex instability, parasympatheticotonia and sympatheticotonia, somatic hyperkinesia, vasomotor instability, pre-disposition to sensorial aberrations, undue cerebrovisceral or viscercerebral inter-reaction, psychosomatic overtones, etc.
>
> All this compels the awareness that the human organism, the nervous system and its elements of physiological quality relates di-

rectly or indirectly to practically every physiological process or compilation of process that may incur.

In a 1978 article, Dr. Janse draws more heavily upon the intricacies of the central nervous system to expand his theories of the controlling effects of the nervous system and results of disturbances to the system. The complexity of detail is beyond the scope of this chapter, however, his summary statements show the preservation of his early conceptualization of the relationship between the nervous system, mechanical disturbance and resulting dysfunction and eventually disease. He often quoted from the foreword of Boyd's, *Textbook on Pathology*, "Disease is function gone wrong."

1. In man, homosapiens, the nervous system is pre-eminent in controlling, conditioning and maintaining the life function homeostasis within the body and its relations to the environs.
2. In man, homosapiens, as in any other organism, adaptation, coping with the impositions of the environs, and maintenance of the survival thrust are priority absolutes. Only through the maintenance of adaptation and reproduction imperatives can he define survival. Yes, the very complexity of his physical make-up, compels the integrative musts assigned to and defined by the nervous system.
3. This integrative imperative mandates the awareness that out of necessity there cannot be a factual or true localization of effect within the nervous system. What happens at one level or area definitely imposes integrative effect elsewhere.
4. The sentient cerebral affectivity (intelligence) of man is primarily for purpose of providing him with a more singular capacity of adaptation. Mental exercises, therefore provoke homeostatic physical responses.
5. Thus we are compelled to sense that there is no such a phenomenon as 'physiological separatism.' 'Functional checker boarding' does not exist within the body. 'Pigeon holing' physiology and neurological conduct is not possible and attempts at such should be abandoned.

6. It is not to be forgotten that essentially man is a sensorial organism. He functions by virtue of the inputs he experiences via the cutaneum, the subderma, the myofacial planes, the diarthrodial complexes of the musculoskeletal system, especially the spine; the relating proprioceptive phenomena. To all of this is added the protopathic and not too well understood visceral sensory inputs. Superimposed upon this conglomerate are the exquisite encounters of the special senses with their charismatic inputs of sight, sound, smell and taste providing the cosmetic overtones to everything. And then as a final conditioning factor are the feedbacks from the cerebral centers.

7. So indeed we are compelled to become philosophical and simply state, "the whole is a great deal more than the sum of its parts." Hence an isolated study of the part, as important as this may be, is not, cannot and does not define the profile of the total.

8. Furthermore it has become a most obvious fact in experimental neurophysiology that within the nervous system there is no such a thing as 'Localization of effect.' Inter-neuronic connections bring every area of the body into intimate integrative or disturbing contact with all other areas, segments or units of the body and that integrated neurological conduct equals homeostasis and health, and that disturbed neurological conduct results in pathophysiology, disintegraton of homeostasis and eventually the intrusion of disease.

9. We find ourselves, therefore, in confrontation. What has been done, as erudite and sophisticated as it might have been, has not spelled out a satisfactory direction. It would seem that other formats, other conjugations, other patterns of investigation have to be designed and initiated, seemingly on a more holistic basis.[15]

From the late 1930s to the late 1970s, the nervous system remained the bedrock of Janse's explanation and justification of chiropractic. Though his knowledge of the structure and function of the nervous system expanded greatly over this forty-year span, the fundamental application of the controlling and integrating function of the nervous system continued to reign supreme in Dr. Janse's dialogue on the discipline of chiropractic.

MECHANICAL ASPECTS OF CLINICAL PRACTICE

Cervical spine

The summation of Dr. Janse's writing on the cervical spine is contained in Chapter 14 of *Principles and Practice of Chiropractic: An Anthology*, edited by R.W. Hildebrandt (1976). Herein, reference is made to an original article published by Dr. Janse in the October 1954 issue of the *National Chiropractic Association Journal* titled, "Cervical and Occipital Involvements and Their Management."

His writings follow a pattern common to his organized approach to a subject. The article leads off with an in-depth analysis of the anatomical elements within and related to the cervical spinal region. The depth of presentation defines an ardent student of the dissection lab. Not only are the anatomical structures described in detail but the relationship between the skeletal, myological, vascular and neurological elements are laid out with precision. This style of writing and teaching established Dr. Janse as one with structural and functional knowledge sufficient to apply respected clinical applications.

His clinical applications begin with a description of the mechanical pathologies or subluxations found in the cervical region. Not only are these mechanical aberrations meticulously described anatomically but their mechanical properties that define motion and displacement are clearly stated. These clinical applications conclude with a description of the roentgenological or X-ray evaluation of the anatomical and mechanical displacements previously presented.

The practitioner typically receives a complete profiling of the region in preparation for a discussion on the treatment or management of the condition. Dr. Janse describes the clinical presentations of patients with a variety of conditions ranging from whiplash to shoulder, arm, hand syndromes. The symptom picture is tied to the anatomical, mechanical and roentgenological findings and treatment becomes an obvious outcome of removing the mechanical disturbance. For a detailed review of his presentation, see the work of Hildebrandt.[16]

311

Drawing on the theoretical concept of the all-controlling nervous system coupled with a thorough knowledge of anatomy, physiology and mechanics, Dr. Janse was able to tie many clinical problems of the head and neck to subluxations of the Atlas and Axis, the two uppermost cervical vertebrae. "The structures affected by all vertebral lesions *(subluxations)*, in order of frequency, are the ligaments, veins, arteries, nerves, and muscles."[17]

From this premise, he attributed the possibility of disorders of the brain to disturbance in the normal flow of cerebro-spinal fluid that was caused by a lesion of the Atlas or Axis. Disturbed venous flow would have an effect upon the various reflex centers of the brain stem and abnormal arterial blood flow would affect all higher brain functions. Direct motor and sensory nerve involvement along with disturbance in the sympathetic and parasympathetic ganglia could lead to numerous symptoms and conditions. He listed disorders of vision, motor function of the eye, secretory functions of the glands of the eye and nose and the salivary glands, ear disturbances, hay fever, and congestion of the tonsils as some of the conditions that could be the result of a mechanical disturbance to a neurological function. The obvious postulate is that corrective chiropractic care can resolve the lesion, remove the neurological disturbance and allow normal function to return.

Lumbar spine

It is difficult to separate the lumbar spine from the pelvis from a chiropractic point of view.

In Hildebrandt's *Anthology* (p. 165) reference to Janse's work on the lumbar spine was in the January 1953 issue of the *National Chiropractic Association Journal*. His work on lumbar disc disease was published in the January and May 1946 issues of the *National College Journal of Chiropractic* and reprinted in the February 1947 issue of the *National Chiropractic Association Journal*. These fundamental works were modified over the years to some degree but the underlying principles remained steadfast in his writings.

Typical of Janse style, his work begins with an in-depth review of the anatomical structures of the lumbar spine. He divides the prob-

312

able pain-causing structures into congenital and acquired alterations. Each is described as a mechanical pathology due to its deviation from normal structure. Once the effects of the mechanical alteration are delineated a full discourse on appropriate therapeutic measures follows. These measures include adjustive and manipulative procedures along with such adjunctive activities as heel lifts, relaxation and reflex technics and traction. The conditions highlighted in this area are 1) asymmetrical facing of the lumbo-sacral facets, 2) spina bifida occulta, 3) spondylolisthesis, 4) Kummel's Snydrome, 5) Scheuermann's Kyphosis, 6) sacralization and pseudosacralization, and the piriformis snydrome. All of the above conditions were considered to have a mechanical impact on the neurological element and thus were amenable to chiropractic care.

The concept of the central nucleus pulposus of the intervertebral disc bulging or herniating beyond its normal confines and thereby putting pressure on spinal nerves began its popularity as a cause for low back pain in the mid-thirties. Dr. Janse is again thorough in his anatomical descriptions of the normal and abnormal with clear emphasis on the mechanical effects of the abnormal on the spinal nerves. He provides a literature review, discusses the etiology and epidemiology, describes the examination findings to be looked for and concludes with a differential diagnosis. This depth of presentation was uncommon in the chiropractic literature of the mid-forties.

Always an advocate of conservative care, Dr. Janse discusses a lumbar disc problem:

> ...The redeeming feature about conservative treatment is that if properly employed it cannot harm or result in adverse effects. With this fact in mind, it appears that resorting to the radical measures of surgery without the intelligent use of conservative procedures would be an abuse of clinical integrity.
>
> Enforced rest and the assumption of corrective positions with the avoidance of aggravating activities are always contributory to correction.
>
> Support by means of properly designed braces may serve at times as temporary but effective aids to the weakened mechanical

state of the spine, its joints and musculature.

Paramount, however, is the fact that the chiropractic adjustment, when properly administered, may and frequently does, cause a replacement of the herniated portion of the nucleus pulposus into its normal confines of the annulus fibrosus.[18]

Dr. Janse then describes numerous massage and manipulative procedures considered effective and beneficial to the treatment of lumbar disc problems. He expressed confidence in the effectiveness of chiropractic treatments based on positive clinical results from colleagues and the work Dr. Illi was performing in Europe. Apparently, with the use of contrast media and X-rays, Dr. Illi was claiming to reduce lumbar disc herniation into the spinal canal with chiropractic adjustments.

...[Illi] has authenticated records of the clinical histories on a number of cases which, by means of neurological examinations and the use of contrast media as related to the taking of roentgengrams, were definitely diagnosed as having herniations of the disc, and which, after a series of careful adjustments, were relieved of their symptoms. Furthermore, these cases, upon post-adjustive roentgen studies, no longer exhibited the obstruction of the contrast media in its attempt to fill the epidural and subdural spaces so characteristic of intervertebral disc herniation.

Obviously, the adjustments had reduced the protrusion and thus dissipated the obstruction to the contrast media in completely filling and outlining the vertebral canal.[19]

Pelvis and Sacro-iliac

Dr. Illi, while practicing in Switzerland, undertook serious investigation of the mechanics in the lumbar spine and pelvis. He constructed a multi-tube X-ray machine that allowed him the ability to take full-spine radiographs at great distances, an advantage for decreasing projection distortion and patient exposure. Dr. Illi was convinced that the authorities and the texts they had written were incorrect with respect to the sacro-illiac joints. The prevailing belief was that the sacro-illiac joints were only partially moveable (amphiarthrodial). Dr. Illi believed they were freely moveable (diarthrodial).

Part of Dr. Illi's investigation necessitated three trips to the National College of Chiropractic and access to cadaveric specimens and the able assistance of a young anatomist named Janse. His first trip occurred in 1940. Subsequent trips took place in 1942 and 1949. In addition to numerous papers, Dr. Illi wrote and Dr. Janse helped translate *The Vertebral Column: Life Line of the Body.* It is difficult to say at this juncture in time who influenced who in their thinking but the combination of these two creative investigators did much to establish foundations for future biomechanical teachings that would impact an entire profession.

The depth of detail contained in the research work of Drs. Janse and Illi extends beyond the scope of this work. Dr. Janse gives the following summary, however, in an early publication on Dr. Illi's work:

Besides the discovery of a new ligament of the sacro-iliac articulation, not heretofore mentioned by anatomists, Dr. Illi sets forth a number of significant new facts and new information. He gives a thorough description of the mechanics and articulating nature of the auricular surfaces of the sacrum and ilium respectfully. He gives the first actual and exacting description of the movements of the sacrum. The real mechanism of walking, according to the principle of a moving sacrum, is covered. He attempts for the first time to locate geometrically, according to existing mechanical devices, a center of body gravity with an explanation as to how it is held over the supporting structures.[20]

In the early 1950's, Dr. Janse published articles relating to the mechanics and their associated disturbances in the pelvis and the sacroiliac joints. He continues to refer to the nervous system as the basis for conditions and cures:

...In other words, regardless of where the stimulus may arise, the sensation of pain is conducted only by nerve fibers. The mechanical factors which give rise to pain must, therefore, directly affect nerve fibers. Essentially there are two such factors to be

315

considered in problems of faulty body mechanics.

1. Tension of structures containing nerve endings sensitive to deformation as found in stretch or strain of muscles, tendons or ligaments, especially those of and about joints. The pain may be slight or excruciating depending on the severity of the strain.

2. Pressure on nerve roots, trunks, nerve branches or nerve endings caused by some adjacent firm structure such as bone, cartilage, fascia, scar tissue, taut muscles and congestive swelling. Pain resulting from the osseous encroachments of subluxation, facet syndrome, enlarged capsular ligament or protruded disc exemplifies nerve root pressure.[21]

The remainder of this article tackles the problem of mechanical disturbances beginning with the feet and extending through the ankle, knee and hip joint. At each level, an anatomical description followed by meticulous description of mechanics and resulting disturbances ensues. The article concludes with a detailed explanation of general and specific measures to be taken in the care and management of lower extremity problems. Such measures include heel and sole lifts, manipulations of the various joints at all levels, exercises and adjunctive therapies to include hydrotherapy, electrotherapy, and hot and cold packs.

Further discussion relates to the pelvis becoming highly complex based on the anatomical structures and their mechanical relationships. Dr. Janse's approach to this area was shaped by his experiences with Dr. Illi. He describes both "intra" and "extra" pelvic deviations and relates them to associated mechanical problems such as a "functional short leg." As with other descriptions, treatment is based on improvement of the mechanical disturbance, thereby relieving the nervous system.

The reader is referred to the original work for a more detailed description of the manipulative procedures employed for pelvic corrections.[22]

It should not be forgotten that Dr. Janse was a strong advocate of soft tissue procedures that extended beyond the more typical osseous manipulative procedures of which he was also a master. In an undated and unpublished paper, *"Soft Tissue Involvements in Spinal and Pelvic Trauma,"* he stresses the importance of the ligaments, spinal discs, fascia and muscles. Each contains nerve endings and are sensitive to mechanical disturbances that can elicit noxious impulses that could lead to reflex responses leading to pain and dysfunction. He always advocated care for the soft tissues contiguous with the more forceful osseous adjustive procedures.

CLINICAL PRACTICE

Manipulation and adjusting

In 1940 Dr. Janse published an article explaining how "manipulations" could be an aid to giving an adjustment. He then demonstrates a variety of soft tissue manipulations for the relaxation of the musculature contractions and for the purpose of reducing edema in the tissues affected by or related to the subluxation.[23]

After being on the lecture circuit for a couple of years, Dr. Janse describes his encounters with many who claimed special dispensations tied to their 'special technic.' He chides the profession for claiming to be 'spinal specialists' when many could not even explain, "...the exact dynamics and correlated relationships existing between the musculature of the spine and pelvis... ." He concludes that with his knowledge of the anatomy, physiology and neurology of the spine, "...it just won't permit me to become that brave in defense of nay one single technic [sic].[24]

Dr. Janse takes to task those who advocate a singular adjustive method.

> It is an unsound policy to seek to interpret chiropractic as a system of healing in the form of a special technic [sic]. Sooner or later when the glamour of far fetched promise wears off and clinical necessities are not fully coped with, disillusionment will be great and much loss of faith will be experienced. A policy of this type constantly necessitates propagandizing to keep it alive.[25]

317

Finally, to talk of technic [sic] writing, one must not neglect the 1947 edition of *Chiropractic Principles and Technic* authored by Janse, Houser and Wells.[26] This was a standard textbook at National and was an expansion of an earlier version in which Dr. Janse is featured in some of the photos but is not attributed to being an author.[27] Preceding and very similar to both these textbooks was Forster's *Principles and Practice of Chiropractic*[28], also a standard text book at National College, surviving through three editions. In each of these texts, the details of adjustive procedures were very well defined.

Female disorders and body mechanics

Dr. Janse related poor body mechanics and posture to dysfunction in females. Noting the long-term awareness in medicine of functional female problems he chides them for failure to advance in this area.

>...there is no reason why, as the result of instituting a few simple public health measures entailing the teaching of proper body mechanics, that the suffering among our young and middle aged women couldn't be effectively prevented.

>This is but another example of how the guardians of public health and the administrators in the field of human welfare, especially physical well-being, have failed to fully live up to their trust. They have permitted themselves to be fitted with the blinders of a straight-laced medical and surgical profession, the members of which seldom permit themselves or anyone else any freedom of thought or to see further than the orthodoxy of internal medicine and the usage of the knife. As the result of this combination, women have never been thoroughly educated to the fact that faulty body mechanics, spinal distortions and failure to develop correct posture habits are perhaps the most important contributing factors to their common ailments and distresses.[29]

Dr. Janse makes reference to a 1930 publication in the Journal of the American Medical Association[30],[31] where 785 young women were examined for posture. Only 20% were found to have good posture.

318

Forty-seven percent had dysmenorrhea along with other gynecological problems. Two years later following training on good posture, only 20% had dysmenorrhea. Posture had improved to where 57% were found to have good-to-excellent posture.

After commenting on the success of chiropractic care for posture problems and the related female disorders, he concludes his article with the following:

> ...one cannot help but wonder why it is that something isn't specifically done about it [bad posture] by the medical profession. Is it so rooted in the dogma of doling out pills or cutting into the body tissues that it is blind to many of the necessities and obligations confronting it?...Why is it that they must continually reject and decry the helpful adminstrations of the chiropractor who has made the study of body mechanics his specialty? Aren't they supposed to be possessive of the idealism that whatever is good for the ailing patient they will endeavor to administer or get for him?
>
> And thus we dare the orthodox school to recognize manipulative therapy as a distinct aid in gynecologic practice. WE [sic] call upon public sentiment to insist upon the recognition of this fact, namely, that manipulative therapy as taught and practiced within the Chiropractic profession is uniquely equipped to help prevent the common disorders of the female.[32]

EDUCATIONAL PERSPECTIVES

Accreditation and Improving the Quality of Chiropractic Education

Dr. Janse was an advocate of quality chiropractic education. In a September 1945 article, he made reference to what is later referred to (in the 1990's and beyond) as evidence-based health care.

> The most pressing responsibility confronting the chiropractic profession today is that of unifying and clarifying, according to known facts, what should be included in the teaching of chiroprac-

319

tic. In the teaching of chiropractic principles and concept, both in our schools and by the 'special technician,' there often is a tendency to overstate and to dabble in conjecture rather than adhering to strictly scientific procedure. Mind you, this is said not in a sense of fault-finding, but in recognition of a common tendency which, if continued to be indulged, may lead to condemnation of our academic integrity. In chiropractic, as in any other true science and clinical art, everything we profess and do should find its verification in the known facts of the sciences.[33]

HUMANISTIC AND POLITICAL PERSPECTIVES

History and Development of the Profession

Dr. Janse spoke to the Women's Chiropractic Auxiliary of Western New York and published his speech in two issues of the National College Journal of Chiropractic in 1952. Hildebrandt's Anthology draws from two issues of the 1952 Journal of the National Chiropractic Association. Both articles dealt with the history and development of the profession.

Dr. Janse's approach to the subject begins with a definition of what a profession is, followed by a brief review of the professional development of the other health professions. The ground work for a review of scientists who advanced ideas before their time is laid with the following:

> Whenever a new thought, a new contribution to science, a new but great human benefit was introduced to the societies of man, resistance, condemnation and even destructive aggressiveness were encountered.[34]

This condemnation of such historical notables as William Harvey or Joseph Lister justifies, for Dr. Janse, the ridicule heaped upon D.D. Palmer as he introduced chiropractic. A brief comment regarding the use of "Rachiotherapy" by the Greeks, the Phoenicians and the Egyptians lends further credence to the concepts of Palmer.

From the earliest beginnings of the profession, he reviews its development by making reference to challenges encountered by the early practitioners and the colleges. References to, "a great professional melting pot," "a profession always in a state of flux," "a crusading fervor," "so much to be done with so little with which to do it," are examples of his style of expression. He spoke of the original development of the profession on an empirical basis supported by the allegiance of decidedly sincere people. He felt, however, that many sincere people bring individual interpretations not always based on scientific fact nor rooted in strong educational backgrounds.

He spoke of the early efforts to obtain licensure in numerous states, the challenge of meeting basic science requirements, and the need to increase the standards of education within the profession. He spoke negatively towards efforts to hold back on the implementation of standards and of the tendency to cling to personalities rather than principles and fact:

> All pioneering minority groups, sustaining a new and not fully established premise, lend themselves to daring and courageous leadership—a leadership of pugnacious extraversion, ready to set aside the conventional and strike out into pathways unexplored and undelineated. All of us know the great personalities of our early professional history. They represented a leadership vigorous and unprecedented. Fully objective in their attitudes, they felt that survival resided in proselytism, indoctrination, and the maintenance of a crusading fervor. In fact, these methods represented much of the basis of early chiropractic education; an educational process based upon the development of convictions through emotional promptings and the teaching of empirical conclusions.
>
> Such a type of leadership among a small pioneering group always leads to great hero worship. Possibly no professional group has afforded its early leader greater adulation than the peoples of our profession. Unfortunately, this did lead to an overemphasis of personalities. Professional attitudes and interpretations were developed, not always in terms of chiropractic as a science, a premise, or

321

a profession, but according to the teachings and opinions of those under whose leadership they had developed.

This led to the rather detrimental tendency of professional sectarianism. Intense loyalties were developed, resulting in the establishment of ideological groups and dividing our professional population into followings of various types. This process usually had its beginning in the privately owned chiropractic schools, which usually were headed by one of the leaders of the profession; consequently, the chiropractic graduates went into practice supporting not necessarily the premise of the profession as a whole, but the ideology of the institution from which he was graduated. All this resulted in diversions of opinion, procedure, and intent. This served as the nidus [nexus] for great differences of concept. Group organizations resulted, one vying with the other for professional control. When society in general, or governmental and legislative agencies came to make inquiry as to what our profession stood for and what the principle of chiropractic included, they were baffled by the various ideas they encountered and the differences of opinions displayed by our people. In chiropractic they found little that was standard and so they shied away from our solicitations for understanding, saying in substance, "Here is a people without a singleness of direction.[35]

In all his formal publications, there is no mention of individuals with whom he may have disagreed. Exceptions can only be found in his later personal writings.

Philosophical concepts of practice

Dr. Janse was open to new ideas that were founded on scientific merit and demonstrated clinical effectiveness. Early in his career there was a flood of new reflex and pressure technics advocated by many in the profession. The following statements depict his attitude.

...I found much of real scientific and therapeutic worth, yet at the same time a panorama of variable ideas and notions as to its physiological premise and exact application. In other words, very few definite and clear cut interpretations as to the 'how' of the results of these technics could be found. Each technician or school of thought had its own explanation and theory. Each advanced its own type and brand of technic, and to the amazement of many doctors each system brought results in application. This set me to thinking and led to the conclusion that essentially underlying all these technics must be certain basic anatomical and neuro-physiological principles that constituted the reason for the comparative success of all. I determined to find out and form my own conclusions. Investigation proved to me among other things something I had long believed, namely, that **no man or technic has a patent on any curative measure, and that if one knows the underlying physiology he frequently can devise his own technics.**[36]

Politics of health care and chiropractic

It is interesting to note the concern both Dr. Janse and Dr. Illi had with the politics of the pharmaceutical industry and medicine in their efforts to suppress chiropractic and chiropractic's responsibility to conduct research to justify its claims. This is especially insightful when one considers the date this concern was expressed, 1940:

> ...The public has as much right to an accurate analysis and correction of spinal distortion by the specialist as the specialist must have a right to deliver it. The protection of the public health then, does not lie in the abolishment of such a specialty, but in its promotion.
>
> If such a principle is detrimental to medico-pharmaceutic finance then the latter, not the former, should be made to conform; the health of the public should not be considered in the light of stock market value.
>
> If medicine has failed to recognize the importance of corrective manipulation, it has failed to fulfill a part of its obligation toward the human community, and if it refuses to rectify this failure because of the recourse that it might incur from the big business of pharmacy, the people should have the right to look elsewhere for the necessary aid.

This situation, on the other hand, places greater responsibility on that group which professes the knowledge of corrective manipulation. We see then that a challenge is made: chiropractors need to do more extensive research work to harmonize their interpretations of manipulative treatment with science...They need to stop making fantastical, unsupported theories, as some do, advancing unfounded, extra-ordinary technics. Either chiropractors must clean their ranks of such undesirable elements, and advance scientific chiropractic, or they will lose their identity and eventually become absorbed by orthodox medicine.

If, on the other hand, the issue is squarely faced and all investigations, interpretations and advancements placed upon premises founded through research, they will force the state and people to give them the recognition which they will deserve, and orthodox therapy will be forced to acknowledge the merits of a new specialty in the domain of the healing arts, and renovate many of their impressions and interpretations as set forth in their manuals of body mechanics...Thus the irrefutable therapeutic merit which chiropractic offers will be put to highest and best use for the benefit of humanity.[37]

There is much more that could be included, but the foregoing excerpts are a representative overview of his scholarship. It could easily be argued that Joseph Janse's legacy, not only as an orator, but as a writer, is unequaled in quality and applicability to any of his contemporary colleagues. Had he lived longer, his insight may have helped us more effectively tackle our professional challenges today.

1   Hildebrandt, R.W. *J. Janse: Principles and Practice of Chiropractic: An Anthology.* National College of Chiropractic, 1976.

2   J. Janse. "Interrelation Between Psychic Disturbance and Body Balance." National College Journal of Chiropractic. Vol. 14, No. ?, Dec. 1941.

3   J. Janse. "Mental Disorders." National Chiropractic Journal, March, 1942.

4   J. Janse. "What The Study of Psychology Has To Offer The General Practitioner." National College J. of Chiropractic. Vol. 19, No.2. Sept. 1947.

5   J. Janse. "War Nerves." National Chiropractic Journal, May 1942.

6 J. Janse. "Your Emotions." National Chiropractic Journal, Aug. 1942.

7 J. Janse. *The Spine is the Life Line.* National College Journal of Chiropractic. Vol. 13, No. 2, June, 1940.

8 J. Janse. "The Teaching of True Chiropractic Science." National College Journal of Chiropractic. Vol. 17, No. 1, Sept. 1945.

9 J. Janse. "The Vertebral Subluxation." National College Journal of Chiropractic. Vol. 20. No. 1. Feb. 1948.

10 J. Janse. "Man, The Biped." National College Journal of Chiropractic. Vol. 20., No. 2, Sept. 1948.

11 J. Janse. "The Vertebral Subluxation." National College Journal of Chiropractic. Vol. 20, Feb. & May 1948.

12 J. Janse. "Subluxation – An Interpretive Overview." Class notes, 1970. Janse Collection. NUHS Archives.

13 J. Janse. "Segmental Disturbances and Pathologies Which Cause Cord and Spinal Nerve Pressures." National College Journal of Chiropractic. Vol. 12, No. 4, December, 1939.

14 Ibid., pg. 9.

15 J. Janse. "The Nervous System." Journal of Manipulative and Physiological Therapeutics. Vol. 1, No. 3, Sept., 1978, pp. 182-191.

16 Hildebrandt, R.W. *J. Janse: Principles and Practice of Chiropractic: An Anthology.* National College of Chiropractic, 1976.

17 J. Janse. "Disturbances Resulting from Atlas and Axis Subluxations." National College Journal of Chiropractic. Vol. 13, No. 1, March 1940.

18 J. Janse. "Suggested Care and Treatment of Intervertebral Disc Herniation." National College Journal of Chiropractic. Vol. 18, No. 2, May 1946.

19 Ibid., pg. 5.

20 J. Janse. "Forward." To "Sacro-Iliac Mechanism Keystone of Spinal Balance and Body Locomotion." By F.W. H. Illi. National College Journal of Chiropractic. Vol. 13, No. 4, December 1940.

21 J. Janse. "The Relationship of the Mechanical Integrity of the Feet, Lower Extremities, Pelvis and Spine to the Proper Function of the Various Structural and Visceral Systems of the Body." National College Journal of Chiropractic. Vol. 26, No. 2, May 1954.

22 J. Janse. "A Common Pelvic Mechanical Pathology." National College Journal of Chiropractic. Vol. 22, No. 2, May 1950.

23 J. Janse. "Manipulations Which Aid Adjustments." National College Journal of Chiropractic. Vol. 13, No.3, Sept. 1940.

24 J. Janse. "The Need and Value of Various Chiropractic Technics." National College Journal of Chiropractic. Vol. 14, No. 3, Sept. 1941.

25 J. Janse. "First Things Must Come First." The National Chiropractic Journal. Feb. & Mar. 1945.

26 J. Janse, R.H. Houser & B.F. Wells. *Chiropractic Principles and Technic.* National College of Chiropractic, Chicago, Illinois, 1947.

27 W.A. Biron, B.F. Wells & R.H. Houser. *Chiropractic Principles and Technic.* National College of Chiropractic, Chicago, Illinois, 1939.

28 A.L. Forster. *Principles and Practice of Chiropractic, 3rd. edition.* The National Publishing Association. Chicago, Illinois, 1923.

29 J. Janse. "Body Mechanics: Its Relation to Common Female Disorders." National College Journal of Chiropractic. Vol. 21, No. 2, September 1949.

30 F.N. Miller. "Posture Studies in Gynecology." JAMA, Vol. 89, pg1761, 1927.

31 F.N. Miller. "Dysmenorrhea Problems." JAMA. Vol. 95, pg. 1796, 1930.

32 Ibid., pg. 11.

33 J. Janse. "The Teaching of True Chiropractic Science." National College Journal of Chiropractic. Vol. 17, No. 1., pp. 3-10, Sep. 1941.

34 J. Janse. "The Development of a Profession." National College Journal of Chiropractic. Vol. 24, No. 2, May 1952.

35 R.W. Hildebrandt. *J. Janse: Principles and Practice of Chiropractic: An Anthology.* Chp. 1, "The History and Development of the Chiropractic Profession." National College of Chiropractic, 1976. Pg.4-5.

36 J. Janse. "Reflex and Pressure Technics." National College Journal of Chiropractic. Vol. 15, No. 2, June, 1942.

37 F.W.H. Illi. "Sacro-Iliac Mechanism Keystone of Spinal Balance and Body Locomotion." Translated by J. Janse. National College Journal of Chiropractic. Vol. 13, No. 4, December 1940.

APPENDIX A

Pedigree Chart

1 Jozias "Joseph" Janse
B: 19 Aug 1909
P: Middelburg,Zeeland,Netherlands
M: 24 Jun 1938
P: Salt Lake City,Salt Lake County,UT
D: 18 Dec 1985
P: Lincolnwood,IL

Gloria Juliana Schade
(Spouse of no. 1)

2 Pieter Janse
B: 28 Nov 1870
P: Veere,Zeeland,Netherlands
M: 20 Jan 1897
P: Vrouwe Polder,Zeeland,Netherlands
D: 25 Mar 1949
P: Huntsville,Weber,UT

3 Geertje DE Voogd
B: 3 Mar 1876
P: Vrouwe Polder,Zeeland,Netherlands
D: 16 Aug 1937
P: Huntsville,Weber,UT

4 Adriaan Janse
B: 7 Oct 1822
P: Grypskerke,Zeeland,Netherlands
M: 3 Apr 1861
P: Vrouwe Polder,Zeeland,Netherlands
D: 17 Feb 1874
P: Veere,Zeeland,Netherlands

5 Debora Matthysse
B: 29 Sep 1853
F: Aagtekerke,Zeeland,Netherlands
D: 29 Mar 19?3
P: Veere,Zeeland,Netherlands

6 Jozias DE Voogd
B: 3 Oct 18?1
P: Aagtekerke,Zeeland,Netherlands
M: 30 Apr 1875
P: Oostkapelle,Zeeland,Netherlands
D: 10 Oct 1921
P: Middelburg,Zeeland,Netherlands

7 Adrana Jobse
B: 31 Oct · 851
P: Aagtekerke,Zeeland,Netherlands
D: 13 Nov 1915
P: Middelburg,Zeeland,Netherlands

8 Hendrick Janse
B:
P:
M:
D:
P:

9 Zoetje Willebootse
B:
P:
D:
P:

10 Jan Matthysse
B: 8 Mar 1812
P: Biggekerke,Zeeland,Netherlands
M: 27 Jul 1833
P: Serooskerke,Zeeland,Netherlands
D: 18 Jan 1855
P: Veere,Zeeland,Netherlands

11 Janna Van Der Vate
B: 29 Jan 1812
P: Aagtekerke,Zeeland,Netherlands
D: 1 Dec 1853
P: Veere,Zeeland,Netherlands

12 Cornelis DE Voogd
B: 5 Nov 1819
P: Oostkapelle,Zeeland,Netherlands
M: 8 Mar 1845
P: Oostkapelle,Zeeland,Netherlands
D: 1905
P: Vrouwe Polder,Zeeland,Netherlands

13 Cornelia Meijers
B: 4 Sep 1824
P: Oostkapelle,Zeeland,Netherlands
D: 1878
P: Serooskerke,Zeeland,Netherlands

14 Leyn (Lein) Jobse
B: 25 May 1820
P: Biggekerke,Zeeland,Netherlands
M: 18 Mar 1848
P:
D: 26 Dec 1883
P: Aagtekerke,Zeeland,Netherlands

15 Geertje De Voogd
B: 13 Jul 1822
P: Domburg,Zeeland,Netherlands
D: 1886
P: Grypskerke,Zeeland,Netherlands

16 Adraan Janse
B: 17 Sep 1759
M: 1 Apr 1785
D: 29 Sep 1822

17 Geertje Wouterse
B: 1759
D: 20 Dec 1820

18 Willeboort Willebootse
B: Westkapell, Zeeland, Netherland
M:
D: 19 May 1808

19 Adriana Ieinjse de Priester
B: 1760
D:

20 Jan Matthysse
B:
M:
D:

21 Debora Jobse
B:
D:

22 Peter Van Der Vate
B:
M
D:

23 Sophia De Meulmeester
B:
M:
D:

24 Joost (Joosse) DE Voogd
B:
E:
M:
D:

25 Janna (Johanna) Langebeke
B:
M:
D:

26 Cornelis Meijers
B:
M:
D

27 Johanna Catharina De Groot
B:
D:

28 Leyn (Adriaanse) Jobse
B:
M:
D

29 Cornelia Smeerdyk
B:
D:

3C Jan (Joosse) De Voogd
B:
M
D:

3· Geertje Louwerse Pierens
B:
D:

Appendix B

Favorite Sayings of Joseph Janse

And here's to the men [and women] of my own breed, good or bitter bad as they might be, at least they hear the things I hear, and see the things I see.

Kipling

I am a doctor of chiropractic no more – but incidentally no less.

Ah, great it is to believe the dream as we stand in youth by the starry stream; but a greater thing is to fight life through and say at the end, the dream is true.

Edwin Markham

Hold fast to dreams, for if dreams die life is a broken winged bird that cannot fly.

Langston Hughes

The greatest of all tragedies is that of ingratitude.

Most powerful is he who has himself in his own power.

Lucius Annaeus Seneca

Straight from the mighty bow this truth is driven,
They fail and they alone who have not striven.

Clarence Umery

Set not a side the ancient landmarks which thy fathers have set up.
Proverbs 22:28

Whatever you think that you can do, or dream you can, begin it.
Boldness has genius, power and magic in it.
Goethe

But all the while a sort of whim
Persistently remained with him,
Half admirable, half absurd
To keep his word, to keep his word.

No snowflake ever feels responsible for a whole avalanche
Attributed to Voltaire

Each of us is part of the problem or part of the answer.

No one can make you feel inferior without your consent.
Eleanor Roosevelt

Yesterday is a cancelled check; tomorrow is a promissory note;
Today is the only cash you have on hand; spend it wisely.
Kay Lyons

Without the strength of a personal commitment, your experience of others is at most aesthetic and benign.

How can you expect to keep your powers of hearing when you never want to listen?

Thank God a man can grow
He is not bound with earthward gaze to creep along the ground
Tho his beginnings be but poor and low
Thank God a man can grow!

The fire upon his altars may burn dim,
The torch he lighted may in darkness fail,
And nothing to rekindle it avail...
Yet high beyond his dull horizon's rim,
Arcturus and the Pleiades beckon him.

Florence Earle Coates

A MAN!
O for a living man to lead!
That will not babble when we bleed;
O for the silent doer of the deed!
One that is happy in his height;
And one that, in a nation's night,
Hath solitary certitude of light!
Sirs, not with battle ill-begun
We charge you, not with fields unwon
Nor headlong deaths against the darkened gun;
But with a lightness worse than dread;
That you but laughed, who should have led,
And tripped like dancers amid all our dead.
You for no failure we impeach,
Nor for those bodies in the breach,
But for a deeper shallowness of speech.
When every cheek was hot with shame,
When we demanded words of flame,
O ye were busy but to shift the blame!
No man of us but clenched his hand,
No brow but burned us with a brand,
You! you alone were slow to understand
O for a living man to lead!
That will not babble when we bleed;
O for the silent doer of the deed!

Stephen Phillips 1864–1915

Better be a diamond with a flaw than a pebble without one.
English Proverb

331

Every life is unsatisfactory until its owner has made up his mind what he wants to do with it.

The world steps aside to let any man pass who knows whither he is going.

David Starr Jordan

With ordinary talent and extraordinary perseverance, all things are attainable.

Thomas Foxwell Buxton

He who would build a productive life must cherish the shortest snatches of time, for therein lies opportunity.

The most difficult part of getting to the top of the ladder is getting through the crowd at the bottom

William Arthur Ward

It's not the hours you put into your work that count as much as the work you put into your hours.

The Parish Priest of Asterly
Climbed up in a high church steeple,
To be near God, so that he might
Hand his word down to the people.

And in sermon script he daily wrote
What he thought was sent from heaven,
And handed it down on the people's heads,
Two times one day in seven.

In his day, God said, 'Come down and die'
And he cried from out the steeple,
"Where are thou, Lord, and the Lord replied,
'Down here among the people.

William Croswell Doane

332

To become free and responsible, for this alone was man created.

Taken from a paper written by Janse titled "The Rise and Why of Communism in China." But he exerted it from the text, "*The Third Force in China*" by Carsun Chang.

Over 2000 years, Mencius, the illustrious follower of Confucius recounted the following incident. There was a boy who sang:

> When the water of Tsang-lang is clear
> It serves to wash the strings of my cap:
> When the water of Tsang-lang is muddy
> It serves to wash my feet.

Whereupon Confucius remarked; "Do you hear what he sings my children? When the water is clear he washes his cap strings in it, when it is muddy he washes his feet in it. The difference in the use is brought upon the water itself.

Watch your thoughts, they become words; watch your words, they become actions; watch your actions, they become habits; watch your habits, they become character; watch your character, for it becomes your destiny.

To Teach—to quicken the mind with an understanding of the new and an appreciation for the old. To build within young hearts lofty ideals and bulwarks of courage and to create for those who are weak a strength of faith and belief. To prompt a child to happiness. To stimulate a youth to effort, to quicken the love of a parent and to hearten the spirit of the aged—that is my calling—that is my joy.

I would much rather be involved in seeking an answer than to provoke another cause.

I dream't death came, the other night,
And Heaven's gate opened wide.
An angel with a halo bright
Ushered me inside.

And there, to my astonishment,
Stood folks I'd judged and labeled
As "quite unfit," "of little worth,"
And "spiritually disabled."

Indignant words rose to my lips,
But never were set free,
For every face showed stunned surprise,
Not one expected me!

Len Dean

They do me wrong who say I come no more
When once I knock and fail to find you in;
For every day I stand outside your door
And bid you wake and rise, to fight and win.

Weep not o'er precious chances past,
Wail not o'er golden ages on the wane,
Each night I burn the records of the day,
At sunrise every soul is born again.

Walter Malone

The heights by great men reached and kept,
Were not attained by sudden flight;
But they, while their companions slept,
Were toiling upwards in the night.

Henry Wadsworth Longfellow

334

And the peasant was asked by the King, "If you knew that to-morrow you were to die, what would you choose to do the remainder of your life"? Without hesitancy and looking down on to the freshly turned earth of his plow, the peasant simply answered "Good King, I would choose to keep on plowing." That indeed is greatness.

> Work-Thank God for the might of it,
> The ardor, the urge, the delight of it.
> Work the soarings from the heart's desire,
> Setting the brain and the soul on fire.
> Oh what is so good as the heat of it,
> And what is so glad as the beat of it.
>
> Work-Thank God for the pride of it,
> For the beautiful, conquering tide of it.
> Work-Thank God for the peace of it.
> For the terrible keen swift race of it.
> Oh What is so good as the pain of it,
> And what is so great as the gain of it,
> And what is so cruel as the goad of it,
> Forcing us on thru the rugged road.
> Work-Thank God for the swing of it,
> For the clamoring, hammering ring of it.
>
> *Angela Morgan*

On the day of my uncle's retirement my aunt received a sympathy card from a group of friends. She was puzzled until she noted that every signer was the wife of a man who had already retired.

Progress is not a precipitation. It is the conscience of vision—laborious, arduous work—dedication—courage—and the willingness of people to become involved.

An organization is a mosaic—it is the profile of many contributions. The pattern is never a singularity—it is the fitting and shaping of many pieces.

My approach to this discipline is based on the concept that knowledge is never static, but that it is vibrant and kaleidoscopic, ever evidencing new patterns, combinations and conjugations. Always there is the need for reevaluation and the formulating of more efficient and effective methods of application.

Success, happiness are not matters of luck—they are the consequence of self-sovereignty. They cannot be borrowed nor plagiarized.

"Happiness is to be cultivated at your own fireside and not in the mansions of others."

Ibsen

Happiness is being proud of what you are, and wanting what you have.

Today so many have suffered from the poverty of too much and so they are afflicted with the anemia of indolence.

We are haunted by the ideal life; and it is because we have within us the beginning and the possibility of it.

Nothing is too marvelous to be true. All that man can envision may become a reality.

What men call luck is the prerogative of gallant souls—the fealty life pays for its gallant kings.

Man's business is to work – to surmount difficulties, to endure hardships, to solve problems, to overcome the inertia of his own nature; to turn chaos into cosmos by the aid of system –this is to live.

In character, in manners, in style, in all things, the supreme excellence is simplicity, and sincerity is the main elegance.

Nothing in the world can take the place of persistence. Talent will not; nothing is more common than unsuccessful men with talent. Genius will not; unrewarded genius is almost a proverb. Education will not; the world is full of educated derelicts. Persistence and determination alone are omnipotent, the slogan "Press on' has solved and always will solve the problems of the human race.

Calvin Coolidge

A profession is an occupation for which the necessary preliminary training is intellectual in character, involving knowledge and to some extent learning, as distinguished from mere skill. It is an occupation which is pursued largely for others and not merely for one's self. It is an occupation in which the amount of financial returns is not the accepted measure of success.

Be your own person, do not seek to live in imitation or plagiarism

Yes, a profession must destroy itself before others can destroy it.

Become involved in the concerns and responsibilities of the profession. Don't be a freeloader.

Be a person of promise. Don't be a cynic. Dabbling in negativisms is a pathological conduct and comprises the 'dry rot' of happiness, not only for yourself, but for those who depend upon you.

Be respectful of all reputable health care measures, systems and professions. No single formula indexes the total answer.

Don't waste your time, your talents and your wherewith in ideological and conceptual bickering. There is no such a quantum as a complete or perfect therapy.

Don't lend yourself to self-concern, egocentricity or envy. Success and happiness are not a bequest nor an inheritance. They are the consequence of positive self-actualization.

Don't pursue happiness, design and conjugate it through your own doing. Never forget happiness is what you are and wanting what you have and be certain we, in chiropractic, have so much.

Dag Hammerskjold, former Secretary General of the United Nations, at the conclusion of his writings entitled "Markings" commits himself as follows:
"For all that has been, thanks! For all that will be, yes!
If the center does not hold, things soon fall apart."

Other quotes from the "Markings" include:
On the bookshelf of life, God has a useful work of reference, always at hand but seldom consulted.

Life only demands from you the strength you possess. Only one feat is possible—not to have run away.

The degree of our anxiety is the measure of our distance from God.

To be truly human borders on the divine.

God is to be our Father, yet we are far from being fathers to our own children. We presume to have insight into divine things, and yet we neglect as unworthy of notice those human relations which are a key to the divine.   *B.H. Roberts/Friedrich Froebel*

What is the greatest surprise? That of man who finds God within himself.

Amado Nervo

It is difficult to make a man miserable while he feels he is worthy of himself and claims kindred to the great God who made him.
Abraham Lincoln

Quoting from Boyd's textbook on Pathology:

"Pathology begins as dysfunction. Disease must have a beginning."

A fanatic is one who triples his speed after he has lost his direction.

Appendix C

Sentinel Talks & Papers

This appendix has been created to capture and share some of the more significant talks and papers of Dr. Joseph Janse. These notable works are presented in their unedited form.

I Am A Chiropractor
Dr. Joseph Janse

National College of Chiropractic Journal, 1943
National Chiropractic Journal, March, 1945

Mine is a great and glorious calling. I have been entrusted with the greatest single therapeutic principle that has come to the knowledge and understanding of man. Upon my shoulders rests the responsibility of acquainting mankind with the profound biological truth that in human health and integrity the nervous system reigns supreme and that all physical, mental, and even spiritual capacities are acquired and fulfilled through its mediations.

As a chiropractor, I represent the principle of thought that expresses belief that disease primarily is the inevitable result of dysfunction as induced by a disturbance of the nervous system.

I am of that school of human biology that pioneered the concept that function is dependent on form; that the secrets of health and disease lie in the science of structural anatomy—its integrity or distortion. Life and health reside in the freedom and ease of all joint movement and support—the axiom upon which the essential portion of our therapy is founded.

It was through the work of my profession that the scientific world's belated attentions were attracted to the pertinent fact that all body function relates intimately to the proprioceptive mechanism—the neurology of joints, muscles, posture, and body balance; and any disturbance of the same will rupture the synchronized relationship between the periphery and the viscera, giving rise to disrelated effort in the physiology of each. Then, augmented by other factors such as malnutrition, infection, etc., the pathological changes as described by Pavlow set in and the common symptoms of organic disease are expressed.

As a chiropractor, I find satisfaction in knowing that I am part of that group which introduced into the field of therapeutic thought the basic and primary truth that functional disorder precedes organic alteration in the progress of disease. That the old static idea, of the early pathologists, that no disease exists unless it can be demonstrated as some form of tissue change is as inimical in good therapy as it is obsolete.

As a result of this brilliant contribution, honest therapeutic thinking has again been directed to the realization that prevention, rather than cure, is the doctor's greatest duty and should represent his most conscientious effort.

I am a chiropractor and, as such, I draw the world's attention to the fact that throughout nature the principle of interdependency motivates all biological evolution and integrity. It is with enthusiastic pride that I point to the idea that "essentially there is no such phenomenon in human biology as localization of effect. Throughout the science of neuro-physiology one lesson stands paramount, namely, stimulus cannot be lent to the nervous system at any possible point without its ramifying and spreading in manifold directions to influence, either beneficially or inimically, other parts and organs of the body.

Therefore, with justified disdain; my profession frowns upon the promiscuous practice of interventive therapy.

My profession, Chiropractic, maintains the principle that the body is a great deal more than the sum of its parts. What a dynamic thought!

The capacities and potentials of the human organism are far greater in scope than the simple sum of brain, heart, liver, and kidney function. As a chiropractor, I am a vitalist and as such I look upon man not merely as a mass of correlated protoplasm but as a being capable of intellectual, moral, and spiritual exploration. Dr. Ivy—head of the department of physiology, Northwestern Medical College, sensed this responsible truth when in one of his texts he wrote "Anyone who attempts to serve as a doctor, purely as a scientist, will certainly fail. As a chiropractor I take honest delight in knowing that through the teachings of my profession, society has become cognizant of the principle that correlates mental and physical phenomena. In other words, they are dove-tailed in their final expression. Psychological aspects do not reside nor express themselves independent of organic activities or vice versa. Today, the student of human biology frankly expounds the fact that the manner in which one thinks, feels, and emotionalizes greatly influences organic function. We now definitely know that such organs as the heart, stomach, intestines, and even the eyes can become disturbed by emotional bouts and temperamental escapades or melancholic inhibitions. On the other hand, it is just as obvious that disturbances of the organs and structures of the body will frequently mirror themselves in certain mental and emotional quirks. And thus the science of psycho-somatic or somato-phychic phenomena fond its inception in the principles of chiropractic.

The chiropractor has kept alive the ancient wisdom that nature heals, the doctor at times but serves to mediate the agent. And, as a chiropractor, I am the advocate of the idea that the universal tendency of all organic existence is toward health. Health is spontaneous—it is the legitimate and inevitable result of the normal powers and properties of the living body and its always obtained where the laws and proper conditions of life are observed. As William James said "Health is the undeviating expression of all life, always concomitant where the conditions natural to the organism are undisturbed."

I am a chiropractor and shall continue to be one because in the accumulated experiences and observations of the years the clinical merit of this science and art has been fully revealed to me. Where ever I go and to whoever I speak the therapeutic qualities of chiropractic are to be observed and acclaimed with enthusiasm.

Throughout the country the chiropractor stands as a doctor of repute and importance. His working hours are long and filled, his services are in great demand. And to all this must be added the fact that the majority of his patients are those who failed to gain relief elsewhere. His reputation comes from his cure of the incurable. There is no profession or human activity that can boast of greater service rendered.

Yes, I am a chiropractor—humble in my sense of responsibility, grateful for the advantages that have come to me through my profession. As a chiropractor I am a doctor committed to everything that is sound and logical in content, honest and decent in relation. It is my covenant to my profession to be tolerant to the views and efforts of all honest men, to be ambitious in the desire to intellectually forge ahead, ever seeking to improve, ever striving to learn, and above all to move among men with dignity, sincerity and without prejudice. Then and only then will anyone be worthy of saying I am a Chiropractor.

The Basic Science Issue in Chiropractic Education
Dr. Joseph Janse, Secretary of the
National Council on Education
Annual Meeting of the Association of
Basic Science Boards of America
12 February 1951
Printed in the March and April (1951) issues of the Journal of the National Chiropractic Association

Gentleman, this is indeed a gratifying opportunity. In behalf of the Council on Education to thank you. We are glad to have the opportunity to present our appraisal of the basic science program. In preparing this paper I have consulted a number of the leading personalities of the educational fraternity of our profession. Hence the opinions expressed are not those of a single individual, but represent a cross section of attitudes of members of our profession.

344

It has been my happy privilege to attend these constructive meetings during the last three years, at the personal invitation of Dr. Orin Madison, a man whose sincere interest in the work of this association commands the respect of all who know him.

At these meetings I have sensed a laudable impartiality toward all of the professions of healing. We who have been privileged to meet with you have followed your deliberations and discussions with great interest and our observations have led us to the conviction that this group is inspired by tolerance, sincerity and honesty of intent. This knowledge is most gratifying to the chiropractic profession for reasons which you will understand. Because of this conviction I shall take the liberty of speaking frankly and to the point.

Careful scrutiny of the basic science issue in chiropractic education discloses a number of factors each of which I would like to discuss separately, hoping that by this procedure the ambiguity that now surrounds the whole matter may be brought to a proper understanding. These factors may be designated and listed in the following order:

1—An appraisal of the early history of basic science legislation as it is related to the chiropractic profession.

2—The lack of uniformity in basic science enactments and the difficulties this presented.

3—The basic difference between the clinical methods of chiropractic and other healing professions and how it reflects in the basic science picture.

4—The limitations imposed upon the chiropractic profession and the difficulties they impose upon chiropractic education.

5—The inherent difficulty that confronts the chiropractic profession in qualifying its candidates for basic science boards.

6—Suggestions and recommendations that might mitigate certain elements of severity.

Point I

An appraisal of the early history of basic science legislation as it related to the chiropractic profession and the reaction of the chiropractic profession to the basic science proposition.

At a number of these meetings I have heard the statement that the creation of the basic science program and the consequent legislative enactments were not of your making. In fact there were several times when it was frankly stated here, that the primary impetus behind the basic science movement was the intent of organized medicine to block the growth of so-called "irregular groups," by creating compulsory standards of examination that, it was hoped, would exceed the educational capacities of these groups. It is a generally conceded and well known fact that basic science legislation was initiated and sponsored by organized medicine. In this effort regular medicine based its reason for sponsorship upon the premise that the public must be safeguarded from incompetents.

Whether such was the genuine intent or but the smoke screen from behind which the chiropractors and osteopaths could be hampered and subjugated is a moot question that has no place in this discussion. However, in verification of these insinuations, I would like to read to you an excerpt from an article written by Dr. Walter L. Bierring, of Des Moines, Iowa, the secretary of the Federation of State Medical Boards of the United States entitled, "An Analysis of Basic Science Laws" and appearing in the AMA journal, March 15, 1948:

> "As previously stated the character of the examination questions in the different basic sciences has undergone remarkable changes assuming more and more the type adaptable for licensure examination, especially that of the practice of medicine. The evident original purpose of enacting basic science laws as a pre-requisite for licensure in the healing arts was to exclude chiropractors and other inadequately trained practitioners from being admitted to licensure."

This is but one of several examples that could be cited and referred to. Thus we see that one of the primary motives for the initiating of the basic science program was not without some degree of bias and ulterior intent on the part of a strongly organized majority against a rather helpless minority. Regardless how justified this action might have appeared to some, its intent was rather selfish and somewhat tyrannical and it must be admitted it caused at first, much concern and resentment among both the osteopaths and chiropractors, who came to look upon the program with suspicion and misgiving.

Prejudiced and unethical tactics were resorted to on both sides, which in my opinion, was as unbecoming to one as to the other. Often I have wondered in observing the great and at times vindictive struggle between the healing professions, whether it isn't true that "the pot is calling the kettle black." One is inclined to ask: "Where is the altruism that should inspire the conduct of those groups that follow the Oath of Hippocrates—be they allopaths, osteopaths, or chiropractors." Or is that question so naïve that it appears ridiculous in this modern age of intellectual sophistry? However, I would like it to be clearly understood that the chiropractic profession is not opposed in any unbiased method of procedure that will protect the public health, and further that we agree that all doctors should be made to demonstrate an adequate knowledge of the fundamental or basic biological science in order to secure a license to practice. What we have disagreed with in the past is the perversion of such a purported method.

Point II

The confusion created by the lack of uniformity in basic science enactments.

Conceived in such a complexity of intent and policy the basic science program resulted in the creation of a widely divergent set of basic science laws in some 18 states and the territory of Alaska. This portrays itself in many phases so that the basic science setup throughout the country is very unwieldy, inflexible and incongruous and results in comprising all who are confronted with the necessity of coping with them.

Unfortunately in several states where the political control of organized medicine predominated the resultant basic science boards were definitely brought under allopathic control. Probably the extreme example of this was in the State of Washington. Until recently, it was the openly avowed intent of this board to eliminate the chiropractic candidates. In fact, a number of years ago, one of the members of the board in court and under oath, flatly admitted this intent. I cite this example not in an attitude of resentment but simply in explanation of why you might have encountered animosity on the part of some of the members of the chiropractic profession. I am happy to acknowledge that there are increasing evidences that the Washington situation is being corrected.

In other states the basic science legislation instituted provided for an examining board consisting of a representation of each of the healing groups and two or more college professors. Examples of such a setup are South Dakota, Minnesota, Oklahoma and Colorado. On the whole from our standpoint these boards have been the most suitable for and sympathetic to the profession's problems.

Still other states have basic science boards whose personnel consist of one or two medical men and a number of college professors who are not of the healing profession. As to whether these medical men, motivated by bias, influenced the other members of the boards is a question which cannot be fully answered and is now probably of very little consequence. Yet, unfortunately, it has, in the past, been the subject of much discussion. The greater number of basic science board members as we now are professors teaching basic science subjects. It is not exceptional, but actually quite usual, that these people are members of the faculty of medical schools. This has been another basis for suspicion and misunderstanding. I believe that all of you will grant that the attitude toward chiropractic as ordinarily encountered in the average medical school, or in that college primarily occupied in educating pre-medical students has not always been sympathetic, and this knowledge you will admit might justify the suspicion. Thus there has been the fear that this attitude might have influenced the basic science board members to be somewhat hypercritical of the chiropractic situation. This skepticism paralleled by the unreasoned resistance of certain chiropractic groups presented but another barrier to understanding and co-operation.

Except in the states of Connecticut and Washington the applicant does not have to declare his school of practice. Theoretically he is supposed to remain fully anonymous. However, over the years the medical profession has seen fit to publish comparative statistics on basic science examinations, usually to attempt to show that the basic science laws are eliminating chiropractic and osteopathic applicants because of incompetence. It has often been asked by certain elements in our profession how it is that the medical profession has such ready access to such information concerning those taking the boards. Now, gentlemen, you might say, are you and your associates not placing too much emphasis upon these alleged causes of suspicion? I hardly think so because these allegations are constantly drawn to our attention as evidence upon which we should fight the basic science program without reservation or exception. Those of us who are trying to co-operate have nothing to answer these accusations with except a declaration of our good faith in the members of the boards. Statements such as Dr. Bierring's leave us defenseless in the face of chiropractic skepticism. These are the issues that have caused the great majority of the chiropractic profession to express antagonism toward basic science boards and their personnel.

These, gentlemen, are not my personal interpretations of the matter. Whether you have been aware of them or not, these are the objective facts of a situation that has been thrust upon you and the chiropractic profession. To say that these facts and circumstances do not exist and are not charged with the dynamics of tense feelings would simply be an evasion of the issue. Who is at fault? That is a question the answer to which I am afraid we may not agree upon. Personally, I would attribute it to the pressures arising from the misunderstandings on both sides and possible from the evident ulterior motives which led to the movement for the enactment of basic science laws. However, what has transpired pro or con, in the past, is much less significant than what is the situation we now face, and what it may be in the future. Mistakes were made some of intent, others out of misconception. I would say that it is water over the dam. To the young and sincere student in the chiropractic college the question of the future is much more paramount, and I feel our attentions might well be concentrated on him. In order to assure him the future he deserves and anticipates, there are those of us in the chiropractic profession who have striven to mitigate and eventually dissipate much prejudice, and believe me, gentlemen, it has not been an easy task. We have had to overcome the resistance of apprehension within our own ranks and concurrently merit and gain your confidence and co-operation.

Point III

The basic difference between the professional and clinical aims of chiropractic and other healing professions and how it reflects in the basic science picture.

Now that we have brought the skeletons out of the closet and exposed them, to view the issue as it presents itself today. Briefly, let me draw your attentions to the comparative therapeutic and clinical aims of the three major healing groups. I shall for the sake of brevity consider allopathy and osteopathy together because I am certain that it is obvious to all that the latter has come to parallel in many respects the clinical methods of the former. In contrast, the chiropractic profession has definitely committed itself to the non-medical therapies, with manipulation as its major approach. It is not the desire, nor the intent of the chiropractic profession to invade the field of medicine and surgery. Hence the clinical objectives of the doctor of chiropractic are definite and precise. His methods are unique and effective in a wide range of conditions, primarily of a functional nature in both chronic and acute disease states. And of course, it is common knowledge that our profession restricts itself to this field. Inasmuch as the approach to the problem of disease is distinctly different, emphasis of study in certain aspects of the basic science varies from that required in medical and osteopathic education. This is especially true of bacteriology and hence a distinctly different conceptual approach is made. It is rather difficult to interest a chiropractic student in the detailed information relating to parasitology, venereal infections and the tropical diseases, and the related medical therapeutic control, since such is outside his objective and prerogative. He feels that all that should concern him is a clear understanding of the differential diagnosis of these conditions so that they may be treated accordingly or referred for other attention. Today, unfortunately, the subject of

350

public health has become primarily a science and process of effecting artificial immunization. And however beneficial some people may think this to be it is not a part of chiropractic practice and so the question arises: Why should the chiropractic student learn all there is to know about the methods that are employed in the preparation of a vaccine or the exact procedures involved in the standardizing of the same?

It is not the practice or intent of the chiropractor to treat by medical prescription or the usage of antibodies, it is offensive to him to rationalize the necessity of knowing the formulas of the sulfonamides or the manner of effect of penicillin and streptomyocin simply because questions demanding this information appear on basic science examinations. It represents a situation both unfair and unjust to the chiropractic applicant. We do not object to qualifying by examination in any of their preclinical or diagnostic aspects, but all clinical and therapeutic reference should be completely avoided.

Please be aware, gentlemen, that such is said not in criticism of you or anyone else. It is but an attempt to explain to you that at times the tendency to permit orthodox allopathic concept to overlap into the basic science questions is not uncommon and rather readily indulged in without volitional intent. And of course such obviously constitutes a hazard to the chiropractic examinee. Thus we must conclude that the chiropractic student is, at times, confronted with a paradox of basic science examination "musts" and clinical "thou shalt nots." I am certain that you will agree with me that it is quite disturbing and uninteresting to study the clinical methods of another school of therapy just to qualify for a basic science examination.

Point IV

Limitations imposed on the chiropractic profession and the difficulties imposed on chiropractic education.

Allow me to present still another problem that confronts us in the chiropractic education and which mirrors its effects in basic science qualifications. As all of you know, chiropractors and chiropractic institutions are definitely assigned certain diagnostic and clinical privileges. Yet they are frequently denied access to the means so necessary to make them effective. For instance, isn't it often true that the usage of state laboratories and other public health facilities are denied the doctor of chiropractic, simply because they are under the control of state medical functionaries? There are those that would deny us of the chiropractic profession diagnostic radiology as well as laboratory diagnosis. In some of our colleges we encounter almost insurmountable difficulty in obtaining cadavers for the teaching of anatomy by human dissection. We are not allowed to do autopsies, yet we are required to know all about the gross pathologies revealed through autopsy studies. We do not have access to autopsy, biopsy, surgical and pathological laboratory to enable us to obtain the necessary materials for the preparation of slides for proper microscopic study, yet it is fully expected of our students to know as much about the entire process as the medical student. In many jurisdictions we are denied the diagnosis and treatment of the infectious diseases but in qualifying for practice we are required to know all about the Weil-Felix Reaction Test, etc. As you see, gentlemen, it is a state whereby parity of qualification is demanded without parity of privilege. If society feels that the doctor of chiropractic, in order to practice his method, should qualify at parity with the medical practitioner, society should at least afford the chiropractic profession the right to utilize those agencies, institutions and facilities so necessary to effectively accomplish this. One is prompted to ask the question: Is it proper that organized medicine should control and regulate all public health facilities and public institutions of healing, notwithstanding the fact that they so often are fully supported by the taxpayers' money and public donations?

Of course, gentlemen, you have a full right to say that is your profession's problem and I might say that we have been diligently occupied in solving it. Unfortunately, we haven't received too much encouragement or assistance from these concerned. We of the profession are also cognizant that this situation cannot be corrected at one effort. First, it has been a tremendous task to obtain the cooperation of certain elements of our own profession. Groups and people of influence who cannot understand and see why the program of qualification for medical graduates with unlimited privileges should be considered a fair requirement of the chiropractic graduates of definitely limited privileges. Then we also have had the grave problem of short-term courses to overcome. Finally it was not always too easy to procure entry to the confidence and understanding of you people who after all are the final peers in the basic science issue.

Point V

The inherent difficulty that confronts the chiropractic educator in qualifying candidates for Basic Science Boards.

To complete our interpretation of this basic science issue in chiropractic education there is still another matter that poses a problem. Except in seven states chiropractic statutes require only a high school education or its proper equivalent for entrance into a chiropractic college. Furthermore, the limitations of professional privileges offered to the chiropractor make it rather difficult for us to limit matriculation to those who have pre-professional college training. Hence we find that in our four-year chiropractic course we are compelled not only to cover the material contained in the basic science division of the curricula of the average medical or osteopathic school, but we find it imperative to lend time and effort to the teaching of such pre-professional subjects as physics, inorganic chemistry, general bacteriology, comparative anatomy, fundamentals of physiology and psychology, as well as public health. Thus the exigency of our process of education is somewhat different and at times severely challenging. So we find that it is necessary to condition a chiropractic student, within four years, to meet in scholastic competition with a hand-picked medical student of from six to eight years of training. And inasmuch as I have had a little something to do with this processing of our young people, I must say, with pardonable pride, that many of them have done a pretty good job under rather severe odds and handicaps. I'll say this, gentlemen, one must admire the stamina and effort that many of our students have expended, restricted as their backgrounds have been, in the laudable desire to meet the demands of your examinations.

Here again you might be prompted to ask a very proper question. Why don't your colleges raise their entrance requirements? I am certain that within a few years it may come to that. However, realistically it must be realized that chiropractic as a restricted profession of healing is going to find it somewhat difficult in attracting sufficient students if the pre-professional demands are as extensive as they are in medicine and osteopathy.

This, then, is the basic science picture as we of the chiropractic profession view it. We are aware, gentlemen, that our problem is not your moral concern or responsibility. We are also duly cognizant of the fact that much of the bitterness of feeling that was developed within chiropractic toward the basic science program is certainly not of your making and that some of it found its nidus in the skepticism of our own people. We are not unmindful that you have inherited not only a very unwieldy set of basic science laws, whose inconsistencies make it difficult for you to effect an integrated and uniform administration, but you have also inherited the pressures of competitive healing groups, whose demands upon you may at times have placed you in the middle. Let me say that we are not ungrateful for your consideration of the particular problem we present. We are aware of your sincerity and the integrity of your intent. We know that you are anxious to discharge your duties with a proper attitude to all concerned. We know that your work is often a thankless one, charged with headaches and tedious hours of endeavor without remuneration. We know that you maintain your positions with admirable concern for their civic significance. Believe me, such commands our admiration. These considerations, gentlemen, prompt us to come to you with our problem. Possibly in the hope that you might be able to help us, and possibly in the anticipation that some of the tension that has been built around the basic science issue in our profession might be mitigated. And that out of this may arise an added incentive on the part of all to seek an improvement of the situation.

Point VI

As a concluding phase of this paper I am going to venture a few suggestions that we of the chiropractic profession feel merit careful study and if possible be instituted. Let me say that they are but suggestions, certainly not instructions. We feel that they are not unworthy, that in no way would they compromise your positions but would make your examinations and interboard relations definitely less onerous for the chiropractic examinee. These suggestions may be grouped as follows:

Group A. Those relating to the type of questions in the basic science subjects proper.
1. In the subject of chemistry it is suggested that all questions be confined to the fundamental knowledges of biochemistry and questions be avoided that:
   (a) pertain to qualitative and quantitative analysis.
   (b) pertain to the formulae, usage and toxicology of drugs and medicines.
   (c) pertain to experiments that are limited to pharmaceutical laboratories.
   (d) pertain to special chemical tests reported in restricted literature or are still in the experimental phase.
2. In the subject of public health questions relating to allopathic preventative medicine should be avoided. The following subjects and procedures certainly fall within that category:
   (a) the differential usage of vaccines, sera, toxins and antitoxins, the manner in which they are prepared, employed, and their reactions, their clinical control and their mechanism of immunization.
   (b) advanced methods of laboratory diagnosis and medical control of tropical diseases.
   (c) the treatment of certain contagious and communicable diseases by allopathic measures.
   (d) the detailed explanation of certain laboratory diagnosis tests that relate to uncommon infective and parasitic diseases.
3. In the subject of physiology it is doubtful whether it is beneficial to ask questions that involve detailed explanations in relation to:
   (a) experimentations conducted on laboratory animals, via vivisection.

355

(b) the usage of elaborate experimental instruments, used only in physiological laboratories of great research centers.

(c) questions relating to recent experimentations in physiology, the reports and literature on which are contained in periodicals commonly only available to medical students.

(d) questions relating to pet theories and concepts of the examiner.

4. In the subject of pathology it has been found that the questions oft times are almost exclusively and unfairly limited to:

(a) parasitology

(b) biopsy and autopsy procedures and findings.

(c) surgical procedures and findings.

(d) rare and special pathological states

(e) involved staining and preparation procedures of pathological tissue.

(f) laboratory tests in relation to given pathologies, which can only be performed in the most complete pathological laboratory.

5. The fundamentals of bacteriology are frequently sacrificed for involved questions in:

(a) mycology and parasitology.

(b) special laboratory procedures in bacteriology, mycology and parasitology that are and can only be performed in laboratories supported by tremendous resources from state and government.

(c) the typing of viruses and their pathological effects on bacteria, viruses and protozoa and the resultant altered pathological picture.

Group B. Suggestions relating to possible improvements in the mechanism and administration of basic science laws.

1. Whenever possible increase the privileges of legitimate and proper reciprocity.

2. Whenever possible the ruling should be that when an examinee passes four out of the six, or three out of the five subjects, he may be privileged to retake, within the same year,

356

the subjects that he failed, without having to repeat the ones passed.

3. If at all possible acquaint the examinees with their results somewhat sooner, so that they may go about the business of preparing for their professional boards, or for their retakes.

4. In grading it is possible to be too arbitrary. For example if 75% is passing, an examinee who makes 74% should merit 75. I simply ask the question: Who can always grade that close?

5. In some of the states where but one day is permitted for examinations the pressure of the time element is often disconcerting to the examinee.

6. In the process of grading, not only should there be an evaluation of the technical knowledge required but also an evaluation of the "common sense" and general grasp of the subject displayed.

7. Make the questions of past examinations available as soon as is possible.

8. Carefully check the attitudes, personal prejudices and qualifications of the readers assigned to grade the papers.
   It has come to our attention that senior students in medical colleges have been used to grade papers.
   Our applicants cannot be blamed if they feel uneasy that their fate lies in such possibly biased hands.

9. A continuation of the effort you have initiated to standardize basic science laws and examinations.
   (a) Duly aware of the fact that this will require years of effort.

10. A continuation of the effort to make the examinations as fair, as unbiased and as considerate of the young men and women who take them as is possible.

Gentlemen, this has been a long paper. I hope that its contents have not been distasteful. Whatever has been intimated or suggested has been done, I hope, with a feeling of deference. The issue and problem is not an easy one. Its solution cannot be immediate and complete. We of the Council on Education of the National Chiropractic Association are aware that these matters cannot be satisfactorily answered all at once. We are not asking you to do the impossible. We have come to you in honesty and we stand ready to co-operate and assist wherever possible. We know that in many respects your hands are tied and that some of the compromising circumstances that exist can only be mitigated by legislative amendment or state attorney's decision. Progress in social, professional and educational fields is always difficult to attain. It demands tremendous sacrifice of personal time and effort without recompense. The educator, the individual who qualifies others for the professions is the "forgotten man" in our society. The ideals and integrity that the educator must possess do not "pay off" very handsomely. Yet, we are compelled to persist. Where it is possible to make an improvement, the same must be done. Progress is a mosaic of innumerable contribution improvements. Here a little and there a little. Day in and day out the quest goes on. Every measure helps. The dissipation of small problems eventually leads to the crumbling of the large ones. Progress is the embodiment of repeated effort. You will say that I am an addicted idealist. I am, gentleman, but may I counter by saying that there is no greater morality than that of attempting to support social, educational and professional progress.

We of the chiropractic profession solicit that you grant us a continuation of the privilege to work with you. Permit us to seek your counsel. May we seek your understanding and patience? Help us to find the proper direction of self-improvement. We wish to afford the young man and woman who come under our guidance the assurance of equal rights, parity of consideration and the full privileges of professional status. We recognize the fact that there is much to overcome. Professional education in general needs to experience the warmth of greater tolerance and understanding, idealism and the morality of culture and human kindness and probably a little less pedantic severity and prudery. The doctor today is so saturated with the materialism of his business that human values mean little. As a biologist and as a technician of therapy, he represents a proficiency that is almost frightening but as a doctor and as a human being he is

358

frequently found wanting. Andrew J. Ivy, dean of the School of medicine, University of Illinois, in his manual the "Physiology of Symptoms," wrote the following:

"It is more important to know what kind of a patient has a disease than to now what kind of a disease the patient has."

Every student should understand that any physician who practices medicine solely as a scientist will fail. One of the most important services of a good physician is the bringing of hope and cheer, even in cases where he cannot effect a cure; thus the physician must combine scientific acumen with much of the "milk of human kindness" in his profession.

In closing may I read a definition of a profession.

"A profession is an occupation for which the necessary preliminary training is intellectual in character, involving knowledge and to some extent learning, as distinguished from mere skill.

"It is an occupation which is pursued largely for others and not merely for one's self. It is an occupation in which the amount of financial returns is not the accepted measure of success."

Let's Stop Fighting Windmills
J. Janse, D.C.

The ACA Journal of Chiropractic, May 1966

For twenty-seven years I have been privileged to function in chiropractic education. Such opportunity and responsibility have provided me with a broad spectrum of experience and observation. My duties have taken me all over the States, Canada, the British Isles, Western Europe, Africa, Australia and Japan. Always I have encountered the everlasting attempt to define chiropractic and to announce its scope of practice. Always there was the ambivalence of opinion, concept and semantics. Always there was an associated torpor of misgivings and feelings. Always there were overtones of frustration and divided conclusion leaving but little of benefit and much of detriment.

Often has it been my assignment to appear before legislative bodies, educators and lay groups. Seldom have I been asked to give specific "locked in" definition, but always explanation and interpretation.

Years ago, in my preprofessional college days, I remember so well having to study various definitions of science, of philosophy and of religion. In each instance no one definition was declared the "gospel" and always the source of reference was submitted. I remember so well the great Ralph Chamberlain in his classes stating: "Science is viable and dynamic. It is never static and inflexible. It modifies and alters, it adds and deletes with the increments of research and the complements of other sciences. Man has no right to impose the dogma of the conclusive upon any other man. Truth and fact must always be left to experience the privilege of addition." One generation has no right to enslave another.

So after twenty-seven years I still would not settle upon any single definition or scope of practice. Daniel David Palmer, Bartlett Joshua Palmer, Willard C. Carver, John Allen Howard, James Firth, Fred W. Illi and many other leading chiropractic personalities sought to submit their definitions and interpretations. If, in doing this, they wanted to contribute to the composite of understanding, then indeed their efforts were laudable. If, on the other hand, these efforts were motivated by egocentric conclusiveness and intractable unchangeableness, then indeed they would have to be rejected. Principle, concept, truth, fact, and definition have to remain unabridged. "Truth is the substance of things as they are, as they were and as they will be." It seems that we have been enslaved in the fallacy of the omnipotence of definitions rather than being receptive to the increments of knowledge.

We have for so many years been a divided and segmented people. For decades we have indulged in the practice of professional feudalism. In provincial disposition we have had our feudal sites with the moots of catechismal definitions and then attempted to function in tribal fashion. From time to time breakthroughs were attempted and realized. Gradually, communications in concept and comprehension were effected; terminologies, semantics, postulations were re-adjusted and barriers of prejudice broken down. Conferences on unity have been held as long as I can remember.

Unfortunately, the insinuations of definitions of chiropractic and scope of practice have always resulted in issues and dissensions of a magnitude far beyond any practical significance. Indeed, making issues over definitions and scope of practice is "making mountains out of mole-hills" and conducting the quixotical practice of 'fighting windmills." Believe me, we in chiropractic have no right to procrastinate our time and spend our wherewith in the inept effort to find a basis for professional unity in definitions or scope of practice. We cannot afford to dissipate our talents, potentials and resources. It is time that we differentiate between matters that are germane in progress and those that are ineffectual.

One thing that the sciences of today teach us is "nothing is more constant than change." The mathematics, the chemistry, the physics and the biology of today define themselves much differently than they did in my collegiate days. Furthermore, today, the lines of demarcation between the sciences no longer compartmentalize them. No biochemist can ignore the biologist, and no biologist can remain independent of the physicist. Today man talks about science with its branches that interrelate and of necessity maintain intercommunication. In the laboratory, the biophysicist, biochemist, biologist, and clinician all work together. And so today man has leaned to function and ideate in the atmosphere of change. This has not been a change of revolution or abdication, but the change of addition, of increment, and the modification necessitated by the findings of research.

Of late, another "unity effort" has been conducted. This is laudable. However, the usual snag of definition and scope of practice was encountered and demise of effort will be unavoidable. So let us take inventory of the past; the facts as they are; as they should be; and as common sense dictates. May I be permitted to draw attention to a number of points that might be deliberated by you:

1. Man has always sought to define and will continue to seek to define. His inherent curiosity will always prompt him to interpret. Hence, just as the pioneers of chiropractic sought

361

to provide definitions, so today there are those who are seeking to define and tomorrow there will be others attempting to lend definition to their versions. This is good because it denotes thinking, and thinking promotes progress. It becomes pathological, however, when attempt is made to surround any single definition for declaration with the halo of exclusiveness and conclusiveness. Then we chiropractors become a "locked in people," progress abates, and conviction becomes fanaticism.

2. No progress of professional education dares to limit itself to any single or restricted aspect of practice that relates to the profession in question. Education in law does not limit itself to corporate law. The undergraduate training in medicine does not limit itself to pediatrics or gerontology. Chiropractic undergraduate education must not be limited to any single concept or method, simply because a profession cannot subsist or survive on an individualized procedure. In the past, several attempts have been made and failed. A professional person should always know more than what he seeks to do. He must endeavor to function within margins of knowledge, comprehension and ability. His differential understanding should always extend beyond the scope of practice. No professional person has the right to limit his knowledge to the immediate concerns of his function and similarly none has the right to exceed the privileges of what he is poorly qualified to do.

3. In forty-seven of the fifty states the scope of chiropractic practice is exactingly determined by law. In some instances the practice of chiropractic is strong and statutorily supported and well-disciplined. The doctor of chiropractic functions without hesitancy or hamstring in fulfillment of his diagnostic and therapeutic responsibilities. In those states where statutory definitions are of a "locked in" nature the chiropractitioner is beginning to stand in compromise. His diagnostic viability is too often challenged and his role as a

"doctor" surrounded with a question mark. Furthermore, he depends too severely upon the clinical shibboleths of his restricted concept and is forced to practice with conceptual blinders on.

4. Too often we in chiropractic have indulged in a squabble of titles. Here in the United States a member of one of the legally established healing arts and sciences, upon receiving his diploma and qualifying for a license to practice, will employ either the prefix "doctor" or the suffix "physician" to the clinical designation of his school of healing. Hence, the Doctor of Medicine or the Medical Physician, the Doctor of Osteopathy of the Osteopathic Physician, are designations employed without further question or issue. In chiropractic however, it has been a tongue-in-check matter. At first, the intensity of the "separatism concept" motivated some of our people to employ the designation "Chiropractor," and with rather belligerent reluctance they tolerated the title "Doctor of Chiropractic," notwithstanding the fact that all possess the D.C. degree. The designation "Chiropractic Physician" was considered by some as beyond propriety, having the overtones of medical aspiration. Unfortunately, this actually constituted a misunderstanding in semantics. In a brief prepared by the Committee on the Standardization of Chiropractic Principles, significant thought is given to this issue as follows:

> "Practitioners of the healing art, regardless of their branch, are called physicians since time immemorial."

> "When, in the course of the centuries, formal education became more and more important, specially qualified physicians were honored with the title doctor of medicine."

> "This doctorate was not the first in the development of academic titles, and it wasn't and it will not be the last.

With the inclusion of newly discovered sciences into the academic curricula, further adequate doctorates become a logical necessity. The 'doctor of laws' and the ' doctor of philosophy' were trailed by the 'doctor of medicine.' In like manner the 'doctor of osteopathy' and the ' doctor of chiropractic' were added, thus completing the later developments in the healing arts."

It was only natural that in popular usage 'physician' and the non-specific designation "doctor" became synonymous for the practitioners of the healing art. This holds true even in countries where a medical physician is not required to possess the academic title "doctor of Medicine," e.g., England and Germany.

In the light of these undeniable facts, the competitive tactics to impugn the rights of the doctors of chiropractic to participate in all the privileges that members of the healing art should enjoy, become very dubious.

It seems rather shortsighted, certainly professionally imprudent, to advocate or tolerate the idea that these titles be assigned to the representatives of the other healing arts but not to the practitioners of chiropractic. In the same frame of reference as used in medicine and osteopathy, is the chiropractor a "doctor,' is he a "physician?" If he is not, then what is he? I would say, that he is both. I would say that if we are determined to maintain identity as a distinct and separate school of healing, we had better recognize that the legal connotations of these titles are an essential to such an identity.

5. Still haunting the hinterlands of our profession is the ambivalence surrounding the words "analysis" and "diagnosis." We still sometimes encounter the opinion that the doctor of chiropractic should not seek a diagnostic interpretation of

his patient, but should conclude on a spinal analysis, whether by palpation, instrumentation or X-ray spinography, only.

In many ways this is a laudable disposition because it seeks to emphasize a significant contribution to the total of diagnostic procedure. However, it imposes a limitation that prevents full comprehension of the patient's case. For example, there is still the tendency to restrict spinal and pelvic roentgenology to the detection of subluxation only, with very little attention given to the attending pathological changes and the developmental defects. There are those who still question whether the doctor of chiropractic or chiropractic clinic centers should have or seek the right to obtain blood and certain tissue specimen for diagnostic purposes. We still find certain members of the professions in public appearances, or over radio and television, and before legislative bodies, declare that the doctor of chiropractic is not too concerned about diagnosis but is more concerned about a proper analysis. Really, isn't this somewhat irrational and unwise? Actually, isn't spinal analysis an aspect of physical diagnosis? An aspect of physical diagnosis when coupled with the other measures of physical, clinical and laboratory diagnosis fortifies the doctor of chiropractic in a most handsome manner. Recent issues and happenings in the Province of Quebec and Denmark where the status of chiropractic has been most exactingly evaluated, seem to prescribe the wisdom of our premise. Do we think that as a profession we can maintain our position and the total of our professional autonomy and clinical encompassment on the basis of "spinal analysis only?"

6. Another overemphasized issue is the ever-existing question of scope of practice. It just seems that altogether too much pro and con is made of this. First of all, it appears that because of the assignments of state laws the question, of necessity, becomes geographical and provincial as much as national. Secondly, the practice of chiropractic has definitely acquired

its traditional connotations in the overall comprehension of the public. Thirdly, it seems nearly impossible to properly designate the scope of any practice within the limit of a few words of a categorical definition. Method and scope of practice are the consequences of statute, tradition, clinical need, the compunctions of ethics, and the generic rights that reside among the various schools of healing.

It is my considered conviction that the "role and scope" of chiropractic practice has been rather completely defined by circumstance, event and the assignments of public need. Certainly, there is no need for a third medical profession. The traditional practitioners of medicine and surgery and the now aspiring osteopathic physicians of medicine and surgery commendably fill the bill. Hence, any attempt in that direction would be an untoward intrusion and a compromise. However, in the field of specific manipulative therapeutics, especially as it relates to the spine and pelvis-therein resides definite need.

This need is not being fulfilled in either the medical or the osteopathic professions and never will be, because they are over-involved in the responsibilities of internal medicine and surgery. This need defines itself eventually in the daily lives of most people, and hence cannot be ignored. The most common ailments that beset man are the spinosomatic and the spinovisceral syndromes, and because of them, extended discomforts, reduced daily efficiency, and frequent partial disabilities are incurred.

This, then, is the area in which this profession must function-efficiently and with full prerogative. It represents a broad field and certainly constitutes a scope of need and practice that defines our profession well; that provides it with containment and direction; that assigns it responsibility and line of demarcation.

366

Now, in order to accomplish this we of the profession have no right to indulge in "practice isolationism." We cannot ignore the fact that the causality of a disease pattern does not totally reside in one factor. Certainly, it is often the case that one factor predominates and attention to it constitutes the major therapeutic necessity. However, the secondary contributing factors must not be ignored entirely. We say that spinal and pelvis segmental derangements often constitute a major etiological, or precipitating factor. This cannot and must not be denied; yet matters of nutrition, diet, environment, habit elimination, infection, psychosomatic and local tissue-change often must have concurrent attention. So again the question arises; "What constitutes a rational, effective and ethical scope of practice?" The answer is provided when we contemplate our role in the healing arts world.

Still another issue of concern that needs clarification and understanding is the unwise but common tendency to sponsor intraprofessional ideologies, practice methods and concepts as the messianic vehicle of unity. Unity is not an instrument, it is not a format, nor is it a procedure. It is the consequence of tolerance, understanding, wisdom, comprehension and the willingness to function with others in terms of common denominators rather than personal concepts. It is both disturbing and unwise for certain individuals or groups to propose "unity panaceas." Such actions upset the equanimity of the profession, create false anticipation and intrude upon the programs and their progress, as conjugated by the responsible agencies of our professional government. Concepts, methods, procedures and technics of practice have their place and importance, but only as subsidiary to professional morality and unity; otherwise they are dangerous.

Thus we come to a conclusion of our discussion. Certainly, it has been but precursory and premonitory. In no way does it seek to reflect criticism or assign fault. It does, however, attempt to focus honest attention upon circumstances that cannot be ignored, yet must not provoke dissension. These are circumstances that must be faced, honestly interpreted, and then met with decisions that assure security and progress for the profession.

Significant Facts of Semantics
Joseph Janse, D.C.
Date Unknown

The word medicine historically has been and is used in two distinct manners.

1. Generically and traditionally it has been and is used to relate to all forms and types of primary health care. This connotation of the word has persisted throughout the ages and this comprises a common usage statute and legal interpretation, practically throughout the world.

    It therefore is not an incongruity to use such references as "Allopathic Medicine", "Osteopathic Medicine," "Chiropractic Medicine," "Homeopathic Medicine," and "Naturopathic Medicine." Not uncommonly both the legislative bodies and the courts have upheld such a context of usage.

2. Then there is the more restricted clinical usage of the term "Medicine." Namely, the usage of pharmacological products (medicines) and the intercession of incisive surgery. It is of course understood that the practice of Medicine (Allopathic) has come to assume the privilege and right to practice all forms of health care irregardless of origin.

3. Society, it's legislative bodies, the law and court have consistently emphasized the fact that there may be more than one primary contact profession and that basically one has no right to seek or maintain control and authority over the other. Furthermore, it is not for one profession to determine the scope of practice of that of another health care profession. This is to be concluded upon by the people through their representative legislative bodies. It is a fact, therefore, that chiropractic as a profession, of an independent status, has as much right to exist, survive and grow as medicine, osteopa-

368

thy, dentistry, etc.

4. It has always been acknowledged that the title "physician" in it's generic sense is not limited to one or the other primary contact health care professions. Never has the court nor the federal government restricted it's usage to any single school of health care. It is true that in usage it should be prefixed by a designation as to which school of primary health care the practitioner belongs. Therefore, in factual forthrightness the following designations are correct and should be required: Allopathic-Physicians, Osteopathic-Physicians, Homeopathic-Physicians, Chiropractic-Physicians, and Naturopathic-Physicians, yet always with a modesty and propriety.

5. The title "Doctor" basically infers a "learned person." It relates to one who in consequence to an acceptable scholastic format has evidenced a reputable recognized level of understanding in relation to a given discipline. So in the academic and professional communities the "Doctorate" titling has manifold applications and usages. We speak of the Doctor of the Biological Sciences, the Doctor of the Exact Sciences, the Doctor of Law, the Doctor of Theology, the Doctor of Philosophy and concurrently the Doctor of Medicine, the Doctor of Osteopathy, the Doctor of Dentistry, the Doctor of Chiropractic, etc.

The Matter of Diagnosis

It is the responsibility of any primary contact practitioner, whether a doctor of medicine, a doctor of osteopathy, or a doctor of chiropractic, to seek to come to as complete an understanding of a patient's ailment as is possible within reason. Such an effort comprises a diagnosis and entails measures of physical, laboratory, roentgenological, and other acceptable scientific clinical methods of differential and concluding interpretation.

Because of the fact that the diagnostic and therapeutic practice of chiropractic as a whole has restrictions, certain diagnostic procedures cannot and should not be attempted by the practicing doctor of chiropractic. Herein lies the reason for referral necessity and a responsibility that should never become an issue or a squabble of interprofessional relations. It is for certain that the diagnostic sciences at best are not necessarily always conclusive.

A serious fallacy exists among the primary health care professions and that is the tendency to indulge in the competitive unbecomingness of asserting such bigotries as medical diagnosis, osteopathic diagnosis, chiropractic diagnosis. Let us hope that everyone of the health care professions have contributed and added to the total indices of diagnosis to be available to all qualified licensed practitioners. We in chiropractic hope that we have contributed significantly to the overall field of diagnosis. Let us hope that the concepts of spinal analysis by motion palpation, applied kinesiology, inspection, mensuration, roentgen study, cinemaradiology, and the pioneering work done in innovative investigation of spinal and pelvic biomechanics as evolved in chiropractic, have represented a meaningful input to the field of diagnosis to be available to anyone of the health care professions. Science does not have any ivory towers of exclusiveness. It is therefore, inconsistent with intellectual honesty to indulge in the semantics of medical diagnosis, osteopathic diagnosis and chiropractic diagnosis and make it an aspect of interprofessional controversy. Diagnosis is diagnosis whether relevant to the practice of medicine, osteopathy and chiropractic.

It Is Still A Matter of Personal Decision
Date Unknown

Some concern is being expressed at every level about the seeming increase in technic and concept clubs that sponsor both on-campus and off-campus exposure seminars. Such within itself is not bad at all if kept in containment and properly differentiated.

As I walk down the halls or around campus I am privileged to encounter our students, they say hello and I am pleased, they stop to chat a bit and feel complimented. Some are tall, others are short, some are pudgy, like me, and others are svelte. The females are lovely but each in her own way. The men are handsome and cavalier but also each in his own way. I like, and affectionately admire them all, yet each merit and should have an individual evaluation.

What am I trying to say? Simply that you cannot homogenize humanity whether physically, mentally, emotionally and even spiritually. This is also true in the circumstances of health or ill-being. Cabot stated it well in the forward of his text, "It is as important to know the patient who has the disease as to know the disease that afflicts the patient."

Man will never be able to homogenize "health care." The mode, the type, and the pattern of therapy must be conditioned by the physical, mental, emotional, ethnic, genetic and social indices of the patient. It is our responsibility as undergraduates to effectively study and comprehend clinical biological fundamentals and their variances. It is our responsibility as undergraduates to understand that fact, that in man (homo-sapiens) "the sensorial organism" and physiological correct measures of "hands on" has diagnostic and therapeutic merit.

True indeed these fundamentals may vary from patient to patient, from person to person and any good doctor will condition his technic applications accordingly and according to the artistry of his or her hands. Years ago I was told by my instructor in technic, "Never make your patient fit the technic—always make the technic fit the patient." Someone else said, "the whole is a great deal more than the sum of its parts."

So if you wish, carefully and effectively study and evaluate all technics, comprehend the biomechanical and neurological physiology on which they are based, but never become the "scapegoat" for a "cure all" technic or an all inclusive hands on method. Know your anatomy, know your neurophysiology, know your clinical biomechanics and you can indeed evolve your own technic apropos to the artistry of your own hands.

THE AGE OF REASON
The Mirror (1970 Yearbook)

What a commanding "theme" you have chosen for your year-book. It is so apropos to the calendar of accomplishment that you have been a part of. It is so descriptive of all that is in process and all that is being designed and intended. Not only do I compliment you but commend you for emphasis of maturity that you thus project upon our profession's profile. This is encouraging and defines you well.

This matter of becoming is a process, often laborious and beset with mitigating difficulties and engulfed by the affectivities of dis-couragements, disillusionments and failures. Becoming is an evolution, not a prescription. It is the eventual consequence of persistence, diligence, dedication and certitude. It is a composite of sacrifice, courage, foresight and conviction.

Chiropractic has just concluded its seventy-fifth year of declared existence. They have been years of heterogeneous and complex design. They were years of "revival like" fervor. They were years of the "Big Idea" and the dynamics of charismatic personalities. They were the years of feudalistic chauvinism and mean tribal-like allegiances. They were the years of awakening and emancipation. They were the years of professional civilizing and they were the years of self-realization and the dawning of self-consciousness. They were the years of transition from the business of operating privately owned schools to institutions eleemosynary in status. They were the years of the dawning mindfulness that a profession is a responsibility, a mosaic of discipline, obligation, control, rules and regulations. They were the years of a people sensing the need to define a role, an image and a place in the communities of academies, sciences, research and clinical effectiveness.

Yes, they were the years of mistake and mishap—"locked in" and insular attitudes and concepts. But they were not ignoble years. Always there was courage; always there was dedication and sacrifice; always there was thoughtfulness and concern toward those who sought relief.

372

It is true we are now entering the concluding phase of our "becoming." We are now ready to assume our place in the congress of the professions; to declare the scientific rational for our premise and to index the efficacy of clinical practices. It is the beginning of an exciting, commanding, and vitally significant decade. Imperatives confront us. They are far reaching and salient. As a profession we must tailor ourselves in such a manner that we can assume our role as an effective, significant segment of the healing arts world. We must qualify ourselves as able, conscientious and concerned members of the academic, scientific and clinical communities. We must with integrity and total merit enscribe an impression upon state and federal government and accrue those responsibilities and rights that behoove a profession.

Now some questions—What then is our personal obligation? What are the commitments we must be willing to assume? What evidences of "becoming" must we be qualified to display and fulfill? Probably it might be wise, morally and intellectually honest to contemplate the following:

1. Are we ready now to begin the life, the career and all the relative commands of responsibility, duty, obligation and accountableness of a profession?
2. Do we possess the certitude of convictions that have been processed and tempered by disciplined evaluation and differentiation; that have their strength and motivation in knowledge, comprehension and the modest realization that there may yet be more to know?
3. Are we willing to shoulder the burdens, the cares, the problems and concerns of the profession and in frank honesty help to seek and find solution?
4. Do we define not only the anticipation but the vision of a worthy life of service, of noble deeds, of disciplined conduct and able strong effort, measuring our anticipations with industry, with integrity and with a total honesty in all relations?
5. Are we willing to seek success and affluence through work well done, and service happily rendered? Do we stand ready

373

to be honest and honorable in all our dealings and not resort to either deception or misrepresentation in our effort to make gain and to acquire wherewith?

6. Shall we license and afford ourselves the time to reflect upon the goodness of life and the profound overtones of the infinite as profiled in the beauty of nature and the marvel of all forms of life? We only remain human if we retain the contemplations of hope and faith. Despair is the great pathology.

When indeed we can display these qualities in our daily lives and thus qualify ourselves as professionals, we will merit the title "doctor" and deserve the respect and response of society, its agencies and institutions learning science and government. Then indeed we will be worthy of our assignment and privileges. Then for certain each and every one of us will have arrived and the process of "becoming" will begin to have a glorious fulfilling.

"O for one to lead...one who will not babble when a people bleed;

O for the silent doer of the deed; one that is happy in his height; and one who in a people's plight of night—hath solitary certitude of light."

Memo
To: Board of Trustees
        Corporate Members
Date: October 1985

Gracious Friends and Associates:

I have been instructed to prepare an Annual Report to be submitted at your Annual Meeting. I shall seek to be brief, yet forthright and to the point, and I am going to declare my concerns without qualm and I am going to make some exacting observations which you, as the Board of Trustees an Corporate Members, should carefully deliberate.

1. My illness and surgery has been a compromise. It has become obvious that recuperation is going to be extended and

374

certainly there will be containments to my physical strength and activities.

2. As you know, with your understanding, my wife and I spent nearly six weeks in Australia lecturing at invitation of the School of Chiropractic and affiliate of the Phillip Institute of Technology. It was both rewarding and revealing. All our expenses and my salary were covered by the honoraria that I received.

    For so many good years NCC has been so highly benefited by our alumni and friends overseas. Where would we be today if it hadn't been for this support? Indeed, times are changing and NCC is going to have to make adjustments. For example:

    a. There is now a chiropractic college in France.
    b. The South Africans are planning for a school of chiropractic.
    c. Sooner or later there is going to be one in the Far East.
    d. Other chiropractic colleges, especially of the ICA, are clamoring to establish branches in Italy, Korea and Egypt.

3. I was requested by the Officers of the Council on Chiropractic Education to meet with some of the personnel of the Australian CCE. This I did. Subsequently, representatives of the two bodies have met and consummated some much needed understandings.

4. The NCC does represent a concern to me. We must admit that in some respects there was an over-reach. It must be made to work, and in the meantime every vehicle of public relations must be utilized. I still contend that Dr. Waln had it moving in the right direction, but he received little cooperation.

    a. Is it true the paying out-patient load at the NCCC is less than it was in the Lombard Chiropractic Clinic? Are we indulging in the attempt of too much clinical sophistication rather than actual timely and effective "patient care?"

5. The satellite clinics:
    a. I still regret that we gave up the Mont Clare Clinic. Effective supervisory personnel should have been appointed. Today, I understand it is an active, busy little clinic.
    b. The Brookfield Clinic has such a potential, but it needs better patient-oriented supervision. Regardless of how able Clinicians might be, friendly patient care should always be a priority. This is more so in chiropractic than in allopathy. The "hands on" phenomenon should always be a priority.
    c. The Chicago General Health Service, if the truth were to be known, is still our most active clinic. The personnel should be encouraged and supported at every level.

6. Fund raising comprises another concern. Who is now in charge? Did we do so badly with the programs of TAM, Century Club and the President's Cabinet? Currently, I do not know where we stand, or I stand. So, who is in charge? What are the programs now in effect?
    a. Because of changing times and mitigating circumstances, some of our constituents are redirecting their support; others have become disillusioned.
    b. It is an ever-continuous and changing challenge that must experience the most exacting attention and supervision.
    c. Our Alumni Association over the years has functioned effectively and meaningfully. We should be deeply grateful and we should not be too demanding and we should not seek to condition its programs or activities entirely. Those in the Alumni Office over the years have done a reputable and rewarding job.

(1) It has maintained effective contact with our alumni abroad.

(2) It has spearheaded such "outreach programs" as "Hands Across the Ocean."

(3) I could so encourage a closer understanding and relationship between the Alumni Association and the Administration.

7. Faculty and Clinic Staffs. All in all we have a strong, able technique and clinic personnel and we should be cognizant of that. I do, however, have a concern which I think should be effectively attended to. Teaching, and yes, even clinical function has become too pedantic to the extent where the purpose of the entire process has become overshadowed by book data, etc. In my opinion, every course, whether in the basic or clinical sciences, should have effective and practical references to the concepts and principles of chiropractic.

a. For example, in anatomy (dissection) to expose the sciatic nerve, it should be attended by a modest clinical reference by the instructor. Therein is the reason why all faculty should be exposed to the basic principles of our profession.

8. We should be proud of the Learning Resource Center (Library and Audio-Visual Lab.) It is my hope that the Archives portion of the Library will progressively come to contain all of the texts and papers of historical and genealogical significance. A people without a sense of background loses direction.

9. Research has become a word that, in my opinion, should be complimented by such terms as "critical studies," "innovative investigation." Here, again, we are confronted by the pertinent question, does it pertain and is it pertinent to the principles of chiropractic? Our profession cannot afford irrelevant studies, as interesting as they might be.

    a. Let us not forget that in the health care field there are few irrevocable specifics. Contained empirical efforts will always be part of the profile. Cabot said, "It is as important to know the patient as to know the disease that the patient has."

    b. Yes, indeed, our Research Department should be supported and encouraged as much as possible, but the administration could well be better informed.

10. Our students as a whole are able, talented people. Some of them come to us with exceptional talent and background. They have always evidenced strong support of the College. At times, I think that we should seek their counsel more often.

    a. It has been my privilege during my tenure to experience the understanding and support of the rank and file.

    b. Since my illness, extended expressions of concern and affection have been expressed. For this, I am deeply grateful.

11. Relations with the other chiropractic colleges has increasingly become a challenging responsibility. It is not possible for us to condition the attitude of other institutions. It is our duty to see to it that NCC remains in the forefront in the opinion of our people, government and the other health care professions.

    a. I am certain you recall the inspection visit of the Norwegian Commission sent over by that government, yet there is not one NCC grad practicing in this good land. Why did the Commission, headed by the Immediate Past-President of the Norwegian Medical Association visit? This image of trust and confidence must be retained.

    b. For some time I have been of the opinion that the profession is seeking to sponsor too many chiropractic colleges. For example, California has no need for five colleges of chiropractic. Furthermore, enrollments should be kept in containment.

12. Accreditation and Registration. We of NCC have been foremost in the discipline of accreditation and recognition by the various agencies of licensure and registration. Personnel of NCC spearheaded the founding of the Council on Chiropractic Education and obtained its registration with the U.S. Office of Education, as well as parallel and similar agencies in Canada and abroad. Both the Executive Vice-President and I have served as Secretary and President of the CCE.
   a. Currently, the CCE is being hampered in its effectiveness by political maneuvering. We, in chiropractic, have a tendency to do that. It is neither honest or beneficial. Our profession, as a minority group, cannot afford the cababble of using politics.
   b. I understand that all chiropractic colleges are seeking accreditation status, except one which is seeking to establish another chiropractic accrediting agency. I question whether the U.S. Office of Education would register and recognize two accrediting agencies for the profession.

13. The National-Lincoln School of Postgraduate and Continuing Education. In past years it has served and serviced and provided the College with a reputable source of income. I have been advised that of late there has been a concerned decline in the number of weekend seminars out in the field, as well as on campus. The question confronts us—why? May I make some observations:
   a. Unfortunately, rather sharp misunderstandings have arisen between the administration and the Dean of the PG School. This should not be and must be corrected.
   b. The other colleges are expanding their courses and contacts. This certainly tells us we had better get with it.

14. The College's economics. I know that I am a "penny-pinching" Dutchman, but always we have measured our economic responsibilities and maintained reserves that measure the rules and stipulations of the accrediting agencies –whether the CCE

or North Central. I have not experienced the confidence of those now in charge and hence I am not too knowledgeable about it all. I simply say this, let us not dabble in over-reach whether in additional renovations, adding additional personnel, etc. It is my opinion that a careful penetrating study be made of this matter.

15. I am ready to discuss the foregoing at any occasion that you wish. Yes, indeed, pertinent decisions are going to have to be made. Now we have a house that is divided. This must not continue. If it involves me, then I should be told and if needs by my title and relating affectivities should be changed or discontinued. We are stewards of an educational institution representing a primary health care profession.

Thank you,

J.Janse, D.C.
President Emeritus
JJ:bh

APPENDIX D

PERSONAL PAPERS, LETTERS, AND THOUGHTS

While the world, especially the chiropractic world, may feel an affinity and understanding for "Dr. Janse," few may appreciate the deep-rooted spiritual beliefs, social sensitivities and love of family that were imbedded in "Brother Janse" or just plain "Daddy."

From his humble beginnings, through a childhood of frugality and hard-work and faith-promoting missionary experiences, Joseph Janse, the person evolved and matured. It was his underlying personal characteristics that laid the foundation for the commitment and diligence he applied to all his doings.

He would be the first to admit he fell far short of perfect, in anything. Yet, he sought the concept of perfection in every sphere of his life, almost to a fault. The following are snippets into his personal life. They are an attempt to aid in understanding the inner soul, the spiritual self, the family man and the personal struggles that confronted him.

Our American Heritage
(American Legion Talk, circa late 1940's to a group in Illinois)
Commander Gilliland, honored guest. Gentlemen of the American Legion, I compliment you. I have observed with keen interest the transaction of your business and I have been impressed with the spirit of determination that has prevailed and in it all I sense an element of greatness.

I feel greatly honored by being invited to talk to you this evening. One is always complimented by being asked to address a group of sincere and honest people. A group that lives with a purpose, a group that represents the American spirit. I have come to realize that the Legion constitutes an agency of tremendous good in this country and permit me to encourage you to continue in the all important effort to maintain the American principle.

I was thrilled when in unison you recited the preamble of the Legion constitution. May I read it and repeat it again.

> For God and country we associate ourselves together for the following purposes; To uphold and defend the Constitution of the United States of America; to maintain law and order; to foster and perpetuate a one hundred percent Americanism; to preserve our memories and incidents of our associations in the great wars; to inculcate a sense of individual obligation to the community, state and nation; to combat the autocracy of both the classes and the masses; to make right the master of might; to promote peace and good will on earth; to safeguard and transmit to posterity the principle of justice, freedom and democracy; to consecrate and sanctify our comradeship by our devotion to mutual helpfulness.

Surely you must agree with me that this is majestic in its meaning and inferences. What a gospel of goodness and righteousness is portrayed in those words.

I feel that my position this evening is both unique and extraordinary. I am not a legion man, in fact I am not a service man. Circumstance never necessitated my becoming a member of one of the armed services. Thus you see I am but a layman, and I talk to you not from the experience of participation but rather from the experience of observation.

To some I may seem naïve and void of sophistication and even sound somewhat trite when I say; In my humble opinion the whole of mankind stands sorely in need of the blessings of Americanism. And our most pressing responsibility is the making secure of our American heritage, because believe me there is none better.

It could be that I may be dubbed as a Fourth of July sky-pilot, a chauvinist. Yet, I will challenge anyone to show me a people, a nation that maintains a greater tradition of freedom, liberty and the right to live decently.

Do you know what is wrong with most of us Americans? We have basked so long in the abundance and blessings of our American birthright—that like the rich boy we are no longer attracted by the dessert of ice cream.

Abundance of everything, freedom of speech, press and religion have become so common place that we now seek to be entertained by the paloverings [sic] and seductions of those who sponsor foreign ideologies.

Yes, there are those in this country and who claim to be Americans that stand ready to trade our American birthright for a mess of foreign porridge.

It is true that frequently our public platforms, the pulpits, our radio and movie studies as well as the halls of our colleges and universities are cluttered with those who are paid propagandists and are here to sell us a tripe of European and Asiatic concept.

Not so long ago on a Sunday morning I was mentally nauseated by having to listen to these scavengers of freedom on four different radio programs. And in deceiving and beguiling terminology they belittled the governmental concepts of the Americas and extolled the virtues respectively of Marxism, Fascism, Monarchism and Shintoism.

If these systems are so effective, so utopian, so abundant in their advantages, why is it that in the countries in which they are conceived and flourish we always find the hotbeds of trouble that lead to wars, destruction, hate, distrust, need and hunger?

Why do they constantly seek our aid—financially, intellectually and spiritually? To me it appears that these hitch-hiking groups are condescending to permit those people that have the automobile to have a ride, and believe me as a nation in many respects we are being taken for a ride.

Who has a greater right to speak with priority about human rights than the voices of such great Americans as George Washington, Thomas Jefferson, Patrick Henry, James Monroe, Abraham Lincoln, Theodore Roosevelt and Woodrow Wilson.

It might be well if the lives and the teachings of these champions of the rights of man were a little more frequently portrayed per discussion, narration and story over the radio and in the movie as well as in the classrooms of our educational institutions.

It is with frank authority that we can speak out about better standards of living. Authority is given to those who accomplish in their responsibilities. Show me a nation, a people that has attained greater heights of decency and human consideration.

Who dares take greater pride in his or her country? In whose land is the tradition of equality, of democracy and of peace and good will greater?

Why should we need to apologize for what we are and why should we succumb to something that has not proven its effectiveness.

When I speak like this, do not think that I am steeped in the conceit of Nationalism or Isolationism. I sense the need and the importance of open and frank intercourse with other nations but I feel our country has been the university of human rights and it would be better if the student sat at the feet of their instructor rather than demanding that he favor their many ill-conceived and vacillating ideas.

I am always impressed by that scriptural axiom, "Set not aside the Ancient landmarks which thy Fathers have set up." Let us not set aside the landmarks of Americanism that the Fathers of this country set up, fought and died for.

I was in Europe. I know what it is like over there. I was in Europe from 30 to 34. Thirty-eight long months. Certainly, there is a lot of good over there which merits our recognition and admiration but gentlemen there is also a lot of evil over there that we must guard ourselves against.

I am the son of an immigrant family. I have experienced the contrast. I say that it is not right for those of us of foreign birth to partake of the American Blessing, yet maintain in attitude our foreign allegiance.

Henry Cabot Lodge expressed the proper attitude when he said; "Let every man honor and love the land of his birth and the race from which he springs and keep their memory green. It is a pious and honorable duty. But let us have done with British-Americans, Irish-Americans, German-Americans, Polish-Americans, and Hebrew-Americans, and all be Americans, nothing more, nothing less. If a man is going to be an American at all, let him be so without any qualifying adjectives and if he is going to be something else, let him drop the word American from his personal description."

I have seen the class distinction over there. I have observed the suppression of the common people. I have experienced the ungodliness and moral depravity of the Nazi and Communist. I witnessed the political rise of the psychopath and pervert Hitler and his buffoon like henchman Goering. I listened to the mentally deranged and morally degenerated ego-maniac Goebbels.

I was in Rome and observed the blustering heavy-chested showmanship of that nincompoop Mussolini. I was able to study the infiltrating of the Balkans, the Netherlands and Scandinavians by the Nazi propagandists and I noted the processes of social and political decadence in France and Belgium. I have seen the Russian hordes strive for self expression and individualism against the suppressions of communism.

Believe me there is nothing over there that we need and they have nothing that we want or be envious of.

This month we are commemorating the birthdays of our two greatest Americans. One, namely George Washington spoke accordingly; "Against the insidious wiles of foreign influence the jealousy of the free people ought to be constantly awake; since history and experience prove foreign influence is one of the most baneful foes of Republican government. Excessive partiality for one nation and excessive dislike of another...

[Note: page 4 missing from original ms., so we skip to pg. 5]

...Americans enjoy the heritage of abundance and prosperity. Believe me my good friends our abundance is great. You cannot find a people on this earth more richly favored than we. Just think of our middle west, literally the bread basket of the world. Where can one find finer farms that produce more than in our state of Illinois and the states adjoining. Where does one find the granaries and the dairies filled to a greater capacity. Surely it could be called an actual garden of Eden without exaggeration. We are the best clothed, the best fed and incidentally still the best housed people in the world. I am always filled with amazement at the staggering accomplishments of our automotive industry. We are a people that live on wheels or fly by wing. Our plains, our mountains, our lakes and stream harbor and produce everything that man needs in such a volume that God's generosity seems unlimited.

Then there is the heritage of industrial greatness. Winston Churchill spoke very correctly and with proper recognition when he said, "The United States is the arsenal of democracy." The other evening I was listening to Fulton Lewis Jr. the national famous radio commentator. He made a most striking statement, by saying that he had the figures that would prove that we produced over 70% of all the war materials used by the allied countries during the war. We should take pride in the realization that it was American planes that sustained the British Air Force during the dark and frightening days of the London Blitz. And it was American tanks and trucks that enabled the red armies to chase the Hun across the Steppes. Gentlemen, it was our equipment that refitted the beaten and shattered armies of France and Holland and our men flew the "Hump" from India into China to supply the bedraggled and ill-fitted armies of that Dragon Nation. Remember this, our liberty ship coursing in all of the lanes of the seven seas represented the deciding factor in favor of victory. Let's not forget that it was our coast guard that broke the back of the German U Boat menace. Our Navy, yes our gallant Navy that cut the ever spreading tentacles of the Jap[anese] octopus, and it was our air force that pounded the Nazi into submission.

We are blessed by the heritage of sportsmanship, tolerance and neighborly consideration. I was impressed the other evening as I read the sports page of one of our daily newspaper and noted that there is a definite inclination among our servicemen to favor the participation of the representatives of the belligerent nations in the coming Olympic games. Such is indeed the attitude of fairness toward the

386

vanquished. Never in the history of our country has our government maintained an imperialistic ambition. No foreign lands have been grabbed and no people have ever been subjugated to our rule.

After World War I and now following this second debacle of evil, [I ask] who is feeding the starving millions of Europe and Asia? What a glorious privilege, what a tremendous legacy of good will.

Yet in the same instance and with ironic connotation who is clothing and equipping the communistic armies of Tito?

Ours is the heritage of decency, courage, ingenuity, and self expression. We are a free people and we are clothed in the dignity of this freedom.

Ours is the glorious heritage of great warriors. Americans have always constituted the greatest fighting team in the world. Free men and women always fight with greater virility. Gentlemen, our sons and daughters are brave and therein lies our security.

In closing may I simply say, God grants liberty only to those who love it and are always ready to guard and defend it.

Why I Believe in God

The other day I heard a competent statement. A discussion had been going on about the ills of the world and the damage of atomic warfare. Apprehension and concern saturated the emotional atmosphere. The one person who had but listened and had not participated in the tense discussion, spoke up with clear concise conviction. "I acknowledge that all that has been discussed is possible and probable, but I also know that God is and that He still resides in His Heavens and hence I feel that faith, hope, belief, and prayer are still the mainstay of human anticipation".

It is good and reassuring to now that in spite of everything the privilege of "belief in God" is available to all of mankind.

It seems that as long as man has been able to record his thought and feelings in symbol and in word he has evidenced a possession of the "God Concept".

Goethe, the great German philosopher put it well when he said:
"To know Thee God—what Thou are to me and what I am to

Thee. To know how and where Thou revealeth Thyself—that indeed is the Eternal Quest."

In the study of all peoples and civilization the "God Concept" has prevailed as a primary factor in motivating social, moral and spiritual progress.

The skeptic, the cynic, yes the atheist may ask, "What are the evidences that God is?" Let us briefly review the elements of answer.

1. Every race, every people, every civilization have had their God or Gods. True at times their concepts were warped and ambiguous, but the idea of theism has prevailed amongst all people. It seemed to be an inseparable part of all social evolution.

2. There is the history of the Ancients who claimed that they had spoken with God and that they had seen parts of His body. Such patriarchs included Abraham, Moses, Elijah, and the Brother of Jared.

3. Then as a strong undeniable evidence are the ancient and modern scriptures that bear testimony of the Existence of God and that announce Him as Our Heavenly Father, who loves us and would seek to bless us if we evidence worthiness. The Bible is the most universally accepted of these scriptures. We as Latter Day Saints place alongside the Bible as additional testimony the Book of Mormon, the Doctrine and Covenants, and the Pearl of Great Price.

4. The greatest and strongest evidence that God is—is the wondrous birth, life, death and resurrection of Jesus Christ as the Only Begotten by God the Father, in the flesh. Jesus indeed was the living, tangible evidence of God, not only as a Being but as a personage of parts and passions, which define Him as being related to the human race.

5. In these latter days a boy-prophet with daring conviction announced that he had seen God and the resurrected Christ. In one glorious announcement, he verified all the evidences and testimonies of the past, and without equivocation declared that God was a glorified immortal exalted human Being.

6. However, in my opinion the most intimate, the most personal and probably the most sustaining of all evidences is that God-Feeling that seems to be an inherent quality within man.

   a. It bears testimony to me as he in moments of being alone looks into the starry heavens at night, or upon the endless expanse of the ocean from the bridge of a ship, or over the expanse of the desert at sunrise. It was this awareness that prompted Commander Richard E. Byrd as he was encompassed by the penetrating silence of his artic camp at Little America near the South Pole. At this occasion he wrote:

The day was dying the night was being born, but with great peace. Here were the imponderable processes, and forces of the cosmos, harmonious and soundless. And in that instance I was part of it, belonging to the oneness of the Universe. The conviction came, that that rhythm was too orderly, to harmonious, too perfect to be a product of blind chance. That therefore, there must be a purpose in the whole and that man was part of that whole, and not an accidental offshoot. It was a feeling that transcended reason. The Universe was a cosmos not a chaos. Man was as rightfully a part of that cosmos as were the day and night."

It was this God-Awareness that caused Astronaut Col. John Glenn to say: "As I gazed into the endless and eternal expanse I was filled with an all enveloping awareness that I was a designed ordained part of the Universe and that God was."

Yes, in my opinion this God-Concept which seems to be an inherent part of the human make-up is the most sustaining evidence that God is. To me it is completely irrational to conclude that the God-Concept is the figment of the imagination or the consequence of an emotional digression.

I cannot conceive of a nature or a creative force so able in the design of a Universe, providing each planet with an orbit of time and season and be so indulgingly erratic in creating or evolving a human being with a mentality capable of the God idea when God is not. Is it not but logical to say, mans very inherent ability and desire to know that God is, is the greatest evidence that God is?

In closing my I read a bit from an author unknown.

"There is a God. The herbs of the valley, the cedars of the mountain, bless him; the insect sports in his bean; the bird signs him in the foliage; the thunder proclaims him in the heavens; the ocean declares his immensity; man alone has said, "There is no God.""…

Thoughts on Religion

Religion is the philosophy of right living.
1. To believe in immortality is one thing, but it is first needful to believe in life.
    a. Is my religion making me happier day by day?
    b. Is my religion actually helping me to be a better husband, father, friend, professional person?
    c. Is my religion serving as an insurance in my personal life against marital troubles, hate, greed, intolerance and self-centeredness?
    d. Is my religion causing me to be more neighborly, [have] less avarices and finer in oral and cultural qualities?
    e. Is my religion helping me be more charitable?…

My creed is to assist the weak, forget wrongs and remember benefits; to utter honest words, to cultivate the mind; to be familiar with the right thoughts that genius expresses; to convey hope, to see calm beyond the storm; dawn beyond the night.
Robert Ingersoll

Reason No II
The righteousness of religion is common sense.
1. J. Golden Kimball

I have always heavily frowned upon the tendency on the part of some of our brethren to demand obedience to the principles of the gospel on grounds of fear of eternal punishment and condemnation. I have also always felt that frequently we make too many promises with reference to the hereafter, when ever someone happens to exhibit a certain amount of righteousness. My personal experiences have proven to me that it just happens to be damn good common sense to be fairly proper and that good conduct is a good personal insurance against unhappiness.

2. Even in this life righteousness leads to happiness and success
    a. We do not have to wait until the hereafter to derive benefits from righteousness.
    b. I go to church because I am personally and immediately benefited by my association with [people]
    c. I want my children to go to church and on missions because such will help me in bringing them up to be capable of happy living.
    d. If I keep the Word of Wisdom [Mormon church health code], partially it is because health is a very keen and great factor in my personal happiness.
    e. If I pay a partial or full tithing [Mormons are asked to tithe 10% of their income] it is not out of the fear that I may through misconduct miss the Celestial Glory but because paying tithing is a beautiful lesson in unselfishness. Paying tithing insures my personality against greed and avarice.
    f. If I keep a commandment of the Lord it is because I want to enjoy the blessing that is predicated upon the obedience to this commandment

Doctrine & Covenants Section 130
"There is a law, irrevocably decreed in heaven before the foundations of this world, upon which all blessings are predicated. And when we obtain any blessing from God, it is by obedience to that law upon which it is predicated."

Reason No III
My religion teaches me that prayer is my spiritual prerogative and frequently I feel the need for prayer.
1. Prayer is my personal safe guard against sin. And Satan trembles when he sees the weakest saint upon his knees.
2. Prayer is my greatest source of learning, wisdom and knowledge.

Epistle of James
If any of you lack wisdom, let him ask of God, that giveth to all men liberally, and upbraideth not; and it shall be given him.

A Prayer
Father, inspire and guide me in my search for the larger life. Quicken my insight that I may see beyond the obvious and the trite. Enlarge my vision of the beautiful and the true. Save me from pedantry. Self worship and self pity. Help me to find [the] life the forces in my own nature through which I may most enrich the lives of others. May I never be unmindful that true culture radiates love through simplicity, gentleness and repose. Help me to express graciously the vision I shall find. When I fail, look Thou with compassion into my heart, and read there what I aspired to be and was not. Amen.

Reason No IV
My religion tells me that the end of life is to be like God.
1. Be ye perfect as your Father in heaven is perfect. Matthew 5:48
2. Read Paul again...That in him we live and move and have our being, for we are also his offspring.
3. Heirs of God—a great promise
a. We as latter-day Saints are self satisfied.
   b. We as latter-day Saints are snobbish.
   c. We as latter-day Saints frequently take the assurance of our Celestial Salvation for granted.
   d. We frequently are unmindful of the goodness in people not of our faith.

392

Reason No V

Religion is and should be the source of great courage and consolation.

Jehovah to Joshua

Only be thou strong and of good courage; be not afraid, neither be thou dismayed; for the Eternal [One] is with thee, whithersoever thou goest.

[From the] famous novel "Peasant"

Do not be afraid, do not cry out...life is good. I come home low down, from the cellar of life where darkness and terror reign, where man is half beast and life is only a fight for bread.

It flows slowly there, in dark streams, but even there gleam pearls of courage, of intelligence and of heroism, even there beauty and love exist. Every where that man is found good is, in tiny particles and invisible roots, but still it is there.

Church Talk—Logan Square Ward
[of the LDS Church, Chicago, IL]
10 January 1942

"And I the Lord am angry with the wicked, I am holding my Spirit from the inhabitants of the earth. I have sworn in my wrath and decreed wars upon the face of the earth and fear shall come upon every man."

Such are the words of the Lord as recorded in Section 63 of the Doctrine and Covenants. I refer to them not because I want to fill your heart with forebodance, or augment the apprehensions and vague sense of insecurity that might be present in our hearts.

I refer to these words because I believe that we as the people of God's Church should be fully orientated as to what is confronting us, and what our responsibilities are with reference to the situation at hand.

I refer to them because in knowledge of my own weakness I feel that we as well as the people of the world need to look to our Houses and see whether they are in order.

I make no pretense at harboring the illusion that the Lord was speaking of someone other than myself, or of other groups of mankind other than we right here at home. I don't think that these words have reference solely to the people of far distant lands.

It is with a penitent heart and humble mind that I am aware of the fact that I and perhaps all of us to some degree at least have failed to live up to our covenants, and as a result we find ourselves somewhat bewildered as to the situation at hand and a sense of uneasiness gripping at our hearts.

The other day in a moment of reflection I questioned myself why it was that I didn't enjoy as much spiritual happiness as I did when I was on my mission. Then I came to the realization that I, J. Janse hadn't been living in compatibility to the enjoyment of spiritual uplifting.

The very fact that we are now in the throws of a gigantic struggle of force and hatred against force and hatred seems to bear out the fact that man has forgotten and neglected his spiritual training, because surely no one full of the spirit of Christianity could have instigated such a conflict as we are now confronting.

Are we at fault? That is a question that I cannot answer. I do feel however that we all, that man throughout the world has contributed toward the creation of the present condition. Perhaps our sin was that of indifference rather than frank aggression or renunciation against and of the principles of Christianity. But regardless it all was conducive to the development of the situation confronting us today.

It was announced over the radio the other day that since the U.S. had been forced into the Great Conflict, there had been a tremendous increase in Church attendance and contributions—to me that gives evidence of spiritual negligence.

Our great President asked us to seek Divine Guidance through prayer. Could it be that he was aware that we are not a praying nation? Yes, truly it may be said that God has with-held his Spirit from the world, and man thus rejected finds himself enswamped by evil powers, dent on destroying him. And in the face of it all even the hearts of strong men quiver.

In exact contrast to the foregoing I now read a promise and blessing which is to be the heritage and blessing of those who seek to do "His Will."

"Wherefore, stand ye in holy places, and be not moved; until the day of the Lord come; Therefore let your hearts be comforted for all things shall work together for good to them that walk uprightly, and to the sanctification of the church. For I will raise up unto myself a pure people, that will serve me in righteousness. And all that call upon the name of the Lord, and keep his commandments, shall be saved—Amen."

What a world of hope, encouragement and promise these convey, and should serve as guideposts during the dark days before us.

And now let us see why it is that all of mankind will have to face 1942 in such a dilemma of hatred and bloodshed—and how man may seek Salvation from this situation and enjoy the blessings of peace and happiness. Only too well do I realize that the following proposals are not going to rectify the issue at hand, but I do feel that they can constitute a code of conduct for us as Latter-day Saints that we might honorably and effectively fulfill our duties as Americans as well as the Chosen people of this latter day.

We have just terminated the season commemorating the theme "Pease [sic] on Earth and Good Will toward Men." I'll venture to say that some of you as I have wondered at times during the course of the Holiday Season, whether or not this declaration of Pease [sic] on Earth, wasn't some what of a delusional phrase.

The other day I heard one of our enlisted men say: "Pease [sic] on Earth, Good Will Toward Men—What a Laugh!"

Has God forgotten the promise of peace and good will? It seems that way. Upon further scrutiny, however we find that probably God is not at fault, but man is the offender. To say—I believe in a God [that] is truly praiseworthy—But to know God—where and how He reveals himself—that is Salvation on Earth.

It is my honest opinion that the privilege to worship God, and to know that He exists is an essential to all human progress and joy. There are those who would deny that the desire to worship is an innate quality within the human soul. Personally, I have come to the definite conclusion that to worship and believe in a God is the most natural and innate thing that man can do, and is a definite component of his instinctive, mental and emotional makeup.

Joseph F. Smith in his book "The Progress of Man" writes the following:

Moreover it is also true that the spirit of worship is inherent in man because of his antecedents as the child of God in the spirit world.

It is natural for men to worship, no matter where they live, or when. No matter how depraved or ignorant they become, within their soul is the feeling of worship. It may become very dim and perverted and apparently disappear entirely through yielding to sin, yet it is doubtful if that spark is ever entirely destroyed.

Man may be designated as a rationalizing being, one capable of comparison and as such he is always striving toward that which he interprets as perfection.

It is this ever prevailing tendency to seek and accomplish perfection that leads him necessarily to believe in a personal God. A personal God, possessive of the attributes of man in a state of perfection.

A half a circle suggests a complete circle, man in his imperfect mortal state subconsciously dreams of a perfect state, immortality. It is the essence of his entire life, it is the quest of his life, it is the basis of all his progress.

> The soul grows by leaps and bounds, by tears and throbs.
> A flash, and a glory stands revealed.
> For which you have been groping blindly thru the years,
> That, yes that is the reward of knowing God.

This country was settled by men and women strong in the faith of their fathers. Our constitution was drawn up by those who sought the Lord in prayer. Less than a hundred years ago the Union was saved thru the administrations of one who was humble as he walked before God, in goodness and righteousness, seeking Divine aid and courage to master the problems confronting him.

This Church was founded and organized by one unschooled in the ways of the world, but rich in the Spirit of God.

Sometimes I question whether we, the church of today are as fully humble in our lives, or whether pride and prejudice have crept into our hearts, to the extent where we are blown up in our own conceit.

Today all truth is measured with science as the yard-stick. I question whether science is infallible and whether its postulates will cover all that which we might designate as factual and truth. The scientific approach cannot and should not be applied to establish the infallibility of religious truths.

I consider it rather unfair to continually subject our spiritual convictions to scientific scrutiny. Why is it always necessary for us to try and prove our belief in God—Faith in His Goodness—Hope for an after life—on a scientific basis?

Spiritual truths have a spiritual basis and a testimony of their truth can only be obtained by making a spiritual approach.

We are beginning to sacrifice our heritage of spiritual wisdom for that of worldly learning.

Oh of what little avail is the learnedness of men. For when men are learned they seek nor heed not the counsel of God, and they perish in their own learnedness.

I frequently fear that many of us as members of the church are beginning to compromise too much with the worldly inclinations around us.

President David O. McKay realizing this made the following eloquent plea in the form of verse:

> For right is right since God is God
> > And right the day must win.
> To doubt would mean disloyalty,
> > To falter would be sin.

We are beginning to find excuses for doing things which are basically against the Word of God.

James R. Lowell

Once to every man and nation comes the moment to decide.
In the strife of truth with falsehood for the good or evil side.
Some great cause, God's new Messiah offering each the blow or blight.
Parts the goats upon the left hand and the sheep upon the right.
And the choice goes by forever twixt the darkness and that light.

Inspired by the refining influences of Mormonism:

1. The idea of a personal god.
2. The companionship of the Holy Ghost
3. The declaration that God will yet reveal many great and important things pertaining to the Kingdom of God, is a promise of untold future joys and progressions.
4. The announcement that every man has a right to hold the Holy Priesthood instills within one the desire to feel the strength of this power.
5. The belief in the quality of man should spur us on to greater heights.
   And thus inspired we will develop the gifts within us.
   a. The gift of innate intelligence, permitting us to act and live as the humans we should be.
   b. Power to appreciate the good and the beautiful.
   c. The gift and power of speech—ability to commune one with the other. There is a bit of legend to the effect that Christ when He was about to confer the gift of speech upon a dumb man, paused, looked up into heaven and sighed and spoke the following: O Father grant that he might use it wisely.
   d. The gift of the five senses.
   e. The gift of faith, (the true measure of all spiritual truths, and the basis of all human progress.)
   f. The gift of courage; courage to live righteously, and honestly.
   g. The gift of hope. Hope springs eternal in the human breast. Be a person of promise.
   h. The gift of Love; They who love are but one step from Heaven.

398

Emotional and Spiritual Well Being lead to Sovereign Life (circa 1952)

I. A Prologue

A great man once said: "God is that man might be, and man is that he might have joy."

In the Sankrist the book of the Ancients of India we read: "Self command is the main elegance."

Leonard Da Vinci pronounced: "You can never have a greater or lesser dominion than that over yourself."

The kingly and philosophical Tennyson said: "Self reverence, self knowledge, self control, these three lead life to sovereign power."

II. A Circumstance
1. Today we are confronted by a frustrated, confused, discouraged and ambivalent world.
2. The drums of War are again rolling their thunder in all directions around the world. The War Lords are again sharpening their swords.
3. Insecurity: political, social and economic unrest stalk us at every turn.
4. We of the United States are going through the most severe, economic, ideological, social, moral and spiritual upheaval ever known.
5. Where ever we stand and where ever we go we find people in the competitive effort of an aggressive and pugnacious civilization. A civilization that has made amazing scientific progress. A civilization that has lent itself completely to the philosophy of materialism. Yet a civilization that experiences neither much peace nor lasting joy. A civilization that has forgotten to recognize the fact that science with out philosophy and spiritual prompting is chaotic.
6. Where ever we go we encounter people upon whose faces we see written: Worry and Anxiety; Fatigue and Despair: Cynicism and Futility: envy and Suspicion.

III. The Eventual Outcome
1. How is it all going to end?
    a. The social and political anarchist, finds a perverted and almost sadistic pleasure in the anticipation of the possible chaos. He revels in death and destruction.
    b. The Sophist will contend that it is a good thing. He says, "It is the birth of a new morality, the morality of the libertine, a morality which refuses to recognize spiritual and moral values. The sophist says man is an animal, let his morality be as uninhibited as those of the animal.
    c. The Intellects say: "It is the dawn of a new Order—unhampered by any tradition, dogma or standard of the past. It is the emancipation of the mind from the realm of religions superstitions and dogma to the free agencies of biological concepts.
    d. The Agnostic and Cynic maintains that things are no better or worse than they ever were. To him there is only one virtue, "eat, drink and be merry for tomorrow we may die."
    e. The Fire and Brimstone theologian will in prognostic manner, announce that this is the beginning of the end.

IV. Who is Right?
1. I hardly think that anyone is. I personally feel as if I would not care to lend myself to the Fatalism of any of these concepts.
2. I feel that there is much good in what we have and what we are.
3. I honestly believe that there is a solution to the problem. That the goodness of man might surpass his evil. That his courage might exceed his frustrations. That his love of neighbor might exceed his envy and hate.

V. <u>Where in Lies the Solution?</u>
1. Does it lie in any set, or specific ideology?
2. Does it lie in some new order?
3. Should we set aside the ancient landmarks our fathers set up?
4. I hardly think so:
    a. I am inclined to believe that it lies in the maintenance of individual integrity. I am inclined to believe that it resides in personal character.
5. The common cry is "What is the other fellow doing about it?"
6. The question might well be, "What am I doing about it?" I know that my individual goodness or character will not rectify the Korean situation , but it might be that the prayers and faith of a 150 million Americans would do much to correct it.

If I dare not believe this, I dare not believe anything and all that we sustain as spiritual ideals is so much malarkey.

VI. <u>It is Time That I proceed to Sustain Myself as:</u>
1. A person who lives with courage and perseverance.
2. A man who is honest, in all that he does, not in just what is expected of him.
3. A citizen who concerns himself about the integrity of his community, and the safety of his country.
4. A neighbor who is neither envious or slanderous.
5. An employer who is considerate and charitable.
6. An employee who is appreciative and ready to fully earn his daily keep.
7. A Father who teaches by example as well as precept.
8. A husband who is bond in fidelity and honor.
9. A professional man who seeks more to serve than to accumulate wealth.
10. An office holder, who seeks to represent good government rather than to lend himself to the muck of dishonest politics.

A Personal Letter to His Father While a Student at National
Chicago, Ill.
Nov. 21, '36

Dearest Dad!

I received your letter yesterday and was very happy to hear from you, but regretted to read that you had suffered such a bad fall. I can understand how that must have hurt and how the pain must still be severe, as well as making it very inconvenient for you.

I do hope Dad that by now the condition has improved decidedly, and that you are regaining the use of your feet, because I can assure you that things like that can often develop into serious complications.

May I advise you that if the condition hasn't cleared up yet, that you go to a doctor and have him look at it. True there may not be any bones broken, but there may be a decided dislocation which will have to be corrected by reducing it. Again you may have suffered a lumbo-sacral or sacro-iliac slip and these of course are best corrected by a good chiropractor.

It may be that they will have to take an X-ray of your pelvic region including the articulations of the hip-bone with the pelvis. Sure I know that you will be wondering what the price will be and where you will get the money to pay it, but in cases like this, one must not worry about that, the paramount thing is that you have yourself properly attended to, so that you can eventually go about your work.

Please Dad have the matter properly attended to, and I can assure you that you won't be sorry that you did. Because such injuries are not to be played with. Of course it may be just some internal bruises of the muscularis of your hip and buttocks if so that much better and it will only be a question of time until you are better.

You certainly must have had a real time with old Bess in the ditch. Surely she certainly is a card.

I hope Dad that you won't worry too much about your accident, because it won't do you any good, and I feel that things will come out OK.

I am enclosing a clipping from the Chicago Daily Tribune. It goes to show you that the Church is expanding more and more all the time.

I am getting along fine out here in the Big City. I am well and busy, thus all reasons in the world to be content.

Yesterday I treated a civil engineer from Copenhagen and after finding out that I was a Mormon he stated that he had attended several of the conferences at the chapel in Copenhagen and commended highly on the church and its principles. In fact he showed me a leaflet advertising a spring conference in Copenhagen, which mentioned brother Joseph L. Peterson as the mission president, and who was to be the principle speaker at the conference.

Now I must say goodbye for this time Dad as I have a lot of typing to do. I sincerely pray that the Lord will bless you and that you might enjoy an quick and uneventful recovery from your injury.

I believe that on the 28th of the month you are having a birthday. May I father extend you my prayerful wishes for God's choicest blessings for your well-being and happiness. I know that I very seldom have permitted myself to give any form of expression as to my love and admiration for you, I suppose all boys are like that, but Dad I want you to know that I do love and admire you. When I reflect upon the years of my life, how you worked and slaved for all of us, how day and night you were on your feet, trying to earn a comfortable living for your family, it fills me with gratitude and thanksgiving. Truly you must love your family, because no man would have done what you have done, if the welfare of his loved ones wasn't the cardinal thought of his mind.

I perhaps am beginning to realize that my old Dad with his gnarled hands and drooping shoulders represents the finest type of manhood. One who has given his life for the sake of his loved ones. I have often thought if I could but strive half as well for my family and children as you have I would consider myself a good father.

And so Dad on your birthday may you find joy and peace of mind in the knowledge that you have battled and struggled against the greatest of opposition and won. That you have gained the respect and admiration for your fellow associates. That you have stood up against the world meeting its attacks and have come out of the fight an honest and faithful man, true to yourself, your god and your duties as a husband and father. I hope that you will be happy Dad. I want you to know that we all care a great deal for you, and that we take pride in knowing that you are our father.

    With love to you, Mom and Ad, I remain,

       "Faithfully your Boy, Joe" [closure hand-written]
    Please keep me informed as to how your hip is getting along.

A Letter to His Sister Adrianna [Jana] at the Time of the Dedication of the new National College campus
Jana 5 July 1963

My Precious Jana:

    So much has transpired since I saw you. Your precious Horace has been placed at rest. His spirit has wended its way into the Paradise of those spirits that were strong and valiant and good and noble. I am certain that his reunion with his parents and our beloved mother and father was a joyous one and I know that he must have carried to them a message of your love and wonderful goodness.

    For us it was a privilege to have Bob, Ruth and her family stop by. Bob is such a fine upright man. How very proud you must be. Ruth has been a most courageous and brave woman. Her children are just darling and so well behaved. She is a wonderful mother.

    Jana I did not come home. As you know the last week in June was the week of the National Convention and on the Thursday of that week we had Dedication. The event was beautiful and went off with such handsome decorum. I had a brother Gulbrandsen who taught choral music at the B.Y. And is now working on his doctorate at Northwestern sing the Lord's Prayer and it was so beautifully done. It brought a warmth of the Gospel into the event.

    However, on Friday and Saturday afterwards I thought that I would just drop. Since then I have been about as tired and weak as a kitten. The let down was more than severe.

I pray dear one that you were not offended. I feel certain that you know how I felt about Uncle Horace. Bless you Jana. Bless you for being one of the finest women I have ever known. You are so much like Mom. Be proud and happy in what you are and what you have in your family.

You have reaped the harvest of your goodness in the goodness of your children and the blessed memory of a fine man your husband.

I love you dearly.
Joe

Another Letter to Sister Adrianna in 1963
Jana 22 August 1963

My Dearest Jana:

Thank you sincerely for your precious letter. You are a wonderful courageous sister and I am grateful and proud.

Yes the young people of our house and their mother should have written. I suppose that there is no excuse. Probably it is because our youngsters have never been taught the value of being considerate and thoughtful. Probably it is because their young lives have never really been surrounded by sentimentalities and the discipline of family propriety.

I do know that Julie and Joe were very much disturbed when I told them of the passing of Uncle Horace. They truly did have a deep affection and love for him. One evening I heard them praying and they expressed their hope that the Lord would bless you.

At times my heart is about to break with a great loneliness. Being surrounded all day by those whom you love and wish to prompt and then not being able to reach them is such a desperate feeling of inadequacy that it at times is overwhelming.

So I keep trying. Praying and hoping that some little effort, some little expression, some little example might touch and provoke impression.

They have reorganized the Stake and have appointed me as one of the seven presidents of Seventy, along with Chairman of the Educational committee. This along with my never ending work at the college keeps me busy day and nite. As long as I can keep myself dog tired I can at least fall asleep with the aid of a sleeping pill.

Gloria has been appointed as President of the ladies mutual. Here in Chicago with such great distances that is such a job. Monday morning early we got up and we drove 190 miles to a site in Wisconsin and sought to camp 25 girls, 8 of whom were non Mormon. When we got there the camping site had been occupied so I scoured about and found another some 30 miles away with the help of one of our graduates who lives in that area. By the time we had the tent set up and wood gathered and the girls bedded down it was mid-nite and then I drove home with the windows open to keep me from falling asleep. Two hours of sleep and then to work.

What Jan is going to do I do not know. There are occasions when I feel that he just wants to get away from it all. Then there are times when it seems that he has been touched.

He has been going out with a little high school senior who has been attending Church although she is not L.D.S. She is of German extraction. Her name is Pat. The other day I heard him tell his mother that he had Pat reading the Book of Mormon. Then of course my spirits soar and my heart wells with gratitude. Then a couple of weeks ago he and three other Church boys were given tickets for racing the car in a neighborhood where there were children. The parents had complained. Of course they had to appear for a hearing. Gloria and I were there. The kids got a terrific lacing from the judge and were placed on probation. Afterwards Jan said that he had better join up with the Service and get out of peoples hair as he caused nothing but trouble. Yet I am afraid that if he did join it would possibly cause him to digress further.

He has been trying this summer. He has attended most of his church affairs and did pay his tithing once.

Julie is sweet and loving, but of course full of the youthful desires and interests of a young lady of 17. Jo is more turbulent and resistive in her temperament. She is taller than her mother and resents it so much.

Last evening I met with the Bishopric on Seminary. It means that the class will be held from 6:30 to 7:15 in the morning and the kids will have to get up at 5 or 5:15 AM I pray that they, Gloria and I will be able to carry it thru. It means that we will have to drive 25 miles a day extra to get them there and back and then to school.

True I probably should never have come to Chicago. Or upon graduating I should have gone into practice. Probably I have been entirely wrong in becoming a dedicated person to a struggling profession. Probably it is a great wrong that I have committed. All I know is that I sought to be honest in all that I have done.

Probably all of this writing is but an expression of self sympathy and concern.

Within me there is but one desire and that is to do what the Lord truly wants me to do, to keep my family together, to repent from my wrong doings and to try and correct some of the severe mistakes that I have made as a father and husband.

You have lost your companion yet you are attended by the precious awareness that there was a great love between you and as a result you are surrounded by wonderful sweet memories. Yes this is the result of your own precious efforts and doings. So my dear let me simply say that I love you. That I need your understanding, that I pray to be included in your faith and prayers. God bless and keep you.

Lovingly yours,
Joe

A Letter to His Sister Adrianna in 1970 after Her Surgery
March 1970
Sunday Evening

My Dearest Jana:

Have just talked to Ade and Grace. They advised that the operation went well and that you were feeling as good or better than could be expected. I am so grateful and I so sincerely pray that things will continue to go well.

There is so much that I would seek to relate to you. Above everything I want you to know that your kid brother loves you and is so deeply grateful.

Over all the years your precious goodness, your unremitting sweet thoughtfulness have been a choice and privileged blessing to all of us.

Indeed you are a special spirit and a choice hand maiden of Our Heavenly Father. So as you reflect on all that has eventuated may I hope that you will sense our gratitude.

My own life in so many ways has been such a garble. Now in my latter years there is such a loneliness and such an encompass of responsibility. For me it is so comforting and strengthening to know that you and Ade are always available for understanding and the profile of the early days of our simple family life as immigrants.

Two weeks from today we commemorate the Easter Season. There is so much about life that is not fully comprehendible. My travels to Africa and the South Pacific filled me with the awareness that there are so many of God's children besides us and I am humbled by the awareness that one should not expect too much of life or of Our Heavenly Father because there are so many upon whom His love and His concern must be divided.

I often think of Dad. He asked for so little. His joy was his work and the propriety of his self respect. He asked for but a bed to sleep in, a simple meal to eat, the right to help his neighbors, and to go to church to worship his Heavenly Father without question.

So my dear precious sister may I submit my humble and heartfelt love. May I recommit myself to all the precious intimate ideals of our childhood, may I assure you that I shall seek to maintain worthiness.

Please pray for me and mine. There is such a need in us. Give my love to yours.

I shall seek to call you every week to determine how things are.

With a total of my love.
Joe

JJ Letter to Joey on her Birthday
Wednesday Morning (~June 1970)

My Dearest Joey:

It was so good to talk to you and Mom if but briefly last evening. I am so grateful for the love that all of you offer me, notwithstanding the haste and the compel that I have projected into your lives.

I am so happy that you and mom have been able to have some good days together and to visit Julie and to see Jan. I do hope that they have been good days and that you gals have been able to have some good talks and to enjoy relating to each other.

As I told you over the phone Babaaloo and I have been having a love affair. She is the most loveable old gal when she is alone with me. In the evenings when I come home she is there on the front step waiting and then she rolls and purrs. Of course the first thing that she insists upon when she gets in the house is to be fed. After this she wants to drink out of the wash basin and then she will come to the front room and pester me.

Your birthday is Sunday. My love, my gratitude and my prayers attend you. Although you will be 22 to Mom and me you are still our youngest one and will always hold a special spot in our hearts as that little blonde Dutch girl who had so much trouble with the exczema.

Oh my sweet young lady your Dad in his peculiar old fashioned way loves you so much. He would hope and pray that wonderful precious measures of happiness and fulfillment may attend you and that your heart will be filled with the happy wisdom of life and the strong motivation of staunch convictions and attitudes.

So often do I think of you, of Jan, of Julie and of Mom. So often I could wish that I had done it differently. So often I feel guilty and totally inept. So often I ask myself the question what must I do to merit the Lord's blessings in your behalf. Indeed I have sought to define something worthwhile in my life. I suppose that my ego thus found a satiation but I can honestly say that behind it all I wanted to do something substantial for my loved ones and build and define an image for the family that we could be proud of. I had hoped that I would be able to provide all of you with a good education so that you could all be self-reliant and be able to earn a decent livelihood. I had hoped that probably I might be able to provide Jan with a strong professional education such as law or dentistry, or to set him up in business so that his life and his desire for nice things and the privilege of enjoying a life of friendly out of door living and day in and day out it digs at me that I have not been able to do this for him and now he stands alone in the struggle and this awareness almost drives me out of my mind.

I look at Kirk's dad who is evolving business that his sons can inherit and experience benefit from, what am I in a position to afford my son? Oh my dear sweet girl how can I reach him, how can I assure him that he need not stand alone?

Now my lovely daughter on your birthday may the Lord bless you. May His strength and His understanding attend you. May true joy and true awareness fill your precious heart.

Happiness is the consequence of strong able attitudes. It is the result of a life that is truly organized and disciplined in being able to do things when they should be done and doing them with a sense of willingness and the excitement of anticipation. Happiness comes from living in such a manner that there is no reason for regret. Happiness comes from kindness and thoughtfulness and going out of ones' way to bring encouragement and hope to those who have less and to compel those who are arrogant to remain humble. Happiness is living close to the principles of the Gospel and to be mindful that God is. Happiness is love for animals, and the grandeurs of nature. Happiness is the togetherness of people who understand each other and can relate to each other. Happiness is a respect for life and a desire to contribute to it. Happiness is the fulfilling of responsibilities not as musts but as opportunities. Happiness is love of work and the excitement of trying to do something worthwhile. Happiness is a silent prayer, a tear, a heartache, a desire to help, a kind word, a smile, a hearty handshake. Happiness is faith and belief, it is belonging to a group and being part of a unit. Happiness is knowledge and wisdom and self-containment, Happiness is man's most sentient emotion.

The other day I spoke at the graduation exercises of the college in Toronto and among other things I talked about the grandeur of work:

> Work-Thank God for the might of it-the ardor, the urge, the delight of it. Work the sorings from the heart's desire-setting the brain and the soul on fire. Oh what is so good as the heat of it-and what is so glad as the beat of it. Work-Thank God for the pride of it-for the beautiful, conquering tide of it. Work-Thank God for the peace of it. For the terrible keen swift race of it. Oh What is so good as the pain of it-and what is so great as the gain of it and what is so cruel as the goad of it, forcing us on thru the rugged road. Work-Thank God for the swing of it, for the clamoring, hammering ring of it.

The other day I read something:

> O for a living man to lead-that will not babble when we bleed;
> O for the silent doer of the deed, One that is happy in his height, and one that in a nation's night has solitary certitude of light.

I have always wanted to be that to my family. I have always wanted to be a strength to all of us. I have always wanted to be a recourse and solace and an understanding. I have always wanted to be an example and I have always wanted to be able to help. I have always wanted to be close to all of you and share your problems and your joys.

Please keep in touch with us this summer. Call us every week. If there is anything that you need or would like to have or do let us know. Take occasion to conclude what you would want to do upon graduating. Do you wish to continue in graduate school, do you want to look for a job, do you want to go into another field or teach? I know that these are difficult things to decide but sooner or later some decision has to be made otherwise you will begin disliking yourself and this is such a distress.

May our Heavenly Father bless you. Tell Jan that I love him. Tell

Mom to call me when she is ready to come home.

Happy Birthday Sweetheart. Dad loves you so very much.

Dad [closure, hand-written]

Letter to Jan, Julie, Joey and Mom!
24 October 1983

Dearest Jan, Julie, Joey and Mom!

So much has eventuated of late. So much has taken place pro and con that my head is in a whirl.

It is for certain that my position here at the college is in ambivalence and quandary. Much is going on that I cannot agree with and yet over which I have no control any longer.

It is true that I can remain and continue to draw a relative good salary if I am willing to lend myself to the situation as it is evolving.

If on the other hand I decide to leave campus my salary will of course be markedly reduced, and currently there is need to maintain the family income.

Now I do not want any of you to fret. In no way do I mind being "emeritus." It had to happen sooner or later. The manner it did happen was not an honesty and of course it did hurt.

It is totally true that I have made a world of mistakes. The most regrettable one being that of neglecting you over so many unbecoming years. Now that I am emeritus, may I beg for the privilege of concluding my years trying to evidence my love for you.

Just remember that your Dad, your Husband and Grandpa is getting to be an "old duffer". I have developed serious bad habits. Encourage me to overcome them. Within me their is such a desperate need to be wanted.

I love you. Dad

A Letter to His Sister Adrianna and Grace
(wife of his brother, Adriaan)
Jana, 11 November 1984

My Dearest Jana and Grace:

I am at the college. We are having meetings of the Board of Trustees and Alumni Officers and I am waiting to be called in to make a report and some observations.

It is for certain that Life never stands still and we certainly cannot always predict what is going to happen.

I know that I have caused you concern and for this I apologize. Now let's review the matter frankly and forthrightly.

For some time I have had some trouble with my heart. The stress of so much and the ever lasting demands of work just got the best of me.

After my trip to Japan and subsequent conventions things came to a head. My associates prevailed upon me to go to a cardiologist and a urologist. The cardiologist insisted that I have an implant of a pace-maker and that has been done.

The urologist after two cystoscopic examinations along with X-rays and scans determined that there was a tumor in my bladder sitting on top of the prostate, this being the reason for my difficulty in urinating. Biopsy shows that the tissue was of a malignant nature. So they presented me with these alternatives (1) by means of surgery take out the entire bladder and prostate and put in an artificial outlet for the urinary system. This I rejected. Then there was extensive chemotherapy and I rejected this. So next week I am going to go on a program of controlled radiation.

It has been a concern but my major concern has been my emotional torpor. All the mishaps, all the problems, all the mistakes, and all the wrong doing in my life impounded their recollection upon me until I thought that I was going to loose my mind. I am on a sedative and I am seeking to rationalize it.

I think that Joey and Mitch have postponed their marriage until next spring. If possible Gloria and I want to come to Utah after the Yuletide and see whether we can properly straighten out this Park City property matter for both Jan and Joey.

413

We then would like to look at a piece of land either in the Heber area or in Huntsville, to determine where we might be able to build a modest home for the latter years of our lives.

Whether I will remain at the college is a moot question. Much depends upon how I make the transition from president to emeritus and whether there is a comfortable worthwhile niche for me to fill in.

So I suppose for the next few months it will be somewhat of an open book. I have been invited to go to Australia for 6 weeks to lecture over there and of course Gloria would go along.

I regretted not being able to be at the Utah Convention. I just do not know what it was to be all about, but I just did not feel up to it all.

Maybe sometime in the future I will be permitted to make amends.

I am deeply grateful for your concern. I am ashamed that I have not fully lived up to the principles of our up bringing. Maybe out of all of this a more reputable Joe Janse will evolve.

Love you dearly
Joe

A Letter Sent to Adrianna (sister) and Grace (sister-in-law)
20 October 1985

My dearest Jana [Adriana] and Grace:

It is around four o'clock, Sunday morning. I cannot sleep so I thought that I would try and seek to write you a note.

I so humbly and affectionately hope that you are well. Certainly you Jana have been so involved with the passing of Lester and all that related. Knowing you as I do you have proceeded with loving determination.

I am about the same. I have had a couple of falls that really jarred me. However, I must keep on trying.

I am frank to acknowledge that I miss you Jana, the walks that we took and the chats that we had. Once again you brought me to realize the significance of our heritage.

Yes, I carefully read the remarks made by the General Authorities at the recent conference, and I must acknowledge that I

414

felt such a great need to be forgiven by Our Heavenly Father.

From all over the world I have received letters and cards of condolence. Severe digress has colored my life. Yet, always I have sought to be honest, forth-right.

Just how eventually it will all come out I do not know. What I have done for the profession and the college I am not ashamed; my personal conduct and the indulgence in bad habits and conducts I regret so very much.

However it is said that one must live with what he was, what he is and would seek to be.

Yes, I would seek Our Heavenly Father's forgiveness. Yes, I would seek His aid in the reconstruction of my life. Yes, I would beg Him to bless my family.

I so appreciated your letter Jana and your lovely card Grace and the wordings of encouragement that you both provided me.

In watching T.V. it would seem that there is trouble brewing in the Church. How I wish that people would let well enough alone.

Now I had better close. Grace I am going to send you the carbon copy of this missive. May be you can figure out the mistakes without too much trouble. I am not up to going over it and make corrections.

Typing this letter has been quite a strain and probably I should return to bed and try to get some unwinding.

Let me conclude by saying that I am so grateful to both of you. Ask our Heavenly Father to give me the wisdom and the courage to do the right thing. In these latter days of my life nothing would please me more than to get well enuff [sic] to be able to come out and spend a week or so with [you].

May Our Heavenly Father bless and keep you. May I strive to be worthy of your Love and concern.

So very gratefully and with all my Love
Joe

(Last letter ever sent to Jana from Joe)

LIST OF CONTRIBUTORS

The following individuals and organizations are recognized for their support in the completion of this work. Without their financing and moral support, much of Joseph Janse's personal story would still be sprinkled throughout various letters, journals and papers.

Based on time commitment, out of pocket expenses, large purchases for which he was never reimbursed and for his untiring support (and constant nudging) for this effort, **Terry R. Yochum, D.C.**, DACBR must be placed in a singular category.

Other significant contributors:
$1,000+
Mark Sanna/Breakthrough Coaching
James Cox, D.C., DACBR
Chiropractic Centennial Foundation
Peter D. Ferguson, D.C.
Japanese Chiropractic College
National University of Health Sciences
National University of Health Sciences Alumni Association
Kazuyoshi Takeyachi, D.C.
Lance Thomas, D.C.
Nelson Vetanze, D.C.

$500

Illinois Chiropractic Society
Kenzo Kase, D.C.
Foot Levelers, Inc.

Carol Port, D.C.
Louis Sportelli, D.C.
Mitchell J. Weiss, D.C.

$200–$250

Patricia Brossard, D.C.
John Davidson, D.C.
Dick Leverone, D.C., DACBR
Michael Mastoris, D.C.
Joseph Moretti, D.C.

Specialized Radiology Const.
Paul Mark Sullivan, D.C.
Mark W. Terry, D.C., DABCO
William Thornton, D.C.
Steve Zasadny, D.C.

$100

Joseph Baric, D.C.
Edward Barowsky, D.C.
Gene Bedocs, D.C.
David S. Belknap, D.C.
B M Benchley, D.C.
Steve Bleser, D.C.
Fritz R. Boehm, D.C.
Gary Boyd, B.C.
Gregory Cesul, D.C.
Daniel Coffey, D.C.
Lacy Cook, D.C.
Wally Conard, D.C.
Andrew Costa, D.C.
Susan Decamp, D.C.
Kenneth Dougherty, D.C.
Neil L. Elliott, D.C.
Steve Elliot, D.C.
Kathleen Erickson, D.C.
Faris Chiropractic Health
Franklin Forman, D.C.
Donald Freuden, D.C., DACBO

Shirl George, D.C.
Jonathan Griffiths, D.C.
R. E. Gwynn, DC
John Hanks, D.C.
Brian Howard, D.C., M.D.
Eliot Hodes, D.C.
Eugene Hoffman, D.C.
Andrew Jackson Jr., D.C., DACBR
Sharon A Jaeger, D.C., DACBR
Craig Jordan, D.C.
H.W. Kathan, D.C.
Herman Kathan, D.C.
Karen Konarski-Hart, D.C.
James Laws, D.C.
Stephen Matthew, D.C.
JC McDonald, D.C.
Thomas Montgomery, D.C.
Kevin Mulhern, D.C.
John Neumeyer, D.C.
Richard Olff, D.C.
George Piccolo, D.C.

$100 (cont.)

Roger A. Pope, D.C.
Virgil Potts, D.C.
Powell, D.C.
Alexander Prager, D.C.
Paul Prol, D.C.
William Rademacher, D.C.
Evelyn K. Richie
Tom Rigel, D.C.
Elihu L. Rosen, D.C.
Paul Rubin, D.C.
Burt Rubin, D.C.
John Rupolo, D.C.
David Snyder, D.C.

Norman Spector, D.C.
Alvin Stjernholm, D.C.
Thomas Stotz, D.C.
Anatoly Subota, D.C.
Marvin E. Tazelaar, D.C.
Patrick Tierney
Steven Troeger, D.C.
Allen Unruh, D.C.
Sandra Vaisvil, D.C.
R.W. Walth, D.C.
James Ward, D.C.
David Wickes, D.C.
Matthew Williams, D.C.
Denise Wojciechowski, D.C.

Apologies to those who have given financially or otherwise, but have not been singled out in this work. To those whose names are included but spelled incorrectly, and to those whose achievements or interactions in Joseph Janse's life are inadequately noted, I also apologize. With the records I had in my possession, plus many more that were given to me, I did my best to state things fully and accurately.

Special thanks to the National University of Health Sciences for opening up their library and archives to me for days. This allowed me to retrieve valuable correspondence and reports not otherwise available, and the story was able to be more accurately told.

INDEX

ABOUT THE AUTHOR

Reed Phillips was first transfixed by Dr. Janse's charisma while serving as a missionary for the Church of Jesus Christ of Latter-day Saints (L.D.S.) in the Chicago area during the mid-1960's. It was Janse's influence that helped lead Phillips to eventually seek chiropractic as his chosen profession and National College as his chosen institution for study, following his graduation from The University of Utah.

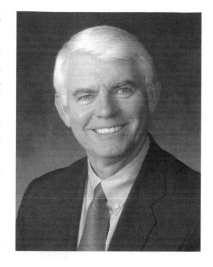

Six years spent at National College of Chiropractic allowed Phillips to become well acquainted and profoundly influenced by Janse. A bond was created that led to the motivation and commitment to preserve his legacy. Janse's example of excellence helped motivate Phillips to pursue a two-year, full-time residency in diagnostic radiology after his initial chiropractic experience at National College of Chiropractic. This lead to his Diplomate in the American Chiropractic College of Radiology. Ten years in practice (1976-86) provided the opportunity to concurrently complete a Master's Degree in Community Medicine from The University of Utah Medical School, and a Ph.D. in Sociology from The University of Utah.

Following the example set by his mentor, Phillips has published extensively, lectured locally and internationally, held numerous leadership positions in various organizations in the chiropractic profession and currently serves as the President of Southern California University of Health Sciences (SCU/LACC).

Reed Phillips has been gently guided and strongly supported by his wife, Sandra. The couple has eight exceptional children.